THE AGE OF ABBESSES AND QUEENS

The Age of Abbesses and Queens

Gender and Political Culture in Early Medieval Europe

Dick Harrison

To my mother, Clary Harrison

HQ
1143
.H37
1998

Nordic Academic Press
Box 1206
221 05 Lund
SWEDEN

© Nordic Academic Press and the author 1998
Cover: Petter Lönegård
Cartography: Alf Dahlberg
ISBN 91-89116-04-6
Printed in Sweden
AiT Falun 1998

The raven himself is hoarse
That croaks the fatal entrance of Duncan
Under my battlements. Come, you spirits
That tend on mortal thoughts, unsex me here,
And fill me from the crown to the toe topfull
Of direst cruelty. Make thick my blood,
Stop up th'access and passage to remorse,
That no compunctious visitings of nature
Shake my fell purpose, nor keep peace between
Th'effect and it. Come to my woman's breasts,
And take my milk for gall, you murd'ring ministers,
Wherever in your sightless substances
You wait on nature's mischief.

Macbeth, Act I, Scene V

Contents

Acknowledgements	14
Introduction	17

Part 1

Theoretical and historiographical background	25
Gender, power and early medieval society	25
Biology, cultural construction and historical manifestations	29
In the shadow of Dark Age misogyny…	34
Sexuality	40
The danger of anachronistic thinking 1: misogyny	42
The danger of anachronistic thinking 2: public and private spheres	45
Early medieval women in current historical research: economy, reproduction and religion	51
Women in politics	55
Political culture and gender	60
Summary	63

Part 2

Analysis of early medieval texts	67
The women of Jordanes	69
Lampeto, Marpesia and Penthesilea: three Amazon queens	70
Honoria	71
Summary	71
The women of Gregory of Tours	73
Basina, searching for ability	76
Chlothild: vengeful daughter, proud grandmother and Catholic saint	77
Chlothar I's women	85

Radegund: the ascetic queen	87
Ultrogotha	95
The women of Theudebert I	95
Charibert I's wives	98
King Gunthchramn's women	101
Audovera and Galswinth: wives of Chilperic I	103
Fredegund: the enemy of God and of mankind	105
Brunhild: a Visigothic princess far from home	130
Faileuba	148
Merovingian daughters	149
Chrodechild, Basina and Leubovera: a scandal in Poitiers	154
Foreign witches: Amalaberg, Amalasuntha, Goiswinth and the others	169
Magnate women	175
Ingitrude and Berthegund	186
Tetradia, Eulalius and their family troubles	194
The good, the bad and the holy	197
Women influenced by Satan	202
Summary	205
The women of Fredegar	219
Brunhild, an evil old queen	222
The women at the court of King Theuderic II	228
The women at the court of King Theudebert II	228
The women of Chlothar II	229
Nantechild and the other women of Dagobert I	230
Women in Lombard Italy	232
Summary	234
The women in the Continuations of Fredegar	237
The women of kings and mayors of the palace	238
Summary	240
The women in *Liber Historiae Francorum*	241
Summary	242
The women of Bede	245
Virtuous followers of Christ	245
Additional information from the *Life of Cuthbert*	252
Women within the political sphere	254
Summary	256
The women of Paul the Deacon	259

Gambara and Frea: the matriarch and the goddess	260
Rumetruda: a Dark Age femme fatale	261
Rosemunda: the avenging daughter	262
Sophia: the arrogant empress	264
Theudelinda: a paragon of virtue	265
Romilda: 'the shameless whore'	267
The construction of political networks through marriage	270
Hostages and exiles: women in trouble	272
Builders of churches	275
Summary	275
Images of female political culture from the Lives of Saints	277
Genovefa, protector of Paris	278
Monegund, a recluse of Tours	279
Venantius Fortunatus and Baudonivia: the two biographers of Saint Radegund	280
Eustadiola, a wealthy saint in Bourges	286
Rusticula, the heiress who was kidnapped	287
Desiderius of Vienne, a martyr produced by Brunhild	290
Jonas of Bobbio: the Life of Columbanus	292
Sadalberga and Anstrude, the saints of Merovingian Laon	298
Gertrude of Nivelles	302
Aldegund, a mystic of the seventh century	305
Balthild: slave, queen and saint	307
Bertilla, Abbess of Chelles	311
The crisis of 675: Bilichild, Chimnechild, Claudia and her daughter	313
Austreberta, Abbess of Pavilly	315
Eddius Stephanus: the Life of Wilfrid	318
Discussion and summary	321

Part 3

Conclusion	335
Women in the four major chronicles	337
Stereotypical images of powerful early medieval women	340
Stereotypes 1: the bad girls	342
Stereotypes 2: the good girls	345

Resources, tactics and strategies	347
Fathers and other biological relatives	347
Husbands	348
Children	351
Aggressiveness and sexual charisma	353
Wealth and generosity	357
Networks of clients and allies	359
The ecclesiastical sphere	363
Dangers	368
Social militarisation	371
Summary	374
Epilogue	381
Bibliography	385
Sources	385
Secondary works	387
Notes	401
Index	433

Western Europe, AD 600

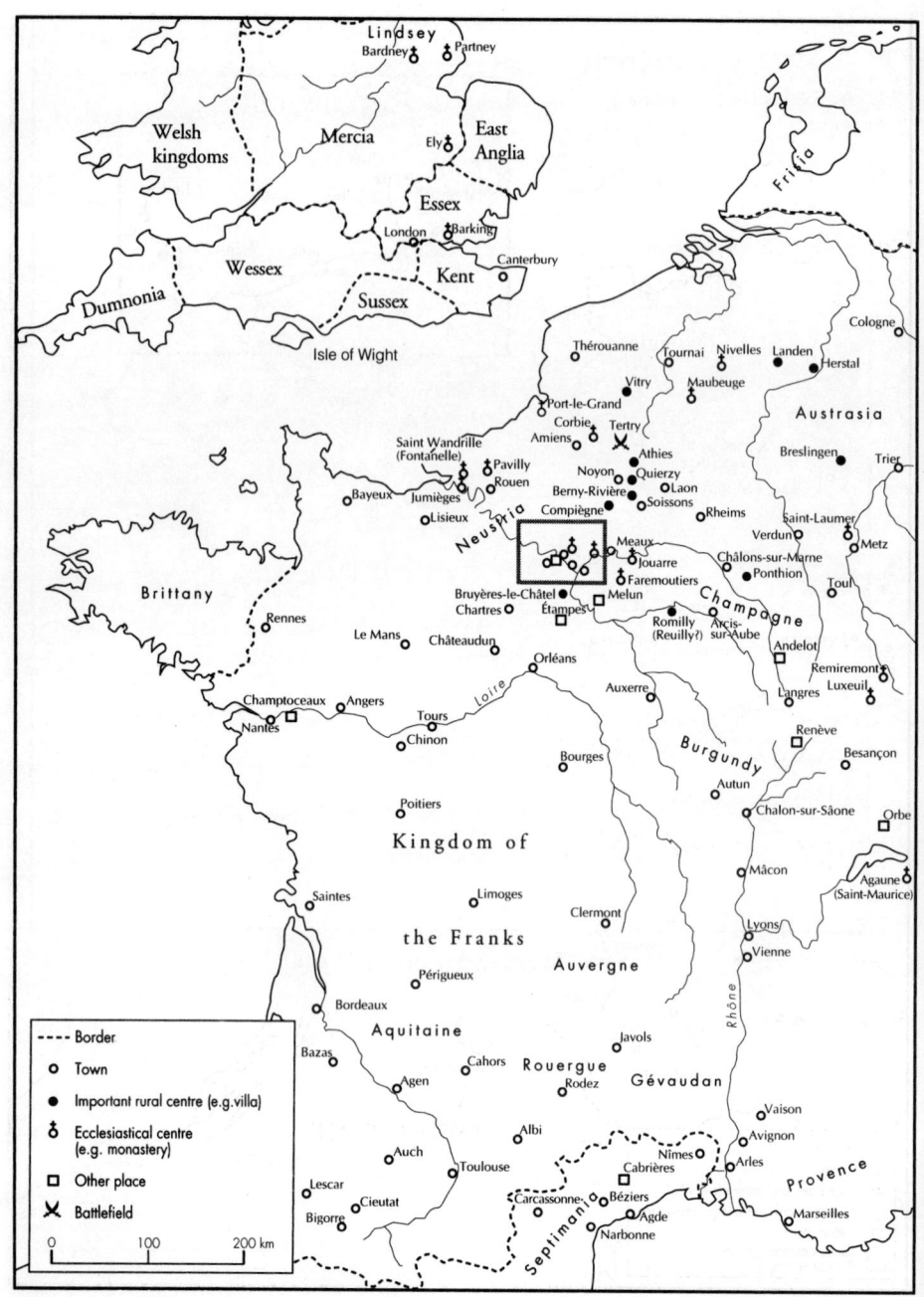

The Merovingian world from the sixth century to the eighth century

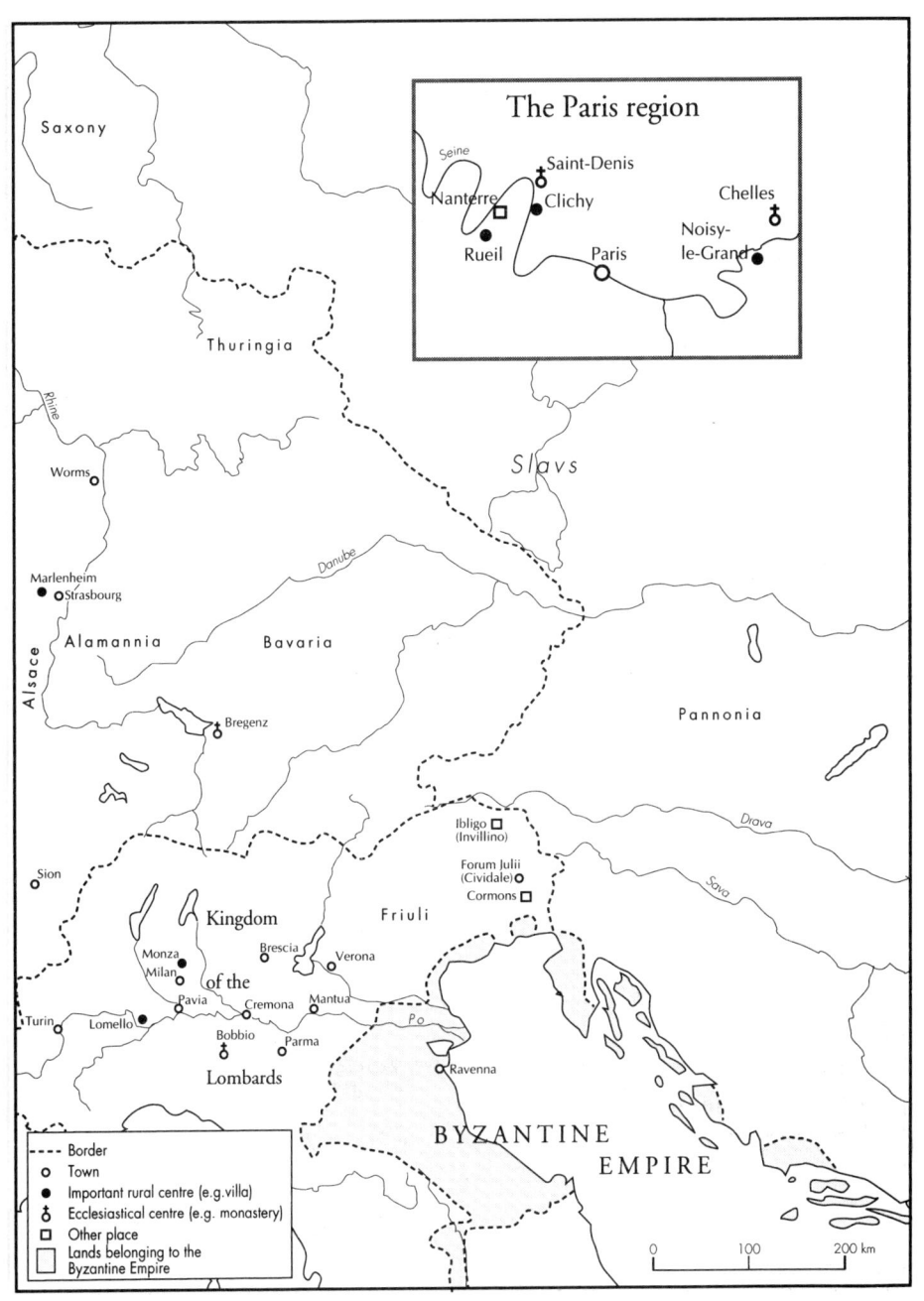

The Merovingian world from the sixth century to the eighth century

Acknowledgements

At the core of this book is an interest in medieval politics. For most people, even for many historians, these two words would seem to be contradictory. The word 'medieval' indicates that something is old-fashioned, more or less Barbaric, and devoid of the particular kind of subtlety that we associate with parliamentary debates, local elections and other elements that are normally thought of as being denoted by the word 'politics'. Nevertheless, there were politicians in the Middle Ages, as in all other known periods of human history. Medieval politics did exist, but the rules were very different from the ones we observe in today's political game. The differences were structural – i.e., the limits for what you could and could not do differed enormously – as well as cultural.

When I first began investigating the history of early medieval kingdoms in the middle of the 1980s, I was chiefly concerned with the structural differences. My doctoral dissertation (*The Early State and the Towns. Forms of Integration in Lombard Italy AD 568–774*, Lund 1993) aimed at elucidating the importance of infrastructural assets to early medieval kings. I then left the topic for a couple of years, focusing my attention on the study of spatial notions in the high Middle Ages. However, in the second half of the 1990s I gradually returned to the political field by way of the late Middle Ages. In a study of Swedish peasant rebellions in the fifteenth century (*Uppror och allianser. Politiskt våld i 1400-talets svenska bondesamhälle*, Lund 1997), I discovered that – although highly illuminating per se – structural perspectives can only provide us with a small part of the big picture. The human beings themselves – their patterns of behaviour, their experience, their tactics and their strategies – should never be overlooked if we want to understand social phenomena such as politics. In other words, I became aware of the importance of studying political culture.

There are several possible avenues of research for someone intent upon studying early medieval political culture. However, a thorough analysis of the early medieval politicians themselves has to take into account the basic distinctions between the various kinds of actors that we encounter in the sources. In the course of the present study, some of these distinctions, such as age, appeared to me as being of less immediate interest than distinctions based on ethnicity, social strata and gender. If any of these basic distinctions can claim some kind of analytical primacy, it is probably gender. After all, it is hard to conceive of any human society in which differences based on gender – separating one half of the population from the other – has not existed. That is not to say that gender has always been of greater historical importance than, say, distinctions based on class. The historical relevance of distinctions such as these is highly relative, constantly subject to cultural change. Nevertheless, I would argue that gender provides a good platform from which to begin. This work is an attempt to make some sense of early medieval politics if seen from a gender perspective.

The publication of this book was made possible by two generous grants, one from the Crafoord Foundation and one from the Swedish Council for Research in the Humanities and Social Sciences, for which I am very grateful. I also need to express my gratitude to all of those who have given me valuable advice on how to develop my ideas further. For someone working in a small country with few medievalists, it is often extremely hard to find out about recent articles and monographs concerning early medieval history, not to mention the difficulty in finding intellectually stimulating venues for discussion. For this reason, my participation in the international project *The Transformation of the Roman World* (European Science Foundation) has been very helpful. Parts of this book have been discussed at ESF-workshops in Isernia and Barcelona in 1997, and I hereby express my sincere thanks to all the participants of the discussions, among others Walter Pohl, Hans-Werner Goetz and Janet Nelson. I especially want to thank Bonnie Effros, who has provided me with good advice on further reading. Other parts of the book have been presented and discussed at seminars in Sweden – in Härnösand, Uppsala and Lund. I thank everybody who attended and contributed to the discussions. Most importantly, I would like to thank Eva Österberg, who scrutinised the entire manuscript, and Christina Carlsson Wetterberg, who read and commented on the chapters devoted to theory and historiography. Malin Lennartsson has kindly provided me with a then unpublished text of her own, for which I am very grateful.

The manuscript has been carefully read and corrected, from a linguistic point of view, by Tim Crosfield and Charlotte Merton. With their help, most of the textual stains of my Swedish accent have been removed from the book. As for the translations from Latin to English that appear in the book (I have tried to provide the reader with quotations in both languages), I personally take full responsibility. However, I have not hesitated to make use of translations that already exist, e.g. J.M. Wallace-Hadrill's translation of Fredegar's chronicle (*The Fourth Book of the Chronicle of Fredegar with its Continuations*, London 1960), L. Thorpe's translation of Gregory of Tours' *Decem Libri Historiarum* (*History of the Franks*, Harmondsworth 1974) and the collection of saints' lives published by Jo Ann McNamara et al. (*Sainted Women of the Dark Ages*, Durham and London 1992).

This book is dedicated to my mother, Clary Harrison, whose interest and loyal support made it possible for me to become a historian.

Uppsala, March 9, 1998

Dick Harrison

Introduction

Once upon a time, on an unknown day, in an unknown year, during the reputedly violent and gloomy era between the fall of the West Roman Empire and the rise of the Carolingians, a girl was born and given the name Chrodochild. We know very little about her. She appears in few sources, and then always in her capacity as consort of King Theuderic III (d. 690 or 691) of the Merovingian dynasty. She is mentioned in the biography of Bishop Audoin of Rouen[1] and in the Neustrian chronicle *Liber Historiae Francorum*.[2] That is all. We do not know what she did, nor do we know what she looked like. We do not even know when she died. Was she a kind-hearted lady or an evil stepmother? She could easily have been both, depending upon from which perspective you looked at her – but the sources are silent.

Still, we can be fairly certain that Chrodochild made an impression on her contemporaries. Her very appearance in the sources testifies to her importance. Persons who were mere ciphers were simply not mentioned in texts such as these; it would have been an unnecessary waste of time and energy. Chrodochild must have had something, some quality, that made her worth remembering, something that prompted the authors of these two texts (written a few decades after the events) to include her name in their brief sketches of Frankish history. What that quality was, we will never know.

At least in Chrodochild's case we are fortunate enough to know her name. We can be sure that many of the powerful and influential women that once existed in early medieval society have disappeared from our view, probably forever, simply because no chronicler was available to record their names for the benefit of posterity. Or, if they did record them, the texts themselves have been irrecoverably lost due to accidental fires in archives, the destructive force of plundering Vikings and Saracens; or simple scholarly neglect on the part of various monks and librarians. Furthermore, many persons of historical significance have been deliberately buried in the dark by order of their victorious enemies. A good example is provided by what French historians have often termed *les rois fainéants*, 'the do-nothing kings'. These monarchs, of whom Chrodochild's husband was one, belonged to the last generations of Merovingian rulers. We know that their immediate predecessors, Childeric II and Dagobert II, had tried to act as powerful kings and that they had paid for their ambition with their lives. Today, in the light of recent scholarship, we also know that *les rois fainéants* themselves, kings such as Chilperic II and Childebert III, were far from the unimportant tools in the hands of their mayors of the palace[3] that historians previously believed them to be. The historical writers of the Carolingian dynasty, eager to display their own glory and the worthlessness of those they replaced, managed to obscure the nature of late Merovingian power for more than a millennium. In many aspects, they still obscure it.

Then what about the women? If the Carolingian historians did their best to make the late Merovingian males invisible, the women, such as Chrodochild, would have become even more invisible. Occasionally, a king such as Chilperic II had to be mentioned since he took part in a campaign, but women seldom went to war. They may have ordered others to do so, but they rarely fought on their own. As a result, a number of late Merovingian queens disappear completely from the texts. We can sense, by reading between the lines, that some of them must have been persons of importance, but all we get is this vague feeling; we can never turn the feeling into political programmes or strategies.

Chrodochild has disappeared from the history books; so have most of her 'Dark Age' sisters – queens and princesses such as Faileuba, Wisigarda, Vuldetrada, Chlodoswintha, Amalaberg, Goiswinth, Chrodechild, Basina and Rigunth. Actually, 'disappeared' is not the correct word: most of these women were never there in the first place. Their names appear in the chronicles, but subsequent historians and editors have forgotten them or even hidden them from our view. The Swedish translator of Gregory of Tours' *Decem Libri Historiarum* considered the entire revolt of the royal nuns of Poitiers in 589–90 (see pp. 154–69) irrelevant and therefore removed it from the edition.[4] In the case of Chrodochild and her generation, we might grudgingly accept this process of 'becoming invisible' as a consequence of the lack of sources. This acceptance, however, is impossible with regard to many, many other queens, princesses, abbesses and magnates of whom we are well informed by contemporary writers. Most of them were powerful human beings deserving of note. Their chief historical fault was that they belonged to the female species and therefore came to be perceived as irrelevant details in the eyes of historians. This book is aimed at unveiling them, to make them as visible today as they once were and as they deserve to be.

A finished product is seldom identical with the idea that prompted the maker to go to work. Projects such as books and similar scholarly endeavours change over time. The present study began as an attempt to analyse gender-specific differences in Paul the Deacon's *Historia Langobardorum*. It soon developed into an analysis of the concept of gender within the political sphere of early medieval Western Europe. Gradually, the focus shifted from both male and female actors to the members of the latter category. There were good reasons for this, as will be explained below. In the end, the work turned out to be an analysis of the political culture of early medieval women in (primarily) Merovingian Gaul and (to a lesser extent) Anglo-Saxon England and Lombard Italy. However, while both the analytical and the theoretical fields of the study were considerably revised during the course of the work, the basic question remained more or less the same. It is linked to the fact that we *know* that many women were highly influential on the political scene of early medieval Europe. Nobody can deny that persons such as Radegund, Brunhild, Theudelinda, Romilda and Hilda wielded power. However, we do not know how this situation should be interpreted. Did these queens, abbesses and duchesses exert their influence on society in the same way as the kings, warlords and abbots? Or should we rather regard the political scene as a gendered arena with distinct sets of male and female resources, tactics and strategies? How, why and towards whom did the powerful women of early medieval Western Europe act in the way they did? Was there a specific female political culture?

In this book, I will try to provide preliminary answers to these questions through an analysis of written sources dating from the sixth century to the late eighth century. For reasons that will be given and explained below, I have chosen to analyse the material both from a gender perspective and from the point of view of political culture. It is my belief that an awareness of gender as a concept in historical research can enable us to understand early medieval politics more than has hitherto been believed possible. Likewise, the concept of gender itself has much to gain from studies based on theories of political culture.

Although most of the events described in this book and most of the persons involved have been well-known to historians and historical writers ever since the early medieval chronicles and saints' lives were written, the present problem has received remarkably little attention by scholars. As will be further demonstrated below, even those modern historians who are interested in gender studies have usually refrained from addressing the issue of medieval political culture. The lack of research can, therefore, hardly be explained by simple reference to the gender-related blindness of previous generations of male historians. Furthermore, while gender studies as such were largely neglected in the past, studies of political history were certainly not. The actions and strategies of kings and princes were already both described and analysed by the writers of Graeco-Roman antiquity. As far as I can see, the absence of studies of female (and male) political culture during the Middle Ages is due both to a neglect of gender as a historical concept and to the theoretical difficulties of analysing politics within a structuralist framework. For historians inspired by the Annales School, political activities are easily (and often deliberately) submerged in *la longe durée* of economic and demographic structures. As a result, human beings themselves have often been reduced to ciphers playing walk-on parts in the vast arena of time. In my view, this attitude is harmful in many ways. Not only does it prevent us from reaching new conclusions concerning political history; it is also unethical towards the members of previous generations. Our ancestors deserve better than to languish in the dark pit of Forgotten History, their actions and thoughts deprived of meaning (other than as examples of structural aspects) and originality.

The book is divided into (1) a theoretical and historiographical background, (2) an analysis and (3) a concluding discussion. In the first section, I will begin by providing a brief outline of theoretical perspectives and models as well as of some of the general discussions of gender theory that are relevant to the present problem. This is followed by an overview of current historiography concerning early medieval gender structures and early medieval women. Particular emphasis will be given to theoretical problems arising from modern research, such as the dangers of anachronistic reasoning. Having discussed the major themes of the topic (gender, cultural construction, historical manifestations, political culture, etc.), I then briefly summarise the theoretical and historiographical background. The second section, comprising the actual analysis of the sources, is divided into a number of chapters on various chroniclers and a special sub-section devoted to an analysis of saints' lives. The selection of sources is, of necessity, traditional. There are, after all, only a limited number of texts to choose from. I have used most of the Western European chronicles from Jordanes to Paul the Deacon as well as a number of *vitae* and *passiones* of saints. Some sources (for instance *Liber Pontificalis* and several of the *vitae* of male saints) have been deliberately left out of the present analysis, since they are of comparatively little use in a study such as this. Finally, at the end of the volume, the analytical results are summarised and subjected to theoretical evaluation and discussion.

Part 1

Theoretical and historiographical background

Theoretical and historiographical background

In many of the studies that have hitherto been published that focus on gender in the early Middle Ages, a theoretical perspective (in the broad sense of the term) is conspicuously absent. The situation is entirely different if we move on to, say, the early modern period. Gender studies of the sixteenth and seventeenth centuries are often accompanied by attempts to place the results within a theoretical framework. As far as I can see, this scholarly difference is mainly due to a lack of theoretical interest on the part of historians studying the early Middle Ages (i.e., historians, not archaeologists; several of the latter often display a considerable theoretical awareness) in general. To someone working in Sweden, as I do, this often quite explicit animosity towards theory – which I have encountered at several conferences, symposiums and workshops – is hard to understand. There are very few medievalists in Sweden, and those there are often work with theories and models borrowed from anthropology, sociology or some other discipline just as historians studying later periods do. When writing this book, I decided not to follow previous early medieval gender studies, thereby refraining from making whatever theoretical perspective I believe in and/or have decided to use invisible to the eyes of the reader. I decided to be as explicit as possible. As far as I can see, nothing is gained by hiding valuable thoughts on the wider ramifications of a study under the textual surface. On the contrary, these ideas should be brought out into the open. In the following chapters, I will try to show some of the theoretical complexities inherent in studies of early medieval politics if seen from the point of view of gender.

Gender, power and early medieval society

A key element in the conceptualisation of the term gender as an analytical and theoretical tool in modern scholarship is the notion of *con-*

struction. The easiest way to explain this is by way of a differentiation between gender as a purely biological category (sex) and gender as a social category. The majority of scholars using the concept of gender have decided that the latter of these categorisations is to be preferred: the actions of men and women should not, and cannot, be reduced to mere biological differences. Rather, the actions should be understood as conditioned by social, economic and political factors. The structures that determine (according to the strict structuralists) or influence (according to the others) how men and women behave in their capacity as gendered individuals are therefore thought of as being created, i.e. *constructed*, on a social and cultural level. To fully grasp the element of construction and the way the gender system works, it is necessary to study both male and female attitudes and actions, not only men's history (as is often, although implicitly, the case in traditional historical research) or women's history. The construction, the true gendering of social relations, is only apparent from a relational point of view.[5]

The complexity of the concept of gender has been further underlined by the important theoretical contribution made by Joan Scott. While maintaining that gender must be regarded as one of the most useful means of articulating power in society, Scott further assumes that gender is constituted on several inter-related yet distinct levels. When used as an analytical tool, the concept comprises cultural symbols, normative concepts, social institutions and organisations as well as subjective identity, all of which should be analysed in order to arrive at a fair approximation of how gender works. Since cultural symbols, normative concepts, various institutions and the vast number of feelings and thoughts that make up our feelings of identity are subject to historical change, we can never take gender for granted. The construction of, and the conceptualisation of, gender varies according to time and place.[6]

Scott's ideas have served as models of inspiration in a way that can only be described as fruitful; a number of good books have been written in the last decade with a theoretical basis similar to hers.[7] However, her views have also been criticised, especially with regard to the difficulty of connecting her various inter-related levels (symbols, concepts, institutions, etc.) with each other.[8] A crucial question, which is not fully answered by Scott, is how social and cultural gender constructions as such should be tied to structures of power. One of the major implications inherent in the idea of gender as a socially constructed phenomenon is that power, just like gender itself, should not be taken for granted.

In the most extreme case, such as in the reasoning of the Swedish historian Yvonne Hirdman, most relations of power are interpreted as preconditioned by gender relations. According to Hirdman, political, social and economic structures are ultimately derived from the gender system. Since men have almost always been able to dominate women by maintaining a cultural and social distance to them (except in situations when the walls between the male and female worlds have broken down in periods of crisis or social transformation), society as a whole has been dominated by a distinctly male hierarchy.[9]

In my view, this attitude is far too extreme to be of much use in a historical analysis. Not surprisingly, Hirdman's theory has been criticised by several scholars. They have accused it of being ahistorical and structuralistic, almost to the point where the individuals hardly appear to have any influence at all over their own fields of action. For instance, Hirdman's argument that cultural and social separation between men and women *always* leads to male dominance is historically untrue. Human societies are a lot more complex than that. Too many conflicting factors influence our lives; too many structures and elements are at work at the same time. True, the variety of choices may be limited due to gender, age, class, etc., but the individual always has the power to act on his or her own.[10] As has been demonstrated in the debate on the fate of women in the early modern period, gender relations in the past were often embedded in other discourses than those apparent from the vantage point of modern history.[11] There is clear a danger in trying to force one big gender system on the historical past. There are, and there always have been, *many* qualitatively different gender systems that should not be interpreted in one single context.[12]

At the opposite end of the historiographical scale, we find historians who almost deny the importance of gender. Far from being seen as a fundamental category within the sphere of human interaction, gender is rather regarded as one among many categories of fluctuating importance. According to this line of thinking, gender systems may have been of crucial importance to the actions and thought of men and women in *some* societies. In others, however, gender is thought to have been less important than, for instance, class, ethnicity or age. If we nevertheless imagine that gender was of primary importance in one of these latter societies, we become, according to these scholars, guilty of dangerously anachronistic thinking. We project our own patterns of thought backward in time to ages that did not share these patterns. A good example of this kind of reasoning is to be found in Hans-Werner Goetz' *Frauen im frühen Mittelalter* (1995). According to Goetz, the concept of gender should not be emphasised in studies of the early Middle Ages, since gender meant very little to the men and the women of that period themselves. The individuals that are mentioned in early medieval texts are judged and valued by their functions not by their sex. Women are not described as women, but as queens, nuns, magnate wives and so on, just as men are described in their capacity as kings, monks and landowners. Goetz even goes so far as to proclaim that men and women actually lived very similar lives during the early Middle Ages ('keine getrennten Lebensbereiche oder gar Lebensformen').[13] He is too good a historian not to admit that there nevertheless were certain gender-specific spheres of society, but he maintains that these were of secondary importance to the individual.[14]

Goetz' ideas are not founded on theoretical thinking but mainly on empirical research into literature from the period in question. Many of his specific results are of great value and will undoubtedly remain influential on students of early medieval gender structures for many years to come. Nevertheless, I have two serious objections. Firstly, Goetz' idea of the secondary importance of the concept of gender in early medieval society is not necessarily valid for all spheres of human life. It might be correct with regard to the very topics he has chosen to study in detail, but it need not be correct with regard to, say, political culture. Secondly, the implicit conclusion from studies such as Goetz' – that gender is not as important as other categories and should therefore not be made the central category of historical research into medieval society – misses the point. Even if we assume that Goetz' evaluation of early medieval society is entirely correct, gender can still be a crucial category in our attempts to understand the period. Regardless of how men and women of the early Middle Ages thought about their gender identities, the concept of gender (as a tool of historical research) may guide us in our search for doors leading to a better understanding of how society worked.

In my view, an awareness of gender as a concept of historical research does in fact help us to understand that, regardless of how men and women themselves might have thought about their positions in society, gender differences were of immense political importance in the early Middle Ages. As will, I hope, become clear in this book, men and women in the past often acted quite differently within the political sphere. The lack of studies of political culture has, however, made this difference hard to specify and thus impossible to explain theoretically. The basic reason why absurd theories about the all-encompassing gender systems of human history (with the all-powerful males and the permanently suppressed females), as well as theories denying the importance of gender, have been able to flourish is the lack of research. Significant parts of the history of gender are still unwritten. While the answer to the question of how power and gender are ultimately linked to each other would appear destined to lie outside the grasp of historians (left to brave philosophers and daring sociologists), it remains up to us historians to try to remedy the lack of knowledge.

Biology, cultural construction and historical manifestations

At this point, we should not forget that the idea of gender as a social construct, an idea to which most gender historians today adhere, is only the outcome of theoretical thinking and is thus open to critical attacks from scholars with a different theoretical perspective. For instance, Jean Grimshaw, in her analysis of feminist philosophers, argues that the relation between biological differences (sex) and social interpretations of gender has not been sufficiently analysed. Gender ought not to be reduced to cultural construction, nor should it be reduced to biology, but biological differences should be emphasised to a greater degree than is usually the case. The distinction between sex and gender should, according to Grimshaw, be understood as a dialectic relation rather than as a dividing line.[15]

The constructivist line of reasoning has also received severe criticism from scholars who attempt to understand gender relations from a psychohistorical point of view. The basis for psychohistorical research is the alleged ability of the historian to understand how the minds of people in the past worked. Naturally, this task is impossible as long as we assume that the people we want to study had structurally different feelings and thoughts than those that we have today. Historians can rarely (if ever), like anthropologists, 'go native' in search of the patterns of thought of the individuals they are trying to observe, understand and describe. However, if we assume that some features of mind and body have remained the same throughout history (or at least during a period that is sufficient for the study in question), the task is no longer impossible. For instance, Arne Jarrick, in a study on Swedish love affairs in the pre-modern era, assumes that love should not be regarded as a cultural construction (although others have argued that it should). On the contrary, love in the eighteenth century was very similar to the concept as we know it today. If that had not been the case, Jarrick would not have been able to study it. In order to provide a theoretical framework to his research, Jarrick argues that relations between men and women have always been determined by biological 'compulsion'. This compulsion has usually resulted in men having (and exerting) more power than women. True, things have changed during the past century, but that should be of little consequence to someone studying pre-modern society.[16]

According to critics such as Jarrick, those who subscribe to the above-mentioned gender theories are 'cultural constructivists' who fail to understand the importance of biology in history.[17] He guesses that the true cause of this failure is the fear that biological reasoning might lead to an acceptance of the dubious fact that women are doomed to remain submitted to male rule forever. Since biology cannot be changed, why should we think that the power structures built on biological foundations should ever change?[18] By neglecting biology, however, Jarrick argues, the problem would appear to have been solved. Gender relations can be interpreted as cultural constructs. Ideas allegedly based upon biological differences (such as 'men are stronger than women and therefore dominate them') then appear as the result of human prejudice, not as the result of nature. In arguing like this, however, the 'constructivists' are blind. They fail to understand that they, themselves, accept several statements as being natural and true, outside the realm of cultural construction. In other words, the 'constructivists' believe in what they want to believe in and unconsciously disregard everything else.[19]

There is a lot to be said for Jarrick's opinion. Some feelings and biological mechanisms, such as love and hate, have undoubtedly remained virtually unchanged since the dawn of mankind. Indeed, in focusing on his enlightened eighteenth century, Jarrick neglects the fact that some patterns of human thought and action (such as attitudes among the members of the judiciary) can be traced significantly further back in history.[20] If someone stabs me in the back with a dagger, I will feel the same pain a member of the Cro-Magnons would have felt, provided that daggers had been invented at the time. Jarrick is also correct in his assessment that many students of gender history take some things for granted but defuse the dangerous issues by making use of constructivist theories. In fact, so does everybody, not merely gender historians. Without assuming that some things are definitely real, our situation would be absurd.

Still, I find something lacking in Jarrick's argument. Agreed, men have always been physically stronger than women, but what does that tell us about history? Very little. Physical force per se does not shape history. Nor does money, shrewdness, imagination, love, hate or anything else. The making of history presents itself to our eyes in the shape of *manifestations* linked to specific events and periods. For instance, although the pain I would feel if someone stabbed me in the back would be the same regardless of whether the event occurred today, during the Middle Ages or in the Stone Age, I would express my anger in completely different ways depending on when it happened. I would adhere to the specific cultural and social codes of behaviour prevalent in the society in question.

Historical manifestations are extremely difficult to fully comprehend. They may depend on any number of factors, such as a certain kind of economic reasoning, a certain political culture, etc. Any single manifestation is far too complex to be understood in terms of biological (or any other) compulsion. The various teleological theories and ideas that have been forced upon our past were never there when history actually happened; these deterministic views are simply the futile attempts of later thinkers to shape the past into what they wanted (and want) it to be. Furthermore, to this set of manifestations should be added another complexity: all manifestations are revealed by one or more historical *transmitters*. These persons, such as the medieval chroniclers to be discussed in this book, must be read and interpreted in their own right. Their ideas of contemporary manifestations need not be the same as the ones we believe ourselves to have identified in the course of our research.

For example: let us assume that a Frankish king falls in love with a servant-girl due to the ever-present psychological mechanisms that make men and women interested in each other. So far so good. But that only tells us that the Frankish king fell in love; it does *not* tell us anything about political and social power. As a manifestation, the event is of little interest to the present study. Let us, however, further assume that the king marries the servant-girl (which many Frankish kings did, as will be discussed later in this book). His marriage, as well as the elevated social position thereby conferred upon the woman, constitutes a historical manifestation of great interest to anyone studying early medieval politics. In trying to understand this manifestation, we quickly find that all sorts of windows are opened towards economy, politics, the military sphere, religion and society in general. True, the various positions and situations constructed by the royal marriage are to a certain extent linked to non-historical elements, such as human biology, but they are also linked to a vast number of other elements. Thus, even if we are able to identify non-changing factors in history (e.g., those associated with biology), we still have to analyse the situation from a broader perspective, taking as much of the manifestation as possible into account. Last but not least, the historical expressions created by the marriage could be conceptualised in different ways by various chroniclers and biographers. The differences contain important meanings that we must at least try to decipher.

These manifestations can be identified with (or linked to) cultural constructs of gender relations. However, the various elements within the construct may vary considerably depending upon the social spectrum in which the construct is manifested and the social spectrum in which *we* decide to view it. Although human emotions and gender differences in physical strength may have remained unchanged throughout history, these non-historical elements of nature have been conceptualised and manifested in completely different ways due to cultural, economic, military and ideological attitudes. For instance, it would appear that sexual desire, a typically non-historical element, was of great importance in the female political culture of Merovingian Gaul. A servant-girl, even a slave, could use her charm to advance all the way to the king's bed-chamber and take charge of the kingdom after his death (see pp.307–11). Desire, however, is only part of the picture. We must also consider how the woman used her power, how she got her allies to do her bidding, how she guarded herself and her children from sexual competitors, etc., etc. By learning to adapt to their role within the political culture of early medieval women, servant-girls such as Fredegund or slave-girls such as Balthild were also capable of changing certain aspects of their structural positions. Thus, by being more successful than was usually the case, they could force their friends and enemies to respond to their power in new ways.

As far as physical strength is concerned, I must confess that I find Jarrick's argument impossible to understand, let alone agree with. That someone is stronger (i.e., has bigger muscles) does not mean that that someone is also more powerful than others are. It is probably true in some extreme cases (the dinosaurs were indeed more powerful than the mammals, because they were bigger), but it is seldom true in evolved human societies and absolutely not in politics. Sometimes, access to ideological sources of influence (temples, churches, saints' graves, etc.) or personal ideological charisma outweighs physical strength completely. In many societies, including our own, knowledge and money (preferably in combination) can turn any weakling into one of the most powerful men (or women) in the country. In the early Middle Ages, any person's real social and political strength ultimately depended upon how many allies he or she could count on, how big their personal networks of saintly bishops, wealthy widows, warlike dukes and influential magnates were in comparison to those of their enemies. Physical strength, this so-called biological 'compulsion', was only one of many, many sources of social influence and human behaviour.

In the shadow of Dark Age misogyny…

The views of women in the period studied here, during the passage from late antiquity to the early Middle Ages, have not been thoroughly elucidated in previous research. Most descriptions of early medieval gender attitudes have tended to focus on the views of those members of the ecclesiastical world, most of them belonging to other centuries than those covered in this book, whose writings are relatively well-known. A careful, theoretically conscious, analysis of gender attitudes among the writers of the sixth, seventh and eighth centuries still remains to be carried out.

First of all, I would like to point out an important aspect that is rarely observed in standard accounts of the history of women during antiquity and the Middle Ages. Anyone who has ever read a book on this subject has met a number of stereotypes: ordinary men are thought to have seen their female contemporaries through a filter of largely misogynic preconceptions of Aristotelian dimensions. I do not dispute that many of these stereotypical images did exist in the minds of ancient and medieval men, but there is more to it. The *real stereotypes* exist in the minds of the historians themselves. We like to build systems, construct images of the past and make bold interpretations. In doing so, we often oversimplify the past to a degree that turns it into something it never was. A famous example is the way the Middle Ages (especially the early part, the 'Dark Ages') as a period has become the object of mythical, mostly false ideas based on a feeling of cultural difference in a very negative sense. This anti-medieval prejudice can easily be traced to fifteenth-century Italian humanists, sixteenth-century Protestant teachers and eighteenth-century French scholars of the Enlightenment, but so what? Even if we shout this as loud as possible over and over again, most people will still continue to believe that the Middle Ages was a dark and gloomy period.

In fact, once we start looking more closely at individual writers and specific periods in the past, many stereotypes dissolve. Thus, there is no reason to suppose that male rhetors and philosophers of antiquity were a priori misogynists. As individuals, they were fully capable of developing their own attitudes. For instance, as has been made clear by Karin Blomqvist, women were not considered as representatives of their sex in the moral code of Dio Chrysostom (d. c. 120). Rather, their moral status (just like that of men) depended upon their social context. Women were seen either as members of a particular social stratum or as individuals in their own right. To Dio, the oppositions between morally good and morally bad people were not the least bit gendered; these oppositions were between the poor and the rich and between the wise and the foolish. Dio's texts testify to a variegated and mostly positive attitude towards women.[21]

For a high medieval example of the danger of believing in modern stereotypes, all we have to do is look at one of the greatest European chroniclers of the Middle Ages, Saxo Grammaticus (fl. c. 1200). True, Saxo (just as he should, according to what the stereotype tells us to expect) did regard women as naturally weak persons who ought to be excluded from political affairs in order to help man by being wife and mother. Saxo's image of a typical woman can hardly be characterised as a positive one. However, his text also displays certain attitudes that do not conform to the standard image. Contrary to patristic tradition, Saxo appears to have strongly disapproved of virginity. As Birgit Strand (now Sawyer) has emphasised, Saxo believed that perpetual virginity was unnatural or even dangerous to women. Women were naturally suited to being wives and mothers, not nuns.[22]

Most patristic authorities, whose writings have been essential in forming our stereotypical image of what learned early medieval men thought about women, would have disagreed with Saxo's attitude. However, the actual images of female individuals in theological literature from late antiquity and the early Middle Ages are not as easy to comprehend as we are often led to believe. In most modern overviews of patristic views on women, we find a very gloomy picture. The Fathers of the Church and the writers whose attitudes conformed to patristic ideas are said to have devoted their texts on women to informing the reader about how bad and dangerous the female species was. These male writers are said to have had, or at least believed that they had, God on their side, quoting one allegedly misogynic passage in the Bible after another. They believed that all women were impure, polluted and polluting. Women, according to the Fathers of the Church, should always be firmly subordinated to their men; anything else would represent a serious danger to society and to Christianity.[23] Eve, the original Temptress, the tool of Satan, was (so we are told) regularly used as a model of what to expect from a woman. Women seduced men and made them fall, just like the sinful Eve had destroyed the virtuous Adam. The only good woman was a woman who denied her femininity and became a virgin for life. Motherhood was worthless compared to chastity; the best thing a mother could do was to keep her daughters safely away from all men. Indeed, if all women managed to suppress their evil lusts, no more children would be born and the Day of Judgement would arrive, bringing glory to all true believers![24] The juxtaposition of Eve (bad) and Mary (good) has been commonplace in many writings on medieval conceptualisations of gender, even appearing in works whose authors argue that the actual image of an ideal woman was to be found somewhere between the two.[25] Best of all, of course, were those women who not only remained chaste but also emerged as bold Christian heroines. These saintly viragos, who made the executioner tremble as they were about to achieve martyrdom, served as shining reminders that women could, if they tried, advance to the high moral level otherwise inhabited only by men.[26] However, even if some patristic writers upheld the view that women were potentially good, they always regarded them as secondary to men. As Klaus Thraede (1990) has remarked: 'Trotz aller dieser Egalisierung bleibt das natürlich immer noch ein stark androzentrischer Gleichheitsbegriff.'[27]

According to Stephanie Hollis (1992), the structural animosity of the male upholders of the early medieval church towards women was even greater than has usually been assumed. After surveying the writings of several ecclesiastical authorities such as Bede and Eddius with regard to their views of Anglo-Saxon women, Hollis concludes that due to ecclesiastical influence the position of women in England declined sharply even before the Norman Conquest of 1066.[28] In most other evaluations, the Conquest has been seen as a negative watershed in the history of English women. It has often been argued, for instance by Doris Stenton (1957) and Christine Fell (1984), that the gender structure during the centuries before 1066 differed sharply from the structure of the high Middle Ages. According to this line of reasoning, the comparatively favourable position of Anglo-Saxon women rested upon the hypothetical fact that patristic conceptions had no real effect on social realities. After 1066, the impact of Gregorian reform and formalised canon law, accompanied by social and military changes, resulted in a deterioration of the status of women.[29] Hollis, however, feels that Fell and the others have underestimated the social actualisation of the pre-1066 church's heritage of doctrines inimical to the female species. In her own opinion, there was a gradual erosion in the position of women (particularly nuns and abbesses) from at least as early as the eighth century.[30] For instance, she interprets the near silence on the activities of reigning queens and the scanty coverage of double monasteries in Bede's *Historia ecclesiastica gentis Anglorum* as the result of a conscious attempt on the part of the author to marginalise women.[31]

In a recent study by Lisa Bitel (1996), the misogyny of the early medieval clergy is further emphasised. Bitel's study covers the opinions of the members of the learned elite in Ireland, all of whom were male and all of whom had received some kind of monastic training. These literati were responsible for the writing of laws, histories and genealogies and the teaching of Latin scholarship; some of them also wrote poems and stories. While disagreeing about several items, they nevertheless implicitly agreed that the women they wrote about should be treated not as independent entities but as persons existing only in relation to men (as wives, lovers, mothers, daughters, etc.). All the texts studied by Bitel assumed a social hierarchy based on blood and wealth, with women languishing at the bottom together with children, foreigners and slaves.[32] Several of the writers suggested that women were different from men not only physically, intellectually and emotionally but also with regard to the very essence of their nature. While men were always assumed to be members of the human race, women were sometimes depicted as entities belonging to the twilight zone between humans and non-humans (i.e., animals and supernatural beings, inhabitants of the *síd*, the Otherworld). In any case, women, whatever their true nature, never attained the full human potential enjoyed by men.[33] Even the most pious nuns imaginable were by nature less than any righteous male.[34] The only way a woman could come close to manly perfection was if she abandoned her femininity and worked hard to become like a man. She should abstain from all the vices that women were closely associated with, such as sex and other bodily lusts.

To do this, she should destroy her own physical beauty: whereas the women of the Otherworld in secular tales were always described as perfectly beautiful, women of the Christian *vitae* (biographies of saints) turned hideous on purpose. Saint Brigit even gouged out her own eye when threatened with marriage. The holiest of early medieval Irish women are said to have mutilated their bodies or fasted until they eliminated all outward signs of their reproductive capacities and the beauty that marked their femininity. Even this was, however, not enough. The only safe way for a woman to become fully immune to the physical world was to leave it entirely, to become one of the living dead. Canonists ordered women who took the veil to obey without question the orders of their male superiors, never dressing to attract any attention, to live as if they had already died and ascended to heaven. – Of course, reality was far different, but misogynic ideas were so accepted in the early Middle Ages that they were taken for granted by all clerically trained writers.[35]

Another aspect of early medieval Irish (and European) misogyny is to be found in tales of warriors and hags. These females used a combination of sex, evil and violence to subvert the formal social roles. In the Irish stories, female warriors and war goddesses (all of them belonging to the pre-Christian past) sought political dominance over men. Their presence on the battlefield drove men to kill each other and ultimately resulted in chaos.[36] Female warriors appear in the literary traditions of several other parts of Europe, all the way from Iceland to the Balkans. According to Carol Clover, they are best understood as imaginative adumbrations of a social reality in which certain women, under specific circumstances, 'became men' for legal purposes. For instance, a brotherless daughter in a society characterised by feuds may have been constrained to function as a surrogate son.[37]

The female Irish spell-casters, who were believed to exist in real life, not merely in the mythical past, were rumoured to be spreading their evil in contemporary society, attacking men with magic, especially of a sexual nature. It is interesting to see that only women appear to have been accused of these acts; the male druids had all disappeared with the coming of Christianity. Penitentials, laws, prayers, and various narratives all assumed women's specialisation in the (always evil) magic of love and sex.[38] The picture is similar if we turn to the Continent. In most early medieval European law codes, non-Christian magical practice is associated with women rather than with men. Although both were believed to be capable of casting spells, only women were ever associated with love magic.[39]

The Irish literati especially feared women acting in groups, e.g. at shrines, mills, feasting halls and during the various phases of cloth production. Since women had their own networks and informal ways of influencing society (see pp. 359–67), their collective actions were structurally different from those of men, and that made them even more dangerous than they already were as individuals. Women had no formal hierarchies (i.e., like those of the men) and no negotiating powers similar to those of the male political actors. They acted according to other principles and displayed a disturbing tendency to ignore the rules of the men. They eloped, seduced, argued and caused all kinds of mayhem.[40] The most dangerous place imaginable was therefore, according to the literati, a mythical island in the Otherworld known as *Tír inna mBan*, the Land of Women. This community of females was not ordered according to male logic: there were no laws, no ties of kinship, no networks of clients, no suits and no feuds. No men lived here, and those unfortunate sailors who ended up on the shores of the island lost their entire world with all that gave meaning to their lives. The women of *Tír inna mBan* were able to deprive the men of their very identity as members of society.[41] In reality, of course, *Tír inna mBan* did not exist. When we analyse tales about the mythical island, however, the fears of male upholders of society become clear: seeing a big group of arguing and shouting women next to a mill or a shrine, they would have instinctively realised that they were approaching a danger zone. These mini-versions of *Tír inna mBan* should be given a wide berth.

Mary Condren, in her study *The Serpent and the Goddess* (1989), links the negative views of women in medieval Ireland to the idea, common in feminist literature, of a huge transformation that is supposed to have turned an originally matricentral Celtic society into a medieval society characterised by patriarchal relations. In Condren's words, 'the Great Mother Goddess Macha vanished from the stage of Irish history following her downfall at the hands of the king and his warriors', a disappearance that symbolised 'the elimination of the possibility of any woman-centered social system, philosophy, or religion.'[42] This transformation was, Condren argues, continued and strengthened by Christianity. The Christian doctrine is said to have promoted a profound dualism between the spirit and the flesh: while the men were believed to inhabit the world of the spirit, women (except those virgins who became 'like men') were relegated to the world of flesh and nature. Those women who clung to the ancient traditions of the pre-medieval matricentral culture were regarded as witches and subjected to persecution.[43] After the Gregorian reform movement in the high Middle Ages, the structural situation for women grew even worse.[44]

The exceptions to the misogynic rule that all women were bad were, as noted above, the religious women. In the Christian religion – by rejecting sex, husbands and babies – women could attain a relatively high level of influence that was not frowned upon by the literati. Still, most Irish nuns remained firmly dominated by male superiors. Their status, like that of secular women, always depended on the status of their male guardians. All the extant Irish penitentials, canons, laws, annals and genealogies confirm women's subsidiary relation to male clerics. Very few women's or mixed-sex communities claimed authority over men's communities, although the complex of Cell Dara (with an abbess and her nuns, a bishop, priests and monks) formed an exception.[45]

Sexuality

As is clear from all the late antique and early medieval writings on the subject, the core of female evil and female weakness was thought to be constituted by sexuality. Basically, the association of women with sex is ridiculously easy to explain: early medieval males, just like modern males, were sexually interested in women. As a result, they thought of sex when they thought of women (especially if they were forced to live in chastity under a monastic rule). If sexuality was condemned (as it was by the male upholders of Christian doctrine), then women would automatically suffer because of their association with the subject.

According to the theological doctrine of early medieval Europe, sex should, if possible, be altogether avoided. Since the Fathers of the Church, for example Saint Ambrose and Saint Augustine, understood that this goal was impossible to achieve, they at least tried to get people to regulate their sexual behaviour and to channel their carnal lusts to one particular purpose: procreation. Ideally, of course, procreation should also be avoided, since it meant that the human species would continue to exist and that the Day of Judgement would be postponed. However, procreation was surely much better than sex for the sake of pure pleasure. As a result of this line of reasoning, the theological authorities maintained that it was all right for men and women to have sex as long as they only did so in order to obey Genesis and be fruitful. Still, they were to engage in intercourse only on certain days of the religious calendar. For instance, some canonists and penitentialists forbade sex on the nights of Monday, Tuesday, Thursday and Saturday except during the three forty-day fasts of the Christian calendar, when they permitted no sex at all. Also, they forbade intercourse during menstruation, pregnancy, or for a month or two after childbirth; they even tried to restrict sexual positions during copulation.[46]

As is clear from the love stories of early medieval Ireland, sexual desire was associated both with extreme danger and with guilty women. When women seized control of a love affair, they turned private passion into a public event, thus driving men to kill each other. The literary message, as Lisa Bitel points out, is obvious: sexually aggressive women threatened men and the society that men had engineered. Women brought passion, and passion brought the kind of ruinous social disorder that always threatened to descend upon unwary men.[47] The women were the guilty ones, not the men, since women were thought to be by nature prone to sexual excess. For instance, the post-800 hagiographer of Saint Ciarán described how the saint temporarily healed the Queen of Mumu of her adulterous passion for the King of Osraige but was incapable of completely cleansing her body of lust. As a consequence, the infection of passion continued to inflame her soul with sin, for which she was eventually punished with death.[48] Likewise, all those tragic couples of the love stories that eloped, believing that they could escape restrictive social networks, died as a result. Desire brought death to the protagonists of the tales because of the pollution and disorder that accompanied illicit sex.[49]

The danger of anachronistic thinking 1: misogyny

While some of the Irish literati would seem to have been even worse than the Fathers of the Church, all Christian thinkers in early medieval Europe appear to have shared a common fear and an implicit hatred of women. At least, that is what most general historical overviews tell us, whether feminist (like Condren's work) or traditional. In this way, modern scholars have attacked medieval (male) writers for being misogynists, for creating an ideological pattern that legitimised male dominance over women for centuries to come. The Fathers of the Church have turned out to be the architects of the patriarchate, and thus perhaps the greatest villains in the history of gender relations. Realising the enormity of this accusation, the historian ought to be suspicious. As was demonstrated above, it is easy to spot attitudes that differ completely from our standard image of ancient and medieval views on women once we take a closer look at the writings of individual authors. The danger inherent in the standard accusation of the patristic authorities, however, is far greater than that. Not only have we anachronistically projected our own stereotypes of what learned male misogyny should look like onto the Middle Ages, we have also failed to understand the early medieval mentality.

Beginning at the core of the problem – the basic biological gap that separates men and women – Joan Cadden (1993) has demonstrated that even the most learned early medieval thinkers, such as Isidore of Seville, had no clear idea of what to believe. Furthermore, they do not even appear to have been aware of their ignorance. While biological differences became the subject of much discussion during the high Middle Ages, the early medieval doctors and theologians were silent. The diversity of information about reproduction and sex-related matters was striking. Isidore repeated old ideas that both denigrate and defend women, offering information that suggests now one view of male and female roles in reproduction, now another. All in all, early medieval intellectuals displayed a considerable lack of concern with discursive science and thereby made room for views based on divergent, even contradictory, assumptions and opinions.[50] Generally speaking, this absence of attempts to relegate women to a specific, and subordinate, biological category would seem to indicate that the structural animosity of early medieval learned men towards women might have been less dangerous than has been argued.

In his thorough analysis of attitudes towards women in early medieval Western Europe, Hans-Werner Goetz (1995) criticises previous writers for being guilty of anachronistic ways of reasoning. Early medieval Christian mentality had nothing whatsoever to do with misogyny or the idea that women were bad and dangerous. A few individual writers may have hated women (some men always have and some still do), but the vast majority shared a completely different pattern of thought. In the eyes of most late antique and early medieval theologians, women were inherently good, since they had been created by God (who was not in the habit of creating forces of evil). In fact, women were neither better nor worse than men. Those women and men that we encounter in the saints' *vitae* should be regarded as exceptional cases, persons who, by virtue of their extraordinary qualities, behaved and thought in ways that would have been impossible for ordinary men and women. When we meet women in other texts than saints' *vitae*, they usually appear to have been highly regarded for conforming to what we are accustomed to interpret as non-Christian ideals. Marriage, not virginity, would seem to have been the norm for all those women who did not join nunneries. The image of an individual woman was based on the social and economic position of that particular person, not on her capacity as a woman. In fact, Goetz argues, gender was *unimportant* in early medieval mentality (see above p. 28). Not even Eve, the original female sinner, was perceived as bad and dangerous. Her position in early medieval theology was, as Goetz convincingly argues, much more complex. Above all, Eve was not perceived as a 'woman' but as a theological being. Thus, she was far removed from any ideas on what human beings, men as well as women, were like.[51]

As is evident from Goetz' study, men and women shared the same views on gender and social structure. Husband and wife agreed that the man was the head of the household, that women were weaker than men, that there were certain social roles that should be performed by men and some that should be performed by women. When confronted by a priest quoting some 'misogynic' passages from a patristic authority, no early medieval woman would have understood these texts as being inimical, let alone dangerous, either to herself or to the position of her sex. Everybody implicitly agreed on what the gender structure should look like, and several women easily used the system to their own advantage.[52]

Looking back at previous research, it is easy to be puzzled. Is it really possible simply to reduce the explicitly negative views on women in early medieval literature to manifestations of commonly held opinions on the nature of extraordinary individuals (i.e., very bad and very good persons, regardless of gender)? Was the male-female consensus on the gender structure really this strong? It would seem that the gap between the different scholarly opinions is too big for us to be able to harmonise them.

Hans-Werner Goetz is undoubtedly correct in accusing previous scholars of neglecting the basic characteristics of early medieval mentality in forming their opinions on theological misogyny. However, it is also clear that several male writers, not only those studied by Lisa Bitel, did fear certain aspects of womanhood. Goetz has shown that the standard image of gender relations was not characterised by an outspoken, harsh misogynic ideology, but he has *not* given us the whole picture. On the contrary, Goetz over-simplifies the early medieval gender structure by arguing that men and women, despite their obvious differences, acted in very similar ways, within the same social spheres and using similar strategies.[53] The different kinds of male and female social networks discovered by Bitel would seem to point in a completely different direction. As already noted, Goetz almost discards gender as a useful analytical tool by maintaining that it was far less important to early medieval people than other social categories. In my view, as I hope to make clear, early medieval reality was more complex than Goetz is willing to admit. There is no reason to suppose that gender differences were incapable of forming the basis of different attitudes towards life as well as different spheres of social interaction and different patterns of strategies. In particular, we should be very careful not to equate a priori the range of actions and tactics available to an early medieval king with those available to an early medieval queen.

The danger of anachronistic thinking 2: public and private spheres

According to a famous anthropological theory, the power and social position of women depends upon the balance between the private and public spheres of society. At the core of this reasoning lies the assumption that the functional division of human activity into private and public spheres accounts for gender asymmetry. The private (or domestic) sphere is usually described as consisting of the various activities connected to the household, while the public sphere consists of politics, judicial institutions, markets and other non-private arenas. If we are to believe the theory, the resources of women are usually to be found in the private sphere, while men easily take control and make use of resources belonging to the public sphere. If a woman wants to attain social influence – including political influence – she is therefore bound to use the resources at her disposal in her own home. A logical consequence would be that the position of women is structurally strengthened during periods that witness considerable growth in the importance of institutions such as the household and the family, as seen from the point of view of society as a whole. Inspired by this line of thinking, some historians have argued that Western European society during the early Middle Ages in fact did experience this change. Compared to Roman antiquity, public institutions – such as law courts – grew considerably weaker during the sixth, seventh and eighth centuries. Power was delegated from the public to the private sphere. Both families and the private networks constructed in local society became important alternatives to the institutions provided by public society. This development must have strengthened the position of women. The fact that women were allowed to hold and possess land, despite various laws to the contrary, serves to illustrate this point.[54] In a famous essay from 1973 (published in 1974 and later reprinted), Jo Ann McNamara and Suzanne Wemple emphasised the relevance of family position (i.e., influence derived from the private sphere) for women with access to public power. Using evidence from early medieval law codes, McNamara and Wemple argued that, since the line between the public and the private spheres was rather indistinct in the early Middle Ages, women could attain more power than in other periods because of their involvement in family and kinship networks.[55]

Another example of how this theory has been applied to medieval history is provided by Megan McLaughlin in an essay on women warriors (1989). According to McLaughlin, female warriors (or rather warlords, since it is impossible to tell whether they actually fought or simply presided over their forces at the battlefield) were more frequent in the Middle Ages than in most other periods of history. She explains this historical anomaly by maintaining that the military life, usually belonging to the public, male-dominated sphere, coincided with the domestic sphere to an unusually large degree during the Middle Ages. Instead of being characterised by huge, professional armies, the warrior society of the Middle Ages was built upon small warbands tied to the private households of chieftains and kings. The daughters of a noble house would have been exposed to military practices and heard military exploits praised from an early age.[56]

While it is true that the theory of private versus public spheres has several interesting features, especially for historians analysing the decline of female influence during the eleventh and twelfth centuries,[57] the theory is unfortunately also hampered by several difficulties. One major problem is that this particular anthropological perspective is hard to accept within the theoretical framework of gender systems as being constructed on a social and cultural level (see above pp. 25–33). This has been pointed out by one of the leading advocates of the private versus public model, Michelle Zimbalist Rosario. The model, according to Rosario, may be responsible for equating women with their biological function because of its focus on female biology, manifested in the idea that family shapes women. Gender structures are, Rosario admits, rather shaped by a multitude of particulars, such as social structure and cultural attitudes.[58]

My own main critical remark, however, is different. By transferring sociological concepts from one period, the twentieth century, to another, the early Middle Ages, anachronistic interpretations are automatically invited. In fact, the early medieval household and the early medieval neighbourhood can hardly be regarded in the same way as we regard their modern equivalents, either from the point of view of empirical analysis or from the point of view of theory. During the

Middle Ages, relationships that we today think of as very private could be thought of as belonging to the public sphere of life by the men and women themselves. The differences between a private sphere and a public sphere are far more difficult to establish for the Middle Ages than for, say, bourgeois society in the nineteenth century. How do we ascertain which aspects were 'private' and which 'public' in the early Middle Ages? For instance, how are we to classify a royal court, especially a court that is dominated by powerful women such as Theudelinda and Brunhild (both of whom we will meet later in this book)? In Janet Nelson's words, 'the distinction between public and private action becomes redundant in the context of the royal hall'.[59] How are we to classify a nunnery? How are certain actions, such as assassinations, linked to the private and/or to the public spheres? Is the juxtaposition of private and public at all fruitful in an analysis of early medieval society?

Even if we assume that these two bipolar spheres always exist, the model would still be of little use if we study a period during which the distinctions between the spheres were blurred. McLaughlin's essay on women warriors is a perfect example of both the usefulness and the dangers of adhering to the theory with regard to such a period. While providing a good background to McLaughlin's reasoning, the theory also masks some important facts. Thus, it makes it easy to forget that violence, the most essential element of warfare, is neither by necessity a public nor a private phenomenon. Today, as is well known, most violent crime in Western society is carried out within the family. In the Middle Ages, violence was considerably more public.[60] Likewise, other aspects of warfare (diplomacy, planning, provisioning, etc.) may also shift from one 'sphere' to another one. Historically speaking, warfare (as a concept encompassing all of these elements) is far too complex a phenomenon to be assigned to one of two bipolar spheres. Another danger inherent in McLaughlin's use of the theory is, in my opinion, that it might obscure several issues of greater historical significance than the particular aspects visualised on the battlefield. What does McLaughlin actually say? Does she argue that warfare was a natural part of women's lives and that powerful women in the Middle Ages should be automatically regarded as female warlords? No, she does not. McLaughlin's evidence, chiefly from the period from the ninth century to the thirteenth, is (as she freely admits) largely anecdotal, and it rarely supplies us with sufficient material to draw wide-ranging conclusions with theoretical implications. It does not help us understand what was regarded as the *normal* female way of acting within medieval politics. True, McLaughlin has remarked, correctly, that women could sometimes lead armies and intervene in feuds, but this information should be placed within a larger framework. How did these women *usually* act when confronted with a political problem? What did their political culture look like? Was warfare a basic tactical element of any conflict, or was it perceived as an emergency action?

For another example of the difficulties inherent in the model, we may look at the gendering of early medieval social arenas that has been revealed in recent research. In her study of early medieval society in Ireland, Lisa Bitel stressed the fact that

(1) Men and women did not usually share the same social arenas and social networks – while the men used various political alliances based upon relations such as kinship, fosterage and patronage, women forged their alliances mainly within the sphere of production (for example weaving).
(2) Even when men and women did use the same social arenas, they often used these places (for example churches) in very different ways.[61]

In other words female networks were based on economic activity rather than on traditional political activity. To understand how female influence worked, we would have to evaluate the roles of production (and perhaps economy in general) within early medieval Irish political culture, regardless of whether the actions we are interested in took place on farms (private sphere) or in the markets (public sphere). Moreover, we sometimes find men and women acting in the *same* social arena (private or public?), but we cannot decide a priori how to interpret the behaviour of groups of men versus groups of women.

Judging from these arguments, it is in my opinion far more fruitful to study early medieval gender structures from other points of view than that of public versus private. Instead, we should focus on subjects such as political culture, economic and cultural contacts, production and spatial conceptualisation. This could lead to far more interesting results than the ones we would inevitably arrive at if we simply attempted to interpret every action as belonging to either a public or a private sphere. The Irish example also clearly demonstrates that male and female power, especially with regard to networks of allies, could take very different forms. This does not mean that male power was more important than female power, even if this is often likely to have been the case, as far as actual politics is concerned. However, the fact that male and female power structures were shaped often in fundamentally different ways means that these structures looked different, were different and had different meanings. To understand society, we must study both the male and the female worlds. For instance, it is impossible to determine who benefited most from the Irish institution of fosterage. While the men gained human resources to be used in the form of future political alliances, the women forged emotional ties that could undoubtedly also be used for a number of purposes if and when the need arose.[62]

As is revealed by these questions and observations, something in the anthropological theory of public versus private is clearly lacking. Actually, this should hardly surprise us. The theory was never meant to be applied to this period. The fact that it is difficult to use in early medieval studies says more about the poverty of theoretical thinking on the part of medievalists than about the weaknesses of sociology. It is all too easy to criticise the theory for being unable to help us understand, let alone explain, the actions of powerful women such as Theudelinda, Romilda, Radegund and their contemporaries, but we have hitherto done very little to remedy this.

At the risk of complicating things even further, I would like to emphasise a point made by Guy Halsall in his study of Frankish grave-goods in the sixth and seventh centuries. Halsall's main observation is that these objects are able to tell us a lot about social tensions and social power – since they undoubtedly represented certain important aspects of status – but he wisely refrains from arguing that they represented *all* aspects of status. Different kinds of status, like different kinds of power, were visualised differently. All societies have several ways of manifesting and using power. For instance, as Halsall points out, status was visualised differently with regard to age: the fact that old people did not have grave-goods does not mean that they were less important, merely that their power was expressed by other means. In fact, in most pre-industrial societies, age was considered to bring wisdom. Finding evidence for this, however, is extremely difficult, since this kind of status was transmitted and felt in ways that we have not yet been able to decode.[63]

Another illustrative example of the fact that different kinds of power were visualised in different ways is supplied by Bonnie Effros' analysis of early medieval rituals. As is demonstrated in her study, the Merovingian queens paid much attention to the way they were buried and the way they were remembered. Saint Balthild, for example, was commemorated in a manner clearly fitting her worldly status as Frankish queen.[64] Gertrude of Nivelles, on the other hand, appears to have been buried in an ostensibly humble way (as far as her mortuary costume is concerned), probably in order to imitate the example of Saint Melania the Younger (d. 439). According to Effros, Gertrude's *vita* thus offers us rare documentation of a woman's conscious choice of burial dress that expressed the values she chose to emulate. Being deprived of the principal avenues of status display in a warrior society, the expression of power assimilated the late antique vocabulary of sanctity. This applies not only to mortuary custom but also to the way women such as Radegund chose to live (and have their lives described by writers such as Venantius Fortunatus).[65] The ideas of sanctity also influenced the way corpses of high-ranking females were cared for. Members of the wealthy stratum of Merovingian Gaul sought to imitate the burials of exemplary Christians and thereby demonstrate the religious orthodoxy of their dead relatives with physical evidence, a strategy from which they themselves could gather strength and influence in local society. For instance, they tried to prevent bodily decay by using linen bandages as well as herbs, particularly myrrh. The accounts of embalming found in saints' *vitae* have been confirmed by archaeological excavations.[66]

These cases should suffice as examples of the enormous difficulties facing a scholar trying to understand early medieval power structures, especially by way of ideas and models constructed for the benefit of research into completely different periods. Any theoretical perspective applied to studies in early medieval history should, therefore, be carefully taken into consideration in combination with an awareness of early medieval mentality. That is not to say that such theories and models should be altogether avoided. On the contrary they should, if possible, reflect the specific cultural manifestations of the historical situation in question. For instance, it is wrong to assess the functions and the roles of female warlords (as McLaughlin does) without taking into consideration the fundamental transformation of value patterns in the *Völkerwanderungszeit*, in the process that I refer to as social militarisation (see pp. 371–73).

Early medieval women in current historical research: economy, reproduction and religion

This is not the place for a detailed relation of all that historians have discovered concerning early medieval women. The range of questions and important issues that have been studied and discussed in recent decades is much too vast for in this book.[67] However, some aspects should be briefly remarked upon since they could, hypothetically, have had an important impact on political culture.

First, it must be made clear that the economic and legal position of early medieval women would appear to have been much better than has usually been assumed. Most women were, it is true, subjected to male rule according to institution known as *mundium*. Also, many early medieval laws in Western Europe (although not in Visigothic Spain) denied women the right to inherit land.[68] In practice many women, especially widows, were nevertheless able to act as individuals in their own right. Furthermore, they could emerge as very wealthy, and thus very powerful, individuals. Frankish fathers, openly contravening legal restrictions, deeded farms to their daughters, and kings had to legislate to stop wealthy landlords from giving away too much land in *morgengabe* (in Anglo-Saxon England known as *morgengifu*) a 'morning gift' to the wife after the consummation of the marriage. Ever since the pioneering work of David Herlihy in the 1960s, a number of studies have illuminated the strong economic position of both Frankish and Lombard women who belonged to the land-owning stratum.[69] The situation was similar in England; the Anglo-Saxon laws all hint at an element of financial independence and responsibility in the wife's status, and English mothers appear to have disputed with their children over their right to bestow fields upon distant kinswomen.[70] Similarly in Ireland families tended to ignore laws aiming to prevent daughters from inheriting property.[71]

However, despite our increasing knowledge of the juridical and economic position of early medieval women, some important questions would appear to be impossible to answer. Most importantly, we do not know whether kings and magnates were monogamists or polygamists. It is often impossible to tell if a certain woman should be regarded as a wife, a concubine or as something else, and, to make matters worse, the situation varied from country to country. While it has been clearly demonstrated that polygamy was legally permitted in Ireland,[72] Janet Nelson has argued that Frankish kings practised serial monogamy.[73] A number of scholars disagree with Nelson and regard the Merovingians as polygamous.[74] In truth, our sources are far too few and give far too little concrete evidence to enable us to reach a final conclusion.[75]

Secondly, it should not be forgotten that women, then as now, possessed one specific asset that can never be appropriated by men: the ability to reproduce. According to virtually all the European literati of the Middle Ages, women's most important domestic task was the bearing of children. Needless to say, women did much more than that; they were essential to the daily survival of a standard household, performing functions that were just as vital to the agricultural economy as the men's. This is obvious to anyone who has ever performed a study of pre-industrial society, and I see little reason in enumerating all the various jobs a woman had to perform on the farm.[76] However, we should be careful not to dismiss motherhood as a key element in understanding the role of women in the household economy. The fact that only women were able to reproduce gave them power; the fact that they reared the children made it possible for them to create affective bonds that, in the end (if we move to the political arena) could provide them with a significant degree of social influence. Biological reproduction may not necessarily be an avenue to power in all societies, but it definitely appears to have been one in early medieval Europe.[77]

Thirdly, several women used the various assets, institutional as well as non-institutional, that were provided by the ecclesiastical sphere of society. So did the men, but past historians have had a tendency to overlook the degree to which early medieval women were integrated into the upper echelons of Christian culture. During recent decades, however, several studies have been published on female monasticism in the Middle Ages, mostly with a focus on periods later than the present concern.[78] Not surprisingly in view of the many aspects of the problem, the evaluation of the role of convents in the lives of early medieval women has differed among scholars. For instance, some writers (such as Jo Ann McNamara and Suzanne Wemple) have argued that the monastic life was not merely perceived as an alternative to life as a married woman but also as an escape route from a world dominated by men.[79] Others, especially Hans-Werner Goetz, have maintained the opposite: that most of those individuals (all in all far more men than women) who joined monastic institutions in the early Middle Ages did so because they were genuinely pious. In other words, we miss the point if we think in terms of male domination and female routes of escape – convents and monasteries were specifically made for religious purposes and should therefore primarily be regarded as such. However, it is impossible to overlook the fact that convents did bring protection to women who were in danger.[80] Dagmar Baltrusch-Schneider has argued that the convents offered the women not so much an alternative to marriage as an alternative to unmarried life.[81]

Scholarly interest in religious women has also led to studies and discussions within two other expanding fields of research: learned women and female saints. It is clear that historians have been prone to exaggeration when imagining early medieval Christian culture as a purely male phenomenon. For instance, it is now well-known that abbesses in the early Middle Ages participated in synods. Many women were distinguished by their impressive learning, such as Hilda of Whitby and Gertrude of Nivelles, and we have several examples of literary works written by women.[82] However, most studies, such as the important work of Janet Nelson, have been directed towards the Carolingian and the post-Carolingian world.[83] As far as the period studied in this book is concerned, the most discussed female author is Baudonivia, one of the biographers of Saint Radegund.[84]

Turning to the explicitly holy women, a significant body of material at our disposal takes the form of saints' lives, *vitae*, most from Gaul.

These have become the objects of intensive research by a number of scholars, and the material is sufficiently rich to keep historians discussing their results and their sources for a long time to come. One specific avenue of research of great interest in the present context is the study of the transformation of views on saintly qualities. As has been demonstrated by, among others, Susanne Wittern, the concept of holiness in the fourth and fifth centuries was not the same as in the seventh and eighth, and this affected the way women were portrayed by their biographers. Thus, it is clear that holy women in the early period displayed a greater degree of participation in secular affairs than in the later, more monastically influenced, period.[85]

Many writers, such as Suzanne Wemple, have judged the early Middle Ages, especially Merovingian Gaul, to have been particularly fruitful in bringing forth specifically feminine versions of holiness and mysticism.[86] In an essay by Jane Schulenburg, the period 650–750 appears as a golden age for female sanctity, when, according to her analysis of the *vitae* in *Bibliotheca Sanctorum*, almost one quarter of all new Western European saints were women (founders of convents, pious royal widows, etc.). For the entire period 500–1100, the figure is 15 percent; for the period 1050–99 the figure is as low as 9.8 percent. Unfortunately, as noted by Hans-Werner Goetz, Schulenburg's analysis does not take into account when the *vitae* (biographies) in question were written. However, it still gives us a clear indication that there were more saintly women in the period covered by the present study than in most other periods. These early medieval female saints often achieved sainthood through their position in a powerful family and their control of economic resources that enabled them to found or endow nunneries.[87] Some of them even had a prestigious background as queens.[88] As a consequence, the typical early medieval saint, as far as we are able to judge from extant sources, appears to have been an abbess. While many monks and abbots were regarded as just as holy as these women, the male saints also appear in other guises (especially as bishops). Since many roads to sainthood and religious influence were barred for members of the female sex, the monastic sphere of life (which *was* open to them) appears to have been comparatively more important for holy women than for holy men. Ambitious religious women could not become bishops, but they could, provided that they were in an economic and social position to do so, rule nunneries.

Women in politics

Looking back at the studies of early medieval women that have been published during the past few decades, it is obvious that some aspects of history have received far more attention than others. Not surprisingly, several of the works hitherto published have dealt with the ecclesiastical sphere of society, not with the secular. The main reason is, of course, that most of our sources were produced within the ecclesiastical sphere and that the writers themselves were primarily concerned with spiritual matters. At first glance, it would appear to be easier and more fruitful to study saints and abbesses than to study those queens and magnate women who remained outside the nunnery walls.

As a result, there is a big gap in our knowledge about women in politics – local and regional politics as well as politics on the level of *regna*.[89] Medieval politics, needless to say, comprised both secular and ecclesiastical aspects, but the former, one that completely dominates the political history of our own age, has been neglected in early medieval studies. Even when the saints in question were necessarily very active in secular matters (as in the case of queens such as Chlothild and Balthild), studies to date have usually neglected the secular aspects of their careers. For instance, there is, to my knowledge, no published study of the Frankish saints' lives read from a political perspective in the secular sense. Although there is a good (but at 248 pages far too short) monograph on early medieval queens by Pauline Stafford, the subject is much too big and the sources far too many for one single work to do justice to the history of an entire era. This is even more evident if we look at a brief survey of Merovingian women by Brigitte Merta, published in 1988: Merta only touches the surface, remarking on obvious features such as ties to the church, the court and the nobility but refraining from a real analysis.[90] According to Stafford, whose book covers the entire period from c. 500 to c. 1050, the power of early medieval queens was completely dependent on the women's (or the women's families') ability to find powerful kings to marry them. 'The queen's position, power, and status derived almost entirely from husband and marriage.' Bereft of her husband, a politically active woman was in a very 'hazardous' position, and her best course of action was often to remarry or to retire.[91] As is obvious from several chapters in Stafford's own work, and as will be demonstrated below, reality was much more complex. For instance, Stafford does not hesitate to admit that royal women could gain considerable influence through their control of wealth[92] and their children.[93] A similar picture emerges in Suzanne Wemple's broad analysis of Frankish women (1981).[94] Janet Nelson, in a famous article on Brunhild and Balthild from 1978, has remarked on the important fact that it was possible for women (at least sexually attractive ones) to climb the ladder towards queenhood without the backing of powerful families. 'The queen's initial offer to her husband of sexual services could obviously serve as a power-base as long as she retained his affections.'[95] Nelson has also emphasised the possibilities available to politically active women through the construction of networks of secular as well as ecclesiastical allies.[96]

In an article on the role of women in the Germanic warbands, Michael Enright (1988) has emphasised the power gained by the queen through her very life and function as a royal consort. The early medieval king's wife, according to Enright, was more than just a hostess carrying around mead cups; rather, she functioned in the royal hall as women do in society where they act as bonds between families who create and embody alliances in order to fashion friendship or restore peace between feuding groups. She was an institutional go-between, a *mediatrix*.[97] In this way, she acquired royal legitimacy that did not evaporate on the death of her husband. Thus, even a childless royal widow could sometimes exert a considerable degree of political influence. 'To all concerned, the old king's wife would have appeared as the most promising bridge to peaceful possession, a conduit to the justifiable power which she symbolizes but cannot exercise in her own name.'[98]

It should be made clear that there is a distinct chronological bias in most of the books and articles on women's roles in early medieval secular politics. There is far more literature on Carolingian and post-Carolingian queens than on politically powerful women before 800. In particular, there has been much research into the tenth century, the age of the Ottonians.[99] Most of the material on politically active women that is analysed in Christine Fell's study of women in Anglo-Saxon England belongs to the period from the ninth to the eleventh centuries.[100] Scholars such as Franz-Reiner Erkens and Kurt-Ulrich Jäschke have also made significant contributions to our knowledge of powerful women in the eleventh and twelfth centuries.[101] Furthermore, there are a number of works on prominent Carolingian women, for example the Empress Judith.[102] The above-mentioned work by Suzanne Wemple (1981) serves primarily to illustrate how the position of women deteriorated during the Carolingian period after having improved during the Merovingian era.[103] As far as Byzantium is concerned, the important contributions to women's history made by Angeliki Laiou deal with the high and the late Middle Ages.[104] According to Laiou, the late eleventh century witnessed the emergence of the aristocratic woman as an important element in the society and politics of the Byzantine Empire.[105]

As far as the period discussed in this book is concerned, however, there is no basic overview and very few thorough analyses. Even the most important article that has hitherto been published on Merovingian queens, Janet Nelson's analysis of Brunhild and Balthild, can hardly be said to have resulted in a wave of studies of pre-Carolingian queens. This is unfortunate, especially since Nelson's study clearly demonstrates that early medieval queens could be very powerful indeed. As a result of their power, the writers of history often painted them in harshly stereotypical colours, turning the female political enemies of their own factions into 'Jezebels', new versions of Jezebel, the evil wife of King Ahab in the Old Testament.[106] The impression of female power evident in Nelson's text has been further revealed by Ian Wood in his book on the Merovingian kingdoms[107] as well as by Enright. All in all, however, Wood's analysis of Frankish queens forms only a minor part of his study, and he makes no attempt to set his results in a wider theoretical framework. Enright's thought-provoking essay has unfortunately not been followed by a more detailed analysis, at least none that has been published.

In the eyes of a non-medievalist, my complaints may seem a bit too strong. After all, we do have many studies of Carolingian and post-Carolingian queens – can we not use these analyses in order to understand how Merovingian and Lombard queenship worked? Judith, Louis the Pious' wife, and the Byzantine princess Theophanu, Otto II's powerful widow, belonged to the early Middle Ages just as much as the Lombard queen Theudelinda and the Frankish queen Fredegund. Is it really necessary to delve deep into the writings of Gregory of Tours, Paul the Deacon, Bede, Jordanes and all the anonymous writers of the 'Dark Ages' to elucidate the situation even more thoroughly than has already been done for other sub-periods of the early Middle Ages?

The answer is yes, and with a good reason. To many students of later history, the Middle Ages as such may appear as one period with only marginal differences between the various constituent centuries. At the very least, the three major sub-periods (i.e., the 'early', 'high' and 'late' Middle Ages) are, according to many non-medievalists, a priori to be regarded as chronological blocks defined by all-encompassing social, economic and mental structures. In truth, however, the period known as 'the Middle Ages' never existed. It is simply an inadequate term used to denote the stretch of time separating antiquity from the early modern era. Thus, the concept known as 'the early Middle Ages', which would appear to be central to this book, is merely a tool of the language; we only use it for practical reasons. The concept does *not* hint at a common set of values, nor at a common socio-economic structure, and certainly not at the existence of a common political culture that would have enabled, say, Empress Theophanu to enter a sixth-century Frankish court with good prospects of assuming power.

The danger inherent in attempts to use tenth-century results to illuminate pre-Carolingian politics is especially evident if we focus on the very institutions that framed the lives of kings and queens. During the centuries studied in this book, the women at the royal courts acted without the backing of a formal framework of queenship. Although they all, in some way, belonged to the royal house – as consorts, mistresses, daughters, aunts or nieces of kings – they never became queens in the post-Carolingian sense of the word. As Janet Nelson has shown, the rites of queen-making and the institutionalisation of queen did not evolve until the ninth century, in connection with the development of the ideology of kingship. The oldest possible reference to the formal elevation of a woman to queenship is the reference in Fredegar's *Continuationes* for the year 751, when Bertrada benefited from Pippin's elevation to king (p. 239). This reference is, however, far too vague to be of any use in the present study. The real evidence belongs to the world of Charlemagne's successors, especially Charles the Bald.[108] The world of Fredegund and Theudelinda was very different from that of the dominant women of post-Carolingian Europe, such as Theophanu, who found her position as queen, royal widow and regent ready-made.[109]

The lack of studies has resulted in strange, diverging descriptions of the roles of women in early medieval society. Even in the 1990s, one writer may (often, it would seem, unconsciously) paint a political picture of early medieval women that is widely different from that of another. In some works, women may be described as very powerful, while in others they are shown to have been structurally weak and submissive. For instance, Clarissa Atkinson (1991) argues that, since there is much legal evidence for the necessity of keeping women safe, women in general were extremely vulnerable. She even goes so far as to regard the early medieval queens as 'peripheral'.[110] In his ambitious attempt at summing up what we know of early medieval queens, Hans-Werner Goetz (1995) argues against the existence of a specific female way of exercising and holding on to power. On the contrary, it would appear to follow from his argument that queens (when they were in a position to do so) ruled in a way similar to the way the kings ruled. There were few, if any, structurally gender-specific tactics and strategies that were instrumental in forming the career patterns of kings and queens. Rather, these patterns depended on circumstance (such as good relations with the king) and individuality (see above, pp. 28–29), on Goetz' evaluation of gender as being of secondary importance during the early Middle Ages).[111] However, note that Goetz does not undertake a study of female politics: the various chapters of his book deal with monastic life, marriage, the peasantry, learned culture and images of women. His inability to discern gender-specific political tactics thus reflects, at least to a certain extent, the lack of published research at his disposal.

Despite the lack of studies of pre-Carolingian queens and female magnates, a few important aspects would seem to have been elucidated. Judging from the studies that have been carried out so far, early medieval female politics appears to have been closely associated with biological reproduction. The queens were dependent on their ability to produce male heirs and on the latters' survival. They used their sons to secure their own positions and as stepmothers often did what they could to make life hard for the sons of other royal women. This is apparent in the history of most Western European countries, in Anglo-Saxon England as well as on the Continent. A queen's power depended on her relations with her husband, on her wealth and on her role as the one responsible for the birth of the next king.[112] Royal women could more easily acquire and wield power through motherhood than through marriage. In Clarissa Atkinson's words, 'the king's mother was much more secure than his consort'.[113] Another aspect that is too obvious not to be noticed is the fact that royal women lived insecure lives. For instance, Brigitte Merta has remarked upon the physical dangers to Merovingian queens in her 1988 article.[114] Still, the influence exerted by the queens themselves, in their capacity as powerful human beings in their own right, can, in view of what has been written by scholars such as Stafford, Wemple, Nelson and Enright, hardly be denied. It remains, however, to be explained.

Political culture and gender

The sub-title of this book is 'Gender and Political Culture in the Early Middle Ages'. So far we have briefly surveyed and discussed some of the current thoughts and theories on gender as well as some of the results of recent early-medieval studies. Before venturing into the sources, it is also necessary to approach the third concept in the subtitle: political culture.

The concept of political culture originated among sociologists in the beginning of the 1960s. It served as a means to bridge the gap between micro- and macroanalysis in sociological research. Lucian Pye, Gabriel Almond, Sidney Verba and others defined political culture as a certain pattern of attitudes towards politics that provide a meaning to political action. Political culture, according to them, denoted the individual's psychological orientation towards political objects.[115] The concept has since been modified through research and the need to respond to criticism. Gradually, the term has come to refer to what we might describe as political mentality: patterns of political behaviour shared between those who participate in politics.[116]

A significant contribution to the study of political culture was made by Nicolas Demertzis in 1985. Demertzis assumes an actionalist rather than a behaviourist approach to the concept. According to Demertzis, political culture should be understood as political practice; the actor's point of view is regarded as essential. Thus, political culture expresses the recursive process whereby individuals and social groups contribute to the making of politics; it also shows how politics is understood and conceptualised by individuals.[117] It should not be confused with political structure. While it is true that structures to a certain extent determine political action, political action as such engenders the possibility of reshaping the structures. Inspired by Giddens' structuration theory, Demertzis defines political culture as 'the complex way political structures are structured and structuring at the same time. They determine political action and at the same time they are determined by it, mediating each other constantly in a plurality of modalities and potentialities.'[118]

In this way, political culture becomes something more than just the reflection of (or the opposite to) political structures. The concept of political culture turns into a description of a vast number of actions, whether innovative or based on routine, actions that actively mould and change the political structure of which they form a part.

Since the concept is a sociological one, political culture can hardly be said to have been embraced by historians in general. There are, of course, a few exceptions. For instance, scholars such as Eva Österberg and Peter Aronsson have made use of the concept in their studies of pre-industrial Swedish agrarian society; Österberg in particular has remarked upon its usefulness to historians.[119] As far as the early Middle Ages are concerned, the lack of available data for the period makes most of the inherent analytical possibilities of the concept impossible to realise. However, the basic theoretical approach is just as interesting from the point of view of a study of sixth-century Gaul as it is for a study of contemporary society. Persons such as Sigibert, Chilperic, Brunhild and Fredegund all acted within a political structure that awarded them a set of roles and cultural attitudes, but none of these Merovingian protagonists on the historical scene lacked the power of improvisation. As actors, they could attempt to turn and twist politics into something that suited their own purposes. If faced with a structural problem, a smart king or queen could discover a solution. If he or she were successful, the structure would bend and allow other individuals similar opportunities. Likewise, by routinely conforming to a certain pattern of action, this pattern would be strengthened and possibly incorporated within the structure.

Demertzis does not make a point of gender; nor do the medievalist gender historians make a point of political culture. There is, however, no reason why the two concepts could not be used together in an attempt to broaden our view of early medieval society. Furthermore, the marriage of political culture and gender enables us to narrow the theoretical issues of the present study into a more clearly defined, and hopefully fruitful, analytical problem. Instead of trying to uncover and analyse early medieval political culture as such (or early medieval gender structures as such), the aim of this study is to interpret political actions from a gender perspective. The theoretical implications of political culture, if we accept Demertzis' actionalist approach to the concept, also serve to weaken the deterministic reasoning that accompanies many of the current ideas of the structural position of women in the early Middle Ages. Regardless of whether we assume queens, princesses and magnate women to have been firmly subjugated to male domination or whether we regard them as Dark-Age versions of Margaret Thatcher, they always retain their ability to act on their own and, through their very participation in politics, change their structural positions.

The issue also contains an ethical aspect. By focusing on the actions and actors instead of on the structures, we emphasise the contribution made to history by the human beings themselves. Structures and political patterns do *not* shape history; history is shaped by individuals, whether acting in groups or on their own. This fact, which is, or should be, self-evident to most of us, is nevertheless often obscured in medievalist research. One of the reasons, of course, is the immense impact of the structuralist thinking of the French Annales School on medieval studies in general. We have been led to believe that 'medieval man' (meaning everybody who lived in the Middle Ages) behaved and responded in a certain fashion. His or her actions were determined by the thoughts and patterns of life that made up the mental world of everybody who lived during those centuries. Whether consciously or unconsciously, many medievalists still base their assumptions of how people acted, and why they acted the way they did, on this structuralist model. The actors – the human beings – are submerged in a sea of structural preconditions. However, by perceiving them as actors with a political culture that enabled them to respond to, to mould and to change the political structure, the unethical negation of the impact of human beings in medieval history is done away with.

Summary

The study of gender in the early Middle Ages, in particular with regard to politics, suffers from both a lack of empirical research and a lack of theoretical awareness. As has been pointed out above, there is no scholarly consensus on the importance of gender in early medieval society. Several recent attempts to analyse the position of women in early medieval Europe point in widely different directions. For instance, it would appear to follow from Goetz' study that men and women acted within the same social spheres and used similar strategies. Bitel, however, arrives at a completely different conclusion. It should be noted that both of these works were published in the middle of the 1990s – in other words, this particular field of research must still be regarded as being in its infancy. It is doubtful whether many of those who discuss early medieval gender structure in journals and at conferences are aware of the wide range of opinions and latent conflicts inherent in the topic.

Those gender studies that have been carried out by early medievalists have mostly focused on other aspects than politics. Due to this scholarly neglect, very few structural features of the lives of early medieval queens and magnate women have been thoroughly elucidated. I remarked upon three aspects that form exceptions to the rule: (1) that the economic and legal position of early medieval women appears to have been much better than was previously assumed, (2) that the reproductive ability of women was of great social and political importance, and (3) that several women used the various assets that were provided by the ecclesiastical sphere of society. We have learnt that royal and magnate women could hold land and influence society (including politics) by way of their sons, their bishops and their convents, but we have also been taught an important lesson: that they lived very insecure lives.

In this book, I study the early Middle Ages, more precisely the period from the sixth century to the late eighth century, from a gender perspective and from the point of view of political culture. I believe that an awareness of gender as a concept in historical research can help us to understand early medieval politics to a larger extent than has hitherto been believed possible. While men and women in the past often acted quite differently within the political sphere, the lack of studies of political culture has made this difference hard to specify and thus impossible to explain theoretically.

For practical purposes, I focus upon what the written sources can tell us about royal and magnate women. Ideally, of course, one might argue that the study ought to encompass all political actors, male as well as female, but there are several good reasons why this would be impractical. First, the study would become too large and consume too much time. Secondly, it is doubtful whether such an all-encompassing study would prove as stimulating from the point of view of scholarly research as it is my intention that the present study should be. To introduce a hitherto little studied topic and a theoretical combination that has so far been neglected, it is often more fruitful to narrow the field of research to specific groups rather than try to grasp an entire society. By directing my efforts to illuminating the political culture of early medieval women, the importance of research both into medieval political culture and into early medieval gender structures is highlighted in a way that would hardly have been the case if these aspects had been submerged in a large synthesis.

As far as political culture is concerned, it should be made clear that the concept, as explained by Demertzis, is hardly a key to new questions and new models in medieval history, but rather serves to provide a general perspective from which to analyse individual actors. For full benefit from Demertzis' conclusions, we would need far more information about the particular historical structures (in the present case early medieval gender structures) than medievalists usually have to hand. For instance, it is impossible for me to 'decide' exactly when a certain female political actor began to transform the political culture by her own actions. However, the concept of political culture helps me to understand her societal activities as such. The political culture that is revealed and mirrored in her activities should be understood as an integrative process. In the end, the analysis will reveal not a static system of roles and patterns but rather a development – history in motion. The particular incidents that we are able to read about and study should be regarded as concrete manifestations of this process of political culture. My aim here is to search for patterns linking these manifestations. Hopefully, I will then be able to reach a preliminary conclusion as to how women acted on the political scene.

As far as gender theory is concerned, the present analysis is founded on the belief that gender is to a large extent based on cultural construction more than on biological differences. Those who study gender relations with the help of axiomatic 'truths' about non-historical elements such as physical strength and psychological impulses should be read with caution. Although human emotions and gender differences with regard to physical strength have remained unchanged throughout history, these non-historical elements of nature have been conceptualised and manifested in completely different ways because of cultural, economic, military and ideological attitudes.

Construction is of less importance to the present study than the *manifestations* that are linked to specific events and periods. As remarked above, historical manifestations are extremely difficult to fully comprehend. Any single manifestation is far too complex to be understood in terms of biological, or any other, compulsion. However, the manifestations can be identified with, or at least linked to, cultural constructs of gender relations. By analysing the concrete manifestations of gender in politics, we have the opportunity to grasp the complexity of resources and tactics that were available in the early Middle Ages.

Since all the manifestations studied in this book are revealed by specific transmitters (such as Gregory of Tours, Paul the Deacon, Bede and Jordanes), we must be very careful not to study the various events and persons as if they belonged to one and the same early medieval spectrum. They did not. For instance, what Gregory tells us about Queen Brunhild is entirely different from the picture of Brunhild as it is painted in most seventh-century works. Therefore, the structure of this book has been built around the sources. Each chronicler and biographer must be read and interpreted in his or her own right. I have used the most important Western European chronicles from Jordanes to Paul the Deacon as well as a number of hagiographic works. These sources have been studied strictly from the point of view of the female gendering of politics. Not wanting to confine my reading of the chronicles to a traditional search for pieces of evidence, I have also made a point of elucidating the various stereotypical images of women that are present in the texts. The stereotypes themselves tell us much about society, but they are also valuable in our attempts to decode political attitudes. A stereotype indicates how a certain number of people liked to imagine that a particular kind of individual (in this case a powerful woman) would act in a certain situation. Thereby, if we are able to interpret it correctly, a stereotype – such as an evil stepmother – may develop into a window to early medieval mentality.

Part 2

Analysis of early medieval texts

The women of Jordanes

We know very little about the man Jordanes. He appears to have belonged to a prominent Gothic family, and he probably lived in Constantinople during the first half and middle of the sixth century. His most famous work, *De origine actibusque Getarum*, a history of the Goths, was probably written in 551. The work is relatively short and is largely based on what other writers, especially Cassiodorus, had already produced.[120]

In *De origine actibusque Getarum*, we encounter 333 individuals, not counting those who only appear as anonymous members of groups and peoples. Of these 333, 299 individuals are men, 34 women. In other words, approximately 89 percent of all the individuals that Jordanes thought worth mentioning were male, only 11 percent female. To this should be added that most groups (the members of which were not counted separately) are distinctly male. There are only two textually prominent female collectives: a group of warlike Amazons[121] and a group of witches (*quasdam magas mulieres, quas patrio sermone Haliurunnas is ipse cognominat*, 'some female witches that he called 'haliurunnas' in his own language') whose children are said to have been the ancestors of the Huns.[122] In fact, Jordanes explicitly tells the reader that his book is a tale of Gothic men, not Gothic women.[123]

Looking more closely at the 34 women of *De origine actibusque Getarum*, we find that most of them are mere names (such as Medopa, Sunilda, Ababa and even famous Ostrogothic women of the sixth century such as Matesuentha). Only four women have what we might refer to as personalities of their own: Lampeto,[124] Marpesia,[125] Penthesilea[126] and Honoria.[127] It is true that a couple of other female protagonists in Jordanes' work appear on more than one occasion, but we only get glimpses of their activity, and their contribution to Gothic history is never explained. For example, the important female regent Amalasuintha (referred to by Jordanes as Amalasuentha) is only mentioned in passing as a woman whose unimportance made her easy to get rid of. Jordanes even hints that Amalasuintha understood this herself, referring to her supposed suspicion that the Ostrogoths would refuse to accept her rule because she was a woman (*ne pro sexus sui fragilitate a Gothis sperneretur, secum deliberans...*, 'since she feared that she would be rejected by the Goths due to the weakness of her sex, she considered...').[128] Most women of Jordanes' world are mentioned either as mothers, wives or daughters or, especially on one occasion,[129] as victims of male cruelty.

Lampeto, Marpesia and Penthesilea: three Amazon queens

The chief exception to the rule of the unimportance of women in Jordanes' text is his story of the Gothic Amazons. Of course, what Jordanes has to say about these women has nothing whatsoever to do with history in the way we use the term; the events are supposed to have taken place a long time ago in a heroic age of myths, adventurous wanderings and martial exploits. Nor did Jordanes invent the Amazons himself; they had been a feature of classical literature for several centuries.

Jordanes explains that the existence of the Gothic Amazons was the result of an accident. Women were not supposed to use weapons and form armies, but they were on one occasion forced to act in manly fashion in order to protect themselves from being forcibly abducted by another tribe. Having won the battle, they realised that they liked fighting so much that they wanted to continue living the lives of warriors. They chose the two bravest women they could find, Lampeto and Marpesia, to act as chieftains. Lampeto remained at home to defend the country from attack, while Marpesia and her warriors set out for Asia. Both Lampeto and Marpesia are implicitly characterised as good women: Jordanes uses the word *audentiores* to indicate their warlike superiority.[130]

Later, Jordanes' attitude towards the Amazons grows increasingly more negative. In writing about the whole group of female warriors, he uses words such as *crudelitas*.[131] However, he does not refrain from admitting that their leaders could still perform individual acts of greatness, especially mentioning Queen Penthesilea's actions during the Trojan war.[132]

Honoria

Honoria appears in Jordanes' text at a critical moment in the history of Italy. Attila and the Huns were about to begin a major raid but were stopped by papal diplomacy and fears for the safety of Attila himself. Attila promised to return to his own lands, but he demanded that the Roman government send him the imperial princess Honoria and all her riches. There was nothing unusual about this demand, and Jordanes does not emphasise it further.[133] However, he does give us a short description of Honoria's character. Due to her position at court, she was forced to live in chastity. Disapproving of this, Honoria had secretly dispatched messages by way of a eunuch to Attila, offering herself as a diplomatic tool to be used in his future negotiations with the Roman court. She did this, according to Jordanes (who perceived her behaviour as shameful), in order to be able to indulge in sinful living, not caring that she might bring ruin to her country.[134]

Summary

The results from the analysis of Jordanes' work are disappointing. True, the main reason for this is undoubtedly the fact that *De origine actibusque Getarum* is a relatively short work, but this does not wholly explain the absence of individual women from the text. We would have expected that someone such as Amalasuintha might have been the object of at least a basic characterisation (i.e., whether she was good or bad), but all we are told is that she was conscious of her own frailty in her capacity as a woman.

Jordanes' decision to paint the world of the Goths and the Romans in male colours is, furthermore, explicit. He tells us himself that he was conscious of a gender perspective when working on the book, almost apologising for writing too much about the Amazons and promising to devote the rest of the work to the history of men. In other words Jordanes perceived women's history as *less important* than the history of men. From his point of view (and, we might assume, from the point of view of most members of the Late Roman social class to which he belonged), empresses, queens, princesses and the like were politically inferior to their male counterparts. Their actions counted for less.

When we do encounter female individuals in *De origine actibusque Getarum*, they are either morally inferior, sex-hungry beings whose actions are dangerous to their own country (Honoria), or they are mythical Amazons or witches from the past.

The women of Gregory of Tours

In the year 579, a Parisian woman was accused of adultery. The woman would appear to have come from a wealthy family; her husband – whom she had left, for reasons that will remain unknown to us – was certainly a man of some importance. The husband had not been able to prevent her from leaving him, but he, or at least his family, objected to the fact that she appeared to be sleeping with another man. This not only made the husband look stupid; it was a disgrace to the entire family. A troop of armed Franks appeared outside the house of the woman's father, shouting that he must prove his daughter's innocence or else let her die. The father responded that his daughter was completely innocent, and he volunteered to swear an oath to clear her name. Both parties then went to the church of Saint-Denis, where the father raised his hands over the altar and swore that his daughter had done nothing wrong. However, the husband's supporters had no faith in the oath that they had witnessed; they openly accused the man of having perjured himself. An argument ensued, and everybody drew their swords. Soon, the church had turned into a battlefield: men of noble birth, some of whom belonged to the court of King Chilperic I of Soissons, set upon each other in front of the altar. Many received severe wounds, the holy church was spattered with human blood, the portals were pierced with swords and javelins, and weapons were drawn in senseless anger at the very tomb of the saint. Eventually, with great difficulty, a measure of peace was restored, but no services could be held in the church until the king had been informed about the event. The father's men and the husband's men both rushed off to court, but Chilperic did not forgive any of them. He sent them to the local bishop with orders that only if they were found not guilty were they to be admitted to communion. Eventually, after they had paid their fines, Bishop Ragnemod had them readmitted. The woman, the cause of the entire scandal and all the bloodshed, was then summoned to trial. However, she never appeared in front of the tribunal. Instead, she hanged herself.[135]

In 581 (or possibly 582), a citizen of Tours called Lupus expressed a desire to enter the church. His wife was dead, as were his children, and secular life had lost its savour. However, Lupus' pious desire could have serious economic repercussions, at least from the point of view of his relatives. His brother Ambrosius was afraid that Lupus might be persuaded to leave all his goods to the church. The solution to Ambrosius' dilemma was to find a new wife for Lupus, someone who could lure him into remaining outside the ranks of the clergy. In the beginning, Ambrosius' plan seemed to be working well. Lupus was certainly not unwilling to try out this second woman, once Ambrosius had found her and arranged a meeting when they were to exchange wedding presents. Together, Lupus and Ambrosius went to the town of Chinon, where they had a house. At this point in the story, the villain enters the stage in the guise of a woman: Ambrosius' wife. For some unexplained reason she hated her husband and was consoling herself with an adulterous relationship with another man. The trip to Chinon was, in her eyes, a golden opportunity not to be wasted. Together with her lover, she laid a trap for Ambrosius. After the two brothers had eaten and got drunk, they lay down to sleep in the same bed. In the middle of the night, the lover came creeping in under cover of darkness. He lit a handful of straw, so that he could see what he was doing. Then he drew his sword and severed Ambrosius' head from his neck with a single blow. Lupus, of course, was instantly awakened, and found himself wallowing in his brother's blood. He began to scream and shout for help, but the lover (who was actually on his way out but had to return to silence Lupus) was too strong. When the fight was over, Lupus was more dead than alive. However, before he died he was able to tell the members of the household what had happened. Not that it mattered much: the plan had succeeded. Ambrosius' widow wasted little time mourning her dead husband. Only a few days later she joined her lover and left the neighbourhood.[136]

These horrible stories are, unfortunately, good examples of the treatment of women in Gregory of Tours' *Decem Libri Historiarum*, 'Ten books of history'. Firstly, the women are seen as the root of the ensuing evil. Whether they are guilty or innocent (in the first case we would suspect her of being guilty, in the second case she definitely is, unless Gregory's source is lying) is not as important as the fact that the two, as women, provoked rumours and laid plans that led to murder and to feuds between men. Women were dangerous; their appetites, in these particular cases their sexual desires and lust for blood, made them necessary to avoid if one aspired to a good life. Secondly, the women are anonymous: we are never told their names. The same is true of many members of the female gender in *Decem Libri Historiarum*, even queens and princesses. Thirdly, the women are only conceptualised as members of a fundamentally male collective: they are associated with their husbands (and their relatives) and possibly with their fathers (and their relatives). We do not see them as women in their own right, at least not until they, like the woman in the first example, finally grab hold of the rope and hang themselves. Only in death does the Parisian woman of 579 achieve a degree of individuality. We do not meet her mother, her sisters, her friends or any other members of the social networks within which she must have acted. They surely existed, but they were not interesting to Gregory of Tours.

Gregory was born in 538 or 539 as a member of a wealthy Gallo-Roman senatorial family. Relatives of his had been or were bishops of several cities in Gaul (Tours, Lyons, Clermont and Langres). In 573, he was himself appointed to the bishopric of Tours. During his lifetime, he managed to produce the famous *Decem Libri Historiarum*, generally considered as his *chef-d'œuvre*, seven books on miracles, one book on the 'Lives of the Fathers', and various other ecclesiastical works. Most of his work has been preserved and has been the object of intense study among latinists, historians and others.[137] Here, I limit my study to *Decem Libri Historiarum*, although some other texts (for example on Saint Monegund) will be dealt with later.

All in all we encounter 1 346 individuals in *Decem Libri Historiarum* (not counting those who only appear as anonymous members of groups). Of these 1 346, 1 149 are men, 197 women. In other words, approximately 85 percent of all the individuals that Gregory thought worth mentioning were male, 15 percent female. Looking more closely at the 197 women of *Decem Libri Historiarum*, we soon realise that most of them are mere names, if that, for again a significant number are completely anonymous (referred to as 'a woman', 'the mother of', 'the daughter of', 'the wife of', and the like). 59 women (that is, some 30 percent of all the 197) have what we might regard as characters of their own. Looking more closely at these, we find that 27 of them are depicted as bad women and 24 as good women, while 8 are difficult to place in either category. These eight persons, among others Abbess Leubovera and Princess Rigunth, are either described in too few words to allow us a chance to really grasp Gregory's view of them, or his descriptions are simply too complex, showing them to be good women in some parts of the text and bad women in other chapters.

In the following, the female world of *Decem Libri Historiarum* will be revealed in different stages. At first, the Frankish queens will be dealt with in more or less chronological order, followed by the Merovingian princesses and the queens of other kingdoms. Then, a survey will be made of women belonging to the magnate stratum (wives of warlords, aristocratic founders of nunneries, etc.) followed by short overviews of Gregory's description of women associated with the ecclesiastical sphere of society and of women influenced by various evil powers.

Basina, searching for ability

Childeric I, one of the first known Merovingian kings, lived a century before Gregory of Tours. A century is a long time – it is impossible to decide which parts of Gregory's account of the fifth century are true and which are based on vague rumours. In any case, the stories of Childeric were definitely *regarded as* trustworthy by Gregory and his contemporaries, which makes them useful in a study aiming to elucidate early medieval political culture.

According to Gregory, King Childeric's life was one long debauch. He seduced one Frankish girl after another, and eventually the Franks grew so angry that they forced their notorious king into exile. Childeric fled to Thuringia, where he took refuge with King Bisinus and his wife Basina. Eight years later, however, he was able to return to his Frankish throne. Shortly afterwards, Queen Basina deserted Bisinus and joined Childeric. The Frankish king questioned her closely as to why she had come all the way from Thuringia to be with him, and she is said to have answered: 'I know that you are a strong man and I recognise ability when I see it. I have therefore come to live with you. You can be sure that if I knew anyone else, even far across the sea, who was more capable than you, I should have sought him out and gone to live with him instead.'[138] Childeric was very pleased and married her. She became pregnant and bore him a son, Clovis, commonly regarded as the greatest of all Merovingian kings.[139]

What does this tell us? Why did Gregory chose to include this passage in his chronicle? One is reason is surely that he wanted to praise the greatest hero of Frankish history, the horrible but Catholic King Clovis, founder of the Merovingian kingdom of Gaul. By making his mother Basina sing his father Childeric's praise, he further enhances Clovis' status. Clovis' father was a more capable king than the king of Thuringia; he was worth Basina's desertion of Bisinus. Basina herself appears as a strong-willed queen with a mind of her own. Only the best, Clovis' father, was good enough for her. In other words, Basina might be regarded as a convenient tool in the literary creation of Clovis. Just as important, for our purpose, is the fact that her own attempt to make a fruitful alliance (i.e., her desertion of Bisinus) was regarded as believable by Gregory of Tours. He saw nothing extraordinary in the fact that a powerful woman wanted to become even stronger by leaving one king for another. Seen from this angle, Gregory's description of Basina becomes not only a literary tool but also a fore-runner of later descriptions of powerful women, such as Brunhild and Fredegund.

Chlothild: vengeful daughter, proud grandmother and Catholic saint

Chlothild (or, more correctly, Chrodechildis) was born in c. 475 and died in 544 or 545. She is regarded as a saint by the Catholic church and is officially celebrated on 3 June.[140]

Originally, Chlothild was a Burgundian princess, daughter of King Chilperic. However, in the second half of the fifth century, the Burgundians had many co-reigning kings. One of Chilperic's brothers, Gundobad, killed both Chilperic and his wife in an eventually successful attempt to dominate the entire kingdom of the Burgundians. According to Gregory, Chlothild's mother was drowned after Gundobad had had a stone tied around her neck. Chlothild and her sister Chroma (who became a religious) were exiled – it is not known where, but it is clear that Chlothild remained within the Burgundian kingdom.[141]

The Frankish king Clovis I, the founder of the kingdom of the Franks in Gaul, often sent envoys to Burgundy. According to Gregory of Tours, these envoys saw Chlothild and were delighted. 'They observed that she was an elegant young woman and clever for her years, and they discovered that she was of royal blood.'[142] Having heard their reports, Clovis asked Gundobad for her hand in marriage. Afraid to refuse, the Burgundian king agreed and handed Chlothild over to the Franks. Clovis then made Chlothild his real wife, placing her above his mistresses, one of whom had already given him a son, Theuderic.[143]

The picture we get of young Chlothild is a nice one: elegant, clever and royal. This is Gregory's way of introducing someone he likes, a woman from whom good deeds are to be expected. Not surprisingly, the good deeds in question are closely linked with religious affairs. Having related the story of Chlothild's early years and her marriage, Gregory immediately informs his readers about Chlothild's Christian zeal. After the birth of her first son, she wanted the baby baptised. It would seem that Clovis, still a pagan, was reluctant to agree to this; at least, this is the impression Gregory wants to convey. In *Decem Libri Historiarum*, Chlothild is allowed to give a long speech (probably invented by Gregory himself) to Clovis concerning the worthlessness of pagan religion. For example, she points out the lack of morals among the old gods: 'Take your Saturn, for example, who ran away from his own son to avoid being exiled from his kingdom, or so they say; and Jupiter, that obscene perpetrator of all sorts of mucky deeds, who could not keep his hands off other men, who had his fun with all his female relatives and could not even refrain from intercourse with his own sister...'.[144] Of course, Gregory also has her tell her husband that he ought to convert to Christianity as soon as possible ('You ought instead to worship Him who at a word and out of nothing created heaven, and earth, the sea and all that is therein...', *Sed ille coli magis debit, qui caelum et terram, mare et omnia quae in eis sunt verbo ex non extantibus procreavit*). She kept repeating this, but Clovis remained a pagan, replying that 'your God can do nothing, and, what is more, there is no proof that he is a God at all'.[145]

Nevertheless, her first son was baptised and given the name Ingomer. Chlothild ordered that the church be decorated with hangings and curtains in the hope that Clovis might be brought to the faith by ceremony. Despite her good intentions, Chlothild's attempt ended in complete disaster. No sooner had Ingomer been baptised than he died in his white robes. Clovis was furious, blaming Chlothild and her so-called God for Ingomer's death ('if he had been dedicated in the name of my gods, he would have lived without question...', *si in nomine deorum meorum puer fuisset dicatus, vixisset utique...*). Chlothild replied by giving thanks to Almighty God for having deigned to welcome a child of hers into His kingdom.[146]

Chlothild's second son was also baptised and given the name Chlodomer. Very soon, the baby began to ail, and Clovis was not the least bit surprised. What else was to be expected if Chlothild were foolish enough to have the child baptised? Chlothild, however, prayed to God and, in the words of Gregory, 'at His command the baby recovered.'[147] She continued to pray that her husband might give up his idol-worship, but nothing could persuade Clovis to accept Christianity. In the end, in one of the most famous episodes of Gregory's History, Clovis was nevertheless forced to accept God's Truth when threatened by military defeat. During a war against the Alamans, the Frankish troops were rapidly being annihilated. As he saw this, Clovis is said to have raised his eyes to heaven and felt compunction in his heart. He spoke directly to 'Jesus Christ, whom Chlothild maintains to be the Son of the living God' (*Iesu Christi, quem Chrotchildis praedicat esse filium Dei vivi*), promising to be baptised if Jesus would grant him victory and give evidence of his miraculous powers. Immediately, the Alamans turned on their heels and began to run away. Returning home, Clovis told his wife how he had won a victory by calling on the name of Christ.[148]

Chlothild then ordered Remigius, Bishop of Rheims, to be secretly summoned to her. Instructed by Chlothild, Remigius urged Clovis to forsake his idols and believe in the one true God. Clovis replied that it would be politically difficult to do this, since the people under his command would not agree to forsake their gods. When he arranged a meeting with his people, however, all those present are said to have shouted their support of Remigius' idea. Shortly afterwards, Clovis was baptised 'like a new Constantine' (*procedit novos Constantinus ad lavacrum*), while Remigius uttered his famous words: 'Bow your head in meekness, Sicamber. Worship what you have burnt, burn what you have been wont to worship.'[149]

After this, Chlothild disappears from view for the rest of Clovis' reign. We only learn that she, together with her husband, was responsible for the building of a church in Paris (later the church of Sainte Geneviève), where Clovis was buried after his death in 511.[150] Gregory informs us that Chlothild went to live in Tours after the death of her husband. She served as a religious in the church of Saint Martin in Tours, and she is said to have remained in that place for the rest of her life, becoming famous for her great modesty and kindness. However, Gregory remarks, she did spend some time in Paris.[151]

Thus far, our impression of Chlothild is that of a typical saintly figure within the Catholic tradition. There is nothing surprising about the way in which Gregory describes her piety and her Christian zeal. Chlothild seems unreal, a model queen with little or no historical foundation other than her name. Then, suddenly, the image of the female saint in Saint Martin's church changes abruptly. The religious woman in Tours is transformed into a bloodthirsty royal widow in Paris.

Gregory describes how Chlothild arranged a meeting with Chlodomer, who became King of Orléans after the death of Clovis, and her other sons. She is reported to have said, in a manner hardly suitable for a future saint, 'My dear children, do not give me cause to regret the fact that I have brought you up with such care. You must surely resent the wrong which has been done to me. You must do all in your power to avenge the death of my mother and my father.'[152] In other words, Gundobad's son and heir, King Sigismund of the Burgundians, must be punished for his father's actions against Chlothild's family. The events Chlothild referred to had occurred several decades before, but she had not forgotten them.

Chlothild's sons immediately declared war on the Burgundians. King Sigismund and his brother Godomar were defeated. While trying to escape to the monastery of Agaune (Saint-Maurice in present-day Switzerland), Sigismund was captured by Chlodomer. Together with his wife and sons, the Burgundian king was imprisoned near

Orléans. However, Godomar rallied his forces and reconquered Burgundy. In this situation, Chlodomer decided to eliminate any threat posed by Sigismund by having him and his family wiped out before resuming the war against Godomar. On Chlodomer's orders, Sigismund and his wife and children were murdered and thrown down a well at Saint-Péravy-la-Colombe, a small township in the Orléanais.[153]

This happened in 523. Chlothild had had her revenge, but she paid a terrible price only a year later. In a battle against the Burgundians, Chlodomer became isolated from his troops and was killed. Godomar's men had his head hacked off and stuck on a stake. Chlothild mourned the death of her son, and when the period of mourning was over, she took Chlodomer's sons into her own household and brought them up.[154]

Unfortunately, there is more to the story. Gregory's text sheds further light on the reputedly pious old queen. The three sons of Chlodomer – Theudovald, Gunthar and Chlodovald – could in theory be regarded as heirs to their father's portion of the Frankish kingdom, and if their grandmother did a good job of bringing them up, they would probably be Chlodomer's heirs in practice as well. This fact did not escape the notice of Chlodomer's brothers Childebert I of Paris and Chlothar I of Soissons (who were also sons of Chlothild), who wanted the lands for themselves. While Chlothild was living in Paris, Childebert observed that she was lavishing all her affection on the three boys. Afraid that this would bring them into the line of succession, he sent a secret message to Chlothar, asking him to come to Paris to discuss what they were going to do to get rid of the threat posed by their nephews: 'Ought we to cut off their hair and so reduce them to the status of ordinary individuals? Or should we have them killed and then divide our brother's kingdom equally between us?'[155] According to Gregory, Chlothar was delighted by the opportunity and quickly made his way to Paris. Childebert, meanwhile, began to spread a rumour that he and his royal brother were holding a meeting to plan the coronation of the young princes. They sent a message to Chlothild (still resident in Paris) that she should send the princes to them, 'so that they may be raised to the throne'.[156]

This pleased Chlothild. She is reported to have felt great pride in the fact that her grandsons were to succeed Chlodomer; in fact, this succession would virtually eliminate the grief she felt for Chlodomer's death ('Once I see you succeed him on the throne, I shall forget that I have lost my son', *Non me puto amisisse filium, si vos videam in eius regno substitui*). The three princes set off, but their uncles had them seized and separated from their households and their tutors. Childebert and Chlothar then sent a man called Arcadius to Chlothild with a pair of scissors in one hand and a naked sword in the other. Coming into the queen's presence, he held them out to her and asked her what fate she preferred for her grandsons: 'Do you wish them to live with their hair cut short? Or would you prefer to see them killed?'[157] Chlothild was terrified but – Gregory makes a point of this – primarily angry. The sight of the drawn sword and the scissors made her furious. Her proud reply was hardly that of a saint: 'If they are not to ascend the throne, I would rather see them dead than with their hair cut short.'[158] Not wanting to see if she, on due reflection, would change her mind, Arcadius hurried back to Childebert and Chlothar. Chlothar immediately killed Theudovald and Gunthar (one of them ten years old, the other only seven) together with all their attendants and tutors. As planned, Chlodomer's former kingdom was partitioned between the two kings. When everything had been taken care of, Chlothar climbed on his horse and rode away, feeling no remorse, and Childebert skulked off to the outskirts of Paris. Chlothild placed the two small corpses on a bier and followed them in funeral procession to the church of Saint Peter, where they were buried side by side.[159] The third son of Chlodomer, young Chlodovald, was too well guarded for his uncles to kill. However, it turned out that he preferred a religious life to that as a king. He cut his hair short with his own hands, became a priest, and after his death in c. 560 was venerated as Saint Cloud.[160]

The next time we hear of Chlothild, she is back in politics. After the death of King Theuderic I of Rheims, Clovis' son by another woman, in 533 or 534, he was succeeded by his son Theudebert, who entered into an alliance with Childebert against Chlothar. When he understood the danger, Chlothar took to the woods. He constructed a great circle of barricades and prepared to resist the combined forces of his brother and his nephew. When Chlothild heard about these events, she decided to intervene. According to Gregory, she went to the tomb of Saint Martin in Tours, where she knelt in supplication and spent an entire night praying that war might not break out between her sons. Martin listened. As Childebert and Theudebert were preparing to storm Chlothar's barricades, a great storm suddenly blew up over the spot where they were encamped. Their tents were blown down and their equipment was scattered. Threatened by hailstones, thunder and lightning, the two kings did penance to God and begged Him to forgive them for having attacked their own relative. Everybody went home, and 'none can doubt that this miracle was wrought by Saint Martin through the intercession of the queen.'[161]

Since Chlothild lived before Gregory's time, we rarely observe her acting in the same way as people such as Brunhild and Fredegund. However, we do get some glimpses of her activity outside the sphere of Merovingian family politics. She definitely gave land to various individuals, whether for pious reasons or in order to create a network of clients. Anastasius, a priest in Clermont, owned property that had been granted to him by Chlothild. Apparently, this land was regarded as very important, since Bishop Cautinus of Clermont did everything he could (including burying Anastasius alive) to make him surrender the title-deeds given by the then deceased queen.[162]

More importantly, Chlothild was also able to exert considerable influence over the appointment of bishops. Gregory tells us that she commanded that Theodorus and Proculus be appointed bishops of Tours in c. 520. Theodorus and Proculus were old men who had accompanied Chlothild from Burgundy, where they had already been consecrated as bishops but had been expelled from their cities after incurring hostility there). Together, Theodorus and Proculus governed the church of Tours for two years. When they had died, Chlothild appointed another of her Burgundian friends to the bishopric, Dinifius (who held it for ten months). She endowed him with a certain property from the royal domain and empowered him to do with it what he wished.[163]

Gregory clearly regarded Chlothild as a holy woman. He rarely misses an opportunity to describe her pious nature, regardless of what he has just described her as doing. For instance, despite Gregory's assertion that Chlothild's words to Arcadius about the sword and the scissors were spoken in a sudden fit of anger (and therefore not to be regarded as representing her true feelings on the subject), he nevertheless makes it plain that she did refrain from saving her grandsons, just as she had, in a bloodthirsty manner, urged Chlodomer to attack the Burgundians. However, *immediately after* this horror story of early medieval politics and family life, Gregory goes on to give his own verdict on Chlothild, and again the image is reversed:

> Queen Chlothild earned the respect of all by her bearing. She gave alms to the poor and spent her nights in prayer. In chastity and virtue she lived out her blameless life. She endowed churches, monasteries and other holy places with the lands necessary for their upkeep; her giving was so generous and so eager that already in her lifetime she was looked upon not as a queen but as the handmaiden of God whom she served with such zeal. Neither the royal status of her sons nor her worldly goods nor earthly ambition could bring her into disrepute. In all humility she moved forward to heavenly grace.[164]

Moreover, as Chlothild finally dies, Gregory describes her as 'full of days and rich in good works' (*plena dierum bonisque operibus praedita*). Her body was carried from Tours to Paris with a great singing of psalms. Childebert and Chlothar had her buried in Saint Peter's church at the side of her husband Clovis.[165] Thus, her departure from *Decem Libri Historiarum* is just as good as her introduction. In Gregory's opinion, Chlothild was a heroine.

Looking at Gregory's description of Chlothild, it is hard to accept her as so genuinely pious as he obviously wants us to believe. She is rarely reported to have actually *done* anything that we might regard as a clear example of piety. We may assume that the church of Tours nourished a tradition of Chlothild as a pious and generous queen (after all, she did appoint some of the local bishops herself, and she did give land to at least one of them), but this does not mean that Chlothild was more pious than the rest of the Burgundians and the Franks. As a Devil's advocate, I could easily argue that Chlothild was trying to create a basis of power for herself in Tours by controlling the most important office of the city. The story of how she managed to get Clovis to accept baptism is pure legend, and the story of Chlothild's and Saint Martin's intervention to stop a Frankish war leaves much to be desired. We cannot even be sure that she lived as a religious in Tours for the greatest part of her life after 511; this may be nothing more than a local tradition. It is perfectly possible that she preferred her palace in Paris, only visiting Tours occasionally. Her alleged donations to ecclesiastical institutions probably took place, but we will never be able to ascertain her actual reasons for being generous.

What is primarily important, in the present context, about Gregory's constant attempts at making us believe in Chlothild's saintly virtues is the fact that these virtues had by his time, only a generation after the queen's death, become intimately linked with the memory of Chlothild. In retrospect, they made her powerful in her capacity as a model of a good Christian queen. As such, she could be consciously or unconsciously used, and her life could be imitated by other queens and royal widows.

When we do see Chlothild in action, we see a powerful woman with much land and several good friends (clients, agents, etc. – we know too little to be sure of their status). We also see a woman who cares about her family – her sons and grandsons as well as her dead parents – and the fact they were of royal blood. She was supposedly eager to have her rightful revenge for the death of her parents, and Gregory even makes her responsible for the war that led to King Sigismund's death. She preferred to see her grandsons whom she brought up herself killed rather than deprived of the right of succession to Chlodomer's kingdom.

Chlothar I's women

Chlothar I was a son of King Clovis I and Chlothild. When Clovis died in 511, his kingdom was divided between his sons, and Chlothar received northwestern Francia with the city of Soissons.[166]

Chlothar's first known woman was Guntheuc, who had previously been married to his brother, King Chlodomer of Orléans. Chlodomer was, as described above, killed in battle against the Burgundians in 524, and Chlothar eventually married his widow.[167] However, it is hard to believe that Guntheuc was actually Chlothar's first wife. Gregory of Tours was not a contemporary of Chlothar's, and it is impossible to reconstruct the events in his court from the few pieces of information that we receive from Gregory's work. In any case, when

Gregory on one occasion decides to sum up the various wives of the king, it becomes clear that there must have been considerable competition among Chlothar's women. In book IV, chapter 3, we are told that Chlothar had several sons by his wives:

(1) by Ingund he had Gunthar, Childeric, Charibert, Gunthchramn, Sigibert and a daughter called Chlodoswintha
(2) by Aregund (Ingund's sister) he had Chilperic
(3) by Chunsina he had Chramn[168]

Add to this Guntheuc, Vuldetrada (see below), the anonymous mother of the pretender Gundovald,[169] and the most famous of all Merovingian queens of Chlothar's generation, Saint Radegund (pp. 87–95, 280–85), not to mention various other unnamed mistresses and servant-girls, and we can easily imagine the court of the kingdom of Soissons as an archetypal Barbarian harem.

Gregory has a story to tell about the fact that Chlothar married two sisters, Ingund and Aregund. Ingund was originally a member of his household. When she had been elevated from servant-girl to royal woman, Ingund asked Chlothar to choose a wealthy and competent husband for her sister Aregund, who was also a member of his household. Ingund's reason for this request had nothing to do with her wanting Aregund to be successful. On the contrary, she was thinking of herself. As long as Aregund remained a servant-girl, she would be constantly ashamed of her. If, on the other hand, Aregund were married to a Frankish magnate, she would become a source of pride to her. Unfortunately, Ingund did not know her husband very well. In Gregory's words, Chlothar was 'too much given to woman-chasing to be able to resist this' (*cum esset nimium luxoriosus*). Filled with desire for Aregund, he instantly hurried off to the villa where she lived and married her. Returning to Ingund, he explained that his search for a wealthy and wise husband for Aregund had led him to the inevitable conclusion that the best possible choice was himself. Therefore, he had married her. Ingund did not complain, but she asked Chlothar to let her retain his favour.[170]

Not satisfied with all the wives he already had, Chlothar continued his search for women wherever and whenever there was a fresh opportunity. In 555, after the death of King Theudebald of Rheims, he quickly took over not only Theudebald's kingdom but also his widow Vuldetrada, daughter of King Waccho of the Lombards. He does not appear to have married her, but he definitely seduced her, a fact that aroused complaints among the clergy. To get the bishops off his back, Chlothar handed Vuldetrada over to Duke Garibald of Bavaria.[171]

The image we get of Chlothar's wives and mistresses is a hazy one. Obviously, no woman could capture the interest of the king sufficiently to construct a basis of power for herself. If one of his wives had done so, she would undoubtedly have made a more significant mark upon history than Chlothar's wives did. Guntheuc, Ingund, Aregund, Chunsina and Vuldetrada all disappear from view as quickly as they are introduced in the chronicler's text. The one we see most of, Ingund, only appears as an anxious woman trying to secure her own position and that of her family.

However, there is one important exception: Queen (and Saint) Radegund. Her history is entirely different from that of Chlothar's other wives. To be analysed according to her importance, she definitely needs a section of her own.

Radegund: the ascetic queen[172]

Radegund (d. 587) is one of the major female saints of the early Middle Ages. She was originally a Thuringian princess, daughter of King Berthar. During a Thuringian civil war, Berthar was killed by his brother, King Hermanfrid.[173] When Thuringia was attacked by the Franks at the beginning of the 530s, Hermanfrid was in his turn defeated by the Merovingian half-brothers Theuderic I of Rheims and Chlothar I of Soissons, who subjugated Hermanfrid's territory, which was to remain under Merovingian rule for about a century until Thuringian independence was restored following a successful revolt in 639. When the time came to return home, King Chlothar took Radegund with him as his share of the booty. Later, he married her.[174]

Apparently, the marriage between the King of Soissons and the Thuringian princess turned out to be a mistake. It is hard for the reader to see how Radegund could have appreciated her husband, whose brutality and cruelty, at least according to Gregory's text, were notorious. For instance, he arranged for Radegund's own brother to be assassinated.[175] In few words, Gregory informs us that Radegund turned to God, took the habit of a religious and built a nunnery for herself in Poitiers. She became famous for her prayers, her vigils and her charities, 'and she became so well known that the common people looked upon her as a saint'.[176] Gregory quotes in full a letter from seven bishops to Radegund from the time of the foundation of the convent. The bishops praised Radegund for following in the footsteps of Saint Martin, himself, just like her, an outsider in Francia. According to the bishops, a number of women from several dioceses flocked to accept Radegund as their leader in the new nunnery ('they hasten in their zeal to quench their thirst at your soft bosom's fountain', *raptim festinant avide in caritate Christi fonte vestri pectoris inrigare*). The bishops granted Radegund's petition concerning the nunnery and the fact that it would be run according to the Rule of Saint Caesarius of Arles. If any nun were to escape from the convent, the bishops decided that she would be excommunicated.[177]

Fortunately, Gregory also decided to insert a personal text of Radegund's in his chronicle. In the letter, which was sent to a number of bishops at an unspecified date after the death of Chlothar I (d. 561), Radegund explained her reasons for founding the convent in the following way:

> Some time ago, when I found myself freed from earthly cares, with divine providence and with God's grace to inspire me, I turned of my own volition, under Christ's guidance, to the religious life. I asked myself, with all the ardour of which I am capable, how I could best forward the cause of other women, and how, if our Lord so willed, my own personal desires might be of advantage to my sisters. Here in the town of Poitiers I founded a convent for nuns. Chlothar, my lord and king of glorious memory, instituted this and was its benefactor. When it was founded, I made over to it by deed of gift all the property which the king in his munificence had bestowed upon me.[178]

These are important words. What we see is a queen (*and* a king) creating a place of power. Radegund says that she did it all to help other women and to serve the Lord – but there is a lot more to it. She freely admits that it would hardly have been possible to create such an impressive convent if she had not been financially supported by her husband. Chlothar helped her with the resources that were needed to make the convent a reality and not merely a pious dream. However, the fact that Chlothar was intelligent enough to understand the potential rewards (both in this life and after death) of having a big, wealthy convent on his side should hardly surprise us. What is more important is that Chlothar, despite understanding this, did not found the convent himself. Radegund did it; it was apparently her idea, and she was sufficiently charismatic to make it work. Chlothar supplied the means, but Radegund controlled the process.

Returning to Radegund's letter, we can also, quite easily, see what she feared. True, she had been successful in establishing a place of power, but she could never be certain that it would remain the way she wanted it. In this, she did not only refer to the danger of her successors forgetting about the Rule or basic Christian beliefs. She also feared for the institution in the same way as king feared for his kingdom: that rebels would try to assume control, that outsiders would attempt coups. In fact, her fears for these future threats were her main reasons for writing the letter:

> If perchance after my death any person whatsoever, either the bishop of this city or some representative of the king, or any other individual, should attempt, in a spirit of malevolence or by some legal subterfuge, to disturb the community or to break the Rule, or to appoint any Mother Superior other than Agnes [the Abbess appointed by Radegund; see below], my sister in God...; or if the community should rise in revolt, which is surely impossible, and wish to make a change; or if any person, possibly even the bishop of the diocese, shall wish to claim, by some newfangled privilege, jurisdiction of any sort over the nunnery or over the property of the nunnery...; or if any nun shall wish to break the Rule and go out into the world; or if any prince, bishop, or person in power, or even any individual from among the nuns themselves, shall attempt with sacrilegious intent to diminish or to appropriate to his or her own personal possession any part or parcel of the property which our most noble Chlothar and the most glorious kings his sons have bestowed upon me, and which I, with his express permission and injunction, have made over to the nunnery, for which

conveyance I obtained confirmation by letters from noble lords and kings Charibert, Gunthchramn, Chilperic and Sigibert, by the swearing of an oath and the subscribing of their sign manual, or which others have donated for the saving of their souls..., may that person incur the wrath of God and that of your holiness and of those who succeed you, and may all such persons be shut off from your grace as robbers and despoilers of the poor.'...'If any person whatsoever, in defiance of the will of God and of the king's authority, thus contravening the conditions here set out and before our Lord and His holy saints commended in my prayers to your protection, shall do aught to harm any individual or to despoil any property, which God forbid, or shall attempt in any way to harass the aforesaid Abbess Agnes, my sister, may he incur the wrath of God and of the Holy Cross and of the Blessed Mary, and may he be assailed and pursued by Saint Hilary and Saint Martin, to whose especial care, after God, I have entrusted these nuns, who are my sisters.'

Si casu post meum obitum, si quaecumque persona, vel loci eiusdem pontifex, seu potestas principis, vel alius aliquis, quod nec fieri credimus, congregationem vel suasu malivolo vel inpulsu iudiciario perturbare timtaverit, aut regulam frangere, seu abbatissam alteram quam sororem meam Agnitem...; aut ipsa congregatio, quod fieri non potest, habita murmoratione, mutare contenderit, vel quasdam dominationes in monasterio vel rebus monastirii quaecumque persona vel pontifex loci, praeter quas antecessores episcopi aut alii, me superstite, habuerunt, novo privilegio quicumque affectare voluerit, aut extra regulam exinde egredi quis timtaverit, seu de rebus, quas in me praecellentissimus domnus Chlotharius vel praecellentissimi domni reges, filii sui, contulerunt, et ego ex eius praeceptiones permisso monasterio tradidi possedendum, et per auctoritatem praecellentissimorum dominorum regum Chariberthi, Guntchramni, Chilperici et Sigiberthi cum sacramenti interpositione et suarum manuum subscriptionibus obtenui confirmari; aut ex his, quae alii pro animarum suarum remedio...contulerunt..., ita vestra sanctitatem successorumque vestrorum post Deum pro mea supplicatione et Christi voluntate incurrat, ut, sicut praedones et spoliatores pauperum extra gratiam vestram habeantur'...'Quod si, quod absit, contra Dei mandatum et auctoritatem regum aliquis de suprascriptis condicionibus vobis coram Domino et sanctis eius praecabiliter conmendatis agere aut de persona aut substantiam minuenda voluerit, aut memoratae sorore meae Agnite abbatissae molestias aliquas inferre timtaverit, Dei et sanctae Crucis et beatae Mariae incurrat iudicium, et beatus confessores Helarium et Martinum, quibus post Deum sorores meas tradidi defendendas, ipsos habeat contradictores et persecutores.'[179]

Radegund further asks, or rather orders, the bishop to appeal to the king or to the city of Poitiers if the nunnery should in any way become endangered in the future.[180] She fully understood that dangerous moments were to be expected. The nunnery was rich and powerful; any king, bishop or lay magnate who wanted to enhance his position could benefit by controlling the convent, for instance by appointing a new abbess and by appropriating lands. Not even the nuns themselves were to be trusted. To some modern readers, Radegund may appear as an overly anxious old woman, but we know from Gregory's own work that she was not the least bit paranoid; Radegund had good reasons to worry. As we shall see (pp. 154–69), a severe crisis erupted only two years after her death, involving a conspiracy of rebel nuns, a hostile bishop and a small army of cut-throats. Already in 590, the convent was attacked and plundered. If it had not been for the support given to the convent by the Frankish kings, it is doubtful whether it would have been able to survive as the kind of powerful spiritual centre that Radegund had wanted it to be. In other words the link between Radegund's convent and the Merovingian royal house was of fundamental importance both to its foundation and to its survival.

This link between secular and spiritual Frankish royalty is also made clear by the fact, evident from Gregory's work, that Radegund's nunnery was regarded as a suitable spot for the location of potentially troublesome female Merovingians. In or before 584, Queen Fredegund, wife of Chilperic I of Soissons, used it to get rid of her husband's daughter Basina shortly after the murder of Basina's brother Clovis (see p. 109). At the same time, she also had Audovera, the mother of Clovis and Basina, assassinated.[181] Basina clearly did not like being locked up in Radegund's convent. Together with her cousin Chrodechild, who had also ended up within the walls, she was to become a leader of the famous rebellion of the nuns in 589–90.

We know something of the life of the convent and the reputation it had acquired in the 570s and 580s. Most importantly, we know that it remained a very royal, very Merovingian convent completely dominated by Radegund until her death. True, she did appoint a nun (the Agnes mentioned in the letter above) as Mother Superior, but it is clear from Gregory's text that this abbess was merely a puppet. All important decisions were dictated by Radegund.[182] Also, we know that the nunnery quickly became regarded as a place of holiness, of heavenly visions. A nun called Disciola, the niece of Bishop Salvius of Albi, was noted for her saintly death, which is described in detail by Gregory of Tours. Before her death, she is said to have spread her hands wide and asked for the benediction of an invisible messenger from God. According to Gregory, a man possessed by a devil, who had come to the nunnery to be cured by the relic of the Holy Cross, dragged at his hair and collapsed on the ground immediately after her death. Furious, he (or rather the demon within him) shouted that a disaster had struck: Disciola's soul had been snatched away 'without those on our side being able to look into matters first'.[183] When asked what he meant by this, he explained that the Archangel Michael had carried away Disciola's soul, completely removing it from the influence of 'my own master, he whom you call the Devil'.[184] Another nun reputedly saw a vision, in which she found the Well of Living Water. Moved by her vision, she asked to be shut up in a cell for ever and to live there as a recluse. This was granted, and Radegund personally led her to the cell as the other nuns sang psalms.[185]

However, Radegund was not satisfied by simply having a wealthy convent of her own. She clearly intended the nunnery to be of as great significance as possible compared to other monasteries and nunneries in Western Europe. In the reign of King Sigibert I (561–75), she sent clerics to the east to search for pieces of wood from the Holy Cross and for relics of the apostles and other martyrs. Sigibert is reported to have given her written permission to do this. The mission was a success: most importantly, a piece of the wood of the Holy Cross was sent to Radegund by Emperor Justin II and his consort, Empress Sophia.[186]

Radegund's attempt to create an ecclesiastical place of power was undoubtedly successful, at least during her own life-time. Her success is evident from the opposition she aroused in the diocese of Poitiers.

To Bishop Maroveus, her convent – soon known as the Convent of the Holy Cross – was a threat to his own position as ecclesiastical leader. When the relics arrived in Poitiers from the east, Radegund asked Maroveus if he would deposit them in the nunnery with all due honour, but Maroveus refused even to discuss it, preferring to leave the city and visit one of his country estates rather than argue with Radegund. Radegund then wrote to King Sigibert and begged him to order one of his bishops to deposit the relics with the honour due to them. Since Maroveus had refused to co-operate, Sigibert deputed Bishop Eufronius of Tours to do what Radegund had asked. When Eufronius came to Tours and performed the ritual with much chanting of psalms and burning of incense, Maroveus deliberately stayed away.[187]

Maroveus continued his spiritual feud with Radegund, never missing an opportunity to deny her the help she wanted. He did not give her the Rule of Caesarius, so she had to turn directly to Arles for it. Ordinarily, Maroveus would have been protector of the nunnery, but his negative attitude made Radegund instead look to the king for protection. Even in the middle of the 580s, as Radegund was near her death, the disagreement between Maroveus and Radegund was daily growing worse.[188] Radegund finally died on 13 August 587 and was buried three days later; Gregory informs us that he was present at the burial himself. He assures us that Radegund's death was the cause of great lamentation in the nunnery. However, the conflict between Maroveus and the Convent of the Holy Cross continued and reached its climax in the great rebellion of 589–90 (pp. 154–69).[189]

Although Radegund lived in a nunnery and thus was prevented from moving around and influencing contemporary politics in the same way as secular queens and royal widows such as Fredegund and Brunhild, it is obvious that she wielded considerable power. When King Chilperic, in 584, considered the idea of fetching Basina from the nunnery to have her marry a Visigothic prince, Radegund refused: 'It is not seemly for a nun dedicated to Christ to turn back once more to the sensuous pleasures of this world.'[190] In other words, she intervened in what we would refer to as foreign policy, preventing a Franco-Visigothic marriage alliance. Another example of Radegund's reputation is evident in the way she was referred to by the pretender Gundovald. In his attempt to be accepted as a true Merovingian king in 585, he once told his enemies to ask Radegund and Ingitrude of Tours (see p. 187) if they did not believe that what he said was true.[191]

Summing up Radegund as she appears in *Decem Libri Historiarum*, we must not forget that she was originally a prisoner of war, a part of Chlothar's booty in the war against the Thuringians. Even in Thuringia, Radegund had been one of the less fortunate members of the royal house, since her father had lost the struggle for power against King Hermanfrid. This meant that she, in her capacity as a Frankish queen, had no personal resources, no firm basis of power and no Thuringian relatives that she could count on as allies in times of need. She built her position at the court of Chlothar and at the nunnery in Poitiers entirely on her status as a Frankish queen and as a charismatic individual.

It is important to realise that Radegund's withdrawal to the religious life made her no less powerful than she had been at court. She kept her contacts with the kings of Francia (both Chlothar and his sons, especially Sigibert), who supported her nunnery with the resources it needed. Her agents went all the way to Palestine and Constantinople in search of relics that would make the convent even more important than it already was. She could and did intervene in political matters.

In fact, her withdrawal to Poitiers appears to have strengthened her position considerably. What could possibly have happened to Radegund if she had chosen to stay at Chlothar's side? She would hardly have been able to dominate Frankish politics to the same extent as the male Merovingians were already doing, especially since her fortunes in Francia depended heavily on Chlothar himself. Furthermore, Chlothar did not die young; he outlived his royal brothers, and his sons succeeded him as adults. There was no period of royal minority, with all the possibilities that this situation might present to greedy magnates and intelligent widows. Also, Radegund could not escape from the fact that she was a political outsider. At best, she could have influenced politics in a way similar to the influence exerted by Fredegund during the reign of Chilperic I of Soissons – but only if her personality resembled Fredegund's and if she was willing to employ the political means (such as assassination) necessary for such a life.

Radegund chose the life of a religious; she became a holy woman. She used the ideological assets at her disposal, and she did it in a way that made her one of the most prominent women in sixth-century

Western Europe. With the convent at her back, she could act in a way that would hardly have been possible at the court of Chlothar. When she talked, bishops and kings listened. Due to the power of the Convent of the Holy Cross (in terms of ideological assets, economic resources and, perhaps most importantly, political alliances to other members of the royal house), no one could afford to ignore Radegund, regardless of what they may have thought of her as a person. Bishop Maroveus behaved as if she were a threat to his own position, and he was probably correct; any bishop confronted by a convent such as the one at Poitiers could easily have been tempted to react in a similar manner.

Ultrogotha

Ultrogotha was married to King Childebert I of Paris. We are very poorly informed about her life as queen, but it appears that she had officials of her own – Gregory mentions a referendary of hers called Ursicinus (who later became Bishop of Cahors).[192] In any case, she was wholly dependent on her status as Childebert's wife. She had no surviving sons of her own, and the weakness of her position was instantly revealed when Childebert died in Paris in 558. Childebert's brother Chlothar I immediately took over the kingdom and the royal treasury, sending Ultrogotha and her two daughters Chrodoswintha and Chrodoberga into exile.[193]

To learn more about Ultrogotha, we have to turn to other sources. It would appear that she acquired a reputation for holiness. Gregory himself (in another of his works) mentions her as a pious pilgrim,[194] and Venantius Fortunatus wrote a poem about her (and about her garden!).[195] The author of Saint Balthild's *vita* says that she comforted the poor and helped monks.[196]

The women of Theudebert I

Theudebert I was a son of King Theuderic I of Rheims and thus a grandson of Clovis I.[197] His father, who had personally preferred to marry a Burgundian princess (the daughter of King Sigismund),[198] betrothed him to Wisigarda, daughter of the Lombard King Waccho.

This was strictly an element of a political alliance; for several years, it would appear that Wisigarda remained at her father's court.[199]

During a war against the Visigoths in the south, Theuderic sent his son to win as much land as possible. Theudebert advanced as far as Béziers, captured the fortress of Dio and sacked it. He then sent messengers to the fortress of Cabrières to say that, unless the inhabitants surrendered, the whole place would be burnt to the ground and they themselves made captive.[200] A married woman in Cabrières called Deuteria, described by Gregory of Tours as a person full of energy and resource, sent her own messengers to Theudebert, saying: 'No-one can resist you, noble prince. We accept you as our ruler. Come to our town and do with it what you will.'[201] Theudebert did this; nobody resisted his troops as they took command of the fortress. Deuteria, whose husband had gone off to Béziers, greeted Theudebert personally, and he found her very attractive. She became his mistress, and it did not take her long to give him a daughter.[202]

During his stay in the south, Theudebert received news that his father was dying. Realising that he had to hurry home in order to stop his uncles from cutting him off from inheriting Theuderic's kingdom, he abandoned the campaign and headed north, leaving Deuteria and her daughter in Clermont. When Theuderic had died (in 533 or 534) and Theudebert established himself on the throne, he sent for Deuteria, had her brought home and married her.[203]

Gregory describes Theudebert as a great and virtuous king who ruled justly and earned the respect of his bishops.[204] Deuteria's position would seem to have been strengthened by the birth of a son, who was given the name Theudebald.[205] Nevertheless, Deuteria was never sure of Theudebert. She knew that other women could capture his heart just she had once done, and this would mean the loss of all her influence. When a daughter of hers had grown into a woman, she began to fear her as well. Theudebert might begin to desire her and take advantage of her. To prevent this from happening, she put the daughter in a cart drawn by wild oxen and had her tipped over a bridge near Verdun. The poor teenager fell into a river and was drowned.[206]

A far more potent threat to Deuteria's position, however, was the Lombard princess Wisigarda. When seven years had passed since the betrothal without anything happening, Theudebert began to be publicly criticised for having abandoned his fiancée. Faced with political necessity, Theudebert deserted Deuteria and married Wisigarda. She died shortly afterwards, but Theudebert did not recall Deuteria. Another, anonymous, woman filled her place.[207]

As to the actual degree of influence exerted by Theudebert's women, our only piece of information relates to Wisigarda's short period as queen. Gregory informs us that two educated magnates at the court of Theudebert, called Asteriolus and Secundinus, developed an intense enmity towards each other. Secundinus had led several embassies from Theudebert to the East Roman emperor (Justinian I), and this made him very boastful. Eventually, the animosity turned into violence, and Theudebert had to intervene to preserve the peace. The king supported Secundinus and put Asteriolus in a subordinate position under him. Suffering from disgrace and loss of power, Asteriolus then appealed to Queen Wisigarda. The queen managed to have him restored to grace. When Wisigarda died, however, Asteriolus was killed by order of Secundinus.[208]

We do not know if they ever met, but it is clear that Deuteria and Wisigarda were rivals. They both wanted to be Theudebert's consort. Deuteria's only known assets were her beauty and her charisma; in fact, she appears to have planned her own seduction during Theudebert's siege of Cabrières. Wisigarda's chief asset was political power: her family ruled the kingdom of the Lombards and thus constituted an important key to Theudebert's growing power in Central Europe. In the struggle between Wisigarda and Deuteria, Wisigarda was bound to win. After all, a king such as Theudebert could always get hold of beautiful women for his bed, but he could not afford to neglect a political alliance.

Deuteria's position as Theudebert's queen must have been considerably weaker than Wisigarda's, despite the fact that they were both strangers in north-eastern Francia (Deuteria from the south, Wisigarda from the east). Deuteria apparently did not control the upbringing of young Theudebald (if she had done so, she would undoubtedly have been able to remain powerful), and she is even, as we have seen, thought to have feared her own daughter. Gregory's tale of the horrible murder at Verdun may not be true, but it is nevertheless of great interest in the present context, since the story was considered believable by the people of sixth-century Gaul. Gregory readily accepted the story as something that could easily have happened in a situation such as Deuteria's. Wisigarda, on the other hand, appears as a powerful queen with her own clients – her intervention on behalf of Asteriolus is proof of her ability to exert influence.

King Charibert's wives

Charibert was a son of King Chlothar I and Ingund.[209] When Chlothar died in 561, his kingdom was divided between his sons, and Charibert received the part that had previously been ruled by his uncle King Childebert I, with Paris for its capital.[210]

Charibert's first known wife was called Ingoberg; they had a daughter who was eventually married to King Ethelbert of Kent (reigned c. 560–616).[211] Unfortunately for Ingoberg, Charibert fell in love with two of her servants, the sisters Marcovefa (who wore the habit of a religious) and Merofled. They were not members of the nobility but the daughters of a poor wool-worker. Realising the danger they posed to her position at court, Ingoberg grew jealous of them. Gregory tells us that she made a secret plan to set their father to work, in the hope that when Charibert saw this he would come to despise the two girls. However, things did not work out as she had planned. As Charibert watched the man preparing wool for the royal household, he became so angry that he dismissed Ingoberg and took Merofled in her place.[212] Charibert is also reported to have had another woman called Theudechild, the daughter of a shepherd who looked after his flocks. They had a son, but the child was buried immediately after its birth.[213]

Despite the fact that he had already married a couple of women, Charibert also decided to marry Marcovefa. By this time, at least some members of the clergy openly protested against the king's behaviour, and Bishop Germanus of Paris even went so far as to have the king excommunicated, probably because two of his wives were sisters. Marcovefa was also excommunicated. Charibert ignored the excommunication, but Gregory informs us that God quickly took his revenge. Marcovefa 'was struck by the judgment of God and died'.[214] Shortly afterwards, in 567, Charibert died as well.[215]

We do not know much about the extent of the power wielded by

Charibert's women, but Gregory informs us of one illustrative incident after the marriage of Charibert and Marcovefa. A young man called Leudast, who was later to become Count of Tours, fled to Marcovefa after having been punished (by having one of his ears slit) for his behaviour. Marcovefa received Leudast with kindness (*quae libenter eum colligens*), promoted him and put him in charge of the finest horses in her stable. Shortly afterwards, he acquired the important post of Master of the Stables. Although Gregory describes Leudast during this period as an arrogant man living a loose life, he also makes it clear that he remained the special favourite of Marcovefa. He did everything she wanted, hurrying here, there and everywhere to see to the queen's affairs (*in causis patronae alumnus proprius huc illucque defertur*). When Marcovefa died, Leudast had to bribe Charibert to allow him to retain his post.[216]

Charibert's death created a crisis for his queens. Their king was dead; the basis of their power and of their influence had disappeared. Immediately, Theudechild tried to save her elevated social status by offering her hand in marriage to one of Charibert's brothers, King Gunthchramn. Having received her message, Gunthchramn replied: 'She may come to me and bring her treasure with her. I will receive her and I will give her an honourable place among my people. She will hold a higher position at my side than she ever did with my brother.'[217] Theudechild was delighted; she collected all her possessions together and set out to join Gunthchramn. We can easily imagine her surprise when it turned out that Gunthchramn was not the least bit interested in her, only in her treasure. Meeting her, he is supposed to have said: 'It is better that this treasure should fall into my hands than that it should remain in the control of this woman who was unworthy of my brother's bed.'[218] He then seized most of her goods, left her a small portion and sent her to a nunnery in Arles (obviously the nunnery of Saint Jean).[219]

Theudechild hated her new life as a nun, especially all the fasts and vigils to which she was subjected. Her only way out of the convent, however, was by making a new alliance with a (preferably powerful) man. She sent secret messages to a certain Visigoth, promising him that, if he agreed to carry her off to the Visigothic kingdom and marry her there, she would escape from the nunnery with her remaining wealth and join him. The man readily promised to do what she had asked of him. Again, Theudechild collected her possessions together and made them up into bundles, but her attempt to escape failed. The abbess (probably a woman called Liliola, who had succeeded Caesaria II as abbess in 559) caught her and had her beaten mercilessly. Theudechild was locked up in her cell, where she remained until her dying day, 'suffering awful anguish'.[220]

As for Queen Ingoberg, she appears to have suffered a kinder fate than Theudechild, but we do not hear of her wielding any actual influence after her dismissal from Charibert's bed. In 589, a few months before her death, Gregory of Tours was summoned to her to carry out certain orders for the benefit of her soul. Gregory describes the dying Ingoberg as a woman of great wisdom, devoted to the religious life, constant in her vigils, her prayers and her alms-giving. When Gregory had arrived, she called a notary and, having discussed her plans with her visitor, left a legacy to the cathedral of Tours, another to Saint Martin's church and a third to the cathedral of Le Mans. By deeds of enfranchisement she also freed many serfs.[221]

The sexual and marital conditions at Charibert's court during the years 561–67 form an excellent example of the difficulties attached to the careers of royal women in Merovingian Francia. Charibert himself is hardly worth analysing in the present context; he was just another lusty young king whose political position was secure – but his women were fighting for social and political survival. Ingoberg is a typical case: although Gregory, who knew her personally, describes her as a pious and wise woman, he also admits that she tried to defend her status with dirty tricks when threatened by the beauty of her own servants. Unfortunately, we do not have enough information to be able to analyse the conflicts that undoubtedly existed between Marcovefa, Merofled and Theudechild.

The story of Leudast makes it clear that Charibert's bed was worth fighting for. Whoever slept with the king, preferably in the capacity as wife, would automatically gain access to wealth and power. This could be used to recruit clients and allies (such as Leudast), who in their turn could be used to influence and dominate others. Given time, Marcovefa would probably have constructed an impressive network of grateful officials, magnates and (why not?) assassins. We know that other royal women (such as Brunhild and Fredegund) did; Charibert's wives failed because their husband died too soon. He reigned for only six years, and none of his wives managed to use these years to enrich themselves and to strengthen their own positions. There was too much competition and too little time. Had Charibert lived ten years more, one of his women would probably have emerged as winner.

From this point of view, Theudechild's appeal to Gunthchramn is not the least bit surprising. In 567, Theudechild had only three assets: her sexual attraction, her past as such (after all, being attached to a Merovingian king was a merit) and her property. She gambled on her ability to use these assets to catch Gunthchramn: his sense of responsibility towards his family, his hormones and his greed would serve to secure her immediate future in a nice little palace or on a royal estate. If Gunthchramn had been the same kind of man as Charibert, Theudechild might have succeeded. However, since he was only interested in her property, Theudechild's attempt failed. Even after that, she still possessed enough property to be able to afford a second chance. If she had not been caught trying to escape from the convent, her future would still have been very hard to predict. The unstable nature of her assets could just as easily have resulted in a carefree existence on an estate somewhere in present-day Spain as in a premature death once the anonymous Visigoth had stolen her valuables.

King Gunthchramn's women

Gunthchramn was a son of King Chlothar I and Ingund.[222] When Chlothar died in 561 and his kingdom was divided between his sons, Gunthchramn received the part that had previously been ruled by his uncle King Chlodomer, with Orléans for its centre, together with the old kingdom of the Burgundians.[223]

Gunthchramn's first known woman was called Veneranda. He is said to have made her his mistress, and she bore him a son called Gundobad. We know nothing about Veneranda apart from the fact that she was a servant-girl employed by one of Gunthchramn's subjects.[224] When Gunthchramn later married Marcatrude, daughter of the magnate Magnachar, Gundobad was sent from the royal court and placed in the city of Orléans. Although dismissed from court, Gundobad nevertheless remained a Merovingian prince and thereby a latent threat to Marcatrude and to the son she herself soon gave birth to. To prevent Gundobad from growing up to become dangerous, Marcatrude is rumoured to have sent him poison to drink. Gregory piously remarks that God made her pay dearly for this: soon after Gundobad's death she lost her own son. As a result, Gunthchramn was estranged from Marcatrude and dismissed her; she died shortly afterwards.[225] In his third known attempt to find a suitable woman, Gunthchramn married a servant-girl of Magnachar's called Austrechild, also known as Bobilla. She gave him two sons, Chlothar and Chlodomer, who both died (probably of dysentery) in 577.[226]

Apparently, Magnachar's family found it hard to accept that Marcatrude had been unable to hold on to her position. Magnachar's two sons are reported to have made 'hateful and abominable remarks' about Queen Austrechild and her children (*pro eo quod in Austregildem reginam eiusque soboles multa detestabilia adque exsecranda proferrent*). In return, Gunthchramn had both of them killed, seized their possessions and added them to the royal treasury.[227]

Gregory of Tours appears to have disliked Austrechild. He mentions her very seldom, and his short evaluation of her (at the time of her death in 580) is a negative one. He describes her as a wicked woman and an evil consort (*nequam spiritum, iniquae coniugis*). According to Gregory, when she began to realise that there was no hope for her, her last wish was that others should die with her. At her funeral, she wanted the sound of others bewailing their dead. She is said to have asked Gunthchramn to avenge her death by killing the doctors she accused of having caused her death by giving her bad medicine: 'Give me your solemn word, I beg you, that you will cut their throats the moment that my eyes have closed in death. If I have really come to the end of my life, they must not be permitted to glory in my dying. When my friends grieve for me, let their friends grieve for them, too.'[228] Having said this, she died. Gunthchramn did what she had requested: the two doctors were executed.[229]

Gunthchramn was an unfortunate man. None of his sons managed to stay alive; there was no one to succeed him at his own court. This might have been because of the actions of proverbially evil stepmothers such as Marcatrude, but the king's problem could just as easily have been caused by ordinary diseases. In any case, his dilemma was hardly unusual in the Middle Ages. There was always a great danger of the children dying, a danger that helped shape the political structure at court. Children were valuable assets: female children could be married off to a foreign ruler, while the birth of male children was a blow to any magnate or rival king who had his own plans on what to do to the kingdom once the king was dead. This fact, as is clearly shown in the case of Gunthchramn's court, had great significance for the king's women. To any Frankish queen, the son of another woman by the king was a threat both to herself and to her sons. This was obvious to everybody; in fact, a queen in that position appears to have been *expected* to strike at her rivals by whatever means possible. We do not know if Marcatrude did actually poison Gundobad, but Gregory and everybody else clearly thought her capable of it. She was protecting herself and her son.

Audovera and Galswinth: wives of Chilperic I

Chilperic I was a son of King Chlothar I and Aregund.[230] When Chlothar died in 561, Chilperic received the part that had previously been his father's original kingdom, (before Chlothar conquered all the other Frankish lands), with Soissons as its centre.[231]

Chilperic is said to have had many wives. The first one was probably Audovera, who gave him three sons Theudebert, Merovech and Clovis,[232] and a daughter called Basina.[233] Later, Audovera apparently lost the king's favour. However, she maintained a residence in or near the city of Rouen, and it would appear that she continued to have contact with her sons.[234] As will be related later (pp. 106–07, 109), both Merovech and Clovis suffered from her loss of power, since Audovera's successor in Chilperic's bedchamber (Fredegund) regarded them as threats to her own position and to that of her children. When Clovis was murdered in or before 584, assassins (possibly in Fredegund's employ) killed Audovera as well.[235]

Audovera was probably of humble birth, but another of Chilperic's wives, Galswinth, belonged to one of the most important families in Western Europe.[236] Chilperic was obviously jealous of his brother Sigibert for having married a Visigothic princess, Brunhild, daughter of

King Athanagild (pp. 130–31). Wishing to have a queen of equal rank, he promised to dismiss all his other wives if he could have Brunhild's older sister, Galswinth. Athanagild believed him and sent his daughter north. At first, Galswinth was heartily welcomed (probably in 567), and Chilperic 'loved her very dearly, for she had brought a large dowry with her'.[237] Galswinth was quickly converted from Arianism to Catholicism. However, another of Chilperic's low-born wives, Fredegund, refused to surrender her position at court, and Chilperic did not send her away. Galswinth never stopped complaining about the issue, constantly accusing Fredegund in front of Chilperic of having insulted her. Finally, Chilperic got tired of her complaints and had her murdered by one of his servants (at least, this was the cause of death that Gregory states that Chilperic's brothers suspected). Gregory reports that Chilperic wept for Galswinth's death, but only for a short time. According to Gregory, God performed a miracle after Galswinth's death. A lamp suspended from a cord burned in front of her tomb. One day, the cord broke and the lamp fell to the stone floor. The stone withdrew at the point of impact and the lamp penetrated it just as if it had been made of soft material.[238]

Despite her short time as queen, Galswinth is of great interest. The reason is her impressive *potential* for powerful action. This potential was probably the reason why Chilperic and/or Fredegund realised that they had to kill her instead of simply disregarding her. Chilperic's great mistake was not the marriage itself but his munificence towards his bride. Probably as an attempt to show off, and thereby raise his own status, he gave Galswinth the cities of Bordeaux, Limoges, Cahors, Lescar and Cieutat as *morgengabe*. These cities, with all their royal lands, troops and revenues, were hers (not Chilperic's) to do with as she pleased.[239] Given time, Galswinth could easily have become a formidable power; no sane king could afford to disregard her. In fact, Galswinth would seem to be the most wealthy woman we encounter in *Decem Libri Historiarum*. Wealth could be used to buy clients and allies; wealth made a person important and dangerous. Add to this Galswinth's status as Visigothic princess with a kingdom to support her in her hour of need, and her death becomes fully understandable. The only safe way to get rid of her was to have her murdered.[240]

Audovera and Galswinth suffered from two completely different problems: Audovera was too ordinary, Galswinth was too extraordinary. Audovera could be dismissed from court without her sons being able to help her; Galswinth had to be killed as quickly as possible, before she had any chance of using her own vast potential. They were both latent threats to the most important of Chilperic's women, Queen Fredegund, but Audovera's position was closely linked to that of her children. She obviously lacked the resources necessary to make her dangerous in the same way as Galswinth apparently was at the time of the marriage.

Fredegund: the enemy of God and of mankind

Fredegund is a major character in Gregory's work, a person no reader can forget having read *Decem Libri Historiarum*.[241] Her prominence in the text of a contemporary historian automatically makes her one of the most important individuals in any attempt to analyse the roles of politically important women in the early Middle Ages. From the middle of the 560s until the second half of the 590s, Fredegund appears to have exerted a considerable amount of influence in the northwestern part of Francia, a region that was developing into the kingdom of Neustria. Her influence, however, was far from static. It varied according to her ability to use the various resources at her disposal as well as to the varying degrees of formal standing within the Merovingian royal house that she experienced during more than three decades of power.

Despite the eventual importance of Fredegund, she is hardly introduced as a particularly interesting individual. Rather, Gregory shows us the young Fredegund (in book IV, chapter 27) as a person of merely secondary importance, a low-born woman who had gained access to the bedchamber of King Chilperic of Soissons and acquired the status of wife.

As related above, King Chilperic, who, it would seem, had acquired a number of low-born wives, was jealous of his brother Sigibert for having married a Visigothic princess (Brunhild). This resulted in his own tragic marriage to Galswinth. According to Gregory, the main reason why the marriage between Chilperic and Galswinth failed was Fredegund's refusal to surrender her position. She was sufficiently dear to Chilperic to be able to remain at court, a fact that irritated Galswinth enormously. In the end, as we have seen, Galswinth was murdered. Shortly afterwards, Fredegund reaffirmed her position as the king's sleeping-partner.[242] This event probably occurred in 567. By her very existence, Fredegund had provoked the murder of one of the highest-ranking women in Western Europe. Her career, soon to be filled with real or presumed evil, had begun.

Fredegund's most famous murder occurred in 575. At the time, Chilperic had suffered greatly in the war against his brother Sigibert. Before inflicting final defeat upon Chilperic (who was residing at Tournai with Fredegund), Sigibert assembled his army at the royal villa of Vitry, where he was raised on a shield and hailed as king. Fredegund, however, dispatched two assassins to Vitry, carrying scramasaxes which they had smeared with poison. Pretending to want to discuss something with Sigibert, they attacked him from two sides and killed him.[243] In her position as Chilperic's wife, Fredegund thereafter continued to take an active part in the war between the two Frankish kingdoms; Sigibert's widow Brunhild and son Childebert II were to be her major enemies for the rest of her life. In fact, Fredegund was in great danger only a short while after Sigibert's murder, as troops from Champagne attacked Soissons where she was in residence. To avoid being captured, she had to flee from the town.[244]

Fredegund was also deeply involved in Chilperic's struggles against Merovech, his son by another wife, Audovera. Basically, there was nothing unusual about the conflict; it was a typical sixth-century Merovingian struggle between father and son. However, the situation was made considerably more serious than it would ordinarily have been because Merovech got married to Queen Brunhild, Sigibert's recent widow. The marriage ceremony was performed by Bishop Praetextatus of Rouen, who apparently was a friend of Brunhild's (at least, he had property entrusted to him by her).[245] Chilperic later had Merovech tonsured and made a priest, but Merovech managed to escape from his monastery and make his way to Gregory's own episcopal city, Tours, where he claimed sanctuary. As Nicetius, husband of Gregory's niece Eustenia, and a deacon from Tours happened to be at Chilperic's court at the same time, Fredegund accused them of spying on behalf of Merovech. She ordered them stripped of all of their possessions and exiled for a period of seven months.[246] Later, she persuaded (i.e., bribed) the magnate Gunthchramn Boso, who was also residing within the walls of Saint Martin's church in Tours, to assassinate Merovech, but the attempt failed.[247] According to rumour, Fredegund was eventually responsible for Merovech's death in 578. In Gregory's text, however, Merovech is described as having been killed by one of his servants at his own request, when he was in danger of being captured and tortured by his father.[248]

One of Fredegund's greatest personal enemies appears to have been Bishop Praetextatus of Rouen. We know very little about the original reasons for the conflict between the bishop and the court of Soissons, but we may assume that it was connected with the feud between Chilperic and the successors of Sigibert, Brunhild's and Childebert's party. As we have seen, Praetextatus had performed the marriage ceremony between Merovech and Brunhild, and this might have been reason enough to make Chilperic and Fredegund eager to get rid of him. At one time, Fredegund tried in vain to bribe Gregory of Tours himself to speak out against Praetextatus when he was standing trial, accused of conspiring against Chilperic.[249] Regardless of what Gregory might have felt about it, Praetextatus was nevertheless exiled after being deposed by the decision of forty-five bishops. The inhabitants of Rouen recalled him after the death of Chilperic in 584. Praetextatus, anxious for royal support, travelled to meet King Gunthchramn of Orléans, guardian of the realm, who was then resident in Paris. He begged Gunthchramn to make a thorough investigation of the case. Fredegund did her best to prevent this investigation, remarking that such an inquest had already taken place, resulting in Praetextatus' deposition. However, Gunthchramn preferred to listen to the advice of Bishop Ragnemod of Paris, who argued that no investigation was necessary; Praetextatus could return to his diocese anyway.[250]

Fredegund, who lived in or near Rouen during the years following Chilperic's death, was very unhappy about this decision. The widowed queen and the bishop appear to have quarrelled often, Fredegund promising that Praetextatus would one day return to the exile from which he had been recalled. Praetextatus literally told Fredegund to go to hell, promising her that she would one day be plunged into the Abyss. The tense situation reached a climax on 24 February 586. Early in the morning, as Praetextatus was resting on a bench during the chanting in his church, he was stabbed under the armpit by an assassin. His followers carried him into his cell and placed the dying bishop on a bed. Fredegund, accompanied by Duke Beppolen and Duke Ansovald (two Frankish magnates who were, at least for the moment, her allies), arrived in order to have a look at him as he lay dying. Pretending to be sorry, she said that she hoped that the murderer would be caught and properly punished; she even offered to bring her own doctors to cure the wound. Praetextatus, however, was not to be fooled. Behaving more like an archetypal Dark Age warlord than as a pious bishop, according to Gregory he used some of his last minutes in life to curse the queen ('...as long as you live you will be accursed, for God will avenge my blood upon your head', *eris maledicta in saeculo, et erit Deus ultur sanguinis mei de capite tuo*).[251]

Fredegund's character as perceived by Gregory of Tours is revealed with extreme clarity in matters pertaining to her own family. It is often a dismal picture, full of rage, anger, murder and persecution. In the middle of everything is Fredegund herself, primarily caring about her own person and destroying (or trying to destroy) those whom she perceives as in some way guilty or dangerous. This negative attitude is even directed towards her own infant son Samson, whom she appears to have blamed for causing her pain at the time of his birth. Gregory tells us that when Samson was born Fredegund was very ill and thought that her end was near. She angrily rejected Samson and tried to kill him. The child was only baptised because of the intervention of Chilperic.[252]

Another illustrative incident is described by Gregory in book V, chapter 34. In this passage, the whole royal family of Soissons is attacked by a fatal disease. Fredegund's sons fall ill and die, Chilperic falls ill and Fredegund reaches the conclusion that God is angry with them. In the words of Gregory, 'she repented of her sins, although late' (*sero penetens*). However, she does not link God's punishment with her own evil machinations. On the contrary, the disease is interpreted as God's way of protesting against Chilperic's fiscal policy. The only cure, according to Fredegund, is to stop amassing wealth to the detriment of the people. Therefore, she is reported to have had the tax demands from her cities burnt to ashes. Having done this, she threatens Chilperic with eternal damnation unless he tosses his own files of tax demands into the fire – which he does.[253]

Unfortunately for Fredegund's reputation, the story did not end with the death of her sons and the burning of the files. True, she spent a month in mourning in the forest of Cuise, but having recovered from her grief she is reported to have begun to regard the disease as an asset, not a threat. If it could destroy *her* children with Chilperic, why not Chilperic's other son by Audovera, Clovis, as well? At the suggestion of Fredegund, Chilperic sent Clovis to Berny where the epidemic was still raging in the hope that he would die of the same disease. He did not. Shortly afterwards, as Clovis was boasting of the fact that he was now Chilperic's only heir, he was foolish enough to make certain remarks about his stepmother. Fredegund heard of this and, according to Gregory of Tours, was terrified. Furthermore, she was led to believe that Clovis (through the magic arts of his girl-friend's mother, who was a servant of Fredegund) was originally responsible for having spread the disease that caused her sons' death. The anonymous female messenger who put these ideas into her head is also reported to have said: 'I warn you: you can expect no better fate yourself, now that you have lost the hope through which you were to have reigned.'[254] Having heard this, Fredegund went to work. She had Clovis's girl-friend thrashed, had her hair cut off and had her tied to a stake which was stuck up outside Clovis' lodging. The girl's mother was tortured into admitting that the charges were true. Adding a few nasty details of her own, Fredegund then presented the 'evidence' to Chilperic and demanded revenge on Clovis. Chilperic had him arrested, but the queen delayed the execution, since she wanted to learn from him exactly what had happened, in other words if he had any co-conspirators who would remain threats to her safety even after his death. Clovis denied all the accusations but admitted that he had many close associates (as was only natural for a Merovingian prince). Having heard this, Fredegund had him stabbed to death at an estate called Noisy-le-Grand. Not satisfied with being rid of Clovis, Fredegund also had his mother (and her own former rival) Audovera cruelly killed (*crudele morte negata*). Clovis' sister Basina was tricked into becoming a nun – she was eventually to rebel together with another reluctant Merovingian nun, Chrodechild (pp. 154–69) – and all their possessions were confiscated by

Fredegund. As a final touch, Fredegund had the woman who had given evidence against Clovis condemned to be burnt alive. As she was dragged off to the stake, the woman admitted that she had lied, but she was soon silenced by the flames. Clovis' treasurer was then arrested and handed over to Fredegund, who condemned him to various forms of torture. He was only saved by Gregory's intervention.[255] The murder of Clovis would seem to have occurred in or before 584.

In book VI, chapter 34, Gregory tells us about Fredegund's actions after the death of her little son Theuderic in 584. She blamed one of her personal enemies, a man called Mummolus, for Theuderic's death, and to prove the allegation, which was clearly false since it would appear that Theuderic died from dysentery, she had a number of Parisian housewives tortured into confessing that they were witches. They were forced to admit that they had sacrificed Theuderic in order to save Mummolus' life during his own illness. Having secured their confessions, Fredegund killed them (cutting off the heads of some, burning others alive and breaking the bones of the rest on the wheel – Gregory's account is very detailed). Satisfied, she went to see her husband at their manor at Compiègne. She told Chilperic what the women had confessed, and Chilperic ordered the arrest of Mummolus. Mummolus was of course subjected to torture and later suspended from a rafter with his hands tied behind his back. Despite the torture, he denied the charges, but he admitted that he had often received unguents and potions from the Parisian women in question. With the logic of a stereotypical witch-hunter, Chilperic concluded that, since the torture apparently did not work and since Mummolus obviously felt no pain, he *must* be a sorcerer. Chilperic therefore told his torturers to continue. Mummolus was racked, flogged with triple thongs and had splinters driven beneath the nails of his fingers and toes. The torturers themselves grew exhausted. Fredegund finally granted Mummolus his life, but all his property was sequestered. He died shortly afterwards from a stroke. As a final act of mourning for the death of Theuderic, Fredegund collected together everything that had belonged to him, even precious clothes of silk and fur, and burned them. Nothing was allowed to remain intact to remind her of her son.[256]

Fredegund also had a daughter, Rigunth. It was arranged that she should marry Recared, son of King Leuvigild of the Visigoths (see p.

152). However, one incident after another wreaked havoc with the plan. Theuderic died, and Chilperic refused to continue the preparations for the wedding, at least for the moment ('I can hardly think of celebrating my daughter's wedding when I am in mourning', *Ecce planctum in domo sustineo, et qualiter nuptias filiae celebrabo?*).[257] Later, on 1 September 584, a great Visigothic embassy arrived in Paris, and this time Chilperic saw no reason to postpone the marriage. To provide Rigunth with an impressive dowry and a following, he rounded up several families of serfs from royal estates and carted them off in wagons. Rigunth was handed over to the Visigothic envoys together with a tremendous dowry, filling fifty carts. Fredegund contributed with a great deal of gold and silver and many fine clothes. When Chilperic saw all the wealth that was about to pass out of the kingdom, he grew very upset. Fredegund, however, publicly stated that all the riches amassed for the benefit of Rigunth and her future husband came from her own purse, not from the royal treasury. According to Fredegund, she had used the manorial and fiscal resources given her by Chilperic and others. When he heard this, Chilperic calmed down. Rigunth set off for the kingdom of the Visigoths together with (according to Gregory) many noble Franks, including a few dukes, and 4 000 ordinary people. However, her huge, poorly protected, wealth was too great a temptation for her followers. The very first night, fifty of her men got up, stole a hundred of the best horses and two great salvers and fled to one of Chilperic's and Fredegund's greatest enemies, King Childebert II, son of the murdered Sigibert. Rigunth's journey developed into a moving disaster for everyone but the thieves. The inhabitants of the cities through which she passed had to provide the entire following with supplies out of their own pockets. Her followers used the opportunity to plunder the countryside, stealing from the poor, ruining vineyards, confiscating cattle, and so on.[258] Meanwhile, Chilperic went off to his manor at Chelles outside Paris. One evening, returning from the hunt, he was struck down by an unknown assassin and died.[259] The news of her father's death reached Aquitaine when Rigunth and her company were staying in Toulouse. Duke Desiderius, a military commander of Chilperic's, immediately entered the city and took the treasure out of Rigunth's hands – she never saw it again.[260] Realising her dangerous situation, Rigunth took up residence in Saint

Mary's church in Toulouse.[261] Her servant Leunard made his way back to Fredegund, who was now claiming sanctuary in the cathedral of Paris. When Fredegund learned what had happened she became furious (*haec illa audiens furore commota*) and ordered that Leunard be stripped of his possessions. All those who had dared return from Rigunth's journey, even ordinary servants such as the pastry-cooks, were stripped of their goods, mutilated and manacled. Furthermore, Fredegund decided to use this opportunity to attack another enemy of hers, Nectarius, brother of Bishop Badegisil of Le Mans. She charged him with having made off with large amounts of Chilperic's treasure and vast quantities of hides and wine from the storehouses. Fredegund's political influence, however, was not what it had used to be due to Chilperic's murder, and Nectarius managed to keep his position.[262]

Eventually, Rigunth was brought back home in 585, humiliated and insulted, by the order of Fredegund.[263] After this, mother and daughter found it increasingly difficult to get along. Rigunth kept remarking that she was of royal blood and therefore a true mistress of the realm, while Fredegund was nothing but a low-born serving-woman, a rank to which she now ought to revert. Furthermore, Fredegund appears to have been furious over Rigunth's habit of sleeping with all kinds of men. Gregory reports that Fredegund and Rigunth frequently exchanged slaps and punches. He even describes how Fredegund on one occasion lured Rigunth into searching for treasure in a chest and then suddenly seized the lid and slammed it down on her neck. Leaning on the lid with all her might, pressing the edge of the chest hard against the girl's throat, she tried desperately to kill her. Fortunately, Rigunth was saved by the intervention of her servants. 'The quarrels between the two were even more frequent after this', Gregory states.[264]

One of Fredegund's and Chilperic's sons did survive and prosper: the future Frankish king Chlothar II (d. 629), eventually one of the most powerful of all the rulers of the dynasty. He was born only four months before the murder of his father in 584 and was originally brought up at the manor of Vitry, far from the sphere of public life. The reason for this (not surprisingly, given the nature of Merovingian politics) is that Chilperic feared that someone would try to kill the infant.[265] After Chilperic's death, Chlothar was Fredegund's insurance against complete loss of power. Chlothar's importance, as well as Fredegund's doubtful reputation, is revealed by explicit rumours, voiced by King Gunthchramn himself, that Chilperic might not have been his real father. On one occasion in 585, Fredegund assembled the leading men of Chilperic's former kingdom (three bishops and 300 laymen) and had them swear a solemn oath that Chilperic was indeed the boy's father.[266]

The greatest crisis in Fredegund's life was undoubtedly the death of Chilperic in the autumn of 584. She had based her entire political career on her ability to influence this one man, and when he was murdered, everything that she had worked for was in danger of collapse. Her bad reputation (by this time, most of the bishops and the lay magnates in Francia appear to have regarded Fredegund with fear and suspicion) made matters worse. In fact, it would seem that rumours immediately began to circulate blaming Chilperic's murder on Fredegund herself. These rumours are only vaguely hinted at in Gregory's text,[267] but they would seem to have been regarded as historical facts by the time of the writing of *Liber Historiae Francorum* ('A book on the history of the Franks', probably composed in Soissons in 727). The author informs us that Chilperic discovered that Fredegund had a lover. To prevent him from harming her, Fredegund had her husband killed.[268] Be that as it may – and there were many other potential murderers who wanted Chilperic dead[269] – when news reached Fredegund that Chilperic was dead, she immediately sought sanctuary with Bishop Ragnemod in the cathedral of Paris,[270] taking with her part of her treasure which she had previously secreted within the city walls. Her weak position was instantly revealed by the way in which the treasury officials (who lost no time in joining her enemy, King Childebert II) confiscated the remainder of her treasure, which had been left behind at Chelles. Alone in the cathedral, Fredegund desperately needed help. If Childebert managed to occupy Paris, her political life would be finished once and for all. Her only real asset, aside from her money and whatever sexual charm she still might have possessed, was her infant son Chlothar II (four months old at the time), in theory the legitimate heir to Chilperic's kingdom. She dispatched messengers to Chilperic's brother, King Gunthchramn of Orléans, begging him to intervene by taking charge of the kingdom in the name of Chlothar. If he did this, she in her turn promised to be 'his humble servant' (*me ipsam eius humilio ditioni*). Fredegund did not have to ask twice – realising the golden opportunity, Gunthchramn quickly summoned his army, marched on Paris and had already taken up quarters within the walls when Childebert arrived from another direction.[271]

The two kings, the uncle and the nephew, immediately began to argue. Childebert demanded that Gunthchramn surrender Fredegund into his hands: 'Hand over the murderess, the woman who garrotted my aunt [Galswinth], the woman who killed my father [Sigibert] and then my uncle [Chilperic], and who put my two cousins [Merovech and Clovis] to the sword.'[272] However, when the request was made, it was too late. Gunthchramn had already been charmed (we can only guess by what means, political or other) into offering Fredegund his protection. Gregory tells us that he frequently invited her to eat with him and promised her that she would come to no harm. According to the text, Gunthchramn's hospitality was *too* generous for Fredegund's health; on one occasion, she rose from the table and begged to be excused, claiming to be sick from a new pregnancy. Gunthchramn was astonished but let her go.[273] Later, when Childebert again requested the surrender of Fredegund, Gunthchramn publicly stated that he did not believe that she was guilty of the evil deeds of which his nephew accused her.[274]

During Gunthchramn's stay in Paris, the leading magnates of Chilperic's kingdom chose to accept the infant Chlothar as their king under the official guardianship of Gunthchramn. Gunthchramn tried to make himself popular among his new subjects (who swore oaths of loyalty both to him and to Chlothar) by making restitution to several people of all those possessions that had been sequestered by Chilperic's adherents. He also made considerable grants to the poor and to the churches, but was careful always to keep an armed escort when walking around in Paris, fearing assassination.[275] He had ample reason for these precautions, since he, like any other new king, constituted a formidable threat to many of those who had benefitted from the former king's rule. In order to create his own power bases, Gunthchramn confiscated much property from Chilperic's supporters.[276]

This policy would appear to have had important consequences for Fredegund, who was, of course, deeply associated with her dead husband's reign. She, like the others, suffered a fresh loss of power. As soon as he felt secure in Paris, Gunthchramn forced Fredegund to settle at the manor of Rueil (near Rouen). She was initially accompanied by many of the magnates of the kingdom who now recognised Chlothar as their king, and by Bishop Melanius, who had held the diocese of Rouen before the reinstatement of the aforementioned Praetextatus. Gregory tells us that Fredegund 'was very depressed, because much of her power had been brought to an end'.[277] It would appear that she remained at Rueil, sometimes residing in the city of Rouen itself, for the next few years.[278]

Although weakened, Fredegund had nevertheless managed to remain alive, and through her son Chlothar had the potential of eventually regaining some of her former influence. If she were to regain her power, however, she would have to begin constructing networks of alliances and removing her enemies all by herself, and she would have to begin immediately. If she waited too long, she risked losing her opportunity; in which case, she would probably remain a widow at Rueil for the rest of her life, unless she chose to enter a convent. In fact, Fredegund *did* begin her struggle immediately. Gregory tells us that she directed her first attack at Brunhild, the influential widow of King Sigibert and mother of Childebert II. She secretly sent a cleric of her household with orders to gain Brunhild's confidence and then assassinate her. The plan worked well at first, but the cleric's real mission was eventually discovered. Having been tortured into confessing everything, Brunhild sent him back to Fredegund, who in her turn punished him for his failure by having his hands and feet cut off.[279]

Meanwhile, King Gunthchramn had begun to investigate the murder of Chilperic. After all, his brother, a Frankish king, had been stabbed to death! Someone, preferably the killer, should pay for it: an end should be put to the abominable habit of murdering kings (*ut per horum necem consuetudo auferretur iniqua, ne reges amplius interficerentur*). Fredegund (who, as we have seen, was suspected herself) decided to make good use of this opportunity by accusing the treasurer, Eberulf. Eberulf was one of those magnates who had begun to neglect Fredegund after her husband's death; he may have regarded her as unimportant and powerless. In any case, Eberulf had refused to come to Rueil to live with her as her lover. In return, Fredegund alleged that it was Eberulf who had killed Chilperic, that he had stolen much of the treasury and then gone off with it to Touraine. For some reason, Gunthchramn believed her. Eberulf's lands and property were confiscated, and Eberulf himself sought refuge in the church of Saint Martin in Tours, blaming Bishop Gregory for his bad luck.[280] Fredegund's position as a politically uncertain factor is clearly revealed when Gunthchramn then tried to circumvent the laws of sanctuary. He recruited 'an empty-headed and greedy fellow' (*vanitati adque avaritiae deditus*) called Claudius, telling him to drag Eberulf out of the church without damaging the building and then either kill him or load him with chains. For this, Claudius would receive a rich reward. Being in the neighbourhood of Paris, Claudius debated with himself whether or not he should visit the widowed queen: 'If I do see her, she, too, may give me some reward. After all, I know very well that she is the personal enemy of the man I am sent to kill.'[281] Of course, being greedy, he paid her a visit. Fredegund was delighted and gave him many presents, promising him much more if he would drag Eberulf out of the church dead or alive. She went much further than Gunthchramn, saying that it was all right to kill Eberulf not only outside the building but also within the very vestibule of the church. Apparently, Claudius preferred Fredegund's orders to Gunthchramn's. The result was a fight inside the church, resulting in much bloodshed. Eberulf and Claudius were both killed. When he heard what had happened, King Gunthchramn was furious, but he quickly calmed down.[282]

It is sometimes hard to figure out exactly what Fredegund did in order to manipulate herself back into a position of real power. Contemporary rumours alleged that the man who brought Rigunth back from Toulouse in 585, Chuppa (who had been Chilperic's Master of the Stables), had actually been sent on a secret mission from Fredegund to the pretender Gundovald (who was killed before the message from Fredegund could be delivered).[283] A more explicit rumour alleged that she was a secret ally of King Leuvigild of the Visigoths. At the time, war was just about to erupt between Leuvigild and Gunthchramn, who longed for the conquest of Septimania, the only remaining Gaulish territory still in Visigothic hands. Suddenly a document, seemingly a letter from Leuvigild to Fredegund, was discovered by some peasants, who sent it to Gunthchramn. Leuvigild asked Fredegund to 'Kill our enemies, that is, Childebert and his mother [Brunhild], as quickly as you can. Make peace with Gunthchramn; buy this peace at whatever price you can. If, as may well be, you are short of money, we will send you some in secret, so that we may be sure that we achieve our purpose. Once we have taken vengeance on our enemies, reward Bishop Amelius [of Bigorra] and the Lady Leuba [mother-in-law of a Frankish duke called Bladast], through whose good offices our envoys have access to you.' We do not know whether Gunthchramn believed that the letter was genuine or not, but he quickly made Childebert aware of the contents.[284]

In any case, it is clear that Childebert and his mother Brunhild would have to be the chief targets of any aggressive policy of Fredegund's. Gunthchramn was comparatively old, being the only surviving Merovingian king of his generation, and it was common knowledge that he intended Childebert to inherit his portion of the kingdom when he died. Childebert and Brunhild already controlled one third of Frankish territory; with Gunthchramn's huge Burgundian territories added to their Austrasian possessions, they would present a dangerous threat to Fredegund and her infant son. The magnates of northwestern Francia could, in that situation, easily shift their allegiance from Chlothar to Childebert. If, on the other hand, Childebert were to die, Chlothar would be in a much safer position and might (if Fredegund made good use of her influence at Gunthchramn's court) take his place as Gunthchramn's heir. Seen from this angle, Fredegund's repeated attempts at killing Childebert make perfect sense.

Immediately after telling us of the alleged letter from Leuvigild, Gregory goes on to describe how Fredegund had two iron daggers made, which she ordered to be deeply grooved and smeared with poison. She gave the weapons to two clerics and told them go to Childebert's court, pretending to be mendicants. When they were begging for alms at the feet of the king, they should stab him from both sides, thereby destroying both Childebert and his mother Brunhild, 'whose arrogant behaviour is encouraged by the support which he gives to her', so that she would cease to be a rival of Fredegund's (*ut tandem Brunichildis, quae ab illo adrogantiam sumit, eo cadente conruat, mihique subdatur*). If this plan proved impossible to carry out, they should instead go for Brunhild herself, 'that woman who is an enemy of mine' (*vel ipsam interemite inimicam*). If they were killed during the mission, Fredegund promised to reward their relatives. The clerics began to shiver at the thought of her plan, realising the danger. To prevent them from backing out, Fredegund had them drugged and packed off on their mission, supplying them with a potion to strengthen their nerves on the day of the killing. However, both clerics were captured in Soissons; during the interrogation, they revealed everything. Childebert later interrogated the would-be assassins himself. Having heard all he wanted, Childebert handed them over to his torturers, who executed them.[285]

Slowly, Fredegund's position at Rueil was definitely strengthened. She used her resources – her property, her son Chlothar, her allies, her assassins, etc. – to reclaim some of the power she had lost in 584. As related above, she had her greatest local enemy, Bishop Praetextatus of Rouen, killed in February 586. By then, she had managed to secure the good-will of Duke Ansovald, previously a servant of Chilperic's, and of Duke Beppolen.[286] The murder of Praetextatus shows that she regarded it as perfectly safe for a woman of her standing to commit such an act despite the unpopularity this might, and obviously did, bring. Gregory reports that one of the Frankish leaders of Rouen went to her after the murder and blamed her for the crime, saying that he hoped that God would be quick to avenge the innocent blood of the bishop. He is also reported to have threatened her: 'We all propose to inquire closely into this crime, to prevent you from committing any more atrocities of the sort.'[287] Fredegund immediately had the man poisoned to death. However, the threat was real: Bishop Leudovald of Bayeux, with the assent of many other bishops, had all the churches of Rouen closed in order to provoke such a general outcry among the inhabitants of the town that the author of the crime would be discovered. Leudovald then had certain individuals apprehended and tortured into confessing that the deed had been committed at the instigation of Fredegund. When she was charged with this, she denied everything and, as Gregory makes explicit, could not be punished (*ea defensante, ulciscere non potuit*). She also appears to have tried to get rid of Leudovald, but he was careful to keep an armed escort with him wherever he went.[288]

Fredegund's strength is also made clear by Gunthchramn's apparent inability to intervene. He was, naturally, in due course informed about the events in Rouen, and he sent three bishops of his own to look into the matter. The bishops met with Chlothar's governors, who promised to investigate the murder. However, they openly refused to let the perpetrator (whenever this person was caught, if ever) be brought to King Gunthchramn. Hearing this, the bishops told the governors that Gunthchramn might show up with an army unless they did as they were told; the bishops then returned to their king. Despite the threats, the only thing Gunthchramn's envoys actually accomplished was to temporarily prevent Melanius, Fredegund's candidate, from succeeding Praetextatus as bishop.[289]

In the end, Fredegund tried to clear herself from the charge that she had been responsible for the murder by instead implicating one of her unfree servants. She accused him of having first killed Praetextatus himself, then spreading evil rumours about Fredegund's guilt. She handed the servant over to Praetextatus' nephew, who put him to torture. The servant now confessed that he had indeed killed the bishop, but he insisted that he had only done this because Queen Fredegund had paid him 100 golden pieces. Others had also wanted Praetextatus out of the way: Melanius had paid him another 50 pieces, the archdeacon 50 more. Furthermore, he had been promised that both he and his wife would be given their freedom if he committed the murder. Having heard the confession, Praetextatus' nephew drew his sword and killed the accused man, thereby putting an end to the investigation. Fredegund remained unpunished, and no-one, not even Gunthchramn, could prevent her from finally appointing Melanius to the see.[290]

By now, Fredegund would seem to have regained most, if not all, of her former power. Her position in young Chlothar's kingdom is made clear to us as we read about her suddenly falling victim of Duke Beppolen's desertion. The Frankish magnates were never known for political constancy, and Beppolen was no exception. Realising the mounting tension between the court of Fredegund and Chlothar and that of Gunthchramn, he left Fredegund and offered Gunthchramn his services. According to Gregory of Tours, he did this because he felt badly treated by Fredegund, not having received the honour he felt due to him. Initially, his desertion seemed a wise choice. Gunthchramn lost no time in appointing Beppolen duke of Chlothar's cities. However, once he tried to enforce his will in the territory, his plan met with serious obstacles. Fredegund, of course, responded to his treachery by sequestering many of his possessions. The people of Rennes refused to admit Beppolen to the town, and Angers could only be taken after he had plundered the neighbourhood, destroyed the harvest and maltreated a number of local inhabitants. Although Beppolen did succeed in taking Rennes at the second attempt and left his son as governor, the townsfolk rebelled and killed the son as soon as Beppolen's army had moved on.[291]

By 586 or 587, Fredegund appears to have felt sufficiently secure to move against Gunthchramn himself. New rumours alleged that she had dispatched secret messengers to Gunthchramn's Visigothic enemies by way of Bishop Palladius of Saintes.[292] In the same year, an attempt was made on Gunthchramn's life. Going to early communion, Gunthchramn suddenly noticed a man sleeping in a corner of the oratory, his sword girt round him and his spear resting against the wall. The man was seized and interrogated. As soon as Gunthchramn's torturers began to work, he confessed that he had been sent by the envoys of Fredegund, among them a man called Baddo, who had been visiting Gunthchramn for the last couple of days. His orders were to kill the king. Fredegund's envoys, however, resisted Gunthchramn's attempts to make them talk. Gunthchramn could not prove that Fredegund was guilty, but he had the assassin wounded and thrown into prison, while the envoys were banished to different places.[293] Later, Gunthchramn ordered that Baddo be brought before him a second time to stand trial in Paris. He made it clear that Baddo would be released only if Fredegund herself cleared him of the charge. When no messenger from Fredegund arrived, Baddo was sent back to prison. In the end, he was released through the intervention of Bishop Leudovald of Bayeux.[294]

Thanks to Gregory of Tours, we actually possess an ear-witness account of Gunthchramn's feelings towards Fredegund after these incidents. Naturally, Gregory may simply be putting his own words in the king's mouth, but there is no reason simply to presume that this is the case. According to the story, King Childebert employed Gregory as an ambassador to Gunthchramn's court at Chalon-sur-Saône in 588. After discussing various issues, Gunthchramn turned to Bishop Felix of

Châlons-sur-Marne, who had accompanied Gregory to the court. 'Tell me, Felix', he said, 'is it really true that you have established warm friendly relations between my sister [i.e. sister-in-law] Brunhild and that enemy of God and man, Fredegund?'[295] Felix replied that it was not. Gregory intervened, saying that Gunthchramn had no reason to worry on that account: 'The King need not question the fact that the 'friendly relations' which have bound them together for so many years are still being fostered by them both. That is to say, you may be quite sure that the hatred which they have borne each other for many a long year, far from withering away, is still as strong as ever. Noble King, it is a great pity that you cannot bring yourself to be less kindly disposed towards Queen Fredegund. We have so often remarked that you receive her envoys with more consideration than you give to ours [i.e., King Childebert's].'[296] Gunthchramn replied that he only received Fredegund's envoys in that way in order to maintain friendly relations with his nephew. Fredegund had nothing to do with his apparent show of friendship – on the contrary. 'I can hardly offer ties of genuine friendship to a woman who on more than one occasion has sent her men to murder me!'[297]

For the rest of her life, it would seem that Fredegund continued to exercise her influence in northwestern Francia, ruling in the name of young Chlothar. She never forgave Duke Beppolen's treachery and did, eventually, get even with him. In 590, when Fredegund heard that Beppolen was leading an army against the Bretons on behalf of King Gunthchramn, she contacted her allies among the Saxons at Bayeux. These one-time pirates, who now inhabited the region known as the Bessin, appear to have been dependent upon the queen, although the details of the relationship escape us. Anyway, she ordered them to cut their hair and to rig themselves out in the Breton fashion and then to march in support of the Breton warlord Waroch. Knowing the territory far better than the Franks did, Waroch managed to shut Beppolen's soldiers in between marshes and narrow lanes. After three days of fighting against the combined Breton-Saxon forces, Beppolen was killed together with most of his men; many perished in the bogs trying to escape.[298] Fredegund also continued her attempts to get rid of Childebert, at one time allegedly employing a whole team of twelve assassins – six to kill Childebert himself, six to kill his son Theudebert.

One assassin was caught (as he was preparing to strike Childebert down at an oratory in Marlenheim) and was forced to confess everything. Under torture, he gave the names of his accomplices. The king had them all arrested and subjected to various forms of painful punishment – Gregory tells us that some of the assassins committed suicide with their own daggers rather than face Childebert's torturers.[299] By now, Fredegund's evil intentions were so well-known that they could be routinely used to incriminate almost anyone, as is clear from the story of how the two rebel nuns Chrodechild and Basina tried to make Childebert suspicious of their enemy, the Abbess Leubovera (pp. 166).[300]

The way in which Fredegund wielded her power over Chlothar's kingdom is clearly demonstrated by an incident in 591. A violent feud had erupted in Tournai,[301] resulting in the virtual annihilation of two Frankish families. As the feud was beginning to spread to more distant relatives as well, Fredegund repeatedly warned the parties to give up their feud and make peace. She could not allow them to create a public nuisance that threatened the rule of law in Tournai. As long as Fredegund merely talked to them, however, nothing happened. Realising this, Fredegund settled the issue by violence. She invited a great number of people to supper and made the three most important survivors of the feud – Charivald, Leudovald and Waldin – sit on the same bench. By nightfall the three men and their servants were completely drunk and unable to defend themselves. At this moment, Fredegund had three men with axes sneak up behind them and quickly decapitate them. The furious relatives of Charivald, Leudovald and Waldin asked Childebert to intervene to arrest and execute their evil queen. It would appear that some kind of action was prepared, but in the end nothing happened. With the help of her supporters, Fredegund got safely away from Tournai.[302]

All the time, however, the boy-king Chlothar remained the chief basis of Fredegund's power. If Chlothar died, she risked losing everything. Any sudden weakness of Chlothar's was a potential disaster. When Chlothar fell seriously ill in 590 (after the battle between Waroch and Beppolen) and was, in fact, for a while presumed dead by King Gunthchramn, Fredegund vowed that she would donate a great sum of money to the church of Saint Martin to save her son's life. She also sent messengers to Waroch, ordering him to set free the prisoners from Gunthchramn's army whom he was still holding in Brittany. Waroch did as he was told, but Gregory, of course, attributes the recovery of Chlothar to Fredegund's vow to Saint Martin's church.[303] In 591, Fredegund decided to strengthen Chlothar's (and thereby her own) position by having the boy ceremoniously baptised in Paris by the most prominent men she could find. She sent messengers to Gunthchramn, asking him to do his duty towards his nephew and arrange for the baptism himself. 'It is for the king [Gunthchramn] to receive him from the baptismal font, and he should deign to treat him as his own son.'[304] This action would both confirm Chlothar as rightful king and as Chilperic's true son *and* symbolically reaffirm Gunthchramn's power in northwestern Francia, a fact that both Fredegund and Gunthchramn must have been aware of. Consequently, since he had nothing to lose and saw no reason not to perform what he regarded as his duty to his family, Gunthchramn agreed. He summoned a number of his bishops and counts and ordered them all to proceed to Paris. Gunthchramn himself was delayed because of an attack of gout in the feet, but he recovered in time and made his way to the manor of Rueil. Meanwhile, preparations for the baptism were taking place in the village of Nanterre. King Childebert, who understood the political implications of the baptism only too well, did his best to stop it by sending messengers to Rueil, accusing Gunthchramn of 'establishing friendly relations with Childebert's enemies' (*cum inimicis eius amicitias conlegaris*) and threatening him with the judgment of God. Gunthchramn dismissed them and continued the preparations. Receiving the boy from the baptismal font, he named him Chlothar and wished him a future full of power. After an exchange of presents, Gunthchramn returned to Chalon-sur-Saône.[305]

This is the last we hear of Fredegund in *Decem Libri Historiarum*. We know that she lived for a few years more, still as powerful as ever, until her death in c. 597.[306]

When analysing Fredegund, it is impossible to overlook the fact that her history was written by a man who made no secret of the fact that he disliked her immensely. Gregory of Tours' history of Fredegund is a Study in Black, a dark tale of a dark woman. Gregory makes it very clear to the reader that, in his eyes, Fredegund is clearly an enemy of

God. Even when she had sought sanctuary in the cathedral of Paris after the murder of Chilperic, 'Fredegund had no fear of God'.[307]

To this should be added that Gregory's fear of the queen was well-founded. Gregory had ample reason to dread both Fredegund and her husband Chilperic. The fact that he was not fond of them appears to have been well known; in fact, his dislike of Fredegund provided his enemies with a weapon to use against him. This is most clearly shown in the story of the slanderer Leudast. This man, who had been deposed as Count of Tours, told Chilperic that Gregory was spreading lies about Fredegund – telling people that she was having a love affair with Bishop Bertram of Bordeaux. At first, Chilperic did not believe the allegation. Leudast was punched, kicked, loaded with chains and thrown into prison.[308] Later, Leudast's story was supported by the subdeacon, Riculf. Both named two witnesses, Gregory's friend Galienus and his archdeacon Plato. After Leudast had been released from prison, he had these men arrested and paraded in front of Fredegund.[309] Chilperic then convened a council of all the bishops in his kingdom and ordered the affair to be thoroughly investigated. When a carpenter called Modestus told Riculf to stop lying and instead ask Gregory's pardon, Riculf began to shout that Modestus was an enemy of the queen. Fredegund, of course, had Modestus arrested, tortured and imprisoned (according to Gregory, he then escaped through divine intervention). At the trial, Gregory managed to clear his name and keep his position.[310]

Leudast then spent a considerable time escaping from one region to another and from one place of sanctuary to another, knowing that Fredegund wanted him dead. He finally managed to obtain a pardon from Chilperic and showed up in Tours with a written order from the king, saying that his wife should be restored to him and that he should be allowed to take up residence in the city. Of greater importance (in the eyes of Gregory) was a letter signed by several bishops, asking that Leudast should be readmitted to communion. The main reason why he had been excluded in the first place was because Fredegund had wanted it, a fact that Gregory was very much aware of. Gregory, fearing what the queen would do to him if he went against her wishes (and probably seeing no reason whatsoever to treat Leudast, his own personal enemy, favourably), refused to readmit Leudast until Fredegund had given her consent. He then wrote to the queen and asked her. Fredegund's reply confirmed Gregory's fears. She wrote:

> I was under such pressure from a great number of people that there was nothing else that I could possibly do, except let him go. I ask you not to make your peace with him and not to give him the consecrated bread, until I have had time to see clearly what my future action should be.[311]

Gregory interpreted Fredegund's reply to mean that she was busy arranging Leudast's assassination. He secretly informed Leudast (by way of his father-in-law) that he should be on his guard. Leudast rejected the advice and instead went to see Chilperic, who was staying with his troops near Melun. Chilperic explained that he could not guarantee his safety, since Fredegund hated him for what he had done. He promised, however, to discuss the matter with his wife and try to restore Leudast to her good graces. Trusting in Chilperic's friendship and power, Leudast then accompanied the king to Paris and threw himself at Fredegund's feet in the cathedral, begging her for forgiveness. This had no effect; the queen was furious and turned to Chilperic, implicitly accusing him of bad judgment. She is reported to have said: 'Things have come to a sorry pass when I see my enemy face to face and I am powerless to do anything!'[312] Leudast was immediately ejected from the cathedral. When the mass was over, some of Fredegund's men attacked him as he was counting money in a shop. After a fight and a failed attempt at escape (which cost him his hair and a broken leg), Leudast was thrown into prison. Chilperic then had him tortured and dragged off to a royal manor. At Fredegund's personal command he was placed flat on his back on the ground, a block of wood was wedged behind his neck and the queen's henchmen started to beat him on the throat with another piece of wood until he died.[313]

Only on occasion does Fredegund behave in a way of which Gregory would seem to approve. When Leudast at one time was claiming sanctuary in the church of Saint Hilary in Poitiers, he had the habit of emerging from the church to break into the homes of various citizens and rob them. He also interfered with women in the porchway of the church. When this was reported to Fredegund, she 'took exception to this desecration of a place consecrated to God' and ordered Leudast expelled from the church. He was immediately driven out and forced to escape to the Bourges region.[314]

In his short analysis of Fredegund, which is almost entirely based on Gregory's writings, Ian Wood (1994) interprets her actions as primarily those of an anxious mother. Wood perceives the pre-584 Fredegund as a woman trying to protect her offspring and to wipe out any conceivable challenge to her children's chance of succeeding to Chilperic's kingdom. Most of her explicit enemies (Clovis, Merovech, Praetextatus) were in one way or another regarded as threats to her own sons. When her sons fell ill and died, this resulted in extravagant displays of grief on Fredegund's part. In Wood's eyes, Fredegund might be seen as 'a model, if somewhat bloodthirsty, queen, whose chief concern was the protection of her immediate family.' After noting that Gregory also describes some of her actions as rather more self-centred (such as the attempted murder of Rigunth and her anger at Eberulf for not wanting to be her lover), he concludes, however, that Fredegund's career cannot simply be reduced to that of a woman concerned only for the survival and inheritance of her children.[315] As for her resources, he does not fail to observe that she made good use of the existence of her son Chlothar, that she must have possessed much treasure and that she frequently employed assassins.[316]

While it is undoubtedly true that Fredegund does appear to have been a self-centred, anxious mother, there is considerably more to be said about her as she appears in Gregory's text. Most importantly, she was a self-centred, anxious mother *acting within the sphere of politics*. It is impossible to fully comprehend Fredegund's actions unless we regard her as a politician as well as a mother.

How, then, did Fredegund behave politically? At the beginning of the present analysis, we saw that her influence was not static; it varied according to her ability to use her resources and to the varying degrees of formal status that she experienced during her long career. Briefly, these degrees can be summarised as:

(1) –567: mistress and wife (one of many) of King Chilperic
(2) 567: former wife, in danger of being thrown out
(3) c.567–84: leading wife (i.e., what we would call a queen)

(4) 584: suddenly made a widow (loss of power)
(5) 584–c.586: widow, fighting to regain her position
(6) c.586–c.597: reigning royal widow with a boy-king under her tutelage

Her resources, as they appear in Gregory's text, can be summarised as:

(1) charisma (sexappeal, beauty, charm, etc.) – undoubtedly the reason why Chilperic recruited her to his bedchamber in the first place
(2) aggressive personality (according to he principle 'do it to them before they do it to you', an admirable quality if you were to succeed as a sixth-century politician in Western Europe)
(3) property (money, treasure, land, etc.), given to her by Chilperic and/or confiscated from her enemies
(4) her husband Chilperic (before the autumn of 584)
(5) her children (especially her only surviving son, King Chlothar II)
(6) her clients, friends and allies (most of whom were recruited with money)

Fredegund's resources and talents were, of course, employed in quite different ways depending upon on what step on the career-ladder she was currently standing. For instance, her purely charismatic resources must have been of far greater use to her in the crucial years 567 (when she risked losing Chilperic's favour) and 584 (when she had to get Gunthchramn to support her) than in relatively calm years such as 583 and 592. During her comparatively strong early period (c. 567–84), her major basis of power was undoubtedly her husband Chilperic, who was commonly recognised as the true Frankish King of Soissons. With his support, she automatically gained access to money, lands and clients. In her later period of strength (c. 586–c. 597), she had to rely on herself.

The major dividing line in Fredegund's career was without doubt the year 584, when she suffered a major setback in the death of her husband. The autumn of 584 shows her using her resources and talents in every conceivable way; she was literally fighting for survival, with the army of Childebert approaching the walls of Paris. The critical years of 584–86 thus form a key to understanding Fredegund in her capacity as a political actor. Sketched along the lines hinted at by Gregory of Tours, her political agenda during this period might look something like this:

(1) Secure property! – The first thing Fredegund did on hearing of Chilperic's death was to hurry to Paris (where she had been smart enough to hide funds), taking with her as much treasure as possible.
(2) Claim sanctuary! – She established a new residence within the cathedral of Paris. Even powerful Merovingians (with the exception of Fredegund herself) hesitated before killing those hiding in prominent churches.
(3) Get a powerful ally! – The most powerful ally possible was undoubtedly King Gunthchramn. Therefore, Fredegund (still in the cathedral) begged Gunthchramn to intervene and, when he had arrived, charmed him into helping her.
(4) After having paid the political price that Gunthchramn will surely demand, try to hold on to as many clients and as much property as possible! – When the immediate political turmoil was over, Gunthchramn had her sent to the manor of Rueil. However, Fredegund managed to retain a number of lay and ecclesiastical clients and allies, such as Melanius and Ansovald. Most importantly, she held on to young Chlothar II. Thereby, she had resources (both landed and human) on which to base a new career.
(5) When you feel reasonably safe, attack your enemies! Having established herself at Rueil, Fredegund began to act in a very aggressive fashion, using her aforementioned resources to gain more strength and political respect (i.e., fear). She repeatedly sent assassins to the court of Brunhild and Childebert; she had Eberulf wiped out; she arranged the death of Praetextatus and reinstated Melanius as Bishop of Rouen.
(6) At the same time, try to attract the attention of other kings and dukes! – According to rumour, Fredegund quickly established good relations with the Visigothic kingdom in the south and with the Breton warlord Waroch. She is also thought to have tried to get in touch with the pretender Gundovald in Aquitaine.

It would appear that Fredegund, having followed these instructions, was back in power by 586. Gunthchramn's inability to intervene in the events following Praetextatus' murder and the fact that he could only postpone – not prevent – Melanius' re-appointment as bishop is evidence of her success. It is clear from Gregory's text that Fredegund's personal aims, her political power and her material resources were already well-known, feared and grudgingly respected during the Eberulf affair. The assassin Claudius made a point of going to see her, despite the fact that he had already agreed to set out after Eberulf anyway.

For the rest of her life, Fredegund controlled Chilperic's former kingdom in her own way: never as completely as Chilperic had done, but still to a greater degree than the theoretical governors of Chlothar, the local dukes and counts and the theoretical overlord, King Gunthchramn, were able to do. She continued to strike at every potential enemy (including Gunthchramn) with assassins, daggers and poison. She hardly needed Gunthchramn any more (except for the baptism of Chlothar), and it is easy to see that his death would only serve to strengthen her position. Gunthchramn appears to have understood this himself. The conversation between Gunthchramn and Gregory in 588 proves that Fredegund was perceived as a strong, independent queen by both the bishop and the king. Gregory, representing Childebert and Brunhild, spoke of Fredegund as being in the same position as these two rulers ('We have so often remarked that you receive her envoys with more consideration than you give to ours...') and Gunthchramn replied by remarking that his so-called friendly relations with Fredegund were merely dictated by political necessity. Any king or magnate who wanted something done in northwestern Francia in the years c. 586–c. 597 would have to go through Fredegund; she was in charge. If you tried to maintain a powerful position in that region of Europe by allying yourself with someone else (such as Gunthchramn), you might end up dead like Duke Beppolen, who obviously misjudged Fredegund's position.

Looking at Fredegund in this way, she becomes far more than an anxious, bloodthirsty, somewhat immoral mother fighting for her and her family's survival. She was not, and for biological reasons could never be, a Frankish *king*. Nor was she a *queen* in the institutional sense that late- and post-Carolingian female rulers were to become a couple of centuries later. The only way to describe her position in c. 586–c. 597 would be to define her as a *reigning royal widow*. There were lots of royal widows thanks to the promiscuity of the Merovingian kings, but few of them managed to hold on to their position in a way that enabled them to inherit de facto a considerable part of their dead husbands' might. Those who did manage this, such as Fredegund, came to occupy a specific position of power that has previously received little attention by scholarly research.

As is clear from Gregory's description of Fredegund's second period of strength, the power of a reigning royal widow was considerably weaker than that of reigning king. She never felt completely secure; she always had to be on her guard, watching for any opportunity to strengthen her position by fresh alliances and daring assassinations. Fredegund did this not merely for the benefit of young Chlothar II, but primarily for the benefit of herself. Chlothar was an integral (and necessary) part of her position and her life, but no reader of Gregory's work can doubt that the most interesting person from Fredegund's point of view was Fredegund. She wanted to rule in the most effective way possible. When an opportunity to gain more land through confiscation arose, she used it, as in the case of Beppolen. She recruited strong clients and allies, such as the Saxons at Bayeux. Also, she fully assumed the responsibility of keeping the peace that was the duty of any king during the Middle Ages. Her interference in Tournai in 591, although hardly the kind of peacemaking effort that we would applaud today, may in fact have saved lives in the long run.

Brunhild: a Visigothic princess far from home[317]

Brunhild was the daughter of Athanagild, King of the Visigoths from 554 to 568, and Queen Goiswinth.[318] She enters the pages of Gregory's History in book IV, chapter 27, when King Sigibert I tries to outdo his Merovingian relatives. Observing that his royal brothers were marrying simple servant girls 'who were completely unworthy of them' (*quod fratres eius indignas sibimet uxores acciperent*), he sent messengers to the Visigothic kingdom in present-day Spain, asking for the hand of Brunhild. Gregory introduces her in the following way:

This young woman was elegant in all that she did, lovely to look at, chaste and decorous in her behaviour, wise in her generation and well-spoken.[319]

King Athanagild was delighted with the prospect of having the powerful Sigibert as his son-in-law. Brunhild was packed off to Gaul with a large dowry, probably in the year 567. Sigibert received her at a banquet together with the leading men of his kingdom. The royal couple were married 'with every appearance of joy and happiness' (*cum inminsa laetitia atque iocunditate*). Gregory remarks that Brunhild, like most Visigoths, was an Arian heretic, but that she was converted by the bishops sent to reason with her and by the king himself.[320]

In this way, the most powerful woman in Frankish history enters the stage. She would stay there for a longer period than most others, men as well as women. In fact, Brunhild was to remain at the centre of Western European politics for 46 years, almost half a century, until her terrible death in 613. Few, if any, early medieval rulers could compete with Brunhild in the quantitative length of her period of influence. In the present context, however, we are primarily interested not in quantity but in quality: how and in what way, according to Gregory of Tours, Brunhild used the foothold she had gained in 567.

We know very little about Brunhild's life between her marriage to Sigibert in 567 and Sigibert's initially successful offensive against his brother Chilperic in 575. Chilperic fled to Tournai, leaving the land around Paris and Rouen at the mercy of Sigibert's troops. Gregory reports that Brunhild and her sons came to join Sigibert in Paris as he was preparing the final assault on Chilperic. However, as we have seen, the king was shortly afterwards murdered at the villa of Vitry by assassins sent by Chilperic's wife Fredegund, thus leaving the north-eastern part of the Frankish realm (the region that was developing into Austrasia) in the hands of his son Childebert II, who was only five years old at the time.[321]

To Brunhild, the death of Sigibert was a disaster. When the news reached her, she was still residing in Paris with her children. In the words of Gregory: 'She was prostrate with anguish and grief, and she hardly knew what she was doing.'[322] Paris was no longer a safe city, and

Brunhild was hardly in a position to be able to guard her children from Chilperic's men once they arrived to take charge of the situation. Realising this, and undoubtedly seeing a good opportunity for himself, Duke Gundovald (one of Sigibert's military commanders, not to be confused with the Merovingian pretender with the same name) removed young Childebert from Brunhild in what to our eyes looks like pure kidnapping. Childebert was proclaimed King and began to reign (in theory) on Christmas Day.[323] The rest of the royal family received no help from Gundovald, nor from any of the other Austrasian magnates. When Chilperic arrived in Paris, he seized Brunhild, banished her to Rouen and took possession of her treasure. Her daughters Ingund and Chlodosinda were imprisoned at Meaux.[324]

At this moment, Brunhild would appear to have lost everything. Chilperic's reason for sending her to Rouen was probably that he did not think she would cause much trouble there. Sigibert's magnates clearly did not want her at their court, and she had no basis of power of her own in Gaul since her family lived in present-day Spain; she appeared to be finished. Had Chilperic and Fredegund known what the Visigothic princess was capable of, they would undoubtedly have killed her in Paris in the autumn of 575 and saved themselves decades of trouble. Since they did not, Brunhild was able to begin her long, successful climb up the political ladder of a royal widow.

She took the first step only a few months later. To everyone's surprise, she got married to Chilperic's resourceful and ambitious son Merovech. After having spent a few weeks in the spring of 576 ravaging the countryside of Tours, he had gone to Rouen, pretending to want to visit his mother Audovera but in fact preparing for his nuptial coup. When he heard of the marriage, King Chilperic was, of course, furious. It must have been clear to him that Merovech was trying to build a position of power for himself, independent of his father. Brunhild might not be powerful at the moment, but she was still a symbolically important princess and a royal widow with a clear potential for future support within her son's kingdom. Chilperic quickly marched to Rouen, scaring the married couple into seeking sanctuary in the church of Saint Martin. After negotiations, Chilperic swore a solemn oath that he would not try to separate them. Believing his words, Merovech and Brunhild stepped out of the church. Chilperic received them according to their rank, had a meal with them and returned to Soissons, taking Merovech with him.[325]

Shortly afterwards, the son was punished for his actions. Fearing a rebellion from Merovech, Chilperic had him imprisoned and eventually made a priest. He was placed in a monastery but escaped in 577 and made his way to Tours, where he claimed sanctuary. Gregory (himself bishop of the city at the time) tells us of Merovech's plans to visit Brunhild. After a couple of months, he did manage to reach her, but (as Gregory writes) 'the Austrasians would not receive him' (*sed ab Austrasiis non est collectus*). Chilperic sent an army to Champagne in search of his fugitive son, but he failed to find him.[326] In other words: Brunhild had by this time been able to return to Sigibert's former kingdom, but she was hardly in a position of power. If she had been able to, she would undoubtedly have supported Merovech against his father. Instead, the *Austrasii*, the Austrasian magnates, could do as they pleased. Merovech had to hide in the Rheims area. After having failed to raise a rebellion against his father, he died mysteriously in 578.[327]

However, we also learn that Brunhild was trying to build a network of allies. Before leaving Rouen, she appears to have made a friend in Bishop Praetextatus (the bishop who had married her and Merovech), to whom she had entrusted property. Praetextatus was reputedly bribing the people to act against the interests of Chilperic (more specifically, to kill him and thus give a helping hand to Merovech). Chilperic had him arrested and the property confiscated; in the end Praetextatus was banished from his diocese and exiled to an island (probably Jersey).[328]

Since Gregory was living in Tours, far from the centres of Austrasian politics, we know relatively little of what went on at the court of Childebert II during these years. It is clear, however, that Brunhild was slowly gathering strength. She appears to have remained in contact with her relatives south of the Pyrenees, and she was able to employ Bishop Elafius of Châlons-sur-Marne as her messenger to the Visigoths.[329] In 581, she forcefully intervened in a feud in order to help her local allies. Duke Lupus of Champagne, who is described as her faithful supporter, was attacked by an army led by the magnates Ursio and Berthefried. Gregory provides us with a vivid picture of Brunhild standing between the two armies, shouting: 'Stop! Warriors, I command you to stop this wicked behaviour! Stop harassing this person who has done you no harm! Stop fighting each other and bringing disaster upon our country, just because of this one man!'[330] Ursio is said to have replied: 'Stand back, woman! It should be enough that you held regal power when your husband was alive. Now your son is on the throne, and his kingdom is under our control, not yours. Stand back, I say, or you will be trodden into the ground by our horses' hoofs!'[331]

In this particular crisis, however, Brunhild managed to overcome her enemies. Ursio and Berthefried withdrew their army. Shortly afterwards, however, they broke into Lupus' houses and stole all his property. Afraid of being killed by the magnates, Lupus left his wife safe inside the walls of Laon and took refuge with King Gunthchramn, thereafter waiting at his court for Childebert to come of age.[332] He felt that he could not rely on Brunhild alone to protect him.

In 584, Brunhild's growing power is demonstrated by the case of Abbot Lupentius and Count Innocentius. Lupentius, who was abbot of the church of Saint Privatus in Javols, was summoned by Brunhild, apparently having been accused by Count Innocentius of Javols of making libellous remarks about her. His case was discussed and he was officially declared innocent. Returning home, Lupentius was seized by Innocentius, dragged off to the manor of Ponthion and maltreated. Later, on the bank of the River Aisne, Innocentius had him beheaded.[333] Of course, this does not tell us much about Brunhild's influence, but immediately afterwards Gregory goes on to relate how Brunhild intervened to have Innocentius elected Bishop of Rodez.[334] In other words, Innocentius was a client of Brunhild's. Whether Lupentius was an enemy of Innocentius' or of Brunhild's is unimportant. What is of interest to us is the fact that Brunhild was creating a network of powerful lay and ecclesiastical clients.

The recently widowed Fredegund (whose husband Chilperic was murdered in the autumn of 584) clearly perceived Brunhild as one of her chief enemies. Gregory tells us that Fredegund compared her own situation to Brunhild's and that she considered herself a better woman. In 585, she is said to have referred to Brunhild as her rival and her enemy. One of the first things Fredegund is reported to have done after having settled down at the manor of Rueil was to attempt to have

Brunhild assassinated. Although the attempt failed, the way it was carried out is revealing. The assassin was a cleric who tried to gain Brunhild's confidence by claiming to be a fugitive from Fredegund. He is reported to have told Brunhild that he sought her protection.[335] By this time (584–85), Brunhild was regarded as sufficiently strong for political fugitives to gather at her court. Otherwise, the cleric would hardly have tried this particular method of gaining access to the royal widow.

Brunhild's growing influence over Austrasian politics made her dangerous. It is unclear how far she was involved in the Gundovald affair (when Gundovald, pretending to be a Merovingian prince, tried to create a kingdom of his own based on Aquitaine) in 584–85, but Gregory reports that King Gunthchramn (Gundovald's chief enemy) warned young Childebert, who was coming of age at the time, not to visit his mother, nor to give her any opportunity of writing to Gundovald or of receiving communications from him.[336] Gregory also informs us that Gunthchramn believed that Gundovald was planning to marry Brunhild.[337] In fact, Gunthchramn used Brunhild's alleged contacts with Gundovald to try to make him disband his troops. Writing to Gundovald, who was at the time safely hiding within the walls of Comminges, and pretending to be Brunhild, Gunthchramn advised Gundovald to order his troops to return home, while he himself took up winter quarters in Bordeaux. Gundovald, however, was not fooled by the letter.[338] When the rebellion had been defeated, the magnate Waddo, one of Gundovald's former supporters who eventually helped betray him, fled to Brunhild. Gregory informs us that 'she received him graciously.'[339] Later in 585, Gregory personally heard Gunthchramn say that Brunhild had threatened to kill him: 'It is true enough that his [Childebert's] mother Brunhild threatened to murder me, but as far as I am concerned that is a matter of small moment. God who snatched me from the hands of my other enemies also delivered be from the snares of Brunhild.'[340]

Nevertheless, Brunhild was clearly far from dominant in her dead husband's kingdom. She was present at various meetings and undoubtedly influenced the young king – in 585, when Childebert's tutor Wandelenus died, she officially took over all responsibility for her son[341] – but many local magnates opposed her plans. This is evident in her attempt to help her daughter Ingund, who had got into serious trouble far from home. Ingund had been married to the Visigothic prince Hermenigild, son of King Leuvigild. In 579, Hermenigild had rebelled against his father, seizing control of a significant part of present-day southern Spain. Although initially successful, the rebellion was ultimately a complete failure. In 584, Hermenigild was captured by Leuvigild's men. Ingund and her young son Athanagild fell into the hands of the East Roman troops stationed in the imperial cities on the coast. The East Roman commander had her sent to Carthage, where she eventually died.[342] At a council at the royal estate of Breslingen (near Diekirch in present-day Luxemburg) in 585, Brunhild pleaded with all the Austrasian nobles on behalf of Ingund, who was then still alive (or still believed to be alive) in Northern Africa. In the words of Gregory of Tours, 'she received little sympathy'.[343] We know from diplomatic letters from Brunhild to the East Romans that she did not give up her attempts to help Ingund and young Athanagild, but to no avail.[344]

Gunthchramn, however, regarded the Ingund incident as a legitimate *casus belli*, a good excuse to attack, plunder and hopefully conquer the last remaining Visigothic province of Gaul, Septimania. According to a letter allegedly sent from King Leuvigild to Queen Fredegund of Soissons in 585, Leuvigild would appear to have regarded Brunhild as one of the main instigators of the war; the Visigothic king asked Fredegund to kill both Childebert and his mother.[345] Shortly afterwards, Fredegund tried, but the attempt failed (see p. 117).[346]

The most conspicuous of Brunhild's enemies among the magnates was a duke called Gunthchramn Boso, previously one of Sigibert's military commanders. Gunthchramn Boso is a very familiar figure to the reader of *Decem Libri Historiarum*, since Gregory makes a point of listing all his many sins against churches, kings, princes and others – for instance, he tried to betray Merovech at the time when they were both claiming sanctuary at Saint Martin's church in Tours.[347] During Childebert's minority, he had (according to Gregory) never ceased to heap abuse and insults on Brunhild, and he had encouraged her enemies to behave towards her in a hostile fashion. In 587, Childebert II decided to rid himself of Gunthchramn Boso once and for all. One may assume that there were numerous good reasons for this, but Gregory explicitly says that he did it 'to avenge the wrongs done to his mother' (*ad ulciscendam iniuriam genetricis*). He ordered the magnate to be pursued and killed. Gunthchramn Boso visited various bishops and nobles, begging for forgiveness, and finally claimed sanctuary in the cathedral of Verdun. The bishop interceded for him at the court of Childebert, and Gunthchramn Boso, led into the king's presence, is reported to have thrown himself at Childebert's feet and confessed that he had sinned against 'you and your mother' (*tibi ac genetrici tuae*).[348] Later, Childebert, Brunhild and Childebert's wife and sister all travelled to King Gunthchramn to have Guntchramn Boso jointly judged by the two kings. They both agreed that the magnate was guilty and should be killed. Hearing this, Gunthchramn Boso chose to fight and died defending himself, pierced by a number of spears.[349] After this, Gregory reports that King Gunthchramn signed a treaty with 'his nephew and the queens' (*cum nepote suo ac reginis*), in other words not only with Childebert, but also with Brunhild and Childebert's wife Faileuba.[350] Brunhild thereby received the city of Cahors with all its lands and inhabitants, which had originally been given by Chilperic to his wife Galswinth, Brunhild's sister, as a part of the *morgengabe* on their marriage in c. 567. Galswinth had also received the cities of Bordeaux, Limoges, Lescar and Cieutat, and they had all, at least technically, passed to Brunhild after Galswinth's premature death. Now Brunhild was given real power over Cahors, and Gunthchramn promised that the other cities which he controlled himself would pass to her after his own death.[351]

At about the same time, a conspiracy was formed between the magnates Ursio, Berthefried and Rauching. They planned to kill Childebert and divide his kingdom between his two young sons, in practice ruling it themselves. Gregory reports that Ursio and Berthefried were full of hostility towards Brunhild and determined to humiliate her once more, as they had done during the early days of her widowhood. However, the conspiracy was discovered and Rauching was quickly killed by Childebert's men. Hearing this, Ursio and Berthefried gathered an even stronger army than they had already assembled, preparing to resist the royal troops at a strong point near Ursio's estate. Brunhild tried to weaken them by secret diplomacy: she sent a message to Berthefried, promising him his life if he deserted Ursio's cause. Apparently, she had stood sponsor to Berthefried's daughter at her baptism, 'and she therefore felt a certain compassion for him' (*ob hoc misericordiam de eo habere voluit*), according to Gregory. Berthefried, however, refused to yield.[352]

As soon as he returned from his aforementioned conference with King Gunthchramn, Childebert assembled an army and ordered it to proceed against the rebels. Ursio was killed in the ensuing fight, while Berthefried managed to reach a church in Verdun and claim sanctuary. Although Childebert's soldiers were forbidden to enter the building to drag Berthefried out, they solved the problem by climbing upon the roof, tearing off some of the tiles and other building materials and dropping them down on Berthefried. He was killed together with three of his companions. Bishop Ageric of Verdun was furious, and he was not to be consoled by the fact that Childebert attempted to distract him by sending presents. Satisfied with the result of the campaign, Childebert made good use of his victory by attacking other potentially dangerous magnates in his kingdom. Certain dukes were demoted from their dukedoms, and many wealthy Austrasians chose to emigrate.[353]

Although Childebert would now seem to have proved beyond any reasonable doubt that he was perfectly capable of ruling his kingdom without the help of troublesome magnates or relatives, it is clear that Brunhild, who was always near her royal son, continued to be present at conferences and remained highly influential.[354] In 587, after the campaign against Ursio and Berthefried, Childebert and Brunhild together received envoys from Recared, who had succeeded his father Leuvigild as King of the Visigoths in 586. The envoys said that their king promised to swear an oath, if necessary, in order to clear himself of the charge that he was inculpated in Ingund's death. He also proposed to pay 10 000 gold pieces for peace and an alliance. Childebert and Brunhild heard what the envoys had to say on the matter, and they then promised that they would maintain unbroken peace and friendship with Recared. Satisfied, the Visigoths also tried to get them to agree to a marriage between Recared and Chlodosinda, another daughter of Brunhild and Sigibert. Brunhild and Childebert together answered the legates that *they* readily agreed to the engagement, but they did not dare to make any promises without the approval of King Gunthchramn (who was very unwilling to end his war with the Visigoths).[355]

In 589, Brunhild had a great salver made out of gold and precious gems. She dispatched it to Recared together with a pair of wooden dishes which were also decorated with gold and jewels. The commission was entrusted to her retainer Ebregisel, who had often been employed in previous missions to the Visigothic kingdom. When Gunthchramn heard that Ebregisel was heading south, he grew suspicious, believing Brunhild to be up to no good. On this particular occasion, he did not fear the Visigoths – Childebert and Brunhild were clear on that account, for they had officially asked him for his approval of the proposed marriage between Recared and Chlodosinda[356] – but rather the heirs of the pretender Gundovald. Was Brunhild trying to stab him in the back by raising a new rebellion? Was she in fact sending presents to Gundovald's sons? Rumour alleged that this was indeed the case, and Gunthchramn apparently expected no better from the queen. He immediately ordered all the roads of his kingdom to be closely guarded, so that no one could pass through without being searched. Travellers' clothes, shoes and possessions were examined to see if any letters from Brunhild were concealed in them. While in Paris, Ebregisel was arrested by Duke Ebrachar and brought before Gunthchramn, who accused him of carrying presents to Gundovald's sons and inviting them back to Gaul 'to cut my throat'. Ebregisel replied that he did not know what the king was talking about, for the gifts were being sent to Recared, who was to marry Childebert's sister. Gunthchramn was eventually convinced and let him go.[357]

The fact that Brunhild continued to employ her own agents and clients all over the kingdom is made clear by Gregory's account of a feud in Tours. As an act of revenge, a man called Chramnesind killed a young man called Sichar, probably in the latter half of 587 or in the beginning of 588. Having committed the murder, Chramnesind hurried to Childebert, threw himself at his feet and explained his reasons for killing Sichar. However, it would appear that Childebert had little to say in the matter, since Sichar had been under Brunhild's protection. As the queen began to rage at him, Chramnesind fled to his home village of Bouges (near Bourges), which was under the jurisdiction of King Gunthchramn. At his second attempt to gain Childebert's pardon, Chramnesind managed to prove that he had killed Sichar in order to avenge an affront. Brunhild, however, had his property sequestered and handed his goods over to Flavinius, one of her retainers. Chramnesind eventually got the goods back with the help of Count Aginus, who supplied him with a letter of restitution.[358]

Brunhild's influence can also be measured by the way she was feared by Gunthchramn, himself by far the most powerful Frankish king at the time. We have already seen that he suspected Brunhild of secretly plotting against him. Gunthchramn's fears reached their peak in the autumn of 589, after a disastrous Frankish defeat in the war against the Visigoths in Septimania. Suddenly, Brunhild was seen as his chief enemy on every political front. Gunthchramn ordered all the roads through his realm to be closed to prevent the passage of people from Childebert's and Brunhild's kingdom through his territory. He blamed his failure in the war on Childebert's alliance with the Visigoths. Hearing that Childebert was planning to send his son Theudebert to Soissons, Gunthchramn suspected that this was merely the first step in an attempt to seize Paris and ultimately deprive him of his kingdom. According to Gunthchramn, all that Childebert had done and was doing was actually Brunhild's fault: she was advising him and, he added, she had once wanted to marry one of the pretender Gundovald's sons. In order to investigate Brunhild's conduct, Gunthchramn summoned a council of bishops to be convened on 1 November 589. Brunhild, however, cleared herself of the accusation on oath, and the bishops went home. The crisis passed, and the roads were again opened for travellers between the kingdoms.[359]

Brunhild's importance is also evident from the continued attempts to get rid of her made by various Austrasian magnates. In 589, Childebert's consort Faileuba uncovered a conspiracy against herself and her mother-in-law; as soon as she could, she informed Childebert and Brunhild about it. Apparently, Septimima, nurse to the royal children, was to persuade Childebert to banish Brunhild, desert Faileuba and marry another woman. In this way, the conspirators would be able to influence the king in a way that was impossible as long as Faileuba and Brunhild remained at court. Should the king prove too stubborn, Septimima's attempts at persuasion were to be followed by witchcraft aimed at ending the king's life. Childebert's young sons would then succeed him, and the conspirators would take over the government, immediately banishing the young princes' mother and grandmother. According to the informers, Sunnegisil, the Count of the Stables, the referendary Gallomagnus and a certain Droctulf, who was Septimima's lover, were privy to the plot.[360]

Septimima and Droctulf were arrested and racked. Septimima confessed that she had killed her husband by witchcraft because she was in love with Droctulf. They both confessed that the charges against them were true and that Sunnegisil and Gallomagnus were guilty as well. However, understanding what was going on, Sunnegisil and Gallomagnus had both escaped to churches and were claiming sanctuary at the time when Childebert's soldiers came looking for them. Promising not to kill them even if they indeed were guilty, Childebert managed to get them out of the churches in order to stand trial. When asked to defend themselves, they argued that they were innocent: Septimima and Droctulf had tried to embroil them in the plot, but they had refused to cooperate with them. Fearing the outcome of the trial – Childebert made no secret of the fact that he did not believe their stories – they again sought sanctuary in a church. In the end, Septimima and Droctulf were severly punished (but not killed), while Sunnegisil and Gallomagnus were stripped of all the property which they had been given by the king. They were sent into exile but, at Gunthchramn's request, were eventually allowed to return to Childebert's kingdom.[361]

Had he known it, Sunnegisil would undoubtedly have chosen to remain as far from Childebert and Brunhild as possible rather than return to his Austrasian home. In 590, Childebert had him tortured again and again. According to Gregory, Sunnegisil was flogged daily with sticks and leather thongs. His wounds festered, and as fast as the pus oozed away and the sores began to mend, they were re-opened by more torture. The constant maltreatment made him confess to anything Childebert asked him about. He readily agreed that he had planned to assassinate the king and that he was guilty of a number of other crimes as well. He also told his interrogators that Bishop Egidius of Rheims had been implicated in the plot made by Rauching, Ursio and Berthefried to kill Childebert. The bishop, although he was ill at the time, was immediately arrested and brought to the city of Metz, where he was locked up in prison. Childebert ordered a council of bishops to be convened for his trial. After various discussions during which Egidius was allowed to return home for a few months, the trial took place in Metz in the middle of November.[362]

At the beginning of the trial, Childebert more or less told the bishops what to do by declaring that Egidius was his own personal enemy and a traitor to the kingdom. Among the crimes listed by the prosecutor, the former duke Ennodius, was the fact that the accused had accepted favours from King Chilperic of Soissons, despite the fact that among other things this man had sent Brunhild into exile (i.e., to Rouen, after the death of Sigibert). Later, letters were produced in court which Egidius had addressed to Chilperic. The king's written replies were also brought forward. The texts written by the bishop contained many insulting remarks about Brunhild. As for Chilperic's replies, Gregory quotes a passage from one of these letters to Egidius: 'The stalk which emerges from the soil will not wither until its root is severed.'[363] This could only mean one thing: that Brunhild had to be killed first, Childebert later. When faced with these pieces of evidence, Bishop Egidius denied ever having written 'his' texts or having received any of the letters allegedly written by Chilperic. However, one of Egidius' own servants, who kept shorthand copies of letters for the bishop's files, confirmed that the letters sent from Rheims to the court of Chilperic were indeed genuine. Eventually, Egidius was convicted. He then confessed his guilt and decided that further lies would serve no purpose. Gregory tells us how his fellow bishops tried to help him, but that Egidius remained firm, confessing that he deserved death for high treason: 'I have repeatedly conspired against the interests of the king and his mother [Brunhild]'.[364] Although Egidius was not executed, he was removed from the priesthood, taken to Strasbourg and condemned to exile.[365]

This is the last we hear of Brunhild in *Decem Libri Historiarum*. When Gregory died, Brunhild's most important years, when she dominated a considerable part of Western Europe in the name of her grandsons, were yet ahead of her. In Fredegar's chronicle, which covers the later part of her career, the picture of an evil old queen, killing and manipulating everyone, forms an interesting contrast to the picture that emerges from Gregory's text. However, it is Gregory's image of

Brunhild that is of interest in this particular chapter. From the point of view of source criticism, it should be noted that Gregory had good reasons to write nice things about Brunhild. Apparently, judging from some of Venantius Fortunatus' poems, Brunhild played a role in Gregory's appointment as bishop of Tours, a fact that Gregory himself never mentions. He had far less reason to be afraid of Brunhild than of, for instance, Queen Fredegund of Soissons.[366] Knowing this, it comes as no surprise that Gregory chooses to introduce Brunhild to the reader as a woman who was 'elegant in all that she did, lovely to look at, chaste and decorous in her behaviour, wise in her generation and well-spoken'. His remark that she wisely abandoned her heretical belief in Arianism and converted to Catholicism further serves to embellish her portrait.

Looking at Gregory's portrayal of Brunhild, one of the first things that comes to mind is her attachment to the members of her family, particularly her daughter Ingund. She was genuinely concerned about the girl, a fact that cannot simply be explained by referring to Ingund's value as a political asset. In fact, after the fall of Hermenigild, Ingund could hardly be considered as such. As a hostage in Carthage, she was more of a liability than an asset.

That Brunhild was a caring mother is hardly surprising; most mothers are. However, Gregory of Tours would have taken her maternal feelings for granted, just as we do. He did not mention Brunhild in her capacity as a good mother simply to prove that this was the case. Rather, he mentioned her actions since he regarded them as *important* to the history of the Franks and of Gaul. Most of Brunhild's actions as a mother went unrecorded; those actions that *were* recorded are only known to us since they occurred on the political stage. As in the case of Fredegund, Brunhild's career cannot be understood unless we perceive her as a politician as well as a mother.

Brunhild's life, as it is described by Gregory of Tours, can be briefly summarised as follows:

(1) –567: Visigothic princess, daughter of King Athanagild
(2) 567–75: wife of King Sigibert I (i.e., Frankish queen)
(3) 575: suddenly made a widow (loss of power) and exiled
(4) 575–c.585: royal widow, struggling to regain her position

(5) c.585–89: royal widow, influencing her son, the adult king of Austrasia, but still fighting aristocratic factions
(6) 589–: royal widow influencing her son with no serious opposition

Her resources, as they appear in Gregory's text, can be summarised as:

(1) the fact that she was a Visigothic princess – this is the only reason she was able to become a Frankish queen in the first place
(2) aggressive personality (refusal to give up and enter a convent or return to her own country, even if she appeared to have lost everything)
(3) property (money, treasure, land, etc.), given to her by her father and her husband and/or confiscated from her enemies
(4) her husband Sigibert (before 575)
(5) her husband Merovech (only briefly, after Sigibert's death)
(6) her children (especially her son Childebert II)
(7) her clients, friends and allies (among whom we should probably count Gregory of Tours)

It is hard to say if, when and how these resources contributed to her ability to act within the political sphere of Francia. For instance, it would probably be wrong to limit the importance of her Visigothic connections only to the first stage of her career. Much later, she continued to send one private messenger after another to present-day Spain (apart from the Ingund affair, Gregory mentions Bishop Elafius of Châlons-sur-Marne and the retainer Ebregisel as messengers south of the Pyrenees).

Being a female stranger in northern Francia, and being in her elevated position merely due to the importance of a Visigothic father who died a year after her marriage, Brunhild was bound to be dependent on her husbands. Once in Austrasia, Sigibert was her main basis of power. In due time, she could probably count on using her dowry to buy herself allies and friends, but her position was nevertheless always insecure. Seen in this light, Brunhild's second marriage to Merovech is hardly surprising, and we should be careful not simply to dismiss the rumours that she contemplated marrying the pretender Gundovald or one of his sons. King Gunthchramn, who apparently helped spread these rumours, was a veteran in Frankish politics; he knew far better than we do how a woman such as Brunhild would have acted to secure and strengthen her position.

However, the period when Brunhild was a married woman was also the darkest part of her political career. It has been justly remarked that she can hardly have been powerless during these years, since she appears to have exercised patronage (for instance by helping Gregory to become bishop) and since Ursio made it clear that she had, in his opinion, exercised too much influence over King Sigibert ('It should be enough that you held regal power when your husband was alive...').[367] Previous studies have also remarked upon the crisis of 575, when Brunhild lost all her influence in Austrasia simply because of the death of her husband, and upon her slow political recovery during the following years. In Ian Wood's opinion, the period between Brunhild's return to Austrasia and the end of Childebert's minority in 585 ought to be characterised as a period in which no single aristocratic faction could maintain control over the young king. Brunhild grew increasingly influential, but she had to cooperate with magnates who were explicitly hostile to her. This situation changed completely in 584–85, when Childebert began to rule as an adult Merovingian king. As Childebert established his own authority, he also established that of his mother. Her enemies among the magnates were eliminated, and by 589 all opposition appears to have been crushed.[368]

I agree with the basic outline of this interpretation. Having lost both Sigibert and Merovech, Brunhild's main asset was undoubtedly her son Childebert. Strictly speaking, Childebert was not hers to control until the death of Wandelenus in 585, when Childebert anyway came of age. Still, Childebert must have felt affection for his mother, and – far more importantly, from our point of view – his political goals largely coincided with hers. The aristocrats who wanted to dominate Childebert and rule in his name were his natural enemies in the same way as they threatened the position of Brunhild. Childebert clearly perceived an attack on his mother as an attack on himself.

However, something is missing from the picture. Why did Ursio, Berthefried, Egidius, and all the others regard Brunhild as a threat? After all, she had lost her husbands, she did not control her son (at least not in theory) and her relatives lived on the other side of Pyrenees, far to the south. In the months following Sigibert's murder, the Austrasian magnates had been able to treat her as a nobody. Still, some years later, Brunhild was clearly a powerful woman, a royal widow to be feared. She does not appear to have been as powerful as Fredegund was after c. 586, but she was sufficiently powerful to be regarded as dangerous.

The answer is, of course, that she made good use of her assets. Firstly, she would have had to have an aggressive, charismatic personality in order to succeed. The Austrasian political sphere was not for weaklings. For instance, if there was the slightest possibility that someone could be got rid of by a trial, an accusation was brought forward and the man in question should be summoned to the tribunal. True, she could never be certain that this would ensure a conviction, but she could at least try. If the trial did not work (for instance, if it was too obvious that Brunhild's enemy was innocent of the crimes she accused him of), the person in question could be assassinated. This method was far more dangerous because it was both highly illegal and doomed to provoke feelings of revenge, but it was nevertheless an option. This particular chain of events is evident in the case of Abbot Lupentius and Count Innocentius. After the failure of the trial, Innocentius (and, we must assume, Brunhild) had Lupentius killed on the bank of the River Aisne.

Secondly, Brunhild needed good friends, clients and allies. Needless to say, she also needed funds to keep her allies from becoming someone else's and thereby weakening her own position. Unfortunately, we only get a few glimpses of how Brunhild manœuvred, but the picture that emerges is still a relatively clear one. For instance, Innocentius (in the example above) was a typical good candidate in this respect; he was exactly the kind of man Brunhild needed in her network of power. As a count, he was able to dominate a significant part of lay and ecclesiastical life in his district. After he had killed Lupentius, Brunhild managed to have him elected Bishop of Rodez, which probably made him even more important. As a client of Brunhild's, Innocentius' position appears to have been strengthened: he became richer and more powerful. At the same time, he contributed to Brunhild's strength in the struggle for power in her son's kingdom.

We can be certain that Innocentius was not alone in his capacity as an agent of Brunhild's. It is clear from Gregory's text that she had many allies and that she tried to get even more. The young man Sichar (who was only about twenty years old when he died in 587 or 588) was under her protection. However, Brunhild did not always succeed. Some of her friends and potential clients (such as Bishop Praetextatus) lived too far away to be able to work efficiently against their common enemies. She obviously attempted to secure the goodwill of the magnate Berthefried by standing sponsor to his daughter at her baptism, but Berthefried still decided to join her enemies. She did get the support of Duke Lupus of Champagne, but she was in the end unable to prevent her enemies among the magnates from stealing his property and scaring him into exile. Despite such setbacks, Brunhild's constant political intrigues must nevertheless be regarded as successful. She regained part of her power, even the tutelage of Childebert, and she was feared by rival kings and queens such as Fredegund and Gunthchramn. During the Gundovald affair, she can hardly have been an innocent bystander – but, to our eyes, she covered her tracks well. Gunthchramn's allegations concerning her secret plans remained rumours.

In the second half of the 580s, when Childebert ruled in his own name, Brunhild had acquired so much personal power that she could hardly be dismissed from conferences and meetings, even if Childebert had wanted to do so. If that had been his plan, he would have had to stage some kind of a coup, and he would have risked a war. Since Childebert's political goals largely coincided with Brunhild's, such a problem never arose. Brunhild had built her bases of power not merely on her close ties to Childebert. True, her position after Sigibert's death was undoubtedly helped by the fact that a son of hers was growing up to become a king; Childebert might have been regarded as an investment for the future, at least in the eyes of the magnates who decided to join Brunhild's cause in the hope of future royal benefits. Her achievement during the years 575–c. 585 was, however, mostly the result of her own actions in her capacity as a *royal widow*.

Like Fredegund, Brunhild had certain resources that could be used to her advantage, provided that she was smart and aggressive enough to use them properly. If she wanted to survive in the polical game, she had to create a network of lay and ecclesiastical clients and allies. She had to use patronage, or at least the memory of past patronage to keep her allies grateful and/or to believe in more patronage to come. She had to use whatever property she possessed to buy herself assassins and fighters (to create fear) and magnate allies (to create goodwill); property in itself was useless unless transformed into human resources, since political power during the early Middle Ages ultimately depended on how many men you were able to command. Just like Fredegund, Brunhild turned out to be a good political player. Her years at Athanagild's and Sigibert's courts had taught her how to manipulate people and how to get things done. The result of her struggle was the creation of a basis of power that made her important as 'the royal widow Brunhild', not only as 'Brunhild, Childebert's mother'. For instance, Sichar was *her* client, not Childebert's. Childebert did not merely allow Brunhild to be present during conferences because she was his dear mother. He also did it because it would have been foolish to underestimate the power wielded by a royal widow.

Faileuba

Faileuba was married to King Childebert II of Austrasia, the son of Sigibert I and Brunhild. She is reported to have accompanied Childebert, Brunhild and Childebert's sister Chlodosinda to the important meeting with King Gunthchramn in Trier in 587.[369] As related above (pp. ~), she was sufficiently important to be perceived as a threat to the Austrasian magnates who conspired with Septimima and Droctulf to have her and Brunhild removed from court in 589. The fact that the plot was discovered was, according to Gregory of Tours, actually because of Faileuba herself. She was recovering from the birth of a child (who had died almost immediately after birth) when she found out about the conspiracy. It is clear from the conspirators' plan that they regarded Faileuba's power as based on her influence over people (Childebert and his heirs), not over wealth. The nurse Septimima was supposed to persuade Childebert to banish Brunhild, desert Faileuba and marry another woman. When Childebert's heirs inherited the throne, Faileuba would be banished from court, thereby losing her influence over her own son.[370]

Merovingian daughters

Audofleda, Albofled and Lanthechild were daughters of Childeric I and thus sisters of Clovis I. We know very little about Albofled and Lanthechild apart from the fact that they were baptised and that Lanthechild was an Arian.[371] However, we have some interesting pieces of information about Audofleda. She was married off to King Theuderic the Great of the Ostrogoths and after his death in 526 appears to have survived him at least for a while. Gregory describes Audofleda as a justly proud queen, although a member of the Arian sect (as was only natural since she lived in Ostrogothic Italy), who was angry with her daughter Amalasuntha for disgracing the royal blood by eloping with a slave. She eventually sent armed men to kill the slave and bring her daughter back. Amalasuntha is said to have had her revenge shortly afterwards: she murdered Audofleda with poison.[372] This, like many other stories that Gregory tells about non-Frankish lands, is hardly true, but it is nevertheless important in the sense that Gregory regarded such tales as trustworthy. If a similar quarrel between a queen and a princess had occurred in Gaul, he would not have been surprised.

Chlothild was a daughter of Clovis I and Queen Chlothild. She was married off to King Amalaric of the Visigoths, probably some time after the death of her father (in 511) and brought a great dowry of expensive jewellery to her new country.[373] According to Gregory, she was very badly treated by her Arian husband because of his hatred of her Catholic faith. Amalaric is said to have had dung and other filth thrown over her several times when she was on her way to church. Finally he struck her with such violence that she sent a towel stained with her own blood to her brother Childebert I, King of Paris. Childebert set off for the south together with a Frankish army, and in the ensuing war Amalaric is reported to have been killed (probably in Barcelona, in 531). Childebert then planned to take Chlothild home to Gaul, but she died on the journey. Her corpse was carried to Paris, where she was buried next to her father Clovis.[374]

Chlodoswintha was a daughter of King Chlothar I and Ingund.[375] She was married off to Alboin, King of the Lombards.[376]

King Charibert I had at least two, probably three daughters. The third, over whom there is some doubt, was none other than the rebellious nun Chrodechild, whom we encounter in another chapter (pp.154–69). The other two were called Bertha and Berthefled. Bertha was married to King Ethelbert of Kent (reigned c. 560–616),[377] while Berthefled joined the Ingitrude's nunnery (p. 187) in Tours. Apparently, Berthefled did not relish her life as a nun. When Ingitrude on one occasion (in 589) left the convent during the conflict between herself and her daughter Berthegund, Berthefled used the opportunity to escape to Le Mans. Gregory clearly disapproves of her: 'she was a woman who ate and slept a lot, and she had no interest at all in the holy offices.'[378]

Chlothild was a daughter of King Gunthchramn of Orléans. We know nothing about her apart from what is said in the text about the treaty of Andelot between Gunthchramn and Childebert II in 587. According to the text, Gunthchramn had donated a lot of property to Chlothild. The treaty stipulated that, come what may, all the men, cities, lands or revenues that had been and that in the future might be donated from father to daughter should remain in Chlothild's hands and under her control. When Gunthchramn died, her guardianship would pass to Childebert II, who promised to protect her interests and her property just as her father had done.[379]

We know the names of two of the daughters of King Sigibert I and Brunhild: Ingund and Chlodosinda. After the murder of their father in 575, they were banished to Meaux, where they were held in custody.[380]

Ingund was eventually married to the Visigothic prince Hermenigild, son of King Leuvigild. When she arrived at the Visigothic court, she was warmly welcomed by her stepmother-in-law Goiswinth, but, as Gregory loses no time in telling us, Goiswinth had no intention of allowing Ingund to remain a Catholic. At first, she talked to her in a kindly way and tried to persuade her to be rebaptised as an Arian. As Ingund stubbornly refused, Goiswinth lost her temper. According to Gregory, she seized the girl by the hair and threw her to the ground; then she kicked her until she was covered with blood, had her stripped naked and ordered her to be thrown into the baptismal pool. Despite this conversion by force, Gregory informs us that there were many witnesses who could testify to Ingund's determined refusal to budge even an inch from her Catholic faith.[381]

Leuvigild handed over a part of present-day southern Spain to his son in 579. Hermenigild took up residence in Seville together with his wife and family. We know from other sources that Hermenigild rebelled against Leuvigild already in the same year. The rebellion had, as far as we can see, nothing to do with religion. Hermenigild, who later became a Catholic martyr, does not appear to have relinquished Arianism until 582.[382] Gregory of Tours, however, writing from far away with a very Catholic perspective, chooses to interpret the Visigothic civil war as a conflict between Catholicism and Arianism. In *Decem Libri Historiarum*, Ingund is said to have begun to persuade her husband to give up his Arian beliefs and accept Catholicism as soon as they were installed in Seville in 579. Hermenigild was, according to Gregory, converted, which is supposed to have made Leuvigild furious. Afraid of his father, Hermenigild started to negotiate with the imperial commanders in the coastal areas that still belonged to Constantinople. Before going to war against his father, Hermenigild tried to protect Ingund by leaving her in his capital. However, Leuvigild bribed the East Roman troops into deserting Hermenigild at a critical moment, and as a result Hermenigild had to seek sanctuary in a church. He was then tricked into leaving it, imprisoned and exiled (in 584).[383]

Eventually, Ingund fell into the hands of the East Romans.[384] Many rumours as to her fate circulated in Gaul; according to one, she had been sent all the way to Constantinople.[385] It was later made clear that she had been sent to Carthage together with her son Athanagild, where she died shortly afterwards.[386]

Sigibert's other daughter, Chlodosinda, continued to live at the royal court of her brother Childebert II and her mother Brunhild. She accompanied them to the important meeting with King Gunthchramn in Trier in 587.[387] In the same year, envoys arrived from Recared, Hermenigild's brother, who since 586 had been the new Visigothic king. The Visigoths had been ordered by Recared to propose a marriage alliance between the two kingdoms: they wanted Chlodosinda to marry Recared himself. Brunhild and Childebert readily agreed to this, but they said that they did not dare to make any promises without King

Gunthchramn's approval. Gunthchramn had ostensibly taken it upon himself to seek revenge for Ingund's fate by going to war against the Visigoths in Septimania, although it would seem that Ingund's fate merely served as a convenient excuse for setting in motion his plans for territorial expansion.[388] When asked about the proposed marriage, Gunthchramn was at first unwilling to approve, but he promised to agree to the plans if Childebert fulfilled certain obligations that had been agreed between the two Frankish kings in the treaty of Andelot in 587.[389] However, it would appear from Gregory's text that Childebert II himself had in fact already promised Chlodosinda in marriage to King Authari of the Lombards.[390] In other words, he used his sister as a tool of political bargaining, first with the Lombards, later with the Visigoths.[391]

Gregory of Tours provides us with the names of two of Chilperic I's daughters. He had a daughter called Basina by Audovera and another one called Rigunth by Fredegund. Basina, who became a nun in Poitiers, will be dealt with later (pp. 154–69). Rigunth first appears in *Decem Libri Historiarum* at the critical moment in 580 when Gregory was standing trial at Berny-Rivière, accused of having slandered Queen Fredegund. She is reported to have felt sympathy for Gregory and for his sufferings; Gregory tells us that she fasted together with the whole of her household while he was clearing his name by saying Mass at three different altars and swearing that he was innocent.[392]

Rigunth was betrothed to Recared, the same Visigothic prince who would later, when he was king, ask for the hand of Rigunth's cousin Chlodosinda (see above). The discussions about the conditions of the marriage led to several embassies from one court to the other.[393] Finally, in September 584, Rigunth began her journey to the kingdom of the Visigoths equipped with a tremendous dowry (see pp. 111–12). Although she was accompanied by several powerful men, it is clear that the expedition was commanded by Rigunth herself: *she* decided where to halt and where to rest.[394] It would appear that she took Waddo, her own mayor of the palace, with her.[395] When they reached Toulouse and Rigunth realised that she was now approaching the border between the two kingdoms, it appears that she used her power to postpone the inevitable for as long as possible. Gregory reports that she began to contrive reasons for delay. Then, suddenly, news reached Toulouse that King Chilperic had been assassinated. Rigunth's situation changed dramatically: by this single blow, she was no longer an influential Frankish princess and she was certainly not a future Visigothic queen. Her dowry was confiscated by Duke Desiderius, and Rigunth went to live in Saint Mary's church in Toulouse, probably seeking to protect herself. A servant of hers called Leunard managed to get back to Fredegund, who was at the time claiming sanctuary in the cathedral of Paris. Fredegund was furious when she heard about her daughter's misfortune.[396] However, it soon got worse: Toulouse was taken by the pretender Gundovald,[397] who seized Rigunth's treasure and had the girl sent into exile together with Bishop Magnulf of Toulouse.[398]

In the end, Rigunth was brought back home by Fredegund's men in 585.[399] The remainder of her life appears to have been spent at court, where she enjoyed the company of many lovers and constantly quarrelled with her mother. Rigunth considered herself a true Merovingian of royal blood, while her mother, in her opinion, was actually a lowborn serving-woman, a rank to which she ought to revert. The two women often fought, and on one occasion, Fredegund even tried to kill Rigunth by choking her, stopped only by the intervention of her servants.[400]

Summing up what Gregory tells us about Merovingian daughters, we are immediatly struck by the difference between these women and their mothers. To be a Merovingian princess was undoubtedly very different from being a Merovingian queen. The queens were women who had achieved their rank through resources and assets of their own: charisma, beauty, powerful parents, intrigues, and murder. They had not inherited their status, and they always had to be prepared to fight and kill for it, for if they did not, they risked losing most of what they had gained. Merovingian daughters, on the other hand, were born into the family and thus equipped with a certain amount of influence from the beginning. This made them self-conscious and proud, just as their brothers took for granted that they were powerful men who enjoyed certain privileges that ordinary Franks were deprived of. When Rigunth set out for the south, she took her own servants and officials, and *she* gave all the orders. Gunthchramn's daughter Chlothild had her own estates, cities and permanent revenues, all of them protected in written treaties at the highest diplomatic level.

When something happened that changed the status of the Merovingian princesses, they were often reluctant to accept their fate. According to Gregory, Rigunth appears to have deteriorated into a violent nymphomaniac at the court of her mother. Her sister Basina, who was locked up in a convent, even went so far as to rebel and gather an army of her own together with Chrodechild (herself probably a daugher of Charibert I), as will be related below. Berthefled, who was also sent to a convent, appears to have grown into a fat, lazy woman who hated being a nun. When she got the chance to get away from it all, she escaped.

The usual fate of the Merovingian princesses, as for most other high-ranking women in medieval Europe, was to be married to someone important, hopefully a king. The Goths and the Lombards were the most powerful Western European neighbours of the Franks; their kings were therefore prime targets in Merovingian marriage policy. The petty kingdoms of the Anglo-Saxons were less interesting from this point of view, but we know that a daughter of Charibert I married a king of Kent. When the Merovingians sent away their daughters to foreign lands, they provided for them by spending huge sums on their dowries, a fact that served both to heighten the status of the father of the bride and to give their daughters a firm financial basis for the creation of networks of power in the kingdoms of their partners. If anything went wrong (as in the case of Chlothild, Clovis' daughter, and Ingund, Sigibert's daugher), the Merovingians were prepared to intervene on behalf of their female relatives, sometimes with troops. Gunthchramn even tried to use one of these occasions, Ingund's problems in Hispania, as a good excuse to wage a major (but unfortunate) war against the Visigoths, hoping thereby to extend Frankish rule to Septimania.

Chrodechild, Basina and Leubovera: a scandal in Poitiers

I have deliberately left out two Merovingian princesses from the analysis above, since their story is both unusual and serves to shed light on the position of powerful women associated with convents. The episode I refer to, which is very illuminating with regard to both the strategy of the nun and the strategy of the lay female magnate, is provided by Gregory of Tours in *Decem Libri Historiarum*, book IX, chapters 39–43, and book X, chapters 15–17 and 20–22. Here, the two patterns collide into one in a way that sheds light on many aspects of the general situation of noble women in early medieval Europe. The story is, of course, far from ordinary (if it *had* been ordinary, it would hardly have received as much attention by Gregory of Tours as it did). Still, the story nevertheless proves beyond doubt that the Frankish nunneries *could* be used as bases for warlike expeditions headed by female magnates.[401]

In 589, two nuns in the Convent of the Holy Cross at Poitiers, Chrodechild and Basina, rebelled against their abbess, a woman called Leubovera. This happened barely two years after the death of the founder of the nunnery, Saint Radegund, Princess of Thuringia and Queen of Francia.

Both rebels considered themselves legitimate members of the Merovingian royal house. Chrodechild argued, on somewhat dubious grounds, that she was the daughter of Charibert I of Paris, while Basina was definitely the daughter of Chilperic I of Soissons and his wife Audovera.[402] However, Leubovera cared little about their family background. She was more interested in forcing the princesses to adhere to one of the three famous vows that all nuns had to swear to abide by – the vow of obedience. Chrodechild and Basina appear to have loathed the very thought of having to obey a common abbess such as Leubovera. Obeying Radegund, herself a holy queen of royal blood, had been easy (at least, it would have been very difficult to rebel against her). Obeying Leubovera was not.

In the end, Chrodechild persuaded a number of other nuns to swear an oath of allegiance to herself. Having proclaimed an open rebellion against Leubovera, a small band of between 40 and 50 nuns, led by Chrodechild and Basina, left the nunnery and went out into the Poitevin countryside. The local peasants appear to have been terrified; no-one dared give food to the nuns or offer them shelter. No-one provided them with horses. The band had to proceed on foot in a northerly direction, heading towards the river Loire. As they reached Tours in the beginning of March, the rain was pouring down and the roads were submerged. Bishop Gregory vividly describes how Chrodechild marched into his residence and ordered him to do his Christian duty towards the poor women. 'I beg you, holy priest, that you keep an eye on these nuns', she said, 'who have have been greatly humiliated by their abbess in Poitiers! See to it that they have regular meals! I am off to visit my royal relatives to explain what we have suffered. I will be back.'[403]

At first, Gregory tried to talk some sense into Chrodechild. Why not go back to Poitiers with him? He could help her negotiate with Bishop Maroveus of Poitiers, and everything could be settled in a calm and peaceful way. There was no need for any of this violence. Chrodechild, however, refused to change her mind. After a heated discussion, Gregory threatened to excommunicate her if she did not relent, while Chrodechild affirmed her wish to visit those of her noble relatives, who had not yet suffered the unfortunate accident of being locked up in a convent. In any case, she remarked, Bishop Maroveus of Poitiers was under no circumstances to be trusted. It was, Chrodechild said, wholly due to his incompetent way of running his diocese that conditions in the convent had become intolerable.[404]

Gregory appears to have agreed with Chrodechild about Maroveus' character. Maroveus was, in fact, something of an old and well-known problem. The bishop of Poitiers had always resented the very fact that the nunnery existed; he regarded it as a threat to his own position as the spiritual head of Poitiers. Saint Radegund had carried on a feud with Maroveus for several years. Maroveus had refused to install and consecrate the famous relic of the Holy Cross which Radegund's agents had brought all the way from Palestine. Eventually, King Sigibert I had been forced to order Bishop Eufronius of Tours to consecrate the new sanctuary in the nunnery, while Maroveus remained conspicuously absent. Maroveus may not even have been present at the funeral of Radegund, despite the fact that she was already on the verge of becoming a recognised saint.[405]

The discussion between Gregory and Chrodechild ended in a rather prosaic way. Apparently, Gregory tried to buy time by babbling on about the weather. Chrodechild, who had just walked all the way from Poitiers in pouring rain, could easily be persuaded to remain in Tours throughout spring. Then, however, she could not be stopped. Leaving Basina in command, she left Tours in early summer and travelled to her uncle King Gunthchramn of Orléans. Gunthchramn heard her out and presented her with many gifts, promising to have his own bishops conduct a careful investigation of the matter. Confident in her success, Chrodechild returned to her nuns.[406]

By this time, the women had spent several months outside the well-disciplined world of the convent. One after another of the harsh rules of Leubovera had been gladly forgotten. The presence of so many unmarried women at one and the same accessible spot at the same time resulted in situations that would never have been allowed behind the safe walls of the nunnery. Several nuns accepted proposals and began to prepare for their weddings. Others, among them Chrodechild and Basina, grew restless. They got tired of waiting for the bishops who were supposed to investigate the matter but who never came. Finally, most of the nuns returned to Poitiers, where they began to transform their band of nuns into a real army. Chrodechild, now behaving more like a Barbarian warlord than a nun, occupied Saint Hilary's church and began recruiting soldiers. Gregory informs us that cut-throats, evil-doers, fornicators, fugitives from justice and men guilty of every crime in the calendar gathered around Chrodechild. Chrodechild and Basina proudly stated that 'We are queens and we will not set foot inside our nunnery until the abbess has been dismissed.'[407]

Four bishops, among them Maroveus, led by Bishop Gundegisel of Bordeaux, went to Saint Hilary's church in order to censure the nuns, presumably hoping to persuade them to return to the nunnery. Gundegisel tried to reason with them, but Chrodechild refused to surrender. In the end, the bishops did exactly what Gregory of Tours had prophesied: they publicly excommunicated all the rebel nuns. This was a serious mistake. Chrodechild's gang, possibly led by an infamous warrior called Childeric the Saxon, attacked the bishops right in the middle of the church. Soon, deacons and priests were seen staggering out of the building with cracked sculls and clothes covered with blood. 'The Devil, I believe, was at work' (*ut credo, diabolo cooperante*), Gregory of Tours wrote in his History. The priests were so terrified that they all panicked and rushed home by the shortest route. Desiderius, a deacon from Autun, jumped into the river Clain and forced his horse to swim across to the other side.[408]

Now, the protest escalated into a military rebellion. Chrodechild had all the lands belonging to the nunnery confiscated in her own name. She appointed her own stewards and forced all the men employed by the nunnery to work for her instead. The nunnery itself was besieged by her gang. Outside the walls of the nunnery, Chrodechild appeared in front of her warriors, yelling to all in hearing that she would toss the abbess over the wall as soon as her forces had seized the convent. Even in the eyes of the tolerant Frankish kings, the situation had clearly got out of hand. They had to stop their warlike female relatives, or they risked losing credibility in their own capacity as guardians of the peace. King Childebert II of Austrasia, a cousin of Chrodechild's and Basina's, ordered the local Poitevin count, a man called Macco, to quell the uprising.[409]

However, there was very little the kings and the counts could do. On the one hand, they had to put down the rebellion and support the bishops. That was their duty as Christian leaders. If they did not, some of the bishops could (at least in theory) excommunicate *them*. On the other hand, the nuns were also religious individuals, and their leaders were Merovingian princesses with powerful relatives all over Gaul. They had to be dealt with carefully, or the kings risked provoking rebellions from God only knows which duke, count or prince that decided to help poor Chrodechild in her just cause. True, the nuns had committed a number of atrocities, but the bishops, especially Maroveus, could hardly be described as models of virtue either. What were the secular authorities supposed to do? King Childebert and Count Macco, who had not lifted a finger, tried to mediate by sending a priest of his own, a man called Theuthar, to the fortified camp of Chrodechild and her nuns. As was to be expected, Chrodechild refused to negotiate unless the bishops immediately withdrew their ban of excommunication. When Theuthar tried to get the bishops to soften their attitude, they turned out to be just as stubborn as Chrodechild.[410]

Autumn turned into winter, and still nothing happened. The weather turned cold, and the nuns began running out of supplies. Some women deserted the rebellion. A few of them went back to their own homes, others to their relatives, and some even returned to the religious houses where they had previously lived. Among those that remained in Saint Hilary's church, Chrodechild and Basina constantly argued over the right of leadership. Chrodechild wanted to remain *the* female warlord of Francia, while Basina was tired of being second-in-command.[411]

In the end, the nuns decided to postpone their internal conflicts in order to make a final assault on the nunnery. In the middle of the night, seven days before Easter, about a year after the start of the rebellion, the attack was launched. The bandits broke through the defences and entered the nunnery, full of riches and relics. With drawn swords and lighted tapers, they rapidly took control of all the buildings. The abbess hid in the sanctuary of the Holy Cross, vainly believing that the renegade nuns and their men would not dare enter such a holy place. Little did she know the minds of her erstwhile sisters and evil Barbarians! She was soon spotted, and the shrine was taken. The ruffians discovered her lying on the ground (she was suffering from an attack of gout) in front of the reliquary which held the relic of the Holy Cross. Fighting broke out, and one bandit actually knifed another one, probably aiming at the abbess. Chaos erupted and the light went out. The bandits grabbed as many non-rebel nuns as they could lay their hands on and started tearing off their habits. The Prioress Justina (Gregory of Tours' niece), who had remained faithful to Leubovera, was mistaken for the abbess. She was forced out of the convent and dragged through the streets of Poitiers towards Saint Hilary's church. As they approached the church, the sky began to lighten momentarily and they realised that they had got hold of the wrong nun. Releasing Justina, they returned to the convent and grabbed the real abbess. She was locked up in a prison not far from Saint Hilary's. After having placed guards on the door to prevent her from being rescued, they went back to the nunnery and continued plundering the place. In a storehouse they found a cask that had once contained pitch but which was now dry. They lit the cask, thus creating a great beacon that aided them in their work. All the valuables were taken and carried away.[412]

Terrified at the turn of events, Bishop Maroveus sent messengers to Chrodechild with a dire message: 'You know what season it is. Unless you order her [Leubovera] to be released from the prison in which she is locked up, I shall refuse to celebrate our Lord's Easter ceremony, and no one being given instruction for baptism will receive it in this town. If you refuse to do what I say, I will rouse the townsfolk and free her myself.'[413] Chrodechild was not impressed. She posted a man with a drawn sword next to the abbess, ordering him to hit her with it as soon as he became aware of any rescue attempt.[414] Bishop Maroveus then appears to have switched tactics. Instead of planning to attack Chrodechild with a mob of his own, he tried to win her over by what looks like bribery. When Easter Day came round, he offered to pay over a sum of money as a surety if the abbess were allowed to watch the baptismal ceremony. Again, Chrodechild, ignored the message.[415]

By now, the city of Poitiers appears to have been in a state of civil war. We know very little of the exact events, but it seems clear that many people were killed, especially in or near the convent. Riots erupted daily. Kings and counts tried to mediate. A daring royal official called Flavianus managed to rescue the abbess, who appears to have been transformed into a female warlord in her own right, setting up her headquarters in the same church that had previously served as a rebel stronghold while Chrodechild appears to have moved into the conquered nunnery. The streets of Poitiers were claimed by gangs and mob leaders that often took matters into their own hands. Basina finally refused to obey her cousin and created a gang of her own. The three women – Chrodechild, Basina and Leubovera – entered into a complex series of negotiations and alliances. The comital administration ceased to function; anarchy ruled. Gregory of Tours tells us that 'scarcely a day passed without someone being murdered, scarcely an hour without some quarrel or other, scarcely a moment without somebody crying.'[416]

Finally, Childebert II and Gunthchramn decided to organise an episcopal tribunal with delegates from all over their kingdoms in order to settle the dispute by canon law. Gregory of Tours, who has told us all that we know of the scandal, was chosen to be one of Childebert's judges, together with Ebregisel of Cologne and Maroveus of Poitiers himself. Before the tribunal could begin its work, however, Count Macco had to make Poitiers a safe place to live and judge in. He was given strict orders from Childebert to do whatever needed to be done, by force if necessary, in order to make Poitiers safe for ordinary people.

Having assembled a band of armed men, he attacked Chrodechild's cut-throats, who had been ordered to guard the nunnery gate. Chrodechild had to watch as Macco's soldiers literally massacred her band with swords and spears. When all hope was lost, she entered the battlefield herself like a mythological Goddess of War, holding the relic of the Holy Cross in her hands, shouting over the clash of weapons and the shrieks of dying men:

> I warn you! Do not lay a finger on me! I am a queen, the daughter of one king and the niece of another! If you touch me you can be quite sure that the day will come when I shall have my revenge![417]

Macco's mob ignored her. They killed all who opposed them and captured the remaining rebels. The captives were brutally tortured and punished. Some were beaten, some had their hair cut off, others their hands, some even their ears and noses.[418]

Now the bishops dared enter the city, and the tribunal could begin its work. Backed by Macco's soldiers, the bishops confronted Chrodechild in front of the cathedral. Chrodechild was far from mentally subjugated; she was still a very angry woman, and was not about to lose what she had spent more than a year struggling for. Coming to the trial, she still carried with her the relic of the Holy Cross, but this was forcibly taken from her in the cathedral.[419] Due to the fact that the historian Gregory of Tours was himself a member of the tribunal and thus an eye-witness to the proceedings, we know quite a lot about the following events. Thanks to Gregory's reports, we can easily see why Chrodechild and Basina had reacted the way they did, why they had deemed their situation so intolerable that they had to revolt.

According to Gregory's text, they had revolted because of the poor food, the lack of clothing and the harsh treatment (in other words the fact that they had been forced to obey the abbess). They had been especially disgusted with having to share their bathroom with other women, and they found it impossible to accept that the abbess enjoyed a number of privileges that they themselves did not share despite their royal blood. They complained that the abbess had been repeatedly observed playing backgammon and enjoying the company of guests. She had organised engagementparties and used a silken altar cloth shot with gold thread as the raw material for dresses and a necklace for her niece.[420]

The abbess, in her turn, explained that the princesses had been treated just like ordinary nuns. In fact, Chrodechild and Basina had possessed more personal items (especially clothes) than they had actually needed in the convent. As to the bathroom, she had to admit that they were partly right. A few years before, a new bathroom had been constructed during Lent, but during the first weeks the new plaster had emitted an awful odour. Queen Radegund, who was still alive at the time, had therefore permitted the servants of the nunnery to use the bathroom until the unpleasant smell disappeared. As far as Leubovera could recollect, the odour had disappeared at Whitsun. At this point, she was rudely interrupted by Chrodechild: 'Yes, but many of them continued using it long after that!' (*Et postea similiter multi per tempora laverunt!*). The abbess replied that this was news to her. If Chrodechild was right, then she herself was in complete agreement with the rebel nuns. However, no one had told her anything about it. If the nuns had seen it happen, it was very wrong of them not to have reported it to her.[421]

As to the accusation of her playing backgammon all the time, the abbess readily confessed that she loved the game. She had done so in Saint Radegund's lifetime. As far as she knew, neither the Rule of the convent nor any other religious sources mentioned backgammon as being a forbidden pastime. If, however, the bishops decided that it was sinful to play backgammon, then she would, of course, do appropriate penance for having indulged in playing it.[422]

The accusation that she had enjoyed the company of guests and had had dinners with outsiders was pure gossip. She had in fact arranged one engagement party, but that had been an official act involving one of her own close relatives, an orphaned niece. She recollected that Bishop Maroveus himself had been present together with a number of priests and city officials. As for the altar cloth, she admitted a certain guilt, but, she quickly added, there were mitigating circumstances. A wealthy girl (now a nun) by the name of Didimia, the daughter of a landed magnate, had given her a silk mantle as a personal gift. Leubovera had cut off a piece of the mantle and kept it for herself, while the rest had been sown into an altar cloth. The part that she kept for herself had been used to make a purple edging for her niece's tunic. Didimia, who was present at the trial, confirmed Leubovera's story.[423]

At this point, Leubovera probably felt certain that she had succeeded. The rebels had not been able to prove a single accusation. The tribunal asked Chrodechild and Basina whether they had any further, really incriminating accusations, such as accusations of homicide or witchcraft, but none of the rebels could (or dared) accuse the abbess of anything like that. However, they did make a point of Leubovera's failure to enforce chastity among the nuns under her supervision who had not joined the rebels. Many of these were, as everyone in Poitiers could see, clearly pregnant. This accusation, however, failed to impress the tribunal. The bishops shook their tired heads and agreed that this was indeed the case, but so what? The poor, innocent girls had been left to their own devices for many months, unguarded in an open nunnery without defences; consequently, they had sinned. Abbess Leubovera, who was not even present at the nunnery during that time, could hardly be blamed for that.[424]

For ordinary people in Poitiers, the trial of the rebel nuns appears to have been exactly the kind of scandal that human beings throughout the centuries have delighted in witnessing or reading about. Gregory of Tours clearly loved it. He painstakingly relates one detail after another, thereby revealing attitudes and behavioural patterns of early medieval life that we normally never have the chance of observing. Despite his personal conviction that rebellions and wild nuns were bad things, he was undoubtedly impressed by the charismatic Chrodechild, who appears to have dominated the entire trial.

Chrodechild used every opportunity to describe the viciousness of Leubovera's dictatorial and sinful régime. She described how the abbess had been unable to keep her lust for carnal pleasure in check; she had dressed her lover in womens' clothes, so that he could pass for a nun or a female servant without risk of being discovered. His only function in the convent had been to sleep with the abbess whenever she ordered him to do so. 'There he is!' (*En ipsum!*), Chrodechild suddenly cried, pointing at a man in the crowd surrounding the tribunal. A man stepped forward, and everyone could see that he was, indeed, dressed in woman's clothing. The audience, fascinated by this unexpected turn of the events, stared at him. Asked why on earth he dressed like that, the man replied that he was impotent, and that his affliction, he felt, made it necessary for him to dress like a woman. Certainly he knew about the abbess. She was a local celebrity; everyone knew of her. But he had never seen here with his own eyes, let alone spoken to her. Besides, he lived far from the nunnery. Having heard this embarrassing confession – we can easily imagine the scoffing laughs of the crowd, as the transvestite confessed his impotence – the tribunal dismissed Chrodechild's accusation.[425]

Chrodechild, however, did not surrender. 'The abbess has a very odd way of proving her sanctity!', she remarked. 'She has men castrated and then keeps them around her as eunuchs, just as if this were the imperial court!'[426] When questioned about this, Leubovera denied everything. She had no idea what Chrodechild was referring to. Chrodechild quickly specified the charge by naming one of the eunuchs. A doctor called Reovalis then stepped forward. He explained that the man in question had suffered severe pain in the groin during his childhood. His mother had taken him to the convent, where Queen Radegund had turned him over to Reovalis. The doctor, who had once seen how a surgeon in Constantinople cut out testicles, now performed this operation himself and thereafter returned the boy to his mother. The Abbess Leubovera knew nothing of this. Again, the tribunal dismissed Chrodechild's accusation.[427]

Having heard all the witnesses, the tribunal declared Leubovera innocent, although not entirely free from blame. She got away with paternal admonitions such as 'Do not let this happen again!'.[428] For Chrodechild and Basina, however, the outcome of the trial was much worse. Their opponents could provide a long list of sins that they were reported to have committed during the past year:

(1) They had disobeyed the bishop when, at the very beginning of the rebellion, he had visited the nunnery and exhorted them not to leave.
(2) They had committed acts of physical violence against the bishop and even trodden him underfoot before leaving him behind in the nunnery.
(3) They had broken locks, burst open gates, started a revolt, and then escaped into the countryside, encouraging others to do likewise.

(4) They had disobeyed Bishop Gundegisel when he summoned them to appear before him in the nunnery, choosing instead to remain in Saint Hilary's church.
(5) They had attacked Gundegisel and the other bishops within Saint Hilary's church, hitting them with sticks and drawing blood.
(6) They had forced their way into the nunnery, built a fire in the courtyard, hurt several of the nuns and sacked the convent.
(7) They had dragged the abbess through the streets as a laughing-stock and imprisoned her.

At this point, Chrodechild intervened. She did not deny that all of this had, indeed, occurred, but she and Basina were entirely innocent. These terrible things had been done without their knowledge and certainly without their approval. Actually, Chrodechild argued, she had personally prevented the thugs from killing the abbess. The accusers continued.

(8) They had most cruelly killed one of the nunnery servants, who had sought refuge at the tomb of Saint Radegund.
(9) They had, when ordered to stop their evil doings, always refused to repent.
(10) They had occupied the convent.
(11) They had refused to surrender the most seditious members of their gang, even when ordered to do so by the kings.
(12) They had persisted in their armed rebellion and fought against both the count and the townsfolk with arrows and javelins.
(13) They had taken the relic of the Holy Cross and used it for their own purposes.

The bishops did not believe Chrodechild's assertion of her innocence. According to them, it was clear that the rebels had planned to kill Leubovera. Furthermore, they did not detect a single element of remorse in either Chrodechild or Basina. The princesses apparently did not regret anything. When they had asked them to beg for the abbess' forgiveness, they had always been met with a flat refusal.[429]

After consulting the canons, the bishops, needless to say, found Chrodechild and Basina guilty. They were immediately excommunicated for the second time in less than a year. The ban was to remain until they had atoned for their sins and done proper penance. As to their immediate future, the bishops wisely decided to leave the matter in the hands of the kings. They did not want to release the unrepentant Chrodechild and Basina into the hands of the abbess in Poitiers, since God only knew what would happen if they went back to the convent, possibly intent on raising another army of angry nuns as soon as Macco's mob had been dispatched. However, the damage that had been done to the convent was in many ways irreparable, unless the kings decided to intervene, as the bishops explicitly asked them to do. Those rebel nuns who had stolen property belonging to the nunnery ignored all requests that they should hand it back.[430]

The verdict was made public, the bishops returned to their cities and Leubovera returned to her nunnery, or what was left of it. The story, however, did not end there. Not before long, Chrodechild and Basina had made their way to their cousin, King Childebert II of Austrasia. By now, they had had ample time to think, and there were no bishops or witnesses present to contradict them. The king was told the names of several men who were accused of having had sexual intercourse with the abbess. Furthermore, these lovers had acted as messengers between Leubovera and none other than the dangerous Queen Fredegund of Soissons. By this time, Fredegund had already disposed of several prominent Franks, and Childebert knew that *his* name was at the top of her present list of future victims.[431] Only a few days previously, he had barely escaped an attack by one of Fredegund's hired assassins as he was going into the oratory in his house at Marlenheim.[432] Not surprisingly, Childebert immediately ordered the men accused of consorting with the abbess and delivering messages to be arrested and brought to his court for questioning. Since there was no evidence whatsoever, they were quickly released and allowed to return to their homes.[433]

At a court in the city of Metz in the middle of November the same year primarily held to deal with Bishop Egidius of Rheims, who was guilty of high treason, the case of the two princesses was again brought up. Basina threw herself at the bishops' feet and begged for forgiveness. She promised to return to the nunnery and to obey the abbess faithfully in all matters. Chrodechild, however, remained firm. She swore that she would never return to the nunnery as long as Leubovera remained there as abbess. Having heard this, King Childebert asked, or rather probably ordered, the bishops to pardon both of his cousins and to withdraw the ban of excommunication. The bishops immediately did as the king asked. Basina returned to the nunnery at Poitiers, while Chrodechild remained free. Childebert gave her an estate that had previously been held by Count Waddo of Saintes, an aristocrat not known for his faithfulness, whose property had been confiscated by the king upon his death. Chrodechild readily agreed to spend the rest of her life as a wealthy magnate. She can hardly have been displeased at the turn of events.[434]

Gregory of Tours certainly did not write this as a moralising episode in his chronicle. In fact, there is no morale at all in the story; if there had been, Chrodechild would not have received a big estate in the end, although the life of a female magnate with an estate of her own must have suited her temperament far better than life in the Convent of the Holy Cross. Rather, she would probably have submitted to Leubovera or faced an awful death. There were many awful deaths to choose from if you were an early medieval chronicler searching for appropriate ways to end the lives of women you disapproved of. Queen Brunhild was torn to pieces by horses; Duchess Romilda of Friuli was raped twelve times and then impaled.

We have every reason to believe that the events described in the story of Chrodechild and Basina actually did occur, that Gregory wrote about them for the simple reason that he was fascinated and felt a need to record what had happened. If there is a tendency to be wary of, it would probably be Gregory's natural tendency to emphasise his own actions and those of his niece Justina, Prioress of the convent. Several parts of the story are clearly based on eye-witness accounts. It is perfectly possible that Chrodechild, when she forced her way into Gregory's chambers in the rainy spring of 589, disturbed him as he was busy writing the very same chronicle in which she herself would turn out to be one of the most fascinating characters. Since Gregory himself died only a few years later, we can be absolutely sure that he must have written the story of the rebellion shortly after the events occurred. The story deserves to be taken seriously. It is neither a piece of political propaganda (as in the case of the stories of Fredegund, Balthild and others), nor a frightening tale thematically related to ghost stories and horror movies (such as the story of Romilda).

What we have is undoubtedly a *cause célèbre*, a scandal of gigantic proportions for its time. In many ways, the story is unique. For once, we actually possess a detailed contemporary account of real-life early medieval bickering, gossiping and what appears to be organised criminality, led by women. But the story is important in more ways than simply as a reflection of sixth-century attitudes and daily life. The story of Chrodechild, Basina and the wild nuns of Poitiers illuminates the possibilities, the strategies of power, that were available to noble, ambitious women in the early Middle Ages. Most importantly, the rebellion demonstrates a sincere unwillingness on the part of the two princesses to be dominated. They were *Merovingian* nuns, not ordinary nuns. For them, as for Radegund before them, the nunnery was not simply a place to live in, praying and venerating relics. They resented the fact the Abbess Leubovera demanded their obedience. To them, piety and political ambition could (and should) be combined. The nunnery was an asset, not a prison. In the early Middle Ages, piety and ambition were never perceived as two separate elements. On the contrary, piety could be employed as a means to secure heavenly support for a number of actions. For members of the Frankish aristocracy, the founding of a convent and life in a convent had (or at least could have) profound political significance. A convent consisted of a concentrate of ideological surplus in society; it was a place of power. Due to the activity of Saint Radegund, the Convent of the Holy Cross at Poitiers was both a very powerful and a very *Merovingian* convent.

Leubovera, however, did not – or did not want to – understand this. She wanted to rule her nunnery as a true abbess, thereby ignoring the fact that she herself was not of royal blood. In other words, Leubovera – not the rebels – made a serious mistake. This had nothing to do with her alleged crimes, with the fact that she enjoyed backgammon and preferred a beautiful dress to a beautiful altar cloth. Her main mistake was her failure to comprehend the specific political culture of Merovingian women. If a Frankish princess or queen could not gain influence by way of a husband or a male child, or alternatively an adult child who remained a faithful son, a convent was by far the most efficient resource available. When Leubovera deprived Chrodechild and

Basina of their influence, she broke an unwritten rule. They, like Radegund, perceived the nunnery of the Holy Cross as a Merovingian monastery, a source of supernatural, divine forces to be used by members of the dynasty. Now that Radegund was dead, they – Chrodechild and Basina – should be the ones in charge, not an upstart such as Leubovera. Leubovera's demands, the very fact that she found it appropriate to govern royal nuns and to enforce the rule of obedience, were both absurd and insulting.[435]

For a politically talented princess in the early Middle Ages, life in a nunnery was not supposed to mean a life in poverty, chastity and, God forbid, obedience – unless, of course, she really wanted this. Chrodechild and Basina refused to behave like ordinary nuns. They wanted to rule. Apparently, their royal uncles and cousins understood this perfectly. King Childebert II and King Gunthchramn hesitated to intervene in order to stop the rebellion until such time when force became absolutely necessary because of the prevailing anarchy in the streets of Poitiers. When it was all over, Childebert appears to have been remarkably lenient. A normal, non-Merovingian, male rebel would certainly not have been awarded an estate as thanks for having spent more than a year robbing, killing and refusing to obey royal commands; but Chrodechild was not a normal rebel. Her behaviour was entirely comprehensible to the members of her family.

Foreign witches: Amalaberg, Amalasuntha, Goiswinth and the others

Gregory of Tours seldom mentions foreign queens and princesses. On the rare occasions when he does, the women are sometimes described as anonymous belongings of their husbands. For instance, the Suebian magnate Andica was married to the sister of the king (who had just succeeded his father on the throne), but after having dethroned the young king and assumed the throne himself in 584, Andica discarded his own wife and remarried the former king's queen (i.e., his father-in-law's widow).[436] This sequence of events does not induce Gregory to give us any single hint as to the characters, the names or the assets of these two women. We are only told that they existed and that they were used by Andica in his struggle for control of the Suebian kingdom of Galicia. The same is true of the wife of Count Waroch of Brittany. We are told that she manumitted some of the captives taken by her husband, but that is *all* we are told.[437] All that we know of the wife of Macliaw, another Count of the Bretons, is that he deserted her when he became a religious and reclaimed her when he re-entered the secular world.[438]

Some foreign queens, however, appear in more impressive textual circumstances. We have already met a couple of them, such as Audofleda in Italy and Basina in Thuringia, both of them closely connected with the Merovingians themselves. We will now meet royal women in Thuringia, Burgundy, Italy, Visigothic Spain and the East Roman Empire.

Amalaberg was married to Hermanfrid, one of the kings of the Thuringians. Gregory describes her as a wicked and cruel woman who longed for war and conquest. When she appears in *Decem Libri Historiarum*, Hermanfrid has already killed his brother, King Berthar (father of Radegund, see p. 87), but Gregory reports that Amalaberg refused to rest until his remaining brother, King Baderic, was killed as well. This would make Hermanfrid the sole ruler of Thuringia. One day when Hermanfrid came in to have a meal, he found that Amalaberg had only ordered half the table laid. When he asked his wife about this, Amalaberg replied that 'a king who is deprived of half his kingdom deserves to find half his table bare.'[439] In the end, Hermanfrid grew tired of Amalaberg's constant goading and decided to follow her advice. He entered into an alliance with King Theuderic I of Rheims, and together they crushed Baderic's forces.[440]

Immediately after the story of Amalaberg, Gregory goes on to tell us about an evil queen of Burgundy. King Sigismund of the Burgundians, who had lost his first wife (a daughter of King Theuderic the Great of the Ostrogoths) remarried a woman whose name is not mentioned in the text. This new queen behaved like an archetypal evil stepmother, maltreating and abusing her stepson Sigeric. On one occasion, she went to Sigismund and told him that Sigeric was planning a rebellion that would result in Sigismund's death ('he cannot rise unless you fall', *nisi tu cadas, ille non surgat*). In the end, she managed to talk Sigismund into having the boy strangled. Gregory describes the Burgundian king as a weak and tragic person, completely dominated by his evil wife. He is said to have regretted the murder instantly, throwing himself on Sigeric's body and weeping, and thereafter hurrying to the monastery of Agaune to pray for pardon. Shortly afterwards, both Sigismund and his wife were struck by God's vengeance in the form of the fury of King Chlodomer of Orléans, who defeated their forces, imprisoned them, killed them and had their bodies thrown down a well.[441]

Moving from the Burgundians to the Ostrogoths, one of the most famous female rulers of sixth-century Europe appears before us: Queen Amalasuntha, daughter of Theuderic the Great and the Merovingian princess Audofleda (p. 149). Hardly any of what Gregory has to tell us about Amalasuntha is correct: what we get from his text is based on loose rumours, lies and propaganda. However, this does not make his story less interesting from our point of view. If Gregory did not regard the story as trustworthy in the sense that it might have happened (at least in sixth-century Gaul), he either would not have included it in *Decem Libri Historiarum*, or he would have made a point of its peculiarity.

In Gregory's eyes, Amalasuntha was both bad and stupid. Her lack of good sense appeared early, when she ignored her mother's advice that she should marry a king's son. Instead, she took as her lover one of her slaves called Traguilla. They eloped to a neighbouring city, where Amalasuntha thought that she would be free to do as she liked. After fruitless negotiations, Audofleda sent a band of armed men to bring her daughter home to court. They accomplished this easily, killing Traguilla and giving Amalasuntha a good beating. Shortly afterwards, Amalasuntha had her revenge in a most ungodly fashion. When on one occasion they approached the altar for communion, Amalasuntha – inspired by the Devil, according to Gregory, who uses the story to show the danger of adhering to the Arian beliefs of the Ostrogothic court – popped some poison into the chalice from which her mother was to drink. Audofleda drank and dropped down dead. The population of Italy was furious with Amalasuntha for what she had done. They summoned a man referred to by Gregory as 'Theudat, King of Tuscany' (*Theodadum regem Tusciae*) to rule over them. Theudat had a hot steam-bath prepared and ordered Amalasuntha to be shut up inside it with one of her maids. Trapped in the scalding steam, the evil princess fell to the stone floor and died immediately. Her relatives, the Frankish kings Childebert I, Chlothar I and Theudebert I, regarded Amalasuntha's death as an act of aggression and demanded a huge sum as compensation. If Theudat failed to deliver the sum, they threatened to invade Italy and submit Theudat himself to the very same treatment he had used to encompass Amalasuntha's death. Theudat agreed to pay fifty thousand pieces of gold, thereby turning the entire affair into a struggle for gold between the greedy Frankish kings themselves.[442]

Later in the same century, Italy was invaded by the Lombards. Only a few sentences after telling us this, Gregory introduces us to the second wife of Alboin, King of the Lombards. He refrains from naming her, but we know from other sources (pp. 262–64) that her name was Rosemunda and that she was originally a Gepid princess. Although not as eloquently detailed as Paul the Deacon's account, Gregory nevertheless provides us with some basic information relating to the wickedness of this woman: longing for revenge for the death of her father, she eventually poisoned Alboin and went off with a servant of his with whom she had become enamoured. According to Gregory, the couple were soon captured and killed.[443]

Goiswinth (probably d. 589) was a Visigothic queen, apparently just as important in Hispania as Brunhild and Fredegund were in Gaul. We learn from Gregory's text that she was the mother of Brunhild, which means that she must have risen to power as a wife of King Athanagild (reigned 554–68). After Athanagild's death, she eventually married King Leuvigild (after the death of his first wife), who reigned from 569 to 586.[444] Gregory's opinion of Goiswinth comes as no surprise to someone who has just read his stories of Amalaberg and Amalasuntha. According to Gregory, the Arian Goiswinth hated the Christians (i.e., the Catholics) of Hispania, persecuting them in every way possible. Many were driven into exile, others were thrown into prison, beaten with sticks and tortured to death. As as result, she was herself the victim of divine vengeance. A white cataract blinded one of her eyes, and in this way 'her eyelids lost the sense that had long before departed from her mind'.[445]

Goiswinth is further described as an Arian villain in her confrontation with the Frankish princess Ingund (a daugher of Sigibert and Brunhild, i.e. Goiswinth's granddaughter), who had come to Hispania to be married to Hermenigild, Leuvigild's son by a former wife (p. 150). On Ingund's arrival at court, Goiswinth is said to have welcomed her warmly, but when it turned out that Ingund refused to accept Arianism, Goiswinth grew angry. Gregory vividly describes how she maltreated her granddaughter until her naked body was covered with blood; then she had Ingund thrown into the Arian baptismal pool.[446]

Goiswinth remained powerful even after her second royal husband's death in 586. When Recared succeeded his father Leuvigild to the throne, he came to terms with his widowed stepmother Goiswinth and agreed to acknowledge her as his own mother. Goiswinth continued to influence Visigothic politics in her capacity as royal adviser. Before sending envoys to Gaul to ask for peace in the conflict that had erupted because of Ingund's fate (pp. 135–36), Recared took counsel with Goiswinth.

The only East Roman empress that we really get to meet in *Decem Libri Historiarum* is Sophia, the consort of Justin II. True, other empresses are mentioned, but only in passing, in short episodes together with their husbands or in relation with a particular deed.[447] Gregory describes Sophia as a greedy woman, who assumed sole power when Justin went insane. The people of Constantinople, however, chose Tiberius as Caesar, a capable man who (unlike Sophia) was dedicated to the care of those in need. When he distributed money to the poor, Sophia complained that he was reducing the state to bankruptcy ('What I have taken so many years to save, you are busy squandering in a prodigal way, and without losing much time about it, either.').[448] As in the case of Paul the Deacon, who tells us the same story (p. 265), the incident is undoubtedly related in order to serve as an example of Tiberius' piety. Sophia's greed is necessary to make Tiberius' charity stand out.[449]

After Justin's death in 578, when Tiberius was crowned emperor as Tiberius II, Sophia broke her promise to accept this and tried to replace him with Justinian, Justin's nephew. Tiberius responded by imprisoning Sophia and confiscating her property. She was only allowed to keep what was sufficient for her daily needs. Her servants were dismissed and replaced by new, faithful ones.[450] Sophia was not, however, deprived of all her influence. As Tiberius lay dying in 582, he consulted Sophia about the succession. Sophia advised him to name a certain

Maurice his successor. 'He is a strong man', she is supposed to have said, 'and a wise one too. He has often fought for the state against its enemies, and he has always won.'[451] In reality, Sophia cared little about Maurice's qualities as a commander – she only proposed him because she thought she had a good chance of marrying him and thus perpetuating her own influence at court. In this, she was mistaken. The dying Tiberius, who agreed that Maurice was a good choice, quickly married off his own daughter to the new emperor.[452]

Summing up what Gregory has to tell us about important women outside Gaul, the dominating image is a very negative one. The non-Frankish queens all appear to have been evil witches, plotting death and behaving stupidly. They wanted to strengthen their own position by inducing their husbands to conquer more territory and kill more enemies, while they themselves got rid of their rivals at home (such as stepsons). If they lived in a country where the members of the ruling class were Arians, they themselves (no doubt inspired by the Devil) were Arians *in extremis*, and they hated Catholics. Nevertheless, they were powerful and were to be treated with fearful respect.

Needless to say, most of what we read about these queens in *Decem Libri Historiarum* is not to be taken seriously. Gregory knew very little about actual events, and his judgment is obscured by his own hatred of Arianism and his tendency to interpret all actions from a theological perspective. From the point of view of Thuringian, Ostrogothic, Burgundian, Lombard, Visigothic and East Roman history, Gregory's tales are of little value. They are, however, of immense importance to Frankish history. The stories of Amalaberg, Amalasuntha and the others make perfect sense if we read them as descriptions of what Gregory thought could have happened in Gaul. Queens who persecuted their stepsons, urged their husbands to kill their enemies and used poison to get rid of their own relatives, were not regarded as unusual by Gregory of Tours. On the contrary, this kind of behaviour was to be expected from any powerful woman that Gregory regarded as bad.

The most interesting foreign queen is undoubtedly Goiswinth, who lived in Gregory's own life-time. Leaving aside his remarks about her being an Arian fanatic who liked to maltreat Catholics, what remains is the picture of a politically wise woman who remained at the centre of Visigothic politics for several decades, influencing at least three kings and exerting a certain degree of influence in Gaul as well through the marriage of Brunhild to Sigibert. Goiswinth would appear to have been one of the most powerful individuals in Western Europe during the second half of the sixth century. From what we learn from *Decem Libri Historiarum*, she based her power on marriages to Visigothic kings and on marrying off her daughters to important Frankish kings.

Magnate women

Having learned what Gregory of Tours thought of women at the very top of sixth-century society, we will now turn to his descriptions of women belonging to the magnate and warlord class, a group of powerful families situated immediately below the royal families. Initially, magnate women will be discussed in general; later, we will look more closely at some of the most prominent members of this group.

Most of the magnate women in *Decem Libri Historiarum* are simply mentioned in one or two sentences each. They only exist in Gregory's text as associates of their husbands or sons: without their men, they would not have been mentioned at all. We know nothing about what they did, what resources they had and whether they were good or bad individuals. Often, we do not even know their names. For instance, when Châteaudun lost its episcopal status in the middle of the 570s, after which it was regarded as a part of the diocese of Chartres, Bishop Promotus of Châteaudun became a mere priest. After having failed to regain his status in 584, he at least managed to get the king to confirm his possession of certain lands, where he lived the rest of his life together with his mother. This piece of information is *all* that we get with regard to Promotus' mother.[453] There are many similar examples: all that we know of the assassin Claudius' wife is that she came from the Meaux area (pp. 116).[454] All that we know of Childeric the Saxon's wife is that she had a property in Auch and that her husband appears to have been very attached to her, since he made a significant effort to win her back when they had been separated due to political troubles.[455] The same situation appears in Gregory's description of the relationship between Count Leudast and his wife.[456] Our information about the daughter and the greedy wife of a wealthy man called Ursus,

175

who lived in Clermont, is strictly related to the parts they played in the conflict between Ursus and a certain Andarchius, who wanted to marry the daughter.[457] Our knowledge of the female members of the family of the Merovingian prince Chramn (d. 560), son of Chlothar I, is limited to the fact that his wife (Chalda) was the daughter of a man (possibly a priest) called Willichar, and that both she and her daughters accompanied Chramn when he went into exile in Brittany where they were all eventually killed.[458]

This willingness on the part of the wives to share the misfortunes of the husbands is evident throughout Gregory's chronicle – whether they wanted to or not, the wives were usually identified with their husbands as far as general social and political aims were concerned. Frankish husbands and Frankish wives were partners in good deeds as well as in bad; as a result, they often shared a common fate. The priest Willichar (possibly Chramn's father-in-law) was joined by his wife as he sought sanctuary (probably in 558) in the church of Saint Martin in Tours.[459] The wives of the rebellious Austrasian magnates Ursio and Berthefried joined their husbands when they shut themselves up in a church in order to evade the royal troops in 587.[460]

Some of the women that do appear in several sentences, not just *en passant*, are nevertheless mentioned more as literary tools than as persons that merit interest per se. For instance, Gregory was painfully aware that many members of the clergy fell far below the moral standards set by the church. In order to warn the clergy not to break the statutes of the canons by having sexual intercourse with strange women (as many priests and monks obviously did), he tells a story of what happened to a sinful abbot called Dagulf. Dagulf is described as a man who liked to rob people of their goods and who was even guilty of a few murders. He greatly enjoyed committing adultery and, on one occasion, made the mistake of sleeping with a woman whose husband came back too early. The husband found his wife and the abbot in bed together, both of them completely drunk. He promptly raised his axe and killed them both; it would seem that Gregory approved of the action.[461] The woman – whose name is not mentioned – is only interesting from the point of view of the moral of the story. She could easily be replaced by something else such as a lot of gold, equally dangerous and tempting.

Sometimes we learn a little more from the few words Gregory deems necessary to illustrate the position of the magnate women of Gaul. Apparently, the position as wife of a Frankish magnate was not considered to be a safe, permanent position of high status that was bound to last until the woman's death. Far from it: wives could be discarded, forgotten or even killed. Murders of wives, or at least rumours of such assassinations, were certainly not unknown. After the killing of a man called Magnovald at the court of Childebert II in Metz in 586, probably by order of the king himself, it was rumoured that it had been done as revenge for his wife's death. Some maintained that Magnovald had murdered his wife after cruelly maltreating her simply in order to facilitate his plans to get into bed with his brother's widow.[462] Another horrible example (again, mainly based on rumour) is provided by the life of the son of Duke Beppolen. Gregory describes him as a libidinous scoundrel whose desire for sexual intercourse drove him to seduce one woman after another (usually servant-girls), marry them, and then behave towards them as if they meant nothing to him. He took against his first wife, rejected her and married another woman, who soon displeased him as well. Thirdly, he married the widow of Wiliulf, a citizen of Poitiers (she had also been married once before, making it the third marriage for both of them), but his manners did not improve.[463]

Reading about men such as Magnovald and Beppolen's son, we get the impression that the early Middle Ages was indeed an era of machismo and male power. Magnates were, it would seem, free to do as they pleased. However, some women did fight back. Once in 589 a typical Frankish magnate called Amalo sent his wife away to one of his estates to look after his affairs. Alone in bed, he was suddenly seized with a desire for a certain young girl of free birth. One night when he was completely drunk he sent his servants to seize the girl and put her in his bed. She resisted but was carried off to Amalo's house by force. The servants punched her so much that Amalo's bed was stained red with the girl's blood. Amalo joined the servants, kicking and punching her himself. Fortunately for the girl, he was too drunk to do much more than that – having taken her in his arms, he immediately fell asleep. The girl then took hold of a sword and dealt him a mighty blow. Amalo screamed, and the servants came running.

As they were about to kill her, the dying Amalo prevented this by shouting that *he* was the sinner – the girl had only tried to preserve her virginity. The girl escaped and made her way to Chalon-sur-Saône, where she threw herself at the king's feet and told him all that had occurred. Duly impressed, the king ordered a royal edict to be drawn up to the effect that she was under his protection and must not be molested by any of the dead man's relations.[464]

The magnate wives were clearly dependent on their men. Their husbands provided them with wealth and with security, as long as they did not begin to look elsewhere for female companionship or, even worse but just as probable, were killed themselves. If that happened, the widows had to act quickly if they wanted to remain rich and influential. We know that Duke Rauching's wife was originally married to a treacherous magnate called Godin. After Godin's death, she remarried and became wealthy, since Rauching appears to have been one of the most greedy magnates of his generation. Gregory provides us with a vivid description of her, as, on 25 October 587, she meets the servant who has come to tell her the news of her second husband's death: she is riding a horse in a street in Soissons on her way to church, bedecked with fine jewels and precious gems, bedizened with flashing gold, with a troop of servants in front of her and another behind. As soon as she sees the messenger, she turns down another street, throws all her ornaments on the ground and seeks sanctuary in the church of Saint Medard. Without her husband, she is powerless.[465] Her situation was very similar to that of Eberulf's suddenly very poor wife, after the murder of her husband in Tours (p. 116). Eberulf's widow lost all the property that had been held by her late husband, and she had to be supported by Saint Martin's church.[466] The widow of Gunthchramn Boso was forced into exile by King Childebert II and King Gunthchramn.[467] Apparently, powerless and wealthy wives were sitting targets for those with swords in their hands. After the military defeat of Duke Ragnovald (a commander of King Gunthchramn's) in 581, the city of Périgueux fell to the forces of Duke Desiderius (a commander of King Chilperic I's) and the hostile army rapidly advanced towards Agen, where Ragnovald's wife was living. She instantly realised her danger and sought sanctuary in the church of Saint Caprasius. However, the saint was not strong enough to help her. She was forced out of the church by her husband's enemies and was subsequently robbed of all her possessions. Her servants were taken away from her, and she was only allowed to set out for Toulouse after paying a sum of money as a surety. Still fearing for her safety, she took up residence in the church of Saint Saturninus in Toulouse.[468] She was only saved from having to spend her days in churches by the return of Ragnovald in 584.[469]

Another interesting example is the story of Mummolus' wife. Mummolus, one of the most prominent warlords of sixth-century Gaul, made a political mistake in joining the rebellion of the pretender Gundovald during the first half of the 580s. King Gunthchramn responded by imprisoning his wife and his children.[470] Eventually, in 585 Mummolus was killed, and his wife was brought forth to be questioned about the wealth that Gunthchramn assumed they must have amassed before the rebellion. In the end, she was forced to reveal everything, including the whereabouts of two hundred and fifty talents of silver and more than thirty talents of gold that had been hidden by Mummolus in Avignon. Gunthchramn confiscated everything and divided it between his nephew Childebert and, at least according to Gregory, the poor. Mummolus' widow got nothing except the property she had inherited from her own relations.[471]

However, we do have examples of magnate women that died without husbands and children but still appear to have been very rich. For instance, Gregory tells us about a relative of Gunthchramn Boso's wife, who died childless in 585 and was buried in a church near Metz together with much gold and a profusion of ornaments. A few days later, Gunthchramn Boso's servants broke into the church, opened the tomb and robbed it of most of the precious objects.[472]

We sometimes encounter women involved in intrigues on the highest political level, although we can seldom paint a complete picture of events and their reasons for acting the way they did. For instance, we have already met Septimima, nurse to the children of Childebert II, who was embroiled in a plot against Queen Brunhild and Queen Faileuba in 589. When she was tortured, she confessed that she had already killed her own husband by witchcraft because she was in love with her co-conspirator Droctulf. In the end, Septimima was severely beaten, her face was disfigured with red-hot irons, all that she had was taken from her and she was sent to the country estate of Marlenheim, where she spent the rest of her days turning the mill and grinding corn to feed the women who worked in the spinning and weaving room of the estate.[473] However, we know virtually nothing about Septimima's background or her financial position. We know even less of Leuba, the mother-in-law of Duke Bladast, who appears to have acted as liaison between King Leuvigild of the Visigoths and Queen Fredegund (p. 117).[474]

Before meeting the most prominent female members of the magnate stratum from the point of view of Gregory's text, we should allow ourselves some time to scrutinise a few of those who, although clearly of less importance than some of the others, are still sufficiently interesting to merit more than just a short reference in *Decem Libri Historiarum*. Alchima and Placidana, Papianilla, Caesaria, Susanna, Tranquilla, Domnola, Constantina, Beretrude, Waddo's unnamed wife, and Magnatrude.

Alchima and Placidana were the wife and sister of Apollinaris, son of the famous fifth-century writer Sidonius Apollinaris, bishop of Clermont. As leader of the Auvergnats, Apollinaris fought on Clovis' side in the war against the Visigoths in 507.[475] His goal was to achieve the same episcopal rank as his father had enjoyed, and both his wife and his daughter did their best to help him. After the election of an old man called Quintianus (who had previously been bishop of Rodez) to the bishopric of Clermont, Alchima and Placidana went to him and are supposed to have said: 'It should be enough for you in your old age, holy prelate, that you have already been appointed to one bishopric. Will you not, who are so pious, allow your servant Apollinaris to hold the episcopate here? If he does gain this high honour, he will obey your command in all things. You will give the orders, and he will carry out your wishes. Please listen sympathetically to this our humble proposal.'[476] Quintianus replied that he had no control over the election. Furthermore, all he really wanted was that the church give him enough to eat each day, so that he might devote himself to prayer. Having heard this, Alchima and Placidana sent Apollinaris to King Theuderic of Rheims with many gifts. Theuderic gave him the bishopric. However, Apollinaris was no longer a young man, and he died only four months after his appointment. Theuderic then ordered Quintianus to be re-instated as bishop.[477]

At the beginning of the 530s, when Theuderic was campaigning in Thuringia, false rumours reached Clermont that he had been killed. One of the leading men of the city, Apollinaris' son Arcadius, plotted to desert Theuderic's heirs and hand Clermont over to King Childebert I. At first, the plan seemed to be working, but it failed when it became clear that Theuderic was still alive and well.[478] Soon afterwards, Theuderic appeared in the Auvergne with an army, intent upon wiping out all resistance to his rule and at the same time giving his warriors good opportunities for plunder.[479] The whole region of Clermont was devastated, and Arcadius fled to Bourges (which was ruled by King Childebert). Alchima and Placidana were arrested in the town of Cahors. All their goods were seized and they were sent into exile.[480]

Papianilla was the wife of the hated tax-collector Parthenius, who worked for King Theudebert I of Rheims (d. 547 or 548). Gregory of Tours was suspicious of the entire concept of taxation and he certainly did not approve of tax-collectors. He describes Parthenius as a voracious glutton who used to eat aloes to give himself an appetite and aid his digestion; also, he used to fart in public without any consideration for those present. When we enter the story, Papianilla has already been dead for some years. After Theudebert's death, an angry mob attacked Parthenius, and he had to flee from his home. He asked two bishops to escort him to Trier and to help quell the riot with their sermons. They agreed, and together the bishops and the tax-collector set off. One night during the journey, Parthenius had a nightmare and cried for help. When asked what was the matter, he explained that he had seen his friend Ausanius and his wife Papianilla, both of whom he had murdered, summoning him to atone for his sins. It turned out that he had suspected Papianilla and Ausanius of having an affair, and he had therefore killed them. This was done despite the fact that Papianilla (according to Gregory) was clearly innocent. In the end, the bishops were unable to protect Parthenius from the anger of the mob: he was tied to a pillar and stoned to death.[481]

Caesaria was the sister-in-law of Count Firminus of Clermont. When the Merovingian prince Chramn, son of Chlothar I, dismissed Firminus from his countship in the middle of the 550s, both Firminus and Caesaria took sanctuary in the cathedral. One day, when the bishop was away, Chramn sent some of his men to drive Firminus and Caesaria out of the building. This was accomplished by careful planning: Firminus and Caesaria were manoeuvred into standing near the unlocked gate of the cathedral, where they could easily be grabbed and removed from the church. They were immediately condemned to exile. The next day, when their guards were sleeping, they took the opportunity to escape and make their way to the church of Saint Julian. Although this saved them from exile, all their goods were confiscated.[482] Caesaria eventually married Count Britanus of Javols and was the mother of his son, Count Palladius, whose suicide she was unable prevent.[483]

Susanna was married to Bishop Priscus of Lyons. She is described as an evil woman, who helped her husband persecute and even kill many of those who had been close associates of the former bishop, Saint Nicetius (d. 573). The reason according to Gregory of Tours was pure envy: Priscus was jealous of the loyalty of these men to his predecessor. Among other things, Susanna and her young women used to enter the very cell in which Nicetius had slept, despite the fact that women were ordinarily not permitted to dwell within this building. In the end, Susanna became possessed by a devil. In her madness she ran through the whole city, with her hair loose about her shoulders, confessing that Saint Nicetius, the holiness of whom she had denied while she still had her wits, was in fact Christ's friend. Desperately, she called upon Nicetius to intervene and save her. The other members of Priscus' family were also punished by the miraculous power of Nicetius.[484]

Tranquilla was married to Sichar, a young man of Tours, who was apparently a client of Queen Brunhild's (p. 139). After Sichar's murder in 587 or at the beginning of 588, she abandoned her children and her husband's property in Tours and Poitiers and went off to join her relations in the village of Pont-sur-Seine. There she married again.[485]

Burgolen was the son of a magnate called Severus. Like his father, he became entangled in the dangerous webs of Frankish political feuds, which eventually resulted in his death. Before that, however, he had possessed vast wealth and enjoyed the status of a very important man.[486] He was married to a woman called Domnola, daughter of Bishop Victorius of Rennes. After his death, Domnola married a certain Nectarius.[487]

In 585, Domnola had an argument with Bobolen, Queen Fredegund's referendary, about a vineyard that they both considered part of their own property. When Bobolen learned that Domnola had visited the vineyard, behaving as if it were hers, he sent messengers to tell her that she should not have the presumption to enter the estate. Domnola disregarded the message completely. She remarked that the estate had belonged to her father and that nothing could stop her from visiting it. On hearing this, Bobolen decided to use force. When he found out that Domnola was at the vineyard, he suddenly attacked her with a band of armed men. After he had had her and all the men and women who were with her killed, he claimed the vineyard and all the movable property for himself.[488] However, two years later, King Gunthchramn punished all those involved in Domnola's death. Bobolen's goods were confiscated to the royal treasury.[489]

Burgolen had a daughter called Constantina, who eventually ended up in the Convent of the Holy Cross at Poitiers. She joined the rebellion in 589 (pp. 154–69) and accompanied the rebel leader Chrodechild on her journey to visit King Gunthchramn in the summer of 589. However, she did not return after the royal audience; Chrodechild left her behind in the nunnery at Autun.[490]

Beretrude was a wealthy woman and the founder of several nunneries. When she lay dying in 589, she appointed her daughter as her heiress. Beretrude also made bequests to her nunneries and to various churches. However, a magnate called Waddo sought to use the opportunity of Beretrude's death to gain more land. In particular, he wanted a country estate near Poitiers that Beretrude had left to her daughter. Therefore, he complained that some of his horses had been stolen by Beretrude's son-in-law; the allegedly stolen horses could be used as a convenient excuse for aggression. He even sent words to the bailiff of the estate to prepare for his coming. The bailiff, however, prepared to resist Waddo; the estate servants were soon armed and ready to defend the property. Waddo's wife tried to persuade her husband not to force his way into the estate, warning him that he risked being killed by the defenders. If that were to happen, both she and her children would find themselves in a very dangerous situation: 'Then I, and my children, too, will be left destitute' (*et ego cum filiis misera ero*). Waddo disregarded her pleas. In the ensuing fight, he was mortally wounded. His son went to the king and obtained possession of his estate, thereby saving himself and his mother from poverty.[491]

Magnatrude was married to Bishop Badegisil of Le Mans. Gregory of Tours regarded both of them as evil, but he makes it clear that Magnatrude was worse than her husband. She is described as having a morose and harsh temper; by constantly nagging Badegisil, she egged him on to commit the most detestable crimes. When Badegisil suddenly died in 586, she did whatever she could to keep all the wealth that her husband had amassed during his episcopate. She retained as if they were her own certain objects which had been given to the church during Badegisil's lifetime ('That was part of my husband's stipend!', *Milicia haec fuit viri mei!*). The new bishop, Bertram, who had previously been archdeacon of Paris, complained about this for a long time. He finally managed to get her to restore everything to the church, although she did so very reluctantly.[492]

Gregory goes on to tell us in detail of Magnatrude's malice and cruelty that was, in his opinion, quite beyond words. On more than one occasion, she cut off a man's penis along with part of the skin of his stomach, and she burned 'the more secret parts' of women's bodies with metal plates which she had made white-hot (*feminis secriciora corporis loca lamminis candentibus perussit*). She was guilty of many other awful iniquities, but Gregory says that he prefers to remain silent about these.[493]

However bad she may have been, Magnatrude was certainly a woman capable of defending herself and her family when the need arose. In 590, when a magnate called Chuppa assembled some of his men and tried to carry off Badegisil's daughter, he discovered Magnatrude to be more than his match. He broke into a country house at Mareil to accomplish his design, but Magnatrude soon appeared together with a band of armed servants. Several of Chuppa's men were killed in the ensuing fight; Chuppa managed to escape, discredited but alive.[494]

All the women discussed in this chapter were, in one way or another, members of the leading stratum of the Merovingian kingdom. Their husbands, lovers or sons were merely one or two steps below the Merovingians themselves on the social and political ladder of Gaul. By all accounts, both the men and the women belonging to this social group behaved in a fashion very similar to that of the members of the royal house. True, we have considerably less evidence for magnate women than for royal women, but all indications would seem to point to similar strategies and similar resources. For example, some of the magnate women developed close ties to ecclesiastical institutions, as did Merovingian queens and princesses. Constantina at first joined the Convent of the Holy Cross and later a nunnery in Autun. Beretrude founded several nunneries of her own.

Like the Frankish queens, the wives of the Frankish magnates were heavily dependent on their men and their families. They always needed male allies. Their positions were usually inferior to those of their husbands. In fact, it would seem that their husbands could even have them murdered without risking much (as is evident from the story of poor Papianilla, the tax-collector's wife). If their male allies died or lost their power, the magnate women had to marry (or remarry) someone important in order to remain influential. Godin's widow married Duke Rauching. Caesaria, sister-in-law of Count Firminus of Clermont, married Count Britanus of Javols after Chramn's confiscation of her and Firminus' property. Tranquilla, Sichar's widow, abandoned both her children and her husband's property to be closer to her own relations and make arrangements for a new marriage. Domnola, Bishop Victorius' daughter and the magnate Burgolen's widow, also remarried after her husband's death. Waddo's wife tried, in vain, to persuade her husband not to risk his life, since his death could easily bring about her own ruin. The danger was real: many magnate women did in fact end up impoverished, such as Eberulf's wife in Tours.

However, despite their constant need for male allies, the magnate women can hardly be described as weak. On the contrary, for many ordinary inhabitants in Merovingian Gaul, women such as Magnatrude and Caesaria were undoubtedly just as difficult to deal with as their male counterparts. If they possessed land and wealth, they could easily summon bands of armed men and attack their enemies. These struggles were just as dangerous for rich women as they were for rich men – Domnola lost her life fighting Bobolen over a vineyard in 585, while Magnatrude's armed defence against Chuppa in 590 resulted in victory and several of Chuppa's men were killed. Septimima was severely punished for her part in the plot against Brunhild and Faileuba in 589.

Just as husbands and the sons were indispensable for the maintenance of the social position of their wives and mothers, magnate women themselves were important as the allies and helpers of their men. For instance, we have seen how Apollinaris' wife and daughter did what they could to further his career. Both of them would seem to have remained prominent members of their powerful family faction in the Auvergne for several decades, and they can hardly have been innocent of Arcadius' treacherous activities at the beginning of the 530s. King Theuderic lost no time in confiscating their goods and sending them into exile as soon as he was able to arrest them. In the case of Caesaria and Firminus, it is clear that she had as much to fear from Chramn as he had; they both sought sanctuary. The greedy (but very capable) Magnatrude must have been a formidable ally to her husband, Bishop Badegisil, as was Susanna to Bishop Priscus.

Ingitrude and Berthegund

Ingitrude and her daughter Berthegund belonged to the Frankish nobility, although their relationship to other important families, such as the Merovingians, is unclear. They do not appear to have been regarded as actual members of the royal house. In the present context, this fact only serves to make them more interesting than would otherwise have been the case. Ingitrude and Berthegund are useful to the analysis in their capacity as *non-royal* but still powerful women in sixth-century Francia.

According to Gregory of Tours, Ingitrude was born in c. 510.[495] She first appears in *Decem Libri Historiarum* as a religious at Tours who was in the habit of collecting the water used for washing Saint Martin's tomb. Gregory relates how a miracle occurred at the tomb, as Ingitrude one day (probably in or near 578) was forced to supplement the water with wine due to a shortage of water. When some of the wine was poured out of the jar and replaced by a single drop of holy water, the jar, which was half empty, was immediately filled to the brim. Ingitrude emptied the jar two or three times, and on each occasion it was replenished by the addition of a single drop of water.[496]

Next, we encounter her in a speech by the pretender Gundovald in 585. As he was trying to be accepted as a true Merovingian king, he told his enemies to ask Ingitrude of Tours and the royal widow Radegund at Poitiers (see pp. 93–94) if they did not believe that what he said was true.[497] From this information, we might infer that if Ingitrude was not actually related to the Merovingians, she was at least someone who had previously been at court. We get more information from King Gunthchramn of Orléans, when in 585 he accused Bishop Bertram of Bordeaux (Ingitrude's son) of having received Gundovald. Gunthchramn said: 'You should have remembered, dear father, that you were my kinsman on my mother's side, and you should not have introduced into your own family this pestilential person from abroad.'[498] In other words, one of Bertram's parents, either Ingitrude or her husband, was related to Gunthchramn's mother, Chlothar I's wife Ingund.

Only in the ninth of his ten books does Gregory give us more precise information on Ingitrude and her position in society. He informs us that she had founded a nunnery in the forecourt of Saint Martin's church in Tours. Apparently, the nunnery was highly regarded. For instance, among the nuns was a woman called Berthefled, a daughter of King Charibert I of Paris. When the convent was originally founded, Ingitrude had sent a message to her daughter Berthegund, saying 'Leave your husband and come, so that I can make you abbess of the community which I have brought together.'[499] Gregory makes no secret of the fact that he regarded the message as stupid. In his capacity as bishop, he personally intervened to stop Berthegund from doing what her mother wanted of her. As soon as Berthegund arrived in Tours, telling her husband that she would never return to her family since 'no-one who is married will ever see the kingdom of heaven' (*non enim videbit regnum Dei coniugio copulatus*), Gregory went to Berthegund and told her that, by abandoning her husband, she was accursed. Berthegund, afraid of being excommunicated, then left the convent and returned home to her husband and her children.[500]

Three or four years later, Ingitrude sent another message to her daughter, asking her to come to the nunnery. Berthegund was not unwilling. One day when her husband was away from home, Berthegund loaded some boats with her own possessions and those of her husband and set out for Tours with one of her sons. As her husband returned home, he quickly realised what had happened and again asked her to come back to him. Ingitrude became worried. She wanted her daughter at the convent, but she was afraid of the consequences; it would appear that she had hoped that Berthegund's husband would simply give in to her wishes. Since he did not, Tours was not a safe place for Berthegund. She was also worried about the charges to which Berthegund had exposed them both by her criminal action.[501]

Ingitrude finally decided to make use of her son Bertram. As bishop of Bordeaux, Bertram was one of the most important ecclesiastical leaders of Gaul; he would be far more difficult to defeat by threats than Ingitrude herself. Therefore, Berthegund was sent away to her brother in Bordeaux. Her husband followed her, but Bertram ignored his complaints: 'You married her without her parents' consent, and therefore she is no longer your wife.'[502] (at this point, Gregory points out to the reader that they had in fact been married for nearly thirty years: Bertram's accusation came a couple of decades too late). The husband revisited Bordeaux several times, but Bishop Bertram refused to deliver up his sister.[503]

The husband then decided to appeal to a higher authority: King Gunthchramn himself. He sought an audience with the king in 585, at the same time as Bertram was out of favour with Gunthchramn because of his reception of the pretender Gundovald. The husband made a bitter attack on the bishop: 'You have taken away my wife and her servants. What is more, and this ill becomes a bishop, you have seduced some of my women-servants and my wife has had intercourse with some of your men.'[504] When he heard this, Gunthchramn was very angry. He reminded Bertram that Berthegund was a relative of his, just as Bertram was, and that it was his own personal duty to punish her if she had done anything wrong in her husband's home. If she had done nothing wrong, why should her husband be humiliated by having his wife taken away from him? Bertram tried to get out of the dilemma by referring to the brotherly love he felt for his dear sister. He had been nice to her and kept her with him as long as she herself wanted to stay. Of course, the husband could come and get her now if he really wanted to. Anyway, said Bertram, Berthegund had already left his buildings.[505]

However, the bishop was lying. He had no intention of surrendering his sister to her husband. In secret, he sent a messenger to Berthegund, telling her to set aside her secular clothes, do penance and seek sanctuary in Saint Martin's church. She did this, thus evading her husband's next attempt to get her back. He arrived with a number of his men to force her to leave her sanctuary. Berthegund, wearing the habit of a nun and claiming that she had taken a vow of penitence, refused to go with him. At this point, the husband apparently grew tired of the vain struggle and returned home.[506]

Then, suddenly, Berthegund changed her mind completely. This was probably because Bishop Bertram died unexpectedly in Bordeaux after developing a high fever.[507] According to Gregory's text, she said: 'What a fool I have been to listen to the advice of my stupid mother. Now my brother is dead, my husband has left me and I am cut off from my children! How unhappy I am! Where shall I go, and what shall I do?'[508] Having thought things over, it would appear that she decided to become a landed magnate, making Poitiers her new base. To become wealthy, she needed as much of her late father's and late brother's lands as she could get hold of. Ingitrude and her greedy nunnery were in the way. Not surprisingly, Berthegund fell out with her mother. As before, Ingitrude wanted to keep Berthegund with her at the convent, but the new Berthegund would have none of it. A quarrel arose between mother and daughter. The two women appeared frequently before the king, Berthegund trying to establish a claim to what her father had left and Ingitrude asking for the estate of her late husband. When Berthegund produced a deed of gift from her brother Bertram, claiming lands that had previously belonged to the late bishop, Ingitrude would not recognise the deed and tried to claim everything for herself. She even sent men to break into her daughter's house and steal everything, including the deed of gift. This was a serious mistake, since it made her guilty of theft in the eyes of the law. Berthegund quickly used this opportunity to force her mother publicly to return all that she had taken.[509]

In an attempt to end the conflict, the king (probably in 589) ordered Bishop Maroveus of Poitiers and Gregory of Tours himself to try to pacify the two women. It was no use: Berthegund came to Tours and appeared in court, but Ingitrude took no notice of what the two bishops were doing. Instead, she went off to the king in a raging temper, determined to disinherit her daughter from all share in her father's property. This turned out to be a wise choice, for without Berthegund to stop her, Ingitrude managed to get a judgment in her own favour. According to the royal decision, one-quarter of the property should be restored to Berthegund, while Ingitrude should receive three-quarters, to share with her grandchildren whom she had from another son. King Childebert commanded the priest Theuthar to make the division, but Berthegund – not surprisingly – refused to accept the judgment. Her refusal made Theuthar's mission impossible to complete. No division was made, and the quarrel continued.[510]

In 590, Ingitrude fell seriously ill. Realising that her end was near, she appointed her niece as abbess. The nuns were not happy about this, but Bishop Gregory managed to silence the complaints. On her deathbed, Ingitrude, apparently angry at not getting the final quarter of her husband's estate, also decided to do whatever harm she still could to Berthegund. She swore that her daughter would never be allowed to offer prayers either in the nunnery or at her tomb. Having said this, she died and was buried on 8 March. Hearing that the old woman was finally dead, Berthegund immediately hurried to Tours, but she was not allowed into the nunnery.[511]

Berthegund now did what Ingitrude had done a year previously: she sought an audience with King Childebert and appealed to him to settle the dispute in her favour without the other party being present. She petitioned Childebert to allow her to replace her mother in the nunnery. Childebert forgot (or decided to forget) that he had already ruled in Ingitrude's favour. He gave Berthegund a new document signed with his own hand, saying that she might inherit all the property that her mother and father had left, and might even go as far as to take everything which Ingitrude had bequeathed to the nunnery. Berthegund lost no time: armed with the order she set out to plunder the convent, despite the fact that the new abbess was a close relation of hers. She removed all the furniture from the building, leaving nothing behind but the bare walls. Not satisfied with the profit from this legal raid, she went on to attack other, illegal goals. Having enlisted the help of a band of ruffians, she stole all the produce from other estates that devout people had donated to the nunnery. No-one dared, or could, stop her. The desperate and apparently quite helpless Bishop Gregory writes: 'She did so many evil things that I find it impossible to set them all down in order for you.'[512] When Berthegund had taken everything she could lay her hands on she returned to Poitiers.[513]

After this, we hear nothing of Berthegund. We may assume that she settled down to lead a comfortable life as a wealthy female magnate, probably in a way similar to the ex-nun Chrodechild after the royal verdict and decisions at Metz in 590 (p. 167). As in the case of Chrodechild, Berthegund's story makes it clear that land and power was not out of reach for greedy single women in the early Middle Ages, even if they were not royal widows with a minor king to bring up. If you were sufficiently persistent and had the right allies, it was perfectly possible to win. We must keep in mind that Ingitrude and Berthegund are not described by Gregory because they were royal women (apparently they were not, although they were in some way related to King Gunthchramn) but because he regarded their various problems as a nuisance to himself and to his city. If Ingitrude had not lived in Tours but in, say, Marseilles or Rheims, we would probably not have known about the existence of her nunnery, nor about her daughter. In all probability, there were many Ingitrudes and Berthegunds in early medieval Francia, but we seldom hear about them due to the general lack of sources and the tendency of the writers to concentrate on events and people in their own neighbourhood.

The lives of Ingitrude and Berthegund demonstrate the resources and strategies available to noble women in general in the sixth century. The following sources of power in particular should be remarked upon:

(1) the fact that Ingitrude and Berthegund belonged to the nobility – if not, their history would have been inconceivable
(2) aggressive personality
(3) property (money, treasure, land, etc.), especially lands inherited from male family members

(4) in the case of Ingitrude, her children (she tried to use both her daughter Berthegund and her son Bertram)
(5) in the case of Berthegund, her brother (she received generous help from Bishop Bertram)
(6) ecclesiastical institutions – Ingitrude's convent contributed significantly to her own standing in society

Ingitrude wanted to establish a convent run by herself and her relatives; she clearly intended the office of Abbess to be hereditary. She identified herself and her interests with those of the nunnery, even to the point of breaking ecclesiastical law. Berthegund's aims are less conspicuous. In the beginning, she appears as a daughter torn between the life of a dutiful wife to a Frankish magnate and the life of an Abbess dominated by her mother. Neither choice would have made her particularly independent, but nothing in Gregory's text hints at this being her primary goal. According to *Decem Libri Historiarum*, Berthegund simply obeyed her powerful mother's wish; she was caught between her duty to Ingitrude and her duty to her own family. Eventually, at the critical moment of Bishop Bertram's death, she began to realise the opportunities, and not only the dangers, of her situation. Her actions in the years after 585 were dictated by her own wishes, not by the wishes of her husband and certainly not by the wishes of her mother.

Why did Berthegund wait until 585–86? And why did her husband not attempt to reclaim her as his wife after this? We will never know the answer to the second question; he may have died or grown tired of hunting her and simply married someone else. The fact that Berthegund chose to break free in 585–86, however, was undoubtedly related to her brother Bertram's death. With the death of a bishop, new lands were suddenly within the grasp of his relatives. It is very possible that the animosity between Ingitrude and Berthegund resulted from pure greed: they both wanted Bertram's property, Ingitrude for her nunnery and Berthegund for herself. With the death of Bertram, the balance of land and power shifted, and the conflict became inevitable. Given the nature of the two women's elevated social positions, the conflict was bound to have serious repercussions and demand the intervention of kings and bishops.

Disputes concerning lands were extremely common in the Middle Ages. Land was the chief source of wealth and influence; everybody wanted as much of it as possible. Seen from this angle, Ingitrude and Berthegund behaved just as we would have expected them to do. The fact that the root of the problem was not particularly spectacular is also evident in the attitude of Childebert. He does not appear to have cared much about the problem: it was undoubtedly only one of many similar disputes among the upper strata of the Frankish population that he had to face almost daily in his capacity as king. Those involved in these disputes were too powerful in local society to be ignored. They could seldom be killed without good reason, since this would make all the other magnates furious. The king needed their support; in fact, the king's own power depended to a large extent upon the goodwill of the Frankish magnates. Childebert fully understood this. He appears to have wanted to escape from the problem as fast and as smoothly as possible by giving (and changing) verdicts in a way that would appease the party that was causing him and his court most legal trouble at the moment. Ingitrude and Berthegund both knew that if you shouted loud enough and were persistent, the king would give you what you desired, if only to get rid of you.

What is particularly important in the present context is that the two struggling magnates were women. We normally envisage the chief combatants of fights such as this one as wealthy male landowners, usually accompanied by small but efficient armed forces. The women are supposed to have remained at home, preparing meals and beds for the return of their dear warriors. Arguing and fighting over the right to property and land are normally regarded as *male* activities. In fact, it has often been taken for granted that early medieval Frankish women were not even permitted to inherit land, let alone fight about it. Berthegund's behaviour after Bertram's death clearly demonstrates that the genderbarrier with regard to property disputes is an illusion. If an ambitious and aggressive daughter, sister or mother saw an opportunity to strengthen her social position and acquire land, she obviously behaved just like a man would have done in a similar situation. Both Berthegund and Ingitrude recruited men (fighters, thieves, etc.) to do the dirty work while they themselves negotiated with the king. Despite her position as a religious, Ingitrude saw nothing wrong in having her ruffians break into Berthegund's house and steal everything they could lay their hands on. Her last recorded action – her oath that

Berthegund would never be allowed to offer prayers in the nunnery – sounds more like the curse of a dying warlord than the last pious words of an old nun.

The example of Ingitrude and Berthegund shows that the resources and strategies available to women at the very top of society (such as royal widows) were also available to other, usually less textually conspicuous, female members of the magnate class. True, it was more difficult for women than for men to get hold of lots of land, but it could definitely be done if the right male relatives died and if you were not afraid of fighting for what you perceived as your right. Soldiers and thieves could be hired, kings could be persuaded. As in the case of Queen and Saint Radegund, Ingitrude also managed to strengthen her position by founding a nunnery and running it as her own institution, appointing the abbesses herself and using the convent as a basis for her social and political influence. Furthermore, Berthegund's life *before* Bertram's death indicates that even married women could make a stand against their lords and husbands, provided they had access to the right allies and the right resources (economic, ecclesiastical, political, etc.). Berthegund had both Ingitrude's convent and Bertram's episcopal office, and this was enough to make her husband eventually give up all hope of ever getting her back.

Tetradia, Eulalius and their family troubles

The story of Tetradia and her husband Eulalius provides us with a good example of marital troubles among the members of the magnate stratum of Gaul. Eulalius was born into a wealthy family and became Count of Clermont; his wife Tetradia was of noble blood on her mother's side, but of humbler origin on her father's.[514]

As a young man, Eulalius is said to have behaved in an irresponsible fashion. His mother often complained about this, and Eulalius gradually grew to hate her. One day, his mother was found murdered in the oratory; she had obviously been killed while praying. No one knew who the culprit was, but her son was strongly suspected. Bishop Cautinus of Clermont (d. 571) was one of those who believed that Eulalius had had something to do with it, and as a result he excommunicated him. Eulalius complained that this was wrongly done, since he had not been given a proper hearing. Eventually, the bishop allowed him to take communion, leaving the judgment to God.[515]

After he had married Tetradia, Eulalius neglected her and spent most of his nights with his women-servants. Not only that, he also abused and maltreated her. He used to knock her about when he returned to her late at night. To make matters even worse, he stole Tetradia's jewellery and money to pay his own debts, which were entirely due to his wild excesses. As Tetradia lost all standing in her marital home, she became increasingly desperate. On one occasion, when Eulalius had gone off to see the king, a nephew of his called Virus, who had fallen in love with Tetradia, promised to rescue her from her husband's evil clutches and marry her himself, his own wife having died. However, this action would undoubtedly be dangerous, since Eulalius in his capacity as Count of Clermont was far more powerful than Virus. Afraid of what his uncle would do to them both, Virus sent Tetradia off to Duke Desiderius, a magnate even more powerful than Eulalius, still intending to marry her later on. Tetradia took with her all her husband's belongings, gold, silver and clothing. She also took the elder of her two sons, a boy called John (who later, apparently of his own free will, returned to Clermont).[516]

When he came back from his journey to the king, Eulalius was surprised; he clearly had not believed Virus and Tetradia capable of such an act, and he could not hope to win a fight against Desiderius. At first, he took no action at all. Then, suddenly, he sought out Virus in the Auvergne and killed him. When Desiderius (who had also lost his wife) was told that Virus was dead, he married Tetradia himself, making her even less accessible to Eulalius' revenge than before.[517]

Realising that Tetradia was gone for good, Eulalius instead abducted a nun from a convent in Lyons and made her his wife. Gregory further reports a rumour, according to which the other women with whom Eulalius was having relations grew jealous and used witchcraft to cast a spell over him. As a result, Eulalius' behaviour deteriorated from bad to worse. He assaulted and killed a man called Emerius, a cousin of the abducted nun. He also murdered Socratius, the stepbrother, and committed various other crimes.[518] As for Tetradia, Eulalius did plan to bring a law-suit against her in 585, but this only resulted in him becoming the subject of so much ridicule and humiliation that he decided to remain silent for the time being.[519] Instead, he entered into an alliance with Bishop Innocentius of Rodez, to whom he sent his son John to be made a priest. Innocentius helped Eulalius recover some of his lost property.[520]

As long as Desiderius was alive to protect her, Tetradia was out of Eulalius' reach. However, Desiderius made a serious political mistake when for a while he supported the pretender Gundovald in his struggles against King Gunthchramn. A few years after the rebellion, probably in 587, Desiderius grew afraid that Gunthchramn intended to do him harm. He left the town of Albi and crossed into the territory of Toulouse, taking with him Tetradia and all his property. Having divided all of his possessions between his wife and his sons, he raised an army and made preparations to march against the Visigoths. Shortly afterwards, he was killed in a battle near Carcassonne.[521]

Desiderius' death weakened Tetradia's position, and Count Eulalius did not hesitate to re-open the case. He brought a law-suit against her for restitution of the property that she had taken with her when she left him. In 590, a council of bishops and prominent laymen was convened on the borders of Clermont, the Gévaudan and the Rouergue to decide the issue once and for all. Eulalius pleaded his own case, while Tetradia was represented by a man called Agin. In the eyes of the tribunal, Tetradia was clearly the guilty party: *she* had left her husband, and *she* had stolen his property. The verdict was that Tetradia should repay fourfold all that she had taken, while the sons that she had borne to Desiderius were declared illegitimate. If Tetradia did as she was ordered, she would be allowed to return to Clermont and have free use of what she herself had inherited from her father. It would appear that Tetradia obeyed the decisions of the court.[522]

Analysing her history, it is clear that Tetradia realised her own limits. She knew that she needed the support of a strong man (Duke Desiderius), and she could not even defend herself at her own trial without a male representative (Agin). When leaving Clermont, she stole as much property as possible, since this was her only way to ensure a small degree of personal power and influence in the years to come. We must not forget that this theft is the main reason why we know anything at all about Tetradia. She and Eulalius were probably quite ordinary members of the magnate class, but her theft gave her control over resources that could be used to accumulate power. Count Eulalius needed those resources and was prepared to fight for them. If he had ignored the theft, Gregory of Tours would have had no reason to include the incident in his chronicle, and neither Eulalius nor Tetradia would have been remembered.

While it is true that Eulalius was a notoriously bad husband with numerous mistresses, and that he had committed heinous crimes such as murder and kidnapping, and a nun at that, he was nevertheless in a far stronger position than Tetradia. Without the protection of Desiderius, she would have lost her case immediately. Indeed, she would hardly have run away from Clermont in the first place without being able to count on Desiderius' help. When Desiderius was dead, however, the assembled court ruled in Eulalius' favour, and no-one appears to have found this strange. Gregory himself, who regarded Eulalius as a very wicked man, fails to display any sign of surprise.

The good, the bad and the holy

Several of the women mentioned in *Decem Libri Historiarum* were in one way or another connected to the ecclesiastical sphere of society. Some of them, of course, belonged to Biblical history and may be left out of the present analysis.[523] That certain women in late antique and early medieval Gaul were thought of in connection with religion does not, however, mean that they were regarded by Gregory as being particularly good, let alone prime candidates for sainthood. We have already met a couple of vastly different royal women, who ended up in convents for very different reasons and who behaved in very different ways with regard to the rules of the nunnery. Gregory's view of Saint Radegund is entirely different from his views of wild female rebels such as Chrodechild and Basina. The same is, not surprisingly, true of Gregory's view of his fellow priests. While some are described as saints, others appear as pure Barbarians not fit to live within the realms of Christendom. For instance, a certain priest in Le Mans is described as just as lusty and libidinous as some of the bad women in *Decem Libri Historiarum*, always keeping with him a woman in disguise so that he could have sexual intercourse with her as often as he liked (the woman was eventually burned alive by her angry relatives).[524]

Generally speaking, we can discern three different categories of religious women. Firstly, there are the good ones: morally correct wives and mothers, who obey the laws of God and of the priests and who will undoubtedly receive their just reward in the life hereafter. Secondly, we have the professionals who have gone to work (whether of their own free will or not) in a convent or a church, but whose actions sometimes leave a lot to be desired; they are not necessarily described as paragons of virtue. They may be rebellious like Chrodechild, ordinary like Leubovera or, in some cases, even quite evil. Thirdly, there are – of course – the saints themselves: pure, holy women destined for a life with Christ.

Let us begin with the first category. Some of the women belonging to this heterogeneous group are anonymous actors, merely mentioned in order to emphasise the holiness of a certain saint or the evil of someone at the opposite end of the moral spectrum. For instance, a certain unnamed woman recognised the spiritual ability of King Gunthchramn of Orléans, abilities that the modern reader of *Decem Libri Historiarum* seldom manages to identify even knowing that Gunthchramn actually did end up a royal saint. She cut a few threads from the king's cloak and steeped them in water, giving the infusion to her sick son to drink. The fever left him immediately.[525] As for women appearing in the text to help Gregory emphasise the wickedness of others, we have a good example in the story of the bad priest from Le Mans mentioned above. When he once tried to seduce the mother of one of his pupils, the woman turned out to be virtuous. She told her husband what the priest was up to, with the result that a band of outraged relatives almost killed the priest, and according to Gregory, they would surely have succeeded if Bishop Aetherius of Lisieux had not intervened to save his life.[526]

One of the first examples of good Christian women in *Decem Libri Historiarum* is the wife of the Roman commander Aetius, who frequently went to the churches of the apostles in Rome and prayed for the safe return of her husband.[527] Shortly afterwards, we encounter a mysterious woman, appearing in a veil, who is said to have played a significant role in the election of Rusticus as Bishop of Clermont;[528] we also meet the wife of Bishop Namatius of Clermont, who was personally responsible for the building of the church of Saint Stephen in a suburb of the city.[529]

As for events that occurred during Gregory's own life-time, one of the first good wives in *Decem Libri Historiarum* appears during the 530s. During the first of half of this decade, when Saint Quintianus was Bishop of Clermont, a local official called Lytigius is reported to have spent his days constantly plotting against the bishop. According to Gregory, Quintianus went so far as to demean himself at the man's feet, but even then Lytigius showed him no deference. One day, as he was making fun of the bishop to his wife, she proved that she had far more sense than he possessed: 'He [Quintianus] may be humbled to-day, but that will never do you any good'.[530] As in all such tales, related basically to demonstrate the power of Christianity in general and a certain saint in particular, she was right. Only three days later royal messengers arrived and had Lytigius bound and dragged off together with his wife and children. Nobody knows what happened to him – he was never seen again in Clermont.[531]

Another morally correct wife appears in Gregory's story of the terrible fire in Paris in 585. She accompanied her pious husband as he, trusting the miraculous power of Saint Martin, moved all his worldly goods inside the walls of an oratory dedicated to this saint. The flames that were consuming Paris came nearer and nearer, but they appeared to lose their heat as they struck the oratory walls. The townsfolk cried out to the couple to get them to escape while there was still time, but they refused. The woman stood firm at the window, through which the flames kept entering, for she was protected by her faith in Saint Martin. According to Gregory, this brave and pious couple saved a considerable part of the city by calling on Saint Martin to prevent the fire from spreading further in that particular direction.[532]

In his story of Saint Aredius, Gregory does not neglect to inform us about the saint's mother, Pelagia. Since Aredius was determined to devote all his time to fasting and praying, he asked his mother to take full charge of all household duties, the servants, the tilling of the fields and the culture of the vines, so that nothing should come between him and his prayer. Later on, when Aredius had built churches and founded a monastery, Pelagia provided food and clothing for all the monks, but, Gregory eagerly points out, she did not allow these heavy responsibilities to interrupt her own prayers to God ('her words rose up like fragrant incense, finding favour in God's sight').[533]

In the second category mentioned above, comprising a number of abbesses and nuns, it is sometimes difficult to discern Gregory's personal opinion. Thus, we are never really given a description of Agnes, the abbess chosen as nominal leader of Saint Radegund's convent in Poitiers.[534] Even more interesting is Gregory's attitude towards Agnes' successor, Leubovera, who played an important role during the violent times of 589–90. It is not clear whether Gregory criticises Leubovera or not. As a member of the episcopal tribunal in Poitiers (pp. 161–66), he did find her innocent, but his actual description of Leubovera and her actions in *Decem Libri Historiarum* makes one wonder whether he really approved of her. She is never praised; we get the impression that Gregory was not entirely satisfied with the way she had performed her duties at the convent. Other abbesses, however, were far worse – but Gregory never explicitly criticises them, although their very actions turn them into bad women in the eyes of the modern reader. A good example of this is an abbess in a convent at Arles, where King Gunthchramn ordered Theudechild to be placed after the death of King Charibert in 567. When Theudechild tried to escape (p. 100), the abbess caught her and had her beaten mercilessly. She condemned the former royal mistress to solitary confinement in a cell, where she remained for the rest of her life.[535] This is how a cruel prison governor is supposed to act towards the heroes in American B-movies, but is it also the way Gregory would have wanted a typical abbess to behave towards a poor woman whose property had been stolen by an avaricious monarch and who had then been sent to a nunnery against her will? We do not know.

One reason why women within the walls of convents were not automatically regarded as good women is, as has been remarked upon previously, that they were sometimes placed there against their will. To many women belonging to the magnate class in Gaul, the convent, while a paradise to others, was merely a prison, cutting them off from the world outside and from the men they wanted to marry. A good example of this is the story of the niece of Bishop Felix of Nantes (d. 582). A man called Pappolen was engaged to marry her, but the bishop strongly disapproved of the proposed union. To gain control of the girl before Felix could prevent their marriage, Pappolen abducted his fiancée from an oratory and took sanctuary with her in the church of Saint Albinus.

Bishop Felix was furious and decided to copy Pappolen's action: by a trick he managed to separate the girl from Pappolen and forced her to put on the habit of a religious. She was shut up in a nunnery at Bazas. A virtual prisoner, she secretly sent messages to Pappolen, asking him to rescue her and make her his. Pappolen did as he was asked: he organised her escape from the nunnery and married her with the king's formal approval.[536] In relating the story of the bishop's niece (whose name we are never told), Gregory refrains from judging her as good or bad. Escaping from a nunnery was certainly not good, but forcing her to live there can hardly be considered a good action either. Both actions were facts of life, and they do not appear to have surprised Gregory. Bishop Felix did what many others did, and his niece behaved as any normal girl would do under the circumstances.

Several women connected with the ecclesiastical sphere of society appear to have kept with them a number of latent sins that could emerge at any given moment. For instance, bishops who were married (but who were supposed to refrain from having sexual intercourse with their wives) were always in danger of being lured into bed by their women, as happened to Bishop Urbicus of Clermont. In the beginning, his wife lived as a religious, apart from her husband, but she was eventually filled with Satan's malice. In the words of Gregory, the Devil 'inflamed her with desire for her husband and turned her into a second Eve' (*quam in concupiscentiam viri succedens, novam Evam effecit*). After much shouting, she did manage to seduce her husband, but he soon recovered his wits and went off to a monastery to do penance.[537] Bishop Sidonius Apollinaris (also of Clermont) does not appear to have suffered from this particular kind of temptation, but his wife did object to the way he removed silver vessels from their home to give them to the poor. To stop her from grumbling at him, he had to buy the vessels back.[538]

Turning to the third category, that of the holy women, we find that most of them are mentioned merely *en passant*, without thorough literary treatment, such as Saint Thecla (originally Melania),[539] Saint Genovefa[540] and Saint Caesaria.[541] Sometimes, Gregory devotes a considerable amount of text to saintly women, as in the case of the chaste wife of a wealthy man in Clermont called Injuriosus,[542] a Catholic martyr in the Arian kingdom of the Vandals,[543] and certain women mentioned in relation to the nunnery of the Holy Cross and the life of Saint Radegund (p. 92), but these cases are exceptional. The reason for Gregory's apparent neglect is undoubtedly that he considered *Decem Libri Historiarum* to be mainly a chronicle of historical events. He wrote other books too, in which the saints dominate completely.

Women influenced by Satan

Men and women alike regularly appear in *Decem Libri Historiarum* as vessels for unclean spirits, demons who have established themselves within their minds in order to cause as much harm as possible to Christendom. For instance, Gregory tells us how a bishop, after having prayed for the well-being of Bishop Theodore of Marseilles, became the victim of a verbal attack by a woman who was possessed of an evil spirit ('You wicked man, grown old in sinfulness, you who petition the Lord for our enemy Theodore, surely you realise that not one day passes without our begging that this man who unceasingly fans the flames which consume us should be exiled from Gaul...').[544] Another woman, who freely admitted that she was possessed by three devils, was ritually exorcised by Saint Hospicius. The same saint also cured a girl, harassed by an unclean spirit, by blessing her.[545] In his relation of the miracles of Saint Aredius, Gregory tells us that the saint cured two women during his own funeral, both of them possessed by evil spirits (immediately after this, the dead saint is also supposed to have cured a dumb woman, who received the gift of speech after kissing his grave).[546] No-one was safe from the attacks of demons: even the daughter of a Roman emperor in Trier fell victim to an unclean spirit.[547]

Gregory relates how Queen Fredegund used suspicions of female black magic to incriminate her stepson Clovis in or before 584. A woman is supposed to have approached her and said that Clovis had fallen in love with the daughter of one of Fredegund's women-servants. According to his accuser, Clovis had managed to encompass the death of Fredegund's sons through the mother's magic arts. As is related elsewhere (p. 109), Fredegund, who was in a state of nervous depression at the time, had the girl severely maltreated and the mother subjected to torture, until she was forced to admit that the charges against her were true. Clovis was killed (p. 109). In the end, even the woman who had given evidence against him was burnt alive. As she was dragged off to the stake, she admitted that she had lied, but this did not save her from the flames.[548]

In 585, Fredegund appears to have behaved much better with regard to another woman, who was believed to possess the magic gift of prophecy. The woman in question was originally a slave, but she gained so much profit for her masters by her prowess in divination that she won their favour and received her freedom. Her speciality was to intervene after robberies, to tell the victim where the thief had fled and to whom he had handed over his gains. She became extremely wealthy, and she would walk about so loaded with jewellery that she was looked upon by the common people as a sort of goddess. Eventually, Bishop Ageric of Verdun had her arrested. During the interrogation, Ageric realised that she was possessed by an unclean spirit which had the gift of prophecy. The solution, of course, was exorcism. Ageric pronounced the appropriate prayers and anointed her forehead with holy oil. Suddenly, the devil within her cried out and revealed his identity. He proved, however, too strong for the bishop, who was unable to force him out of the woman. She was allowed to leave and, realising that she could no longer live in the neighbourhood, made her way to Queen Fredegund and sought refuge with her.[549]

Prophetic ability appears to have been regarded by Gregory as one of the most usual ways in which Satan worked his mischief among men and women. Prophets possessed by demons appear on several occasions in *Decem Libri Historiarum*. In 577, Gunthchramn Boso sent one of his servants to a certain woman who was supposed to have the power of prophecy. He had known her for more than ten years, and he maintained that she had revealed to him before the event the very year, day and hour when King Charibert would die in 567. This time, when asked about the future, the woman told him that King Chilperic would die within the year, that his son Merovech would become king and that Gunthchramn Boso would lead Merovech's armies during the next five years. In the sixth year, he would be appointed to a bishopric. When Gunthchramn Boso heard this, he became very proud, imagining himself the future Bishop of Tours. He hurried off to Gregory to tell him the news, but Gregory only laughed at him and remarked that 'one should put no faith in the Devil's promises' (*credi non debent quae diabolum repromittit*).[550]

Another woman (called 'Mary', a name that Gregory appears to have regarded as an alias) appears in the last book of *Decem Libri Historiarum* as a follower and assistant of a bogus Christ from Bourges, a man gone insane and prompted by the Devil to claim that he was Christ and to spend his days prophesying the future. 'Mary' (whom he pretended was his sister) followed him from one place to another. After the man had eventually been killed, 'Mary' was submitted to torture, and she was forced to reveal all the man's hallucinations and tricks. Still, there were those who continued to believe that he had been Christ and that Mary had a share in his divinity.[551]

Despite these cases, there can be no doubt that Gregory of Tours regarded prophetic ability as such as quite real. True, women who proclaimed that they knew what was going to happen could sometimes be charlatans, but some of them had to be treated carefully. Their messages, at least, should not be ignored. In 585, a woman in Paris announced to the townsfolk that all of Paris was in immediate danger of being destroyed by a conflagration. Everybody should leave the city as quickly as possible, or risk being burned to death. The Parisians laughed at her, but she gave substance to her prophecy by referring to a vision: 'I saw in a vision a man coming out of Saint Vincent's church [later Saint-Germain-des-Près], radiant with light, holding a wax candle in his hand and setting fire to the merchants' houses one after another.'[552] As it turned out, her vision proved true: three days later, as twilight was falling, a house caught fire. The flames spread to other houses with the help of the wind, and Paris was reduced to ashes.[553]

In some cases, it is not clear whether Gregory believed that the women in question behaved as they did because of the direct influence of demons. He may in fact have regarded their actions as fully to be expected from certain kinds of women. Some of them, just like some of their men, were simply bad. There were Biblical precedents, some of which are actually mentioned in texts quoted by Gregory, such as that of Sapphira.[554] Many of the powerful queens and princesses would fall within this category, such as Fredegund and Goiswinth. However, we also find less important individuals, such as the nuns who accompanied Chrodechild and Basina in their revolt against the Convent of the

Holy Cross in Poitiers. One of these followers is given particular treatment by Gregory. She is described as 'a certain recluse' (*reclusa quaedam*) who lived in the nunnery but often found it impossible to coexist with the abbess. At a time when Saint Radegund was still alive, she had herself lowered from the wall and fled to Saint Hilary's church, accusing the abbess (probably Agnes) of many transgressions, all of which Gregory regarded as false. Later on she had herself pulled up into the nunnery again. She asked permission to shut herself up in a secret cell, saying that she felt a need for doing penance in isolation. However, when the revolt of Chrodechild and Basina began, she broke down the door of her cell in the middle of the night, escaped from the convent and found her way to the rebels.[555]

Summary

We have now reached the end of the analysis of the women in *Decem Libri Historiarum*. It is time to summarise the results, particularly with regard to what they tell us about female resources and strategies. I present the results mainly from the point of view of royal Merovingian women, since these dominate the tales transmitted to us by Gregory of Tours. The resources of all the others – mainly various wives of Frankish magnates – are summarised later, as is the personal view of Gregory of Tours concerning women that he perceived as generally bad.

Relatives (fathers, brothers, etc). Undoubtedly the most important asset for a woman within the royal and magnate strata of Merovingian Gaul was the links that they enjoyed to other people, particularly to members of the opposite sex. Initially, these women were supported (and politically exploited) by their fathers and their relatives, or by their mothers and their relatives, if the mother in question happened to be a powerful royal widow, such as Brunhild. This link to powerful parents and relatives appears to have been of primary importance to foreigners such as Wisigarda, Galswinth and Brunhild, who entered Gaul as outsiders but who could always count on their fathers' families for support. Of course, in their cases, their links to their fathers were often synonymous with political alliances, a fact that served to make them even more important than would otherwise have been the case. If Theudebert had chosen to neglect Wisigarda, his attempts to dominate certain areas east of the Rhine might have been jeopardised.

The same structure that provided for the political power of foreign princesses in Gaul also provided for the well-being of Frankish princesses sent abroad to marry foreign kings and princes. The Merovingians, male as well as female, were quick to react if news reached them that their own girls were in trouble. True, their reactions may sometimes have been little more than thinly disguised wars of aggression (as in the case of Gunthchramn's campaigns against Visigothic Septimania), but they did react. They were sometimes powerless to intervene (poor Ingund did die in Carthage, despite the efforts of the Merovingians), but they always seem to have tried.

The influence derived from the existence of relatives, especially fathers, was, however, far from a permanent feature of the lives of Frankish royal women. This is revealed in some of Gregory's stories of Merovingian daughters – proud girls who despised their often less aristocratic mothers and took their own influence for granted. If their fathers died, they immediately risked losing a considerable amount of their importance. They often had severe problems adapting to their new situations, as is demonstrated by their promiscuity, their attempts to escape from nunneries and their constant conflicts with persons more powerful than they. Fredegund eventually tried to kill Rigunth just to stop her from behaving the way she did. Childebert and Gunthchramn had to use the army to pacify Chrodechild and Basina, who refused to obey an ecclesiastical authority that was not Merovingian (they had obeyed Radegund; they would not obey Leubovera). Still, their inherited status as Merovingians made these princesses far more powerful than ordinary magnate women. Despite her many sins and acts of violence, Chrodechild ended up with an estate of her own, living a life that undoubtedly suited her far better than her previous life at the Convent of the Holy Cross in Poitiers.

Husbands. Having entered the royal court, the queens immediately grew heavily dependent on their husbands. This structural feature of the political life in sixth-century Gaul only affected the royal women. No king had to please his queen the way a queen always had to please her husband.

For a Frankish queen, the king's favour was essential. If the king found himself a new wife or a new mistress, the queen was in danger, as were her children. This structural fact resulted in considerable differences between the various Frankish courts. Some kings appear to have been worse than the rest, such as Chlothar I and Charibert I, who always recruited new lovers to their residences. For such a king's wife it must have been very difficult to construct a permanent basis of power at the court itself, although they did try, as is clear from the story of Marcovefa and her client Leudast. Their links to the king were too weak. The insecurity bred by this kind of competition sometimes resulted in bloodshed and even murder, as is evident from what Gregory tells us of Deuteria's daughter and of Queen Galswinth. However, it was certainly possible for the kings' women to use their own new-found importance in order to build power bases outside the court. For Charibert's women, this proved impossible because of the king's premature death, but one of Chlothar's women, Saint Radegund, managed extremely well.

Despite the insecurity of being a king's wife, the position was definitely one of power. The queen had access to the king and to his treasure. She had more influence over royal decisions such as appointments to important posts than most people in the kingdom could ever hope to achieve. If a conspiracy of magnates wanted to control the king, the queen was always a serious obstacle that had to be cleared. A good example of this fact is the way a conspiracy of Austrasian magnates plotted to get rid of Faileuba and replace her with someone who would ensure their own political ascendancy. Faileuba (and Brunhild) proved too strong, and the conspiracy failed.

Children. In the long run, the most important male assets of Frankish royal women were their sons. As long as they had influence over their upbringing, and as long as they remained in contact with them, they would remain powerful. For instance, Faileuba was not only Childebert II's consort, she was also a royal mother. Even if her enemies within the Austrasian aristocracy had managed to have her replaced by another queen, she would still have been extremely dangerous to their faction in her capacity as mother. It is clear that the conspiracy against Faileuba aimed at removing her from the country entirely, not merely deposing her. Were she allowed to remain at court, or even in Austrasia, she would still be in a position to influence present and, above all, future politics by way of her son.

The importance of children is especially evident if the queens outlived their husbands, as was often the case. The career of Fredegund is a perfect example of this. During her first period of power (until the autumn of 584), she based her influence on her husband Chilperic. During her second period of power she shifted the basis from her now dead husband to her infant son Chlothar II. Without Chlothar, her career might easily have been brought to an abrupt end at the death of Chilperic. Brunhild's career is similar: until 575, she based her influence on King Sigibert. During her second period of power, the basis of her influence shifted to her son Childebert. Despite their difficulties, both Fredegund and Brunhild were lucky, for they had the best possible assets at the most critical moment of their political lives. Other queens were less fortunate.

If their royal husbands died and left them without male children, the queens could easily land in trouble. Thus, Chlothar I easily removed Childebert's widow, Queen Ultrogotha, from her late husband's realm in 558. She had no sons who could help her through the men who owed them allegiance in her capacity as a royal widow. Given time, she would probably have been able to use her own wealth to strengthen her position, but Chlothar, a veteran of Frankish politics, was not the kind of king to allow this. Without husband and sons, Ultrogotha was doomed.

Sometimes, the mere existence of male children was not sufficient to guarantee the queen a permanently secure position at court. Since this kind of asset was, literally speaking, of a personal nature (being based on people, not on land or money), the queen/mother could easily lose her influence if the king/father paid little respect to the ties between sons and mothers. While some kings might have wanted to have the mother around for the benefit of their children, other kings might not have cared about what happened to the queen once she had become too old to be of interest from a sexual point of view. All the Frankish kings, like their queens, were individuals who behaved differently towards each other. The importance of personal attitudes and individuality made the political game at court impossible to determine; the very structure created an atmosphere of insecurity that could have serious consequences. Deuteria, Theudebert I's wife, appears to have been very aware of this, but despite her frantic attempts to safeguard her position and the fact that she was the mother of Theudebald, she failed.

A key strategy for several royal women was the persecution (whether by slander or murder) of the children, and especially the sons of their competitors. Since a normal Frankish king appears to have had a number of women who could potentially provide him with male heirs, any queen who tried to plan her future had to make sure that none of the others' sons became too powerful. The situation at the court of King Gunthchramn was typical: everybody appears to have instinctively believed that Marcatrude had poisoned her stepson Gundobad.

The best example of female competition involving children is, however, the dangerous situation at the court of Chilperic I. Audovera's career as the king's wife was terminated rather early, so in this respect she posed no threat to either Galswinth or Fredegund, but her sons proved to be serious obstacles to Fredegund. To ensure that she was not eventually killed by one of them herself (which could ultimately have brought Audovera back to power, especially if Chilperic was dead by then), Fredegund had to eliminate them completely from the political scene. In the end, Audovera's branch of the royal family of Soissons was almost annihilated. It is hard to think that Fredegund encompassed this out of personal hatred for Audovera; in all probability, she did it to safeguard herself and her sons. She aimed at creating the best possible chances for survival.

Property. Property was, or rather could become, of primary importance to everybody, men as well as women. In itself, property had little value as a political tool, but it could easily be used to construct networks of clients. With the help of land and money, you could buy friends to support you, warriors to fight for you and assassins to kill for you. This fact is clearly demonstrated in the reaction to Galswinth's increasingly powerful position at the court of Soissons. Galswinth appears to have been far richer than any other Frankish queen mentioned in *Decem Libri Historiarum*. No-one could afford to ignore her, least of all her husband Chilperic and her rival Fredegund. Given time, she could have recruited entire armies. The only way to neutralise the threat posed by Galswinth was to kill her, which they did.

Of course, all of the royal and magnate women of Merovingian Gaul had property. If they lost their wealth, they would no longer have been interesting to Gregory of Tours unless, of course, they either embarked on an ecclesiastical career and became saints or responded to their fall from grace by becoming dangerous criminals. Merovingian princesses were automatically provided with a lot of land, servants and sometimes even cities. What is interesting from our point of view is the way they used their landed assets and whether they tried to gain even more. That they were aware of the possibilities inherent in landholding is evident. Chrodechild lost no time confiscating the lands of the nunnery of the Holy Cross when she established herself as a woman of power in Poitiers during the revolt of 589.

Clients and allies. This asset, too, is neutral as far as gender is concerned. The power of the Frankish kings was ultimately based on their ability to get their warriors to fight for them. The same is true of the Frankish queens, even very early ones. For instance, Chlothild, widow of Clovis I, possibly made use of the fact that for a time she controlled the upbringing of her grandsons (the sons of Chlodomer), but her real strength appears to have been derived from the agents and clients she managed to recruit herself, such as the bishops of Tours.

Although Gregory of Tours does not appear to have been specifically interested in providing information concerning the allies of royal women, he often happens to mention them anyway, since they are essential to some of his stories. Thus, we know that, despite her short period as queen, Wisigarda managed to create what appears to be some kind of network of allies in Austrasia (including a man called Asteriolus). The same appears to have been true of other short-lived queens, such as Marcovefa. Gregory's description of Leudast's behaviour at the royal court of the kingdom of Paris makes it clear that Leudast was Queen Marcovefa's client, not King Charibert's. After the queen's death, Leudast stood to lose everything he had achieved and had to bribe the king to be allowed to retain his post.

Naturally, the webs of influence consisting of clients and allies tended to become increasingly impressive as the queens managed to hold on to their positions and use their property and their access to the king to recruit even more supporters. This made it possible for royal widows such as Brunhild and Fredegund to construct networks of clients and allies all over Gaul. In the long run, this shaping of networks was essential to the survival of the royal widows as persons of power. Without the right allies, they could easily lose their influence over (and even their physical access to) their sons. If that happened, their careers were over, and they risked being killed by their rivals, who did not want them to get a second chance – thus, Audovera appears to have been killed *after* having lost her last allies.

Ecclesiastical resources. Several women were intimately associated with the church, whether as nuns, abbesses, founders of nunneries or simply as wealthy benefactors. Their ties to ecclesiastical institutions were established and strengthened by donations, appointments of bishops and the creation of myths, such as Chlothild's legendary persuasion of Clovis in his acceptance of Christianity.

Those who were most successful in their attempts to gain strength through the church eventually came to be regarded as holy women. Two sixth-century Merovingian queens, Chlothild and Radegund, both ended up as saints. True, it is hard to evaluate their exercise of power in their capacity as retired queens and royal widows in churches, nunneries and other residences, but it is abundantly clear that their association with the church strengthened their position within the political structure of Gaul. The royal nunneries, especially Radegund's Convent of the Holy Cross in Poitiers, developed into ideological assets that could be effectively combined with personal charisma and personal links to members of the Merovingian royal house. The kings might ignore a former royal mistress looking for a new king to seduce (as in the case of Gunthchramn and Theudechild), but they could not afford to neglect a mighty abbess. The collection of relics and the spread of legends of miracles and visions associated with the nunnery undoubtedly served to make Radegund's position even stronger than it already was.

The resources of magnate women. Although considerably less powerful than the royal women and far less prominent in *Decem Libri Historiarum*, the women belonging to the magnate class of Merovingian Gaul appear to have closely resembled the queens and princesses. Their resources were similar to those of the royal women, but at a lower level. They were not quite as rich; their clients are more difficult to discover in Gregory's text. Like the Merovingian women, they needed the help of male allies (fathers, husbands, brothers, sons, etc.) as well as a landed power base to serve as a platform for their ambition. Like the Merovingian women, they risked being shut up in a convent if their fathers or guardians wanted to get rid of them. Without male allies, they usually lost their struggles against male enemies, a fact that automatically resulted in loss of property. Tetradia's case is typical. Without the help of a husband, she quickly lost the fight against Eulalius and was forced to yield up a lot of property. Understanding the weakness of their situation, the widows of magnates often tried to marry another magnate as soon as possible. This would, in fact, often have been relatively easy, since wealthy widows were far from unwelcome in the homes of greedy aristocrats without wives of their own.[556]

Although weaker than queens and princesses and often in danger of losing their power and their wealth, the magnate women still appear to have been able to exert a considerable amount of influence. Basically, their strategies were the same as those of the Merovingians. They founded convents or donated property to various ecclesiastical instutions. They helped their men in planning common strategies. They could, if they had to, order their servants and warriors to attack their enemies. Just as the social position of Radegund was strengthened by her holy retirement at Poitiers, Ingitrude was definitely stronger in her capacity as leader of her nunnery in Tours than she would have been as the wife of a Frankish magnate. She combined the ideological resources activated by her rule of the convent with her personal charisma, and probably with her family ties to the royal house. Furthermore, Berthegund's actions illustrate that a female magnate could behave in a fashion similar to that of a male magnate, provided that her male relatives were dead or in no position to argue about key matters such as inheritance. Both Ingitrude and Berthegund hired ruffians to perform the dirtiest part of their jobs (plunder, theft, etc.), while they themselves negotiated with the king. When she fought her husband, Berthegund proved very capable in activating her alliances with powerful relatives, such as her brother and her mother.

The attitude of Gregory of Tours. As we have seen, Gregory does not display any specific tendency to paint the women of his chronicle as either good or bad. Several of them are much too complex to be categorised in this fashion. The number of purely good women differs little from the number of purely bad. Not surprisingly – Gregory was, after all, a pious medieval bishop who was writing for a Christian audience – the good ones are usually associated with God and the saints, while the bad ones are often associated with demons and Satan. Several bad women behave as such because they are possessed by demons, while the good women walk a path that might, God willing, lead to sainthood. They see visions, they long for an ascetic life in complete chastity or they do whatever they can to get their husbands to act like true Christians.

However, one particular group of women emerges as worse than the rest: the foreign queens such as Amalaberg, Amalasuntha and Goiswinth. With hardly any exceptions, these were, according to Gregory, evil individuals. They are described as being bloodthirsty and eager for more power than they already have (i.e., they want their husbands to conquer more territory). They kill their stepsons and (if they are Arians, which they often are) persecute the Catholic population of their countries. In other words, they act as symbols for all that Gregory disapproved of in powerful women in general. Gregory, of course, had little, if any, information on what kind of action queens such as Amalasuntha really undertook during their political careers, but he used them as literary creations to show what, according to him, could easily happen in Gaul if the Frankish queens began to behave in a way that Satan would have wanted them to. They serve as examples of bad queens *in extremis*, promiscuous witches intent upon poisoning their enemies and killing as many stepsons as possible (that is, behaving like Fredegund, Gregory's chief personal enemy among the queens of his own day). Reading between the lines, we also encounter a few, but important, hints that demonstrate a considerable degree of political influence among some of the foreign queens and empresses. Goiswinth appears to have enjoyed a position in Visigothic Spain similar to that enjoyed by Fredegund and Brunhild in Merovingian Gaul.

Returning to the women of Gaul itself, we may take a closer look at exactly how Gregory depicts the bad ones. It is clear that some sins appear more often than others and may thus be said to constitute parts of Gregory's stereotypical image of bad women in general. For instance, Magnatrude (the wife of Bishop Badegisil of Le Mans) is described as a malicious and cruel person who delights in committing the most detestable crimes and persuades her husband to follow her example.

She persuades *him*, not the other way around. When indulging in sadistic crimes herself, Magnatrude is drawn to features of the human body associated with sexual activities, such as the cutting off of a man's penis and burning 'the most secret parts' of women's bodies. Moving to Queen Deuteria, we find that her worst crime, the killing of her daughter, was prompted by the fear that her husband would soon find the daughter more sexually interesting than he found Deuteria herself. To the reader, these women appear to have been virtually obsessed with sex. The urge to have intercourse could turn even pious and virtuous women into sex-hungry monsters, as is said to have happened to the wife of Bishop Urbicus of Clermont.

When evil women, such as Deuteria and Fredegund, decide to kill somebody, they usually get someone else to carry out the murder itself. They employ assassins with daggers or use some more covert method. For instance, Marcatrude is supposed to have used poison against her stepson Gundobad – poison in particular appears to have been perceived as an excellent way to get rid of somebody without having to go to the trouble of hiring mercenaries and planning a violent ambush. Fredegund, the most active of all the female villains that we meet in Gregory's chronicle, is said to have dispatched several assassins at the same time with orders to kill her enemies. The best (or rather the worst) example of all the murderous activities of Merovingian women is, however, the last wish of the evil Queen Austrechild, who asked King Gunthchramn to kill the doctors who had failed to save her life. Gunthchramn, himself eventually venerated as a saint, did as he was asked.

Generally speaking, the bad women of *Decem Libri Historiarum* (not counting those possessed by demons) are regularly associated with three common vices: they are obsessed with sex, they like to kill their enemies by using agents, and they are indirectly guilty of various sins by talking their men into committing them. Why is this so? Why does Gregory associate women that he regards as sinful with sexuality, incitement to murder and bad advice? We will return to the problem at the conclusion of the book, but note that Gregory's attitude can hardly be interpreted as simply the result of the development of a set of stereotypical misogynist images within the early medieval clergy. Gregory's attitude was rooted in sixth-century society, not only in the ideas that came to him through education and work but also in his experience of everyday politics. Gregory knew many of the protagonists of *Decem Libri Historiarum* personally. He had first-hand experience of Queen Fredegund (whom he had reason to fear) and Queen Brunhild (whom he had reason to thank). In fact, Gregory may be interpreted as one of many members of Brunhild's political network. Had he simply wanted to paint a picture of contemporary sinful women, he could easily have come up with a number of Biblical sins, but he did not. For some reason, he found it natural to assume that a powerful woman acted through her husband by giving him advice, whether good or bad, and that she had to search for others such as assassins and male members of her personal political networks to fight her battles for her. These may not have been her only sins, but they were certainly her most conspicuous ones from the point of view of Frankish politics. The same is true of sexuality: a queen who could not keep her husband permanently seduced risked losing her status and, in some cases, her life and the lives of her children.

Conclusion. Even the most powerful royal women in *Decem Libri Historiarum*, Fredegund and Brunhild, were considerably weaker than their male counterparts. In their capacities as reigning royal widows after the death of Chilperic and Sigibert, Fredegund and Brunhild were forced to be far more careful than their late husbands had ever been. They had to use their gender-neutral resources such as property more efficiently than a king would have done. Thereby, the basic rules (or, one might say, the lack of rules) in the Frankish political game become more accentuated in the eyes of the modern reader.

By far the most important rule of early medieval political culture (as opposed to modern, more bureaucratic and institutionalised forms of politics) is the importance of the individual. Today, if a premier is assassinated in a normal Western country, it is a personal disaster but not a national one. A new premier steps in, and life goes on as usual. If, however, a king was assassinated in the sixth century, chaos erupted. Power was up for grabs; whoever managed to get hold of the royal treasury would be far stronger than all his competitors. The bishops in Gaul could count on the fact that their churches might soon be filled with refugee queens and magnates whose political base had suddenly disappeared. Thus the most important political power bases were of a personal nature: ties of family, friendship, love, patronage and honour. Land and wealth in whatever form were only effective means of influence as far as the owner managed to turn them into human assets by rewarding followers with lands, distributing the plunder after a successful war, confiscating property from rebels and giving it to someone else.

This rule affected everybody. Seen from a gender perspective, however, it is clear that it affected women in a somewhat different way than it affected men. Queens and kings did not respond to the need to gather human resources in the same fashion. While the political structure demanded a certain aggressive personality if one were to succeed, the nature of the aggressiveness varied considerably with gender, age and social position. Queens needed a different kind of charisma than kings, since they used different social and political arenas. An obvious example is sexuality. This factor does not appear to have been important within male political culture: a normal Frankish king could sleep with any servant-girl he wanted, regardless of what his wife or the bishop thought about it. In fact, the more women a king slept with, the greater his chances of getting male heirs. For a queen, however, sexuality was of immense importance, especially if the queen in question was busy climbing the social ladder by way of the king's bedchamber (as Fredegund did). When faced with a political crisis, royal women employed their charismatic assets of sexuality, beauty, and charm to a degree that their male counterparts never had to do. This does not mean that the lives of the queens were calmer and less violent than those of the kings; it simply meant that they fought their battles on different fields and with different weapons.

The varying degrees of influence exerted by widowed queens were, at least partly, related to their own strictly personal natures. For instance, it would appear that Fredegund had more charm and sexual charisma than Brunhild. Fredegund was good at persuading people, using people and getting potential enemies to give her a helping hand when she really needed it (such as King Gunthchramn, who later appears to have regretted that he helped her after Chilperic's death). Brunhild certainly lacked some of Fredegund's talents: she was obviously in a worse position after Sigibert's death than Fredegund was after Chilperic's. As a consequence, Brunhild had to compensate by working harder than Fredegund in her subsequent attempts to gather political allies. Despite her eventual success, she never managed to dominate the entire court of young Childebert. Her personal resources were not yet strong enough to defeat all her opponents among the Austrasian magnates.

As far as female political culture is concerned, ties to male allies (relatives, husbands and sons) can hardly be overstressed and overvalued. The difference between a royal or a magnate woman with powerful male helpers and a woman who was standing all on her own was considerable. The chief ways to counteract a lack of male relatives consisted of (1) the establishment of close ties to the church and (2) the construction of a network of male allies (secular as well as ecclesiastical), both of which were used by many of the Frankish queens that we read about in *Decem Libri Historiarum*. Or rather, they tried to use them. Recruiting allies was difficult and expensive, as was the foundation of a convent. Radegund's ecclesiastical strategy was a life-time commitment, and it could hardly have worked unless Radegund herself had been a very pious woman.

To be successful in their construction of a personal network, the Frankish queens needed both a political platform (such as a husband or a son) and wealth. They had to begin early, when their husbands were still alive and when various local nobles were attracted to the queens in the usually quite correct belief that access to the queen was almost as good as access to the king and the various royal appointments and grants. The building of networks created tensions in local society, for instance if a queen wanted to present her own candidate to a bishopric that another local magnate had already decided was his. We know that Brunhild's attempts to construct a network of aristocratic allies in Austrasia met with significant problems, since the other magnates (such as Ursio and Berthefried) realised what was going on and responded by attacking her supporters (including Duke Lupus of Champagne).

The importance of sons, the male royal heirs, should be repeatedly emphasised. The archetypal evil stepmothers of the early Middle Ages usually regarded male sons of other queens as prime targets for the poisoned daggers of their hired assassins. While certainly evil from a moral point of view, these assassination attempts made perfect sense as elements in the struggle for political survival. Fredegund felt that she had to move against Brunhild before Brunhild moved against her or, rather, against her son Chlothar, on whose life she based her very existence as a woman of power. The royal heir was not only a possible – if by no means a certain – ticket to political survival, he was also (when he had grown up and assumed the throne) the most powerful political ally that any royal widow could ever hope to get. The reason for this, as is clearly demonstrated in the case of Brunhild and Childebert versus the Austrasian magnates, is that the royal mother and the royal son usually had the same enemies. The magnates who threatened the position of the mother (or the wife, who in Childebert's case was Faileuba) also threatened the position of the king himself, since they wanted to control him and use him for their own purposes. While fathers and sons could easily end up as mortal enemies, as did Chlothar I and Chramn, mothers and sons were in most cases natural allies.

The women of Fredegar

After Gregory of Tours, Frankish history becomes considerably more difficult to study. The most important work for the period following immediately after Gregory's death is commonly known as the chronicle of Fredegar. Actually, the historian known by the name Fredegar, or rather 'Fredegarius', never existed. The name was given to an anonymous seventh-century writer, probably working in Burgundy, several centuries after his death. In fact, it would appear that the name was introduced as late as in the 1570s.

In any comparison between 'Fredegarius' and Gregory of Tours the former is bound to come off worse. Fredegar lacks Gregory's verbal ability, superb use of language and literary form that makes the latter as readable today as in the age of the Merovingians. Furthermore, Fredegar is more closely bound by the annalistic arrangement of the sources at his disposal. He jumps from one scene of action to another, devotes much energy to some years but ignores others completely. He is often difficult to understand; his ability to compose a coherent narrative is far worse than Gregory's. Nevertheless, Fredegar's chronicle is a vital link in Frankish history, and anyone interested in seventh-century history has to face his text sooner or later.[557]

I use only the fourth book of Fredegar's chronicle for the same reason that J.M. Wallace-Hadrill refrained from including the first three in his edition of 1960. Books I, II and III are, with a few exceptions, taken directly from other sources, whereas Book IV largely comprises an original chronicle covering the last decades of the sixth and most of the first half of the seventh centuries, until the year 642. I have also made use of the 'Continuations of Fredegar', which were compiled in the eighth century, chronicling events from where Fredegar stopped until the advent of Charlemagne (642–768). The first part of the Continuations, covering the years 642–721, was actually the result of a rewriting of the Neustrian chronicle *Liber Historiae*

Francorum (analysed on pp. 241–43) but the rest of the work is, as far as is known, original.

As in all the other works analysed in this book, many of the women mentioned in Fredegar's chronicle are simply names; they appear in the form of short entries that are difficult to place within a large interpretative framework. Some of them only appear in the text because Fredegar mentions their men. For instance, Sidonia, the widow of the warlord Mummolus, is only mentioned because her husband was killed and she was sent to King Gunthchramn as a prisoner together with Mummolus' treasure.[558] In other cases, the information is hardly relevant to our present purpose. For instance, Fredegar, just like Paul the Deacon, devotes much time to the story of the Persian empress Caesara who wanted to become a Christian. The entry looks exotic and may hint at the importance of queens, their alleged piety and their diplomatic roles in the east, but stories such as these can hardly be effectively used in an attempt to solve the riddles of Western European political culture.[559] The same is true of Fredegar's account of the twelve Wendish wives of Samo, the leader of the Central European confederation that is often regarded as the first Slavic kingdom.[560] Samo's wives may have come from twelve different tribes, and the marriages may have been a way to keep the confederation (which fell to pieces after Samo's death) together. However, interesting though this information is per se, it tells us nothing about the structure of politics in the west.

Another problem with Fredegar's women is that they are almost always intimately connected with the Merovingian royal house itself. While Gregory of Tours provides us with several descriptions of the lives of non-royal (although usually rather wealthy) women, the world of Fredegar is a world of kings, queens and mayors of the palace. Since the first half of the seventh century is often considered to be a crucial phase in the development of aristocratic self-confidence in Gaul, this lack of interest in the history of magnate women is irritating, to say the least. That something important is missing is instantly revealed if we turn our attention to the rich hagiographical material for the seventh century (pp. 286–321).

The closest we get to a description of the condition of women within the non-royal magnate stratum in Fredegar's chronicle are the events outlined in chapter 54, probably referring to the year 626. These problems began when Warnachar, mayor of the palace of Burgundy, died. His son Godinus immediately married his own stepmother Bertha. When King Chlothar II heard of this, he grew furious. Chlothar ordered Duke Arnebert, himself married to a sister of Godinus, to raise a force and kill him. Godinus and Bertha fled to the realm of Chlothar's son, King Dagobert I of Austrasia, but to be on the safe side they also sought sanctuary in the church of Saint-Epvre on the outskirts of Toul. Dagobert petitioned his father to pardon Godinus, and Chlothar finally agreed to spare his life on condition that Godinus gave up Bertha, whom he had married contrary to canon law. Godinus did as he was asked and returned to Burgundy. Bertha, however, began to act in a way that makes one wonder what on earth Godinus had done to her during their exile. Instead of going home, she went straight to King Chlothar and informed him that if Godinus ever appeared in front of Chlothar in the future, it would be with the intention of killing him. Chlothar decided to get his retaliation in first: while Godinus was forced to go to one church after another, ostensibly to swear oaths of allegiance and fidelity, Chlothar's henchmen were watching him every moment, eagerly looking for a suitable spot to kill him. Two of these royal assassins, Chramnulf and Waldebert, finally killed him at a farm near Chartres.[561]

This story gives us a glimpse of what life was like for members of the magnate stratum in the 620s. First of all, we observe that the king was deeply interested in marriage politics. This was not only to protect canon law, it was also to uphold a balance of landholding and power. Women often inherited land, and some widows could be very wealthy. If one family was allowed to marry into too much land, it might become too rich for its own good. Other magnate families might become jealous and afraid. Feuds could erupt, small-scale wars could start, and high-ranking officials, perhaps even kings, risked losing their lives. If the king, on the other hand, could control marriage policy and have his own candidates marry the wealthiest widows, a precarious balance could be maintained. It is a pity that Fredegar does not give us more examples of this, since the tendency (especially of King Dagobert I) to intervene in magnate marriages will become very obvious as we begin to look at the hagiographical sources.

Another interesting observation is that Bertha seems to have been in a position of strength. She chose freely to marry Godinus, and she agreed to follow him to Austrasia. Then, when she could return to her home in safety, she decided to go to the king and accuse Godinus of planning murder. What was she after? Was she sincerely concerned for Chlothar's welfare? Or was she out to get even for something Godinus had done while in Toul? We will never know, but one thing is certain: Bertha was not a cipher. She acted as a free individual with a number of choices available to her.

A third, and equally important, observation to be made from this example is that most people in the story were in some way related to each other. Warnachar was the father of Godinus, who married his own stepmother Bertha. Godinus' sister was married to Duke Arnebert, who was ordered by Chlothar to proceed with his soldiers against Godinus. In the seventh century, the members of the Burgundian and Frankish aristocracies were establishing networks of relatives with access to land, royal offices and various kinds of influence. The kings had to keep up with this and act in a similar fashion if they wanted to remain influential.

Brunhild, an evil old queen

Turning to their attitudes towards specific persons, the greatest difference between Gregory of Tours and Fredegar is their treatment of Queen Brunhild. As we have seen, Gregory paints Brunhild in relatively bright colours, far brighter than those used for Queen Fredegund. Fredegar, on the other hand, in his fourth book, has little to say about the latter, merely pointing out that King Gunthchramn was in contact with her after the death of Chilperic. He also mentions that her offensive (together with her son Chlothar II) in 596 led to the capture of Paris and other cities and to a great victory in the battle of Laffaux against the forces of Childebert II's sons. After that, he simply mentions that she died in 597.[562]

Brunhild is another matter entirely. Like Jonas of Bobbio (pp. 292–98), Fredegar does what he can to make his readers see her as an evil old witch. Both Jonas and Fredegar lived in a post-Brunhildian world, dominated by her political enemies, the descendants of Chilperic and

Fredegund. Their reasons for denigrating Brunhild are therefore obvious, but that does not mean that we should neglect their stories. Reporting bad things about a person is one thing; deciding exactly which elements of evil to use in the text is quite another.

When we meet Brunhild in Book IV, chapter 7, she still appears relatively harmless, although those who have read Book III know that she has blood on her hands.[563] She is mentioned, together with Childebert II's wife and sister, as having been present at the meeting between Childebert and Gunthchramn at Andelot in 587.[564] The next time we encounter her in the chronicle, however, she is already thirsting for blood. In 598, we are told, she was responsible for the assassination of Duke Wintrio.[565] By that time, she was again in a position where she ruled in the name of minors, since Childebert had died in 596 (according to Paul the Deacon, both Childebert and his consort, i.e., Faileuba, were murdered). The joint kingdom of Austrasia and Burgundy had been split between Childebert's two sons, so that Theudebert II ruled Austrasia and Theuderic II ruled Burgundy.[566] Brunhild appears to have continued to base her power upon Austrasia, but in 599 she was chased out of this kingdom.[567] A poor man is said to have found her wandering alone near Arcis in Champagne, and he brought her to her son Theuderic of Burgundy. Theuderic made her welcome and treated her with ceremony. Brunhild is said to have thanked the man who helped her by making him Bishop of Auxerre.[568]

In Burgundy, Brunhild would seem to have responded violently to any real or imagined threat posed by members of the aristocracy. In 602, she had a patrician called Aegyla bound and put to death although, according to Fredegar, he was completely innocent. Her reason was sheer greed: after the murder of Aegyla, his property was confiscated and made a part of the fisc.[569] The next year, Brunhild (acting with Bishop Aridius of Lyons) had Bishop Desiderius of Vienne deposed from his see. Desiderius was exiled to an island.[570] Having told us this, Fredegar immediately moves on to note that Brunhild was in the habit of sleeping with a Gallo-Roman called Protadius. In 604, she did what she could to bestow honours upon her bedfellow. On the death of Duke Wandalmar, Protadius was appointed patrician over the territory east of the Jura and over the lands of the Scotingi (a group of Alamans). At the same time, Bertoald, Theuderic's mayor of the palace, was sent to inspect the royal domains in the districts and the cities along the banks of the Seine up to the Channel. This was allegedly done *vt Bertoaldus pocius interiret*, in other words so that his death could be procured more easily.[571]

The events of 602–04 clearly indicate that Brunhild was busy constructing a new network of power in Burgundy. Her clients were promoted and her aristocratic enemies, whether lay or ecclesiastical, were persecuted. This impression is strengthened if we continue to trace Protadius' career in the sources. Fredegar makes no secret of the fact that he regards Protadius as a wicked man, who (although capable of performing a good job, at least on occasion) extorted as much money as possible for the fisc and used the opportunity to enrich himself as well as the royal treasury.[572] As a consequence, Protadius grew increasingly unpopular in Burgundy. Brunhild, however, used him as an ally in her attempt to win back power in Austrasia. She persistently urged Theuderic to attack Theudebert, claiming that the latter was no son of Childebert's but rather the son of a gardener. In 605, Theuderic was lured into doing as Protadius and Brunhild wanted. An army was mustered, and Theuderic went to war against his brother. However, when the army was encamped at Quierzy (on the Oise near Noyon), a group of Burgundian magnates urged Theuderic to come to terms with Theudebert and to stop paying attention to what Protadius had to say. Apparently, Theuderic disregarded their advice. The magnates then decided to use force. As Protadius was sitting in the king's tent playing dice with the court physician Peter, a troop of Burgundian warriors surrounded the tent while others detained Theuderic himself. When the king told them to stop molesting Protadius, the magnates responded by killing him. Theuderic had no choice but to abandon the campaign and return to Burgundy.[573]

The man chiefly responsible for Protadius' death was Duke Uncelen of the Alamans. He had, according to Fredegar, given the final order for the assassination at Quierzy. Brunhild never forgave him for his betrayal of her cause, and two years later, in 607, she had her revenge. Uncelen's foot was cut off at her instigation, and he was stripped of all his belongings.[574] The patrician Wulf, who had consented to the murder of Protadius, was killed at the villa of Faverney (near Luxeuil) on Theuderic's orders – but, Fredegar points out, on the advice of Brunhild.[575]

Having got rid of these enemies, Brunhild went on to meddle in Theuderic's marriage plans. The king had sent messengers to King Witteric of the Visigoths, asking for the hand of his daughter Ermenberga. The Frankish envoys had sworn an oath that Theuderic would never depose her from her position as queen. Having heard this, Witteric had gladly sent his daughter north, and Theuderic had received her delightedly. Apparently, however, both Brunhild and Theuderic's sister Theudila were against the marriage. We can only guess why; they were probably afraid that Ermenberga would oust them from their position at court. Their constant talk eventually poisoned Theuderic against his bride (*instigantibus uerbis Brunechilde aua et Teudilane germana efficetur odiosa*). After barely a year, in 607, Ermenberga was sent back to the kingdom of the Visigoths without the wealth she had brought with her.[576] Fredegar also tells us that on another occasion several years before this, Brunhild had intervened to stop a planned marriage between Theuderic's father Childebert and Theudelinda, the Agilolfing princess who instead became Queen of the Lombards.[577]

That Brunhild feared her female counterparts in the Frankish courts is obvious. She had good reason to be afraid; her long political life had taught her to be wary of young, ambitious women in kings' bedchambers; no-one knew when a new Fredegund might pop up. Her fear was realised when in 608 King Theudebert of Austrasia married a woman called Bilichild. She had originally been a slave, bought from merchants and taken to the court by Brunhild herself. As Queen of Austrasia, however, she was plunged into a verbal war against Brunhild, using contemptuous letters as her weapons. When, on one occasion, it was decided that the two queens should meet at a conference in order to patch up peace between Theudebert and Theuderic, Bilichild refused to attend.[578]

In 607, Brunhild's old enemy Desiderius, the former Bishop of Vienne, decided to return from his exile. On the wicked advice of Brunhild and Bishop Aridius of Lyons, Theuderic ordered him to be stoned to death. Fredegar does not hesitate to proclaim this evil deed instrumental in eventually depriving Theuderic and his family of their kingdom. Many miracles were reported to have occurred at Desiderius' tomb, and the dead bishop was soon regarded as a saint.[579] An even more conspicuous ecclesiastical enemy, however, was Columbanus.

The entire chapter 36 of Fredegar's fourth book is, in fact, taken verbatim from the *Vita Columbani* of Jonas of Bobbio, with very few additions (but with some omissions) (see pp. 292–95). The image of Brunhild as a second Jezebel, an evil old woman afraid of female competition at court, is thereby strengthened.[580]

In 612, with internal opposition apparently crushed, Theuderic and Brunhild triumphed on the battlefield. The Burgundian army invaded Austrasia and defeated the forces of Theudebert. As king of two of the three Merovingian kingdoms, Theuderic then advanced against Chlothar II of Neustria in 613, but he was prevented from uniting Gaul by his death from dysentery in Metz.[581] Brunhild was with him at his end, and instantly proclaimed one of Theuderic's sons, Sigibert, his father's successor (Sigibert II). The Austrasian magnates, especially Arnulf and Pippin of Landen (the ancestors of the Carolingian dynasty), then invited Chlothar II to enter the country and take command. Brunhild, who was in Worms at the time, sent an embassy to Chlothar telling him to abandon Theuderic's former lands. Chlothar replied that he undertook to abide by whatever decision should be arrived at by a gathering of Franks chosen for that purpose. Brunhild, of course, made ready for war: she sent Sigibert II to Thuringia with Warnachar, mayor of the palace, and other magnates, to gather support from the people across the Rhine. However, she also sent a secret letter to one of the magnates, a man called Alboin, ordering him to kill Warnachar and the others, since she suspected them of planning to desert her cause and join Chlothar. Alboin read the message and then tore the letter into bits. One of Warnachar's men found the bits lying on the ground and pieced them together on a wax tablet. Having read the contents, Warnachar realised that his life was in danger. Shortly afterwards, he *did* desert Brunhild and made secret arrangements to help Chlothar in the ensuing conflict.[582]

Brunhild also sent messengers to Burgundy, but, Fredegar assures us, the bishops as well as the secular lords in Burgundy feared and hated the old queen. They joined Warnachar's conspiracy and laid plans to kill all the members of Brunhild's family.[583] Due to the betrayal of his own army, Sigibert II quickly lost the war. Brunhild was arrested at the villa of Orbe and brought before Chlothar, who resided at the village of Renève, together with Theudila. Chlothar ordered Sigibert II and his brother Corbus to be killed, but he had something special in mind for Queen Brunhild. He publicly charged her with the deaths of ten Frankish kings (Sigibert I, Merovech, Chilperic I, Theudebert II and his son Chlothar, Chlothar's son Merovech, Theuderic II and three of his sons). Brunhild was tortured for three days and then led through the ranks on a camel. Finally she was tied by her hair, one arm and one leg to the tail of an unbroken horse, and she was cut to shreds by its hooves.[584] The woman who had been at the centre of Frankish politics for forty-six years was dead.

Reading about the later phases of Brunhild's career, and trying to forget about the personal feelings of those who dictated Fredegar's attitude, it is obvious that there is a clear continuity from the period described by Gregory of Tours. In both periods, Brunhild acted through intermediaries, trying to establish networks of power both within the secular and the ecclesiastical spheres of society, at the same time striving to secure a landed base to be used in order to buy allies. Protadius is a typical example: he was obviously hand-picked to lead Burgundy and its king on the path that Brunhild intended. Those who were perceived as threats to her position were murdered, by intermediaries of course, regardless of whether they were bishops, dukes or whatever. Other queens in particular were regarded as dangerous. Brunhild disliked Bilichild and she preferred that Theuderic slept with a number of mistresses than with a powerful wife. Fredegar's dramatic tale of the conspiracy that resulted in her downfall has a certain ring of truth about it: we would expect Brunhild to see enemies everywhere, to plot to kill Warnachar and to use all the resources available to gather support. In this particular case, she failed. Someone (or some people) did not do his job the way he was supposed to have done it, probably because he was bribed into deserting her. Needless to say, not all that Chlothar II did in the fateful year of 613 has been put down in Fredegar's chronicle. Fredegar was (and had to be) on Chlothar's side: the winner always gets to decide what the historical accounts will look like in the eyes of posterity.

The women at the court of King Theuderic II[585]

As we have already seen, Theuderic II, King of Burgundy, never really got around to getting himself what proper churchmen such as Columbanus regarded as a real queen. His marriage to the Visigothic princess Ermenberga was not a success, whether or not Brunhild had anything to do with it. The girl was sent back to the Visigoths, and the ensuing scandal almost resulted in war.[586] With the exception of Ermenberga, all of Theuderic's women are described as mistresses; the Latin word used is normally *concubina*, although Columbanus also used the much dirtier *lupina*, 'prostitute'.[587] We have no idea how many they were, since Fredegar only mentions them in connection with their role as mothers. In 602, one of them gave birth to the future Sigibert II.[588] In 603, another one produced a son called Childebert.[589] In 607, one of Theuderic's concubines gave birth to Merovech.[590]

These royal bedfellows, were, however, not the only influential females at the Burgundian court. By far the most influential woman in the whole kingdom was, of course, Queen Brunhild, but at least one other woman should also be mentioned: princess Theudila, Theuderic's sister. We know very little about her, but Fredegar provides us with enough information to enable us to guess that her influence must have been considerable. Like Brunhild, she perceived Ermenberga as a threat and urged her brother to get rid of her.[591] She appears to have accompanied Theuderic and Brunhild to Austrasia in 612, and was certainly a companion of Brunhild's in 613. Together with Brunhild, she was brought to the trial at Renève that ended in Brunhild's horrible execution, but Fredegar refrains from telling us what Chlothar II had in store for Theudila herself.[592]

The women at the court of King Theudebert II

Since 'Fredegarius' appears to have lived in Burgundy, we hear less about Austrasian affairs than about Burgundian ones in his chronicle. As a consequence, we are very badly informed about the personal life of King Theudebert II. In particular, it is frustrating not to hear more about Queen Bilichild. She is only mentioned in two of Fredegar's chapters, but the information provided there is sufficient to make us understand that she must have been something special. She was originally a slave girl bought by Brunhild, probably during the 590s when the widowed queen was still resident in Austrasia. Fredegar describes her as a spirited woman who was much loved by the people because she managed to bear with nobility the simple-mindedness of King Theudebert, to whom she was married in 608 (...*et esset Bilichildis utilis et a cunctis Austransiis uehementer diligeretur, simplicitatem Teudeberti honeste conportans*...). Although she had once been bought by Brunhild, she did not perceive herself to be her inferior. On the contrary, she frequently sent Brunhild contemptuous letters. We also learn from Fredegar's text that Bilichild had an important part to play in the negotiations between the courts of Austrasia and Burgundy, but she is said to have refused to attend a conference with Brunhild that was supposed to ensure peace between Theudebert and Theuderic.[593]

For an unknown reason, Theudebert had Bilichild assassinated in 610. Instead, he took to wife a girl called Theudechild.[594] We have no idea of what happened to her, since her political life was terminated when Theuderic conquered his brother's kingdom two years later.

The women of Chlothar II

Chlothar II, perhaps the most powerful of all the Merovingian kings, is much praised by Fredegar. Chlothar is thought to have been strong-minded, well-read, God-fearing, kindly disposed to all and full of piety. He did however, Fredegar admits, have a couple of faults. First of all, he loved the chase more than he ought to have done. Secondly, 'he took too much notice of the views of women young and old' (*mulierum et puellarum suggestionibus nimium annuens*).[595] In other words, Chlothar did what his women told him to do. This was a bad way for a man to live, according to Fredegar.

The first of Chlothar's wives mentioned by Fredegar was Berthetrude. Fredegar tells us that the king was devoted to her and that the whole court loved her for her goodness.[596] She accompanied Chlothar to the villa of Marlenheim in Alsace in 613, after the execution of Brunhild.[597] Shortly afterwards, she was secretly approached by Bishop Leudemund of Sion, who at the instigation of the patrician Alethius told her that Chlothar would die within the year and that Berthetrude had better send her treasure to Sion, where he promised that it would be safe. He also informed her that Alethius was planning to give up his wife and marry the queen in order to be able to succeed Chlothar as king. On hearing this, Berthetrude was very frightened. She began to cry and took to her room. Leudemund regretted what he had said and began to fear for his own safety; in the end, he sought sanctuary in the monastery of Luxeuil. He was later pardoned by Chlothar and permitted to return to Sion. Alethius, on the other hand, was tried and executed.[598] Berthetrude died in 618 or 619.[599]

Chlothar's second wife was Sichild, the sister of Dagobert I's wife Gomatrude. We know hardly anything about her except that Chlothar suspected that a certain Boso of Étampes, son of Audolenus, was guilty of misconduct with her. Boso was therefore killed in 626 by Duke Arnebert on instructions from Chlothar.[600]

Nantechild and the other women of Dagobert I

Of all the Merovingians it is Dagobert I, son and successor of Chlothar II, who is most known for his lust for women. For example, the late Merovingian author of Saint Amandus' biography is very outspoken in his condemnation of Dagobert's desires.[601] However, the only one of his wives that we really get to know, thanks to Fredegar's text, is Nantechild.

In 625, Dagobert came at his father's order to Clichy (near Paris), where he was married to Gomatrude, sister of Queen Sichild.[602] For an unexplained reason, as early as 628 he abandoned her in the villa of Reuilly and instead married a maiden of the bedchamber called Nantechild and made her his queen.[603] She would eventually give birth to a son called Clovis (II).[604] Not content, he admitted a girl called Ragnetrude to his bed during a tour of Austrasia in 629; she soon gave birth to a son called Sigibert (III).[605] Then Dagobert committed a fatal act in the eyes of Fredegar: he moved to Paris. Here, he surrendered himself to limitless debauchery, having three queens and innumerable mistresses. The queens were the above-mentioned Nantechild and two new ones: Wulfegund and Berchild. But as for the others: 'the names of his mistresses would be wearisome to insert in this chronicle, since there were too many of them' (*nomina concubinarum, eo quod plures fuissent, increuit huius chronice inseri*).[606]

When Dagobert lay dying in 637, he commended Queen Nantechild and their son Clovis II to his trusted adviser Aega (young Sigibert III was already King of Austrasia, at least in theory).[607] Since Clovis was a minor, the regency over Neustria was assumed by Aega and Nantechild.[608] Nantechild appears to have wielded considerable power,[609] a fact that is obvious from her role in the partitioning of Dagobert's treasure. Sigibert III and his advisers lost no time in asking for their share, and a formal partitioning took place at Compiègne on instructions from Nantechild and (formally) Clovis, with the consent of Aega. Nantechild managed to secure one-third of the treasure for herself.[610]

Nantechild's influence is also evident from certain events that occurred at the time of Aega's death in c. 641. Some days before, a man called Ermenfred, who had married Aega's daughter, had killed Count Chainulf during a court session at Augers. Queen Nantechild then permitted members of Chainulf's family, as well as many others, to attack Ermenfred's possessions. Ermenfred was forced to seek sanctuary in a church at Rheims and to stay there for many days to escape his magnate enemies as well as the 'royal wrath' (*rigio temore*), which probably refers to the wrath of Queen Nantechild (it can hardly refer to anyone else, since Clovis was still very young).[611] Meanwhile, Aega was succeeded as mayor of the palace by Erchinoald, a relation of Dagobert's mother.[612]

It would appear that Nantechild's and Clovis' rule had hitherto mainly applied to Neustria, while only in theory extending to the Burgundian kingdom. In 641 or 642, however, Nantechild brought Clovis with her to Orléans and summoned all the bishops, dukes and wealthy landowners of Burgundy to a meeting. She won them over and raised a man called Flaochad to the hitherto vacant dignity of Burgundian mayor of the palace. On this occasion, Nantechild also gave her niece Ragnobertha to Flaochad in marriage. Fredegar is puzzled as to why this happened. According to him, Flaochad and Nantechild had been secretly planning something completely different (*nam alium consilium secrete Flaochatus et Nantildis regina macenauant*) which, according to Fredegar, must have been in some way contrary to the wish of God, since He did not allow it to come to pass.[613] Shortly afterwards, Queen Nantechild died.[614]

Women in Lombard Italy

Events in Italy are mentioned quite often in Fredegar's chronicle, and some of the women associated with Italy are clearly deserving of note. Of course, that does not mean that Fredegar's notions of what Italo-Lombard women did or did not do have anything to do with Italian reality. His description of the world outside Gaul should primarily be interpreted as a collection of images connected with his view of the world as he knew it, as illustrations of what he deemed sufficiently natural to occur in Burgundy, Neustria or Austrasia.

The first woman we encounter in Lombard Italy is Theudelinda, the great heroine of the Italian tradition represented by Paul the Deacon (pp. 265–67). Theudelinda belonged to the Agilolfing dynasty of Bavaria, but according to Fredegar she was a Frank. She is said to have been betrothed to King Childebert II, who rejected her on the advice of Brunhild. Together with her brother Gundoald, Theudelinda then moved to Italy, where she married King Agilulf (in Fredegar's text, Ago). They had two children, a son called Adaloald and a daughter called Gundeperga. Gundoald also married at the same time. According to Fredegar, he married a noble Lombard woman, by whom he had two sons. Fredegar then informs us, rather surprisingly (at least to anyone who has read Paul the Deacon's description of Theudelinda), that Theudelinda and Ago caused Gundoald to be shot with an arrow while he was relieving himself. They are supposed to have been suspicious of him, since he was too popular among the people; it was not safe to let him live.[615]

Gundeperga was eventually married to Arioald, King of the Lombards (in Fredegar's text, Charoald; reigned 626–36).[616] Fredegar has only nice things to say about Gundeperga. She is described as 'in all things good-natured and full of Christian piety, generous in alms-giving and universally loved for her bounty' (*pulchra aspecto, benigna in cunctis et piaetate plenissema christiana, aelimosinis larga, praecellenti bonitatem eius, diligebatur a cunctis*). On one occasion, a man called Adalulf tried to seduce her, but Gundeperga merely spat in his face to show her contempt for him. Realising that he had endangered his own life, Adalulf hurried to Charoald and told him that the queen was plotting with the rebellious Duke Taso. She planned to poison Charoald, marry Taso and place him on the throne. Charoald believed Adalulf's lies and sent Gundeperga to the fortress of Lomello, where she was shut up in a tower for three years. However, the Frankish king Chlothar II, who according to Fredegar was related to Gundeperga, took this action very seriously. A Frankish delegation eventually arrived to enquire into the affair. After some discussion, it was decided that the dilemma should be solved by single combat between Adalulf and a champion of Gundeperga's (according to Fredegar, she was represented by a certain Pitto). Adalulf was killed and Gundeperga was released.[617]

After the death of Charoald/Arioald in 636, Fredegar reports that Queen Gundeperga, 'to whom all the Lombards had sworn fealty' (*eo quod omnes Langobardi eidem fidem cum sacramentis firmauerant*), sent for Duke Rothari of Brescia (in Fredegar's text Chrothacharius) and compelled him to abandon his wife and marry her. She would then, she promised, see to it that he became King of the Lombards. Rothari accepted her offer and swore that he would never abandon Gundeperga nor impair the honour of her royal rank. Rothari turned out to be a good king, but he forgot his promise to Gundeperga. Instead of treating her like a great queen, he shut her up in a single room in the palace of Pavia, where she lived in seclusion for five years. She was kept out of his own part of the palace, since Rothari preferred the company of his mistresses (*concubinas*). Being a good Christian, Gundeperga blessed God anyway and spent her time praying and fasting.[618] Fredegar then proceeds to tell us a strange tale about the eventual release of Gundeperga. According to the story, a man called Aubedo, sent by the Frankish king Clovis II on an embassy to the Lombard court, decided to make a personal effort on behalf of the incarcerated queen. In the course of the conversation with Rothari, he said that it would be unwise to ill-use a queen who was related to the Franks and whom he had to thank for his throne. His actions, should he continue in this way, would be much resented by the Frankish kings and their peoples. Since Rothari was afraid of the Franks, Gundeperga was immediately released. Rothari ordered all the properties and fiscal domains that had been hers to be restored to her. The grateful queen, who lived in the midst of royal splendour for the rest of her life, rewarded Aubedo richly.[619]

Summary

No-one can doubt, having read Fredegar, that early medieval Frankish queens were powerful. Summing up their patterns of political behaviour, we get the following picture:

(1) Queens constructed networks of secular and ecclesiastical agents of their own; this is very obvious in the case of Brunhild, but she was hardly the only one to act in this way. If widowed, they could use their power base to rule the country in the name of their sons and with the help of magnate allies, in Nantechild's case the mayors of the palace Aega, Erchinoald and Flaochad.
(2) To remain powerful (i.e., able to recruit allies), the queens had to be wealthy. They needed land, whether personal or fiscal, and they confiscated what they could. Nantechild took control of a third of Dagobert's treasure during the conference at Compiègne, despite what must have been fierce competition.
(3) When acting against their enemies, they used male intermediaries (assassins).
(4) When acting within the more peaceful sphere of ordinary politics, they did not have to use intermediaries. On the contrary, they themselves appear to have been regarded as natural diplomats, weaving peace between their men. Fredegar thought it worthy of note that Bilichild on one occasion made a point of *not* attending a peace conference.
(5) The queens were also able to exert considerable influence by persuading their men to do as they wished. It would appear that Berthetrude and Sichild were particularly good at this, since Fredegar informs us that Chlothar II paid too much attention to the advice of his women.
(6) When climbing the career ladder, they could literally start from scratch, just like in the days of Gregory of Tours. Fredegund had begun her career as a servant; Bilichild started out as a slave. Their

charm and good looks led them to the kings' bedchambers, and if they were sufficiently smart, they managed to stay there.
(7) Knowing the route to promotion through seduction, the royal women were always wary of competitors. The greatest threat to a Merovingian queen in Fredegar's time was The Other Woman. Brunhild and Theudila both regarded Ermenberga as a threat. Ambitious mistresses were dangerous, but (as Brunhild herself knew better than anyone) a Visigothic princess had a potential for power that was too great to be tolerated.
(8) The queens were never safe. Not only could they be ousted from court through their own failure to keep the king interested in sleeping with them, they could also be killed. Bilichild was allegedly murdered by her own husband.

Several of these elements are also highlighted in Fredegar's tales of life at the Lombard court in Northern Italy. We must keep in mind that Fredegar probably knew very little of what life was really like in Milan and Pavia. His story of the fate of Gundeperga says more about what he thought could happen in Burgundy than about what really did happen in Italy. As such, the story is extremely interesting. For instance, it clearly demonstrates the actual power wielded by a royal widow: Fredegar thought it perfectly logical that a widowed queen should be able to decide the royal succession and promote her own husband to the throne. His tale of the plot of Alethius shows that this strategy was perceived as natural by contemporary magnates. Paul the Deacon has a similar story about the accession of Agilulf in 590 (pp. 265–66); we may be facing an element of political culture that was shared by both the Franks and the Lombards. The story of Gundeperga can also be used to demonstrate the high degree of solidarity within the powerful families of Western Europe. Just as in the case of Ingund (p. 136), the Merovingians did everything they could to help Gundeperga when she was in trouble. Of course, the story may be fictitious, and it is unlikely that Gundeperga was perceived as a Merovingian. Still, Fredegar clearly imagined that the Frankish kings would react in this way, protecting the interests of their family members even if they were married off to kings far from home. However, not only does Fredegar's chronicle show Gundeperga behaving as a typical powerful, generous,

God-fearing Merovingian queen, gathering support from various layers of the population and especially from the church – it also provides us with examples of what might happen to a queen if and when she failed to arouse the king's interest. Gundeperga fell from royal grace twice, both during her marriage to Arioald/Charoald and during her marriage to Rothari. She was sent away from court and placed under what looks like some kind of house arrest. Similar things happened in Gaul all the time. When someone like Dagobert I tired of a wife or a mistress, he simply sent her off to an estate and quite possibly never saw her again.

Last, but not least, Fredegar's chronicle is in itself an excellent example of historiographical politics. Brunhild, a good woman in *Decem Libri Historiarum*, is suddenly transformed into a monster. Fredegar could hardly have written about her any differently, since the political tradition represented by Brunhild and her branch of the Merovingian family had lost out in the political game. The successors of Sigibert I had been killed. The successors of Chilperic I, on the other hand, had triumphed, and their triumph had been closely linked to that of Brunhild's Austrasian enemies, the ancestors of the family that would later be known as the Carolingians. However, and this has not been previously remarked upon as much as it should, another good woman in early medieval politics and literature is also transformed into a negative character in Fredegar's chronicle: Theudelinda. In Paul the Deacon's *Historia Langobardorum*, she is virtue personified. In Fredegar's chronicle, she has her own brother murdered because she is jealous of his popularity. True, Fredegar's picture of Theudelinda is too sketchy to be of much use in an analysis, but it nevertheless gives us an obvious hint as to the existence of an alternative Theudelinda tradition, one in which she may have resembled the post-Brunhildian version of Brunhild. In Brunhild's case, we do know about the image, since Fredegar, Jonas and others have transmitted it to us. In Theudelinda's case, however, the alternative image has been lost.

The women in the Continuations of Fredegar

Most of the manuscripts containing Fredegar's chronicle also contain a continuation of 54 chapters bridging the gap from 642 to the era of Charlemagne that began in 768. This *Continuatio*, or rather *Continuationes*, is actually the product of more than one author, the first of whom was not even conscious of the fact that he was continuing Fredegar's work. This author was trying to continue the so-called B version of the chronicle known as *Liber Historiae Francorum*, a Neustrian chronicle probably written in c. 727. The B version, however, is not Neustrian but Austrasian, clearly modifying the text to suit the Austrasian point of view. This means that chapters 1–10 in Fredegar's *Continuationes* should rightly be regarded as a rewriting of *Liber Historiae Francorum*, while chapters 11–17 contain matter written by the anonymous author who continued the B version up to the year 736. The rest of Fredegar's *Continuationes* is the result of early Carolingian attempts to record history as they perceived it. At some time before 751 or 752, Count Childebrand, a half-brother to Charles Martel and thus uncle of Pippin the Short, had Fredegar's text revised and continued with the help of the local Austrasian version of *Liber Historiae Francorum* to take the story up to the point where his own writers could continue. It would appear that one of them worked on the project until he had finished chapter 21, being followed by another writer. Childebrand probably died at the beginning of the 750s (when the writer had reached chapter 34), but the work was carried on and finished under the supervision of his son Nibelung.[620]

The women of kings and mayors of the palace

The women of Fredegar's Continuations are noticeably fewer in number than in the chronicle proper, and those that are mentioned seldom appear on more than one occasion, usually in connection with their men.[621] Only two women – Pippin of Herstal's wife Plectrude and Pippin the Short's wife Bertrada – are mentioned in more than one chapter. For instance, two clearly important women, Beletrude (wife of the Duke of Bavaria) and her niece Sunnichild (later the wife or mistress of Charles Martel) are mentioned together in one single sentence in their capacity as prisoners of war after Charles' campaign against the Bavarians.[622] After that, Beletrude disappears. Sunnichild reappears disguised as a 'wicked stepmother' (*nefario nouerce*) several chapters later, in 741 or 742 shortly after Charles' death. As such, she advises Charles' daughter Chiltrude (her own stepdaughter) to cross the Rhine secretly and marry Duke Odilo of the Bavarians. The marriage was contrary to the will of Chiltrude's brothers and must be regarded as one element of a much larger political gamble. It would be useful to hear more about Sunnichild's role in all of this, but the chronicler is silent.[623]

Nevertheless, despite the obvious shortcomings of the *Continuationes*, the text clearly shows the power of Merovingian queens in the seventh century and that of the wives of the mayors of the palace in the late seventh and in the eighth centuries. Already in chapter 1, we are told that Clovis II married a foreigner, a former Anglo-Saxon slave called Balthild, who is described as both sensible and attractive. After Clovis' death, she controlled the regency of her son Chlothar III.[624] We also read of Childeric II's pregnant queen Bilichild, who was killed together with her husband in 675. Childeric's aristocratic enemies dared not let her escape from the ambush alive.[625]

Since the *Continuationes* was a work commissioned by the Carolingians, it comes as no surprise that the authors chose (or were ordered to) include a couple of women married to mayors of the palace, something 'Fredegarius' had refrained from doing. The first such woman we meet is the 'noble and vigorous' (*nobilis et strenua*) Anseflid, who was married to Waratto, mayor of the palace in Neustria. After Waratto's death, the position of mayor was taken by Anseflid's son-in-law

Berchar. Having suffered his famous defeat at the battle of Tertry in 687, Berchar was murdered at the instigation of Anseflid (*instigante Ansflede matrona socrui sua*).[626]

The victor at Tertry, Pippin of Herstal, was married to a woman called Plectrude. She was the mother of two of his sons, Drogo and Grimoald. Plectrude is described as 'noble and most intelligent' (*nobilis et prudentissima*).[627] Pippin also had another 'noble and elegant' woman (*nobilem et elegantem*), described in the text as his wife (*uxor*), called Alpaida, who was the mother of his eventually most successful son, Charles Martel.[628] When Pippin died in 714, Plectrude assumed command. In the war that followed between the various aristocratic factions, Plectrude remained a powerful force to be reckoned with in Austrasia. She imprisoned Alpaida's son Charles and did what she could to prevent him from gaining power, but Charles escaped and rallied his own forces. When threatened by the Neustrian troops of Ragamfred and King Chilperic II, Plectrude made them turn back from attacking Cologne by buying them off with treasure. Later, when Charles took Cologne in 717, Plectrude made peace with him and surrendered Pippin's treasure to his forces.[629]

The mayor of the palace Grimoald (d. 714, the son of Pippin of Herstal and Plectrude), had a son called Theudoald, but all we hear about Theudoald's mother is that she was 'a certain mistress' (*quadam concubina*).[630] However, the chronicler also informs us that Grimoald married the daughter of Radbod, Duke of the Frisians, undoubtedly a political alliance aimed at securing the northern frontier.[631]

The textually most prominent woman in Fredegar's *Continuationes* is also the last one to be mentioned in the work: Bertrada, wife of King Pippin the Short and thus the first queen of the Carolingian dynasty. In fact, she is introduced in the text at the very moment when she is proclaimed queen in 751.[632] Although we never actually see Bertrada doing anything important on her own, it is clear from the text produced under the supervision of Nibelung that she co-operated closely with her husband and often accompanied him on his campaigns. In 767, she went together with Pippin across the Loire to Bourges, where she was left in the company of high-ranking nobles, while Pippin waged his seemingly endless war against Waiofar of Aquitaine.[633] Pippin later returned to Bourges, where he spent the winter with Bertrada.[634] As her husband continued the war in 768, Bertrada set out on her own to Orléans and thence by boat along the Loire to the stronghold of Chantoceaux. Pippin joined her for a short while a couple of months later.[635] During the next campaign, which ended with the news of Waiofar's murder, Bertrada continued her journey to Saintes, where she took up residence and greeted the king when he returned in triumph.[636] Later in the same year, she accompanied the ailing Pippin to Saint-Denis near Paris, where he died.[637]

Summary

The evidence from Fredegar's *Continuationes* may appear disappointing at first sight, but it does serve to underline some elements within early medieval political culture that are seen more clearly in other sources. Most importantly, not even the authors of the *Continuationes* can hide the fact that queens, princesses and other wealthy women in the seventh and eighth centuries were political actors in their own right, not just tools of their husbands and fathers. Despite the writers' reluctance to tell us more about them, it is clear that women such as Plectrude, Sunnichild and Chiltrude had enough property and allies to carry out their own political plans. Just as in other early medieval sources, these women used male intermediaries (assassins) when they want to get rid of somebody, as when Anseflid had Berchar murdered.

The women in *Liber Historiae Francorum*

The work known as *Liber Historiae Francorum*, 'a book of the history of the Franks', was probably written at Saint-Denis, Rouen or Soissons in c. 727. If Fredegar's chronicle is regarded as a Burgundian work, the *Liber Historiae Francorum* is definitely considered Neustrian, more precisely the work of an aristocrat from the Paris basin. The work is essentially a history of the relationship between the royal court and the Neustrian magnates. Contrary to Fredegar's *Continuationes*, this is not a work primarily concerned with the Carolingians' rise to power.[638] However, while of great interest for aspects of political history during the decades around 700, the differing tendencies of the Neustrian, Austrasian and Burgundian writers are less important to the present study than the way they paint their pictures of political culture as such. Seen from this angle, the differences are marginal. Since a considerable part of *Liber Historiae Francorum* is taken directly from other sources, I have limited the present study to chapter 35 onwards.

Not surprisingly, the greatest female villain in *Liber Historiae Francorum* (as in *Vita Columbani*, *Passio Desiderii* and Fredegar's chronicle) is Queen Brunhild. She is described as a woman obsessed by thoughts of death and destruction: she is the dominant force behind Theuderic II's war against both Chlothar II and Theudebert II.[639] However, this is only the beginning. Having used Theuderic to get rid of Theudebert, she quarrels with Theuderic and quickly decides to get rid of him too. Theuderic is poisoned. Far from satisfied, Brunhild now turns on Theuderic's children and has them all killed.[640] She then appears to have turned her thoughts to the prospect of sexual intercourse with a man several decades younger than her: Chlothar II. When Chlothar sends for her, pretending that he wants to marry her, she hurries to meet him. Of course, Chlothar has no intention of marrying Brunhild. As soon as she arrives, she is condemned to death and brutally killed.[641] Considering the unrealistic lengths to which the author of *Liber Historiae Francorum* goes to further blacken the already blackened name of Queen Brunhild, it is strange that he does not blame her for Chilperic I's murder too (as does Fredegar, see p. 419). Instead, he argues that Chilperic was murdered at the instigation of his own wife, Queen Fredegund, who was afraid for her safety after Chilperic had discovered her with a lover.[642]

The rest of the women in *Liber Historiae Francorum* are only treated very briefly. We learn that Queen Balthild was a beautiful and intelligent woman (*pulchra, omnique ingenio strenua*),[643] while her husband Clovis II was a man best kept at a safe distance: 'he had every kind of filthy habit – he was a seducer, and a debaucher of women and a glutton and a drunk'.[644] Childeric II's wife is mentioned as being pregnant at the time she was murdered together with her husband.[645] Anseflid, Warrato's wife and widow, is briefly described in a nice way (*nobilis ac ingeniosa*), and her power is evident from the fact that she was a willing key to Pippin of Herstal's rise to the position of mayor of the palace after Berchar's murder.[646] Theuderic III's wife Chrodochild is mentioned in passing,[647] as is Radbod's daughter (and Grimoald's wife) Theudesinda.[648] Plectrude's failure to secure the power of her late husband Pippin during the years 714–17 is described (her initial seizure of Pippin's power base, her imprisonment of Charles, the fact that she was forced to give away some of her treasure to Ragamfred and Chilperic II while staying in Cologne and finally her surrender to Charles), and Plectrude herself is said to have been 'a very noble and very wise wife' (*uxor nobilissima et sapientissima*).[649]

Summary

An admittedly brief analysis of the little text there is of *Liber Historiae Francorum* confirms the conclusion arrived at in other parts of this book: that queens and magnate women (in this case the wives of mayors of the palace) in Merovingian Gaul had a potential for political action and could, if they used their resources wisely, be leading protagonists on the political and military scene. Brunhild, of course, is a special case. By the time *Liber Historiae Francorum* was written, Brunhild's wickedness was already legendary, and little remained of the benevolent queen once described by Gregory of Tours in *Decem Libri Historiarum*. The Brunhild described by the anonymous Neustrian chronicler is not to be taken seriously other than as an example of what might happen to a powerful woman whose enemies decided how her history was to be written and perceived. We have a clear parallel in Paul the Deacon's tale of Romilda of Friuli (pp. 267–70), but in her case there is no Gregory to speak in her favour.

Although *Liber Historiae Francorum* is a short work, the author nevertheless thought it essential to include the stories of Anseflid and Plectrude. Both of them played crucial parts in the Frankish political game during the decades around 700. The author had no reason to disparage their names, and he obviously regarded their political activities as quite natural. If women such as Anseflid and Plectrude wanted to take charge in politics, they could go ahead and do so. They are even provided with specific characterisations that illustrate their nobility and intelligence. The author also found it perfectly natural for a king to be morally depraved while his consort was virtuous: although Clovis II (the husband) is described as being a drunken seducer, Balthild (the wife) is described as beautiful and intelligent. For the writer of *Liber Historiae Francorum*, powerful women were seen as ordinary features of political life. Although they did not fight themselves, they could easily find men to command their armies, and they were essential in forging alliances.

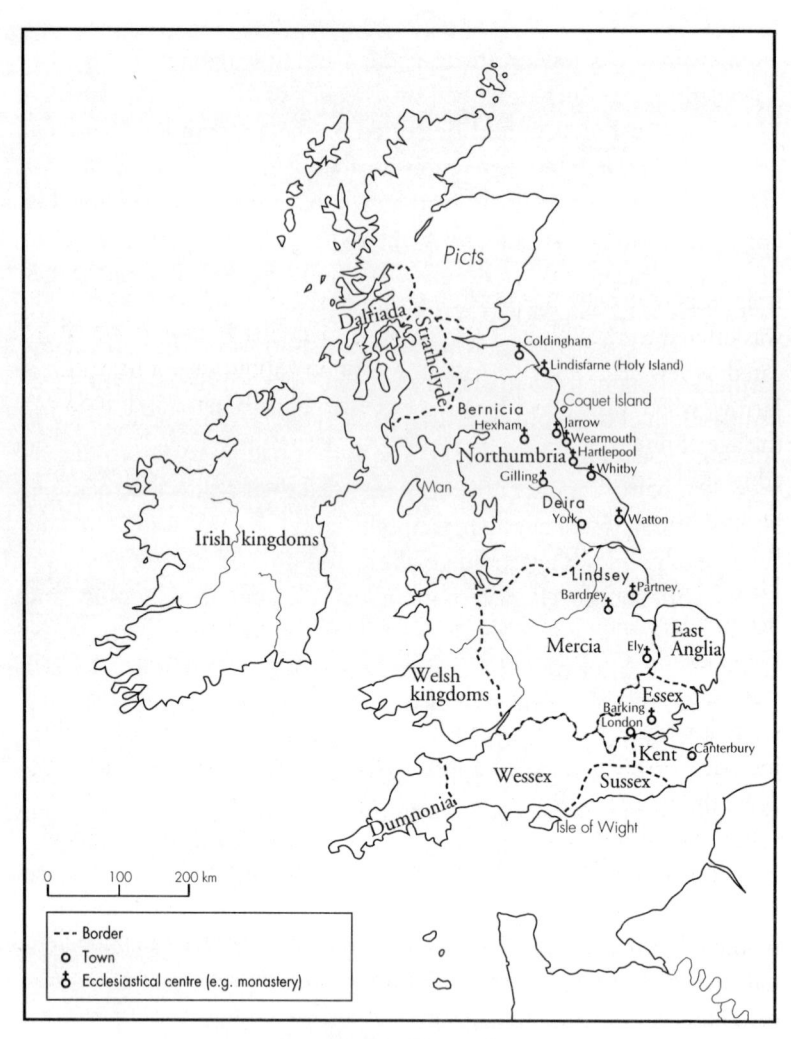

The British Isles, AD 700

The women of Bede

It appears that Bede was born in 673 and died in 735. As a child, he was offered to the abbot of Wearmouth, Benedict Biscop, to be educated. A few years later, he moved to the neighbouring monastery of Jarrow, where he remained until his death. He a became a deacon at the age of nineteen and a priest at thirty. The rest of his life was devoted to study, mainly of the Latin Bible, and writing (Biblical commentaries, chronologies, computistics, hagiographies, etc.). His most famous work, *Historia ecclesiastica gentis Anglorum*, 'The Ecclesiastical History of the Anglian People' (*Anglorum* usually being rendered as 'English'), was finished at the beginning of the 730s, a few years before Bede's death. The work is still commonly regarded as one of the outstanding masterpieces of early medieval literature.[650] The present study is primarily based on the 'Ecclesiastical History', but I have also included Bede's most famous hagiographical work, *Vita Sancti Cuthberti*, the Life of Cuthbert, written in c. 721, in the analysis.

In *Historia ecclesiastica gentis Anglorum*, the reader encounters 626 individuals (not counting those who only appear as anonymous members of groups and peoples). Of these 626, 548 individuals are men, 78 women. In other words, approximately 87.5 percent of all the individuals that Bede thought worth mentioning were male, only 12.5 percent female. Looking more closely at the 78 women of *Historia ecclesiastica gentis Anglorum*, we find that most of them are mere names (such as Breguswith, Cyniburg and Ricula) or not even that, merely appearing as 'mother of', 'wife of', 'a girl'. Only 17 women have what we might refer to as personalities of their own.

Virtuous followers of Christ

A striking difference between Bede's seventeen and the female characters of the historical works of Gregory of Tours and Paul the Deacon, is that most of them are described as *good* women. The reason for this is obvious. Since the work is a church history, most of the people we encounter are in some way connected with the church, thus belonging to a sphere of society that Bede (who belonged to it himself) thought of as being morally superior to the other, sinful and dangerous, secular sphere.

Eanfled. The first of the good women that we meet in Bede's text is Eanfled. She was the daughter of King Edwin of Northumbria and Queen Ethelberga. Bede informs us that she was baptised by Paulinus on Whit Saturday, a few weeks after her birth on the night of Easter Day 626, before the king himself decided to embrace the Christian faith. Thus, she became one of the very first Northumbrian Christians.[651] After her father's violent death, she was taken to Kent in 633 together with Paulinus, Ethelberga and other relatives and associates of the late king.[652] Later in c. 651, she was brought back to Northumbria to become the wife of King Oswy.[653] Bede tells us that she petitioned her husband to grant land to a certain Trumhere (an Anglian cleric and member of the royal house, who had been trained by the Irish and would eventually become Bishop of the Mercians) on which to build a monastery at a place called In-Getlingum (Gilling, near Richmond), where King Oswin of Deira had been killed in 651. Oswin's premature death had been treacherously arranged by his enemy King Oswy of Bernicia himself, who in this way managed to unite the two parts of Northumbria under his rule. Eanfled wanted the monastery to serve as a place where prayers could be offered for the eternal salvation of both slayer and slain. The queen's basic motive, according to Bede, was a longing for expiation for Oswin's unjust death.[654] After telling us this, Bede goes on to inform us that Eanfled, contrary to her husband, celebrated Easter at the correct time of the year according to Roman Catholic practice together with *her* court (not the court of King Oswy) and her Kentish priest Romanus.[655] He also tells us that she supported the pious plans of the young (future bishop) Wilfrid, who wanted to travel to Rome, by sending him to King Earconbert of Kent with a request that he would send him on to Italy. Apparently, she had already helped Wilfrid to become accepted in the monastery of Lindisfarne.[656] Later in her life, she ruled the monastery of Whitby together with her daughter Aelffled,[657] and she was eventually buried in the church of Whitby.[658]

Earcongota. Earcongota was the daughter of King Earconbert of Kent and Queen Sexburg. According to Bede, Earconbert was the first English king to give orders for the complete abandonment and destruction of pagan idols in his kingdom. He also gave specific orders for the observance of the Lenten fast. Earcongota, who shared her father's zeal, joined the nunnery of Faremoutier-en-Brie in Gaul (founded in c. 617). Bede describes her as a nun of outstanding virtue and provides us with an account of her death which she had forseen in a vision, when she is said to have actually been seen going straight to heaven. Many miracles are supposed to have occurred at the time of her death and later.[659]

Ethelberga and Saethryd. Ethelberga was the daughter of Anna, King of the East Angles; Saethryd was his stepdaughter. Bede praises them both for being of such merit that they, although foreigners, eventually became abbesses of Faremoutier-en-Brie. He has most to say about Ethelberga, who remained a virgin all her life. Her holiness was proven when the monks opened her grave seven years after her death and found her body untouched by decay.[660]

Osthryd. Osthryd was the daughter of King Oswy of Northumbria. She eventually became the wife of King Ethelred of Mercia.[661] Bede mentions her in connection with his tale of the veneration of the bones of Saint Oswald, Osthryd's uncle. As Queen of Mercia, she had the bones reinterred in Bardney Abbey in the sub-kingdom of Lindsey, and she helped spread the news of the healing power of the saint.[662] Eventually, in 697, she was killed by some Mercian chieftains while Ethelred was still king.[663]

Ethelhild. Ethelhild was the sister of Bishop Ethelwin of Lindsey and of Abbot Aldwin of Partney; she was herself an abbess of a religious house in the same part of England. Bede mentions her as still being alive at the time of the writing of his book. She is, however, only mentioned in passing. One time, Bede says, she visited Bardney Abbey and talked to Queen Osthryd about the miraculous power of Saint Oswald. Ethelhild maintained that she had seen light reaching heavenwards from Oswald's relics during the night, and Osthryd gave her some healing dust associated with the saint. Later, Ethelhild witnessed a miracle because of her use of the dust.[664]

Aelffled. Aelffled was the daughter of Oswy, King of Northumbria, and Queen Eanfled. Bede tells us that Oswy, before going to war against King Penda of the Mercians in 655, vowed to offer his own daughter to God as a consecrated virgin and give twelve estates to build monasteries if God would grant him victory. Having won the battle, Oswy kept his promise. He dedicated Aelffled (an infant at the time) to God's service in perpetual virginity. She entered the monastery of Hartlepool, at that time ruled by Abbess Hilda. When Hilda founded the monastery of Whitby a couple of years later, Aelffled was taken with her. In time, she became a nun, living a pious life within the walls of Whitby until her death at the age of 59.[665] Bede also informs us that she eventually came to rule the monastery together with her mother.[666] Aelffled was buried in the same church at Whitby as Eanfled.[667]

Hilda. Bede devotes an entire chapter (book IV, chapter 23) to Saint Hilda of Whitby, together with Etheldreda (see below) the most conspicuous religious woman of seventh-century England.[668] She was the daughter of Hereric, nephew of King Edwin of Northumbria, and she was baptised by Paulinus as one of the first of the Northumbrians to accept the new faith. According to a story told by Bede, her mother Breguswith dreamed about her when Hilda was still only a child in the form of a symbolic jewel that emitted such a brilliant light that all Britain was lit by its splendour. When she was 33 years old, Hilda decided to abandon the secular life and serve God, renouncing all that she possessed. In order to facilitate her planned trip to Gaul (where she intended to join the community of nuns at Chelles), she went to East Anglia. Her sister Hereswith, mother of King Aldwulf of East Anglia, had already become a nun at Chelles. After a year of preparations, however, Hilda was recalled to Northumbria by Bishop Aidan of Lindisfarne. She was granted land near the River Wear, where she went to live as a nun together with a few companions. A year later, she was promoted to Abbess of Hartlepool. Aided by Bishop Aidan and others, she spent a couple of years ordering the monastic life at Hartlepool. Then, she set out to found her famous monastery at Streanaeshalch (Whitby), where she established the same regular life as in her former monastery. According to Bede, her wisdom was held to be so great that kings and princes used to come and ask her advice on their difficulties. Whitby quickly became one of the leading centres for monastic training and learned culture in England; five men from her monastery were later appointed to bishoprics. Hilda herself became – just as her mother had dreamed – a shining example to all of England.[669] In 664, Whitby was chosen as the spot for the synod that was to determine at what date Easter was to be celebrated in Northumbria. Hilda participated in the synod, supporting the Irish view against the Roman view. The synod ended in victory for those in favour of Roman practice, but Hilda appears to have accepted this without protest.[670]

When she was 59 or 60 years old, Hilda was attacked by a burning fever that never left her body; Bede interprets this as God's way of trying her soul, so that her spiritual strength might be made even more perfect. If that was indeed God's intention, he appears to have succeeded admirably, since Hilda continued to give thanks to her Maker and to instruct the members of the monastic community both publicly and privately. In the end, the sickness killed her, and she died on 17 November 680 at the age of 66, 'after an earthly life devoted to the work of heaven'. Her death was accompanied by visions of her rising to heaven under the guidance of angels, and an especially wonderful vision was experienced at another religious house by a devout nun named Begu.[671]

Etheldreda. Saint Etheldreda is the chief subject of two chapters in *Historia ecclesiastica gentis Anglorum,* book IV chapters 19 and 20 (actually a hymn written by Bede in her honour).[672] Etheldreda was the daughter of Anna, King of East Anglia. She was married to Tondbert, a prince of the South Gyrwas, but he died shortly after the wedding, and she was instead married off to King Egfrith of Northumbria. According to Bede who had the story from Bishop Wilfrid, who had supposedly heard it from Egfrith himself, she managed to keep her virginity despite the fact that the marriage lasted twelve years. She kept begging her husband to allow her to retire from the secular world and devote her life to the service of God, and Egfrith finally gave his permission. She entered the convent of Egfrith's aunt, Abbess Ebba, at Coldingham. Only a year later she moved to Ely, where she became abbess of a new convent.[673] It is clear from Bede's text that Etheldreda, before she became a nun, must have had a court of her own with thegns bound to her, not to the king. The most prominent of these thegns and the steward of her household was a man called Owini, who had accompanied her from East Anglia. Eventually, Owini renounced the world and became a monk.[674] Another thegn of Etheldreda's was called Imma.[675]

As Abbess of Ely, Etheldreda excelled in piety, never wearing linen, hardly ever washing in hot water, only eating one meal a day, etc. Like so many other holy persons in the Middle Ages, she is said to have been given a special disease by God, in her case a large red tumour under her jaw. According to Bede, Etheldreda interpreted this as God's way of helping her to be absolved from the guilt of having carried needless jewellery around her neck when she was a girl. Some people said that she also possessed the spirit of prophecy, in the end even foretelling the epidemic that was to kill her, as well as the exact number of those who would die with her in the convent. This event occurred seven years after her arrival at Ely. She was succeeded as abbess by her sister Sexburg, who had previously been married to King Earconbert of Kent. Sixteen years later, Sexburg decided to have Etheldreda's bones exhumed and placed in a new coffin (the old one had been merely a simple coffin of wood) and transferred into the church. When the tomb was opened, Etheldreda's body was found to be entirely free from decay, and even her original coffin was discovered to possess miraculous healing powers.[676]

The nuns at Barking: Ethelburga and the others. Ethelburga was the sister of Earconwald, Bishop of the East Saxons. Before becoming bishop in 675, Earconwald had founded two religious houses, a monastery for himself (at Chertsey) and a convent for Ethelburga (at Barking). Ethelburga is described as behaving as she was supposed to behave, constantly planning for the needs of the community,[677] and Bede mentions several miracles that are said to have occurred at Barking.[678] At her death, nobody doubted that her soul went straight to heaven; in fact, her rise to heaven was even foretold in a vision experienced by one of her nuns, Tortgyth. A crippled nun who asked the recently deceased Ethelburga to be released from her continual pain was miraculously set free from her body – she died and went to heaven – only twelve days later.[679] Ethelburga was succeeded in the office of abbess by another devout nun named Hildilid, who ruled the convent with great energy until extreme old age.[680]

Bede clearly regarded the visionary Tortgyth as a holy person. She spent many years helping Ethelburga to maintain the regular observances by instructing and correcting the younger sisters. Eventually, she was attacked by a serious disease that plagued her for nine years. Bede explained this as God's way of burning away any traces of sin that might remain among her virtues through ignorance or neglect. The disease grew steadily worse, until Tortgyth lost the use of her limbs and her tongue. She died three years after Ethelburga, a day and a night after a conversation with her former abbess, who appeared to her in a vision.

Heiu. Heiu is said to have been the first woman in Northumbria to take the vows and habit of a nun. She founded the monastery of Hartlepool but did not stay there long, preferring to settle in a town called Calcaria, in Anglo-Saxon Kaelcacaestir (possibly Tadcaster).[681]

Ebba. Ebba, the sister of King Oswy and thus the aunt of King Egfrith of Northumbria, was Abbess of Coldingham.[682] Although Ebba was a good woman herself, her subordinates appear to have been less religiously minded than they should have been. A pious Irishman called Adamnan was told by a heavenly messenger that the inhabitants of Coldingham, both men and women, were far too sinful for the monastery to be allowed to continue in its present form. The monks and the nuns should have been praying and studying, but instead they were only eating, drinking, gossiping or simply sunk in unprofitable sleep. The nuns in particular were sinful: they spent their time weaving fine clothes, which they employed to the peril of their calling, either to adorn themselves like brides or to attract attention from strange men.

Therefore, punishment would soon follow: the monastery would be destroyed by fire. When Adamnan told Ebba of his vision, she became very alarmed, but Adamnan comforted her somewhat by saying that the monastery would not burn while she was alive. Nevertheless, Ebba did her best to avert the disaster, and the members of the community did in fact undergo penance. After Ebba's death, however, they relapsed into their earlier sins and became even more wicked. As had been foretold, Coldingham was destroyed by a fire.[683]

Heriburg and her daughter. Abbesses such as the ones mentioned by Bede appear to have been true models of virtue, at least at first sight. If we dig deeper, however, we sometimes find that they display certain characteristics that seem more egocentric than we might have expected from holy women waiting for their heavenly reward. One such aspect is the one of hierarchy: the abbesses were not meek and submissive nuns but rather powerful rulers of religious houses. As we have seen, many of them were closely related to one or more of the Anglo-Saxon royal houses. Many of them were princesses, royal widows or retired queens. They might have obeyed God, but they were superiors as far as the other nuns were concerned. This attitude is especially evident if we look at how they arranged the succession. True, Bede seldom informs us about the process of election of a new abbess, but he sometimes does mention what the abbesses themselves thought about it. In the case of Heriburg, abbess of Watton, it is abundantly clear that she intended her daughter Coenburg to succeed her as leader of the convent. The only reason why we know about this is that Coenburg fell ill and was helped by Bishop John of York, whose healing powers were of great interest to Bede. The entire story is transmitted to us to demonstrate the holiness of the bishop; Heriburg's plans for Coenburg's future appear to have been regarded as natural and typical to Bede, something he would have expected from any abbess.[684]

Additional information from the *Life of Cuthbert*

In Bede's hagiography of Saint Cuthbert, we often encounter religious women similar to the ones in his Ecclesiastical History.[685] They are described in much the same way. Abbess Ebba of Coldingham, for instance, is described as being honoured for her piety and nobility alike. Her God-fearing piety made her send for Cuthbert so that he could reinvigorate her community (although they do not appear to have listened very closely, to judge from later events reported in Bede's Ecclesiastical History).[686] Another abbess called Verca is also described as a devout woman.[687]

The description of Abbess Aelffled is more complex. She is said to have been a holy woman who looked after her nuns with motherly care, and she is reported to have felt a deep affection for Cuthbert. She was once cured from a disease with the help of a linen cincture or girdle that was made miraculous by the fact that it belonged to the future saint.[688] However, she also possessed a sense of curiosity that Bede may not have considered entirely proper. On one occasion in 685, she sent a message to Cuthbert begging him to come and talk over some important matter. Cuthbert agreed and set out for the appointed place on Coquet Island, where he met the abbess. During the conversation, Aelffled suddenly flung herself before him, adjuring him by the name of God and the angels to tell her how long her brother, King Egfrith of Northumbria, would live and who would succeed him. 'I know you can tell me', she said, 'if only you will, because the spirit of prophecy is strong in you' (*Scio enim, inquit, quia prophetiae spiritu quo polles, etiam hoc dicere potes, si uis*). Cuthbert tried to avoid the question, but Aelffled, 'with feminine audacity' (*audacia feminea*), kept on insisting that he reveal what he knew. In the end Cuthbert did hint to her that Egfrith's successor would come from an island in the sea, and Aelffled realised that he was referring to Aldfrith, a supposed son of Egfrith's father Oswy, who was living in Ireland at the time. Satisfied, she urged Cuthbert to reveal whether he thought he would become bishop (she knew that Egfrith wanted this). Cuthbert replied that he suspected that might happen, but that he had no intention of remaining a bishop for long, perhaps for a period of two years. Of course, Cuthbert was right on both accounts. Aldfrith did succeed Egfrith, and Cuthbert was appointed to the bishopric of Lindisfarne, but he only served until 687.[689]

Bede's main reason for telling us the story of the meeting on Coquet Island would seem to be his wish to emphasise the prophetic ability of Saint Cuthbert, not the curiosity of Abbess Aelffled. This interpretation is strengthened by a description of a later event. Aelffled again asked Cuthbert, then bishop, to come and see her in order to converse with her and consecrate a church. They met at an estate belonging to Aelffled's monastery. During dinner, Cuthbert suddenly had a vision, and Aelffled begged him to reveal what he had just seen. As on Coquet Island, Cuthbert tried to evade the issue, but Aelffled did not give in. Cuthbert then revealed that he had seen a holy man in Aelffled's own monastery being borne by the hands of angels into heaven; as to the man's name, Cuthbert said that Aelffled would announce that herself the next day. The abbess began to investigate the health of her subordinates, and she soon found out that a shepherd called Hadwald had fallen from a tree and died at the very moment Cuthbert had his vision. She immediately sought out Cuthbert, who was in the middle of the dedication ceremonies, and, 'with woman-like astonishment' (*stupore femineo*), announced the dead man's name and asked the bishop to remember him at mass.[690]

Women within the political sphere

Although very illuminating as to how a monk such as Bede perceived the ideal religious woman, *Historia ecclesiastica gentis Anglorum* is difficult to use to discover patterns of action and culture with regard to powerful women in the secular sphere of society.[691] Bede does not appear to have been interested in writing about them: he wrote a church history, devoted to telling the reader about monks, nuns, priests and pious laymen. As far as political culture touched upon the ecclesiastical sphere, he certainly mentioned the elements in question (in particular the increasingly popular habit of founding monasteries in the middle and second half of the seventh century), but that is all we get. There are traces of other kinds of activity as well, but no more than traces. We can be absolutely sure that royal women did have a certain degree of power in Anglo-Saxon society, since other political actors of their own time behaved as if they were influential. Bede even quotes an entire letter from Pope Boniface V to Queen Ethelberga, the wife of King Edwin of Northumbria and the daughter of King Ethelbert of Kent.[692] In the *Life of Cuthbert*, the future saint is shown visiting the Queen of Northumbria on more than one occasion.[693]

One element of the political culture of early medieval England has already been mentioned: that of founding religious houses. There appear to have been many generous and at least outwardly pious kings and queens in the latter half of the seventh century, after the conversion of the Angles, Saxons and Jutes to Christianity. Even more land was donated to monasteries in the eighth century. Another aspect of Anglo-Saxon political culture, one that is impossible not to mention even for a writer such as Bede, is the importance of marriage as a diplomatic tool. The royal houses (Deira, Bernicia, East Anglia, Kent, Mercia, etc.) were all to a certain degree interrelated by marriage. The kings married off their daughters to potential allies in various parts of the country.[694]

Of greater interest in the present context is the way kings and queens acted when they wanted something done, not counting when they wanted to recruit monks and nuns for a new monastery or have the ones that they had already recruited pray for them. The kings appear to have acted as archetypal Dark Age warlords, killing their enemies as soon as they could lay their hands on them and going from one war to another in their unholy quest for land, wealth and people to govern. Why they did so can, of course, not be discussed here, demanding as it does a thorough discussion of the nature of plunder economy, gift exchange and client relationships, but we should remember the form itself: Bede conceptualised the prime form of secular male political culture as one of warfare. This was certainly not how he conceptualised the prime form of *female* political action. Queens did not go to war when they wanted something done. What, then, did they do?

Firstly, they relied on their men. *Their* men, not the king's men. On some occasions, Bede happens to mention households, courts and thegns associated specifically with certain royal women. We have met a few of them above: Queen Etheldreda had thegns (we even know the names of two of them, Owini and Imma) and Queen Eanfled had a court. There are more examples: Cynwise, Queen of Mercia during Penda's reign, was powerful enough to hold royal hostages.[695] In other words, the queens at least had so much wealth that they could maintain a couple of agents connected with their own households. Whether this was true of all Anglo-Saxon royal houses is impossible to tell, but it is certainly likely. England was small, and many of its dynasties were,

255

as was said above, closely related to each other. Furthermore, the recurrence of political turmoil made it common practice for many princes and princesses to spend a significant part of their lives in exile. The political culture of Northumbria can hardly have been very different from the political culture of East Anglia and Mercia.

Secondly, they had their enemies murdered, probably by making use of their agents. I suspect that Bede regarded such murder as sinful, but he never really provides us with a real characterisation of a murderous queen (probably since his book is not intended to deal with them in the first place). Still, they do appear now and then. Bede reports a rumour, according to which Peada, King of the South Mercians, was assassinated through the treachery of his own wife.[696] Furthermore, he appears to be quite certain (not showing any signs of surprise) that the Frankish queen Balthild, herself an Anglo-Saxon, was responsible for the death of the bishop of Lyons.[697]

Summary

Historia ecclesiastica gentis Anglorum provides us with a picture of the early medieval monastic image of a good woman. She should definitely be a nun; she should live in a religious house and she should devote her entire existence to the service of God, abstaining from fine clothes, gossip, idle sleep and other things that Bede regarded as sinful in the eyes of the Lord. In fact, most activities except praying, fasting, studying, seeing visions and witnessing (or performing) miracles appear to have been forbidden. To the modern reader of Bede's work, the fire at Coldingham would seem to indicate that God had grown considerably harsher and more difficult to please than in Biblical times. The Coldingham episode (and, to a certain extent, the description of the inquisitive and stupefied Aelffled in *Life of Cuthbert*) also serves to shed some light on misogyny. What was specifically bad about the nuns of Coldingham, according to the story, was that they enjoyed fine clothes and that they wanted to attract the attention of strange men; that is, it was expected for ordinary women to want to look beautiful and seduce strangers, but nuns should know better. Like other early medieval writers, Bede seems to have associated sexuality in general and sexual immorality in particular with women, but he does not dwell on the subject as much as other chroniclers.

The reason for this is, of course, that *Historia ecclesiastica gentis Anglorum* is a church history. It is not a political history. Queens and princesses mainly appear in their capacity as abbesses, nuns or benefactors of religious houses. Political facts are submerged in a sea of monasticism and tales of episcopal succession. Nevertheless, there are a few illuminating hints of Bede's view of the political culture of his age. First and foremost, we must never forget that the founding of religious houses as such formed an important element in early medieval politics. Furthermore, Bede makes it clear that queens had their own clients and soldiers (thegns), attached to their own households. He also mentions rumours of political assassinations performed at the instigation of powerful women.

Italy, AD 700

The women of Paul the Deacon

Paul the Deacon belonged to a noble Lombard family from Friuli, not far from the north-eastern border of Italy. He was probably born in the 720s and he probably died in the 790s, but no exact dates are known. Historians have been unable to decide whether he spent the main part of his life as a layman or as a member of the clergy. In any case, we know that he visited monasteries and secular courts in several parts of Western Europe. He appears to have stayed for a while at the court of King Ratchis (744–49) in Pavia (Paul tells us himself that he had been present when Ratchis showed the famous cup that King Alboin had made from his father-in-law's scull[698]); later, he spent some time at the ducal court of Benevento. His first dated poem was written in 763 in honour of the Beneventan duchess Adalperga, to whom he also dedicated his *Historia Romana* (c. 770). In the last decades of the eighth century, he clearly belonged to the learned élite of the Carolingian world. He entered the sphere of Charlemagne at about the same time as Alcuin of York, at the beginning of the 780s. It has been calculated that he probably lived in Francia during the years 781–85. At this time, he wrote his most famous poem, a prayer directed to Charlemagne himself, asking for mercy on behalf of his brother Arichis, who had been exiled after a failed Friulian rebellion in 776. At the end of his life, he returned to Southern Italy and went to live in the monastery of Monte Cassino, where he wrote the work that would make his name immortal, *Historia Langobardorum* ('History of the Lombards'). The *Historia*, consisting of six books encompassing the history of the *gens* from its origins until the reign of King Liutprand (712–44), was very popular during the Middle Ages; more than 100 manuscripts have survived.[699]

In *Historia Langobardorum*, the reader encounters a very male world. All in all, 530 individuals appear in the work (not counting those who only appear as anonymous members of groups, such as *gentes*). Of these 530, 462 individuals are men, 68 women. This means that approximately 87 percent of all the individuals that Paul the Deacon thought worth mentioning were male, only 13 percent female. It should be added that most groups (the members of which were not counted separately) that appear as such are distinctly male: 30 Lombard dukes, 17 Frankish dukes, 12 Avar soldiers, 150 bishops, and so on. The only predominantly female collective is a group of Amazons, appearing in Book I, chapter 15.

Looking more closely at the 68 women of *Historia Langobardorum*, we quickly find that most of them are mere names (such as Hermelinda, Winiperga, Guntrut, Ranigunda, Anna, etc.). Only seven women have what we might term personalities of their own: Gambara,[700] Frea,[701] Rumetruda,[702] Rosemunda,[703] Sophia,[704] Theudelinda[705] and Romilda.[706] Four appear in Book I, while the last two books (V and VI) do not contain any real female personalities whatsoever. Of course, some of the women that appear without being given a true characterisation are still of interest to the present study. They will be dealt with after the analyses of those mentioned above.

Gambara and Frea: the matriarch and the goddess

Gambara was a matriarch. She first appears in the third chapter of the first book of *Historia Langobardorum* as mother of Ibor and Aio, the first chieftains of the *gens* that would eventually evolve into the Lombards. Gambara was known for her great wisdom; members of the tribe often went to her in search of good advice.[707] Her most important contribution to society occurred when the *gens* was threatened by the Vandals. When the Vandals demanded tribute, Gambara advised her sons to defend their freedom with arms rather than submit to the enemy in shame.[708] Before the battle, the Vandals asked Godan (Odin or Wotan) for help. Godan promised that he would give victory to those he first saw at sunrise. Gambara then approached Godan's wife, Frea, with a similar request. Frea advised Gambara to get the women of the *gens* to let down their hair, arranging it to look like beards. Both men and women should then stand next to each other in a prominent place, so that Godan could not fail to see them when he opened his eyes at sunrise, looking out from his window towards the east. Gambara informed the women and the warriors what to do. The next morning Godan was very surprised to find a great many hirsute individuals lined up outside his window. He asked Frea: 'Who are those long-bearded persons?' (*Qui sunt isti longibarbi?*) Frea responded, that since he had now given them a name (hence *Langobardi*, 'long beards'), he should also bring them victory. Godan agreed, and the Vandals were defeated.[709]

Gambara and Frea both belong to the realm of Lombard mythology, bound up in the myths of the origin of the *gens Langobardorum*. The story of Godan and Frea was undoubtedly of great importance to Lombard *Wir-Gefühl*; it would appear to have been a tale that all newly accepted members of the *gens* had to accept. As such, their appearance in *Historia Langobardorum* is of a specific kind. In the eyes of Paul the Deacon, they could scarcely be interpreted and described in the same way as later, more historical, queens and duchesses. In viewing them as politically active (although purely literary, non-historical) persons in society, the element of gender is clearly less important to observe and analyse than other mythical elements, linking the minds of seventh- and eighth-century storytellers to a distant past.

Rumetruda: a Dark Age femme fatale

Rumetruda was the daughter of the Lombard king Tato. If she was a historical person (which she could very possibly be, although Paul the Deacon's tale about her would seem to be largely fictional), she would have lived at the beginning of the sixth century, when the Lombards had left Rugiland (in present-day Lower Austria) to settle in western Pannonia.

According to Paul the Deacon, a brother of the Herulian king Rodulf had visited Tato to discuss issues of war and peace between the two *gentes*. On his way back, the Herulian ambassador passed Rumetruda's house. The king's daughter was impressed by the large retinue. She asked about the troop, and her servants informed her that it belonged to the brother of King Rodulf, who was returning to his brother's kingdom after having concluded the negotiations with King Tato. Rumetruda invited Rodulf's brother to share a cup of wine with her. Unfortunately for him, and for the future of Herulo-Lombard relations, he accepted. Seeing how small he was, Rumetruda, bursting with vanity, looked down upon him and ridiculed him. The Herulian felt greatly humiliated, grew angry and responded in a similar vein. This made Rumetruda furious. Enraged 'in a way that only a woman can be' (*furore femineo succensa*) she began to plan his death. Pretending to be friendly, she smiled and offered him a seat with his back towards a window. The window was covered by an expensive piece of drapery that served to hide an assassin, who was waiting for Rumetruda's signal – the words 'Mix the wine!' (*Misce!*) As she turned to the cupbearer and said the words, the hidden assassin plunged one spear after another into the Herulian's back. When news of his brother's death reached King Rodulf, he immediately declared war on the Lombards.[710]

There is little, if any, reason to search for grains of historical truth in this story. It simply serves as an explanation of the cause of the war that led to the firm establishment of Lombard power in Pannonia. Rumetruda is more or less a tool of the tale, an evil girl who could easily be replaced with something else (slaughtered cows, misunderstood messages, etc.) that would also have made Rodulf angry. Still, it shows us Paul the Deacon describing a woman of the early Middle Ages acting within the realm of politics. Rumetruda appears as a vain, illogical person who should be avoided. When happy, she invites strange men (who look powerful) in for a cup of wine. When angry, she does not hesitate to have them slaughtered by her assassins. She displays a combination of, on the one hand, a character based on vanity and stupidity and, on the other hand, tactics involving what would seem to be attempted seduction and murder through agents. The result of her interference is war.

Rosemunda: the avenging daughter

Rosemunda was the daughter of Cunimund, King of the Gepids. When the Gepids were defeated by the Lombards in 567, she was captured by Alboin, King of the Lombards, who eventually married her. After the battle, Alboin had Cunimund's head cut off and made into a cup, a so-called *scala*.[711]

Rosemunda made her contribution to history five years later, when she avenged her father in a way that Paul the Deacon has described in one of the most memorable and well-known passages of his chronicle. According to the tale, one evening Alboin, who was resident in Verona, had far too much to drink. Seeing the *scala* of Cunimund before him on the table, he had it filled with wine and handed to his wife, telling her to 'be joyous and have a drink with her father' (*eam ut cum patre suo laetanter biberet invitavit*). Rosemunda grew furious. She silently decided that her father's death could only be avenged by the murder of her husband. She managed to persuade Helmechis, the king's *scilpor* ('shieldbearer', a Lombard title) to help her, and they cunningly enlisted the support of another important Lombard nobleman, Peredeo. At first, Peredeo refused to help them, but Rosemunda blackmailed him into giving his consent. Under cover of darkness, she pretended to be the servant girl with whom Peredeo frequently slept. After they had had sexual intercourse, Rosemunda revealed her identity and threatened to inform Alboin about the incident unless Peredeo offered his help in the plot.[712]

The murder took place after a dinner, when Alboin had fallen asleep. Rosemunda removed all weapons from the palace except Alboin's own sword, which she tied to his bed in a way that made it impossible to move. Acting on Peredeo's advice, Rosemunda ('who was more evil than a wild animal', *omni bestia crudelior*) let Helmechis into the chamber. Alboin suddenly awoke, realised the danger and made frantic attempts to grab his sword. Since this was impossible, he tried to defend himself with a stool, but Helmechis proved superior. Thus Alboin died, 'because of the plots of a single little woman' (*uniusque mulierculae consilio periit*).[713]

Helmechis had not committed the murder simply to please Rosemunda. He wanted the throne. In order to achieve this, he married the widowed Rosemunda, a usual tactic under these circumstances. However, the coup failed. When the Lombards in Verona turned against them, Rosemunda asked Longinus, the imperial commander at Ravenna, for help. Longinus sent a ship to Verona. Rosemunda and Helmechis fled during the night, taking with them Alboin's daughter Albsuinda and the Lombard royal treasure. Safely in Ravenna, Longinus attempted to persuade Rosemunda to kill Helmechis and marry him instead. 'Since she was easy to persuade to commit any evil deed whatsoever, and since she wanted to rule Ravenna' (*illa ut erat ad omnem nequitiam facilis, dum optat Ravennatium domina fieri*), Rosemunda immediately agreed to Longinus' plan. As Helmechis one day was stepping out of the bath-tub, she handed him a poisoned drink. Helmechis drank some of it but, when he suddenly understood what was going on, he turned on Rosemunda and forced her to swallow what was left in the cup. Both of them died, 'according to the judgment of the Almighty' (*sicque Dei omnipotentis iudicio interfectores iniquissimi uno momento perierunt*).[714]

Rosemunda appears as an almost archetypal female villain: the evil woman who uses sex and poison to kill one husband after another, a sixth-century Lucrezia Borgia. Yet her basic goal (a fact that Paul the Deacon does not fail to admit) was to avenge her father's death and the way Alboin had treated his corpse by making his head into a cup. She felt insulted, both with regard to herself ('be joyous and have a drink with your father') and with regard to her family. Revenge per se is not a bad thing in the eyes of Paul the Deacon – this is clear from other stories in *Historia Langobardorum*.[715] It is tempting to argue that the negative description of the vengeful Rosemunda is partly (if not wholly) due to the fact that revenge in the positive sense, at least according to Paul the Deacon, was considered a *male* prerogative.

Sophia: the arrogant empress

Sophia was married to the East Roman emperor Justin II. Like the empress Theodora before her, she managed to exercise a great deal of influence over imperial politics. In Paul the Deacon's History, she appears a couple of times in circumstances that give the reader a negative impression of her character.

We first meet her as she opposes the eunuch Narses, the East Roman leader of Italy, during the 560s. Sophia is reported to have said that she would bring him back to Constantinople and set him to work with the textile-producing female servants of palace, a job that should suit him, since he was a eunuch. Fear of Sophia led Narses to invite the Lombards to invade Italy and occupy it – a famous story with little (or no) historical truth in it.[716] Later, we encounter Sophia after the outbreak of her husband's insanity. After Justin's executive power had been taken over by Tiberius, Sophia is reported to have objected to the way the regent gave large sums of money to the poor instead of saving it in the royal treasury. Tiberius defended his action by referring to the Bible; it would seem that the story is related primarily to serve as an example of Tiberius' piety.[717]

When Justin died in 578, Tiberius was crowned emperor as Tiberius II. Sophia (although she had promised to accept this) soon began to plot against him. When the emperor was holidaying at a rural villa during the wine harvest, Sophia summoned Justinian, Justin's nephew, and attempted to have him proclaimed emperor. On hearing this, Tiberius returned to Constantinople, imprisoned Sophia and confiscated all her property. New servants – faithful to the emperor – were assigned to her.[718] Nevertheless, Paul the Deacon makes it clear that she managed to keep some of her influence. When Tiberius lay dying in 582, he is reported to have consulted Sophia before naming Maurice as his successor.[719]

Summing up Paul the Deacon's view of Sophia, we see a woman guilty of arrogance, haughtiness and greed. She has a lot of power, and she is hungry for more. Tiberius II, who is described as a true Christian, becomes her natural enemy.

Theudelinda: a paragon of virtue

Theudelinda was the daughter of Duke Garibald of the Bavarians. On 15 May 590, she was married to the Lombard king Authari. Paul the Deacon describes Authari's quest for a bride in detail: how he travelled to Bavaria disguised as a royal messenger, met the duke and his daughter, and made it possible for Theudelinda to secretly figure out his real identity. During all of this, Theudelinda appears as a young, innocent princess, blushing when the 'messenger' touches her hand. Later, when Garibald was threatened by the Franks, Theudelinda and her brother Gundoald fled to Italy, where they were heartily welcomed by Authari. The wedding took place in a field outside Verona.[720]

The introduction of Theudelinda into Paul's narrative consumes more text than most other peoples' introductions in *Historia Langobardorum*. However, Paul the Deacon has even more to say about the queen's early days. Duke Agilulf of Turin, who was present at the wedding, is reported to have been informed by a seer that the new Lombard queen would soon be his own wife. Agilulf threatened to kill the man if he spread this idea, but the seer remained firm: 'You can kill me, but this woman has for certain come to this country in order to marry you.'[721]

On 5 September the same year, barely four months after the wedding, King Authari died in Pavia, apparently from poison. According to Paul the Deacon, the Lombard nobles left the choice of a new king/husband to Theudelinda, 'since they appreciated her greatly' (*quia satis placebat Langobardis*). She was allowed to choose her next husband from among all the Lombards, provided, of course, that she did not pick someone entirely unsuitable for the royal office. After having consulted wise men she decided upon Duke Agilulf, who was immediately sent for. Theudelinda and Agilulf met at Lomello, where she offered him a cup of wine and he responded by courteously kissing her hand. Smiling and blushing, Theudelinda told him not to kiss her on the hand but on the mouth, since this would be more appropriate in the future. She then informed him about her decision to marry him and make him king. The wedding was celebrated, and Agilulf was formally declared king at the beginning of November.[722]

Agilulf and Theudelinda ruled the Lombards until Agilulf's death in 616. In Book IV of *Historia Langobardorum*, Paul the Deacon provides us with several examples of the queen's virtue. He stresses her good relations with Pope Gregory the Great, who is reported to have sent her a copy of his newly written *Dialogues*, since he knew that Theudelinda was a true Christian committed to doing good deeds.[723] Theudelinda is said to have made King Agilulf benevolent towards the Catholic faith, giving or restoring lands and influence to the Church and the bishops.[724] Later, she is said to have persuaded Agilulf to make peace with Gregory and the East Romans, for which the pope was very grateful.[725] Gregory in fact dispatched a letter of thanks to her, which is reproduced in *Historia Langobardorum*.[726]

Paul the Deacon specifically relates how Theudelinda had the famous church of Saint John the Baptist in Monza built and richly adorned with gold and silver. She provided it with generous grants of land.[727] Near the church, she constructed a palace with paintings showing events in Lombard history.[728] According to Paul, it was here that she gave birth to her son Adaloald,[729] who succeeded his father as king in 616. However, Paul makes it clear that Adaloald, although by this time a teenager, ruled together with his mother. By the time he was deposed in 626 (allegedly after becoming insane), Theudelinda was presumably dead, although Paul says nothing about this. He does, however, tell us that Theudelinda and Adaloald rebuilt many churches and gave significant donations to holy places.[730]

In Italian tradition, Theudelinda is a positive figure: a fair Catholic queen from the north who restores ecclesiastical culture, establishes good relations with the pope, secures the peace and builds churches. She is the model of a good, Christian queen: instead of seducing her men in order to have them commit murder, she blushes, smiles and does her duty. Instead of using her royal power to further her own secular interests, she uses it to build churches and endow them with property. Still, it would appear that Theudelinda was present at the centre of Lombard politics for about 35 years, influencing three kings (Authari, Agilulf and Adaloald), in turn. How was this possible for a queen who is supposed to have spent her days praying, giving away land and reading Gregory's *Dialogues*? Apparently, Paul the Deacon (and the Italian tradition) refrains from telling us the whole story. No woman or, for that matter, man could possibly remain that powerful for so long without getting their hands dirty, especially in the violent decades around the year 600. The tradition of Theudelinda must have been carefully moulded by descendants of the queen's brother Gundoald, the Lombard kings of the so-called Bavarian dynasty during the latter part of the seventh century. In the days of Paul the Deacon, it was already firmly established. That an alternative and considerably more negative Theudelinda tradition once existed is hinted at in Fredegar's chronicle (pp. 232).

Romilda: 'the shameless whore'

Romilda was married to Duke Gisulf II of Friuli, who died in c. 610 trying to protect his duchy from the Avars, who ravaged the province. After the defeat, the Lombards sought refuge in the fortified settlements and *castra* of the region, such as Cormones (Cormons) and Ibligo (Invillino). The widowed duchess Romilda herself remained in the well-fortified town of Forum Julii (Cividale del Friuli) together with numerous refugees, especially widows and children. It would appear that Romilda was in middle age; she had already given birth to eight children, and at least two of her sons had reached manhood.

The Avars soon reached Forum Julii and began to besiege the town. The Avar leader, the khakhan, planned the siege on horseback, searching for weaknesses in the Lombard defence system. As Romilda was looking out from the wall of the town, she became aware of the khakhan's presence. 'As she saw how young and handsome he was, she – the shameless whore – began to long for him, and she had a messenger inform him that she would surrender the entire town to the Avars if he promised to marry her.'[731] The khakhan readily agreed, and Forum Julii was betrayed into his hands. Soon, a vast number of Lombard men, women and children were taken as captives to the plains of Pannonia, where the men were slaughtered and the rest were divided as slaves. Romilda did not care about this; her only desire was to share the khakhan's bed. The Avar leader did in fact fulfill his promise to the duchess, but having done so, he handed her over to twelve of his soldiers, who were given the opportunity to rape her one night. After this, a stake was raised on an open field. Romilda was dragged forward and impaled. Showing her the stake, the khakhan is reported to have said: 'This is the man you deserve!'.[732] Paul the Deacon sums up the story by observing that 'such a death was awarded to this horrible woman who betrayed her country and thought more of her sensual cravings than she thought about the welfare of the citizens and of her relatives.'[733] However, Paul assures his readers that Romilda's daughters remained virtuous. To get rid of the lusty Avars, they put raw chicken-meat between their breasts and thus eventually gave off an awful stench. The Avars came to believe that all Lombard women smelled badly by nature and should therefore be avoided. Romilda's and Gisulf's daughters were later sold to Bavarian and Alamannic noblemen.[734]

I think we can safely assume that many elements of the story are completely fictitious. This is a horror-story, a tale told on cold evenings next to the fire in the farms of north-eastern Italy. It is the kind of tale that was popular among members of the adult generation who wanted to scare and perhaps enlighten the girls of the household. It was in all probability also very popular among members of the younger generation who wanted to be frightened witless – we have, in fact, similar tales today, told in the form of movies about murderous ghosts such as Freddy Krueger in *A Nightmare on Elm Street* and Jason in the all-too-predictable sequels to *Friday the 13th* (in the modern cases, the duchess of the early Middle Ages has been replaced by promiscuous teenagers who pay for their immorality with hideous deaths). In *Historia Langobardorum*, Romilda is described as fundamentally illogical, inherently stupid, insensitive to the fact that people are being murdered and sold as slaves and mainly interested in having sex with a cruel Barbarian. She is, in Paul the Deacon's own words, 'a shameless whore'. If we accept his words as the truth, we would have to agree with him.

But why should we take for granted that Paul the Deacon is telling the truth? He is probably relating a Friulian legend; we must assume that he had once heard it himself on a cold night next to a fire in or near Forum Julii. Let us tentatively forget the explicit motives Paul uses to explain Romilda's action. Let us also agree that the tale has not simply been fabricated to hide the fact that Forum Julii was forced to surrender due to shortage of food (which could easily have been the case, considering the influx of refugees). What is left? (1) The Avars ravaged Friuli, (2) the Avar khakhan and the Duchess of Friuli made some kind of treaty involving the withdrawal of the Avar troops to Pannonia together with their Lombard captives and (3) the khakhan and the duchess were married. This kind of chain of events was far from unusual in medieval frontier areas. Firstly, both the Lombards and their Slavic neighbours made similar plundering expeditions; the Avars only did what everyone else was doing in the area of present-day Friuli and Slovenia. Secondly, the Avars were certainly not strange Barbarians in the eyes of the Lombards: in 567, the Lombards and the Avars had together attacked and defeated the Gepids. A year later, they had entered into a formal alliance when the Lombards left Pannonia in order to invade Italy. Bearing in mind that Romilda had adult sons in the beginning of the seventh century, it is certainly possible that she could have been alive in 567. In any case, she was surely born at a time when the Avar alliance was common knowledge among the Lombards. Furthermore, several other alliances and agreements had been concluded between Lombards and Avars even after the Lombard invasion of Italy. Thirdly, the political development of the Lombard kingdom during the decades around 600 was characterised by the wars between King Agilulf and a number of rebellious (perhaps separatist) dukes. From this angle, it is tempting to argue that the Avar invasion of Friuli may actually have been a result of the alliance between the Lombard king and the Avar khakhan – the latter may have intervened on behalf of the former, so as to weaken the strongest of all the northern Lombard duchies. In that case, the second marriage of Romilda would (like most medieval marriages between members of politically prominent families) also have been an attempt to forge a political alliance to prevent the Avars from attacking the duchy. Paul the Deacon's tale of Lombard captives being taken to Pannonia can be tentatively explained as a part of the usual exchange of hostages between new allies. We have no proof whatsoever that the night of the twelve rapists or the morning of the stake ever existed, but we do know that Romilda's family continued to reign in Friuli for several decades. It is well-known that the Lombard monarchy did not fully subjugate the Friulian dukes until the reign of King Liutprand (712–44), a fact that Paul the Deacon himself admits.[735]

Looking at the problem in this way, the real Romilda is no longer by necessity 'a shameless whore'. Her actions were later explained in a way that made her look like such a person, and we have unfortunately no clues as to why this happened. What is interesting in the present context is, however, not *why* but *how* she turned out as she did in the context of historical memory. In the Friulian tradition related by Paul the Deacon, Romilda is primarily characterised by her inability to reason (if she had been intelligent, she could have figured out the dangers of submitting to the Avars), her neglect of her own people and her strong, almost sick, longing for sexual pleasure. Together, these elements formed her identity in the same way as Christianity and a sense of duty formed the identity of Theudelinda.

The construction of political networks through marriage

Even when the individual characters of the women themselves remain invisible to our eyes, several of the females of *Historia Langobardorum* are nevertheless of great interest to the present study. One aspect of the lives of royal women, that appears already in Book I, is their role as marriage partners. By giving away his daughter to a neighbouring king or duke, an early medieval monarch could construct a network of alliances that could (provided that he built it well) serve as a key ingredient in his attempts to achieve security.

The Lombard king Waccho, who reigned in Pannonia in the beginning of the sixth century, was married three times: to Ranicunda, daughter of a Thuringian king, to Austrigusa, daughter of a Gepid king, and to Salinga, daughter of a Herulian king. Austrigusa gave him two daughters, Wisigarda and Vuldetrada. Wisigarda was married off to King Theudebert I of Rheims (p. 95–98) and Vuldetrada to his son King Theudebald (and, after his death, to Duke Garibald of Bavaria, p. 87).[736] All in all, Waccho's royal in-laws were spread out over a wide area from present-day Transylvania to present-day France. That the family connection with the Merovingians was deemed of great importance is evident from later events: before marrying Rosemunda, King Alboin had already been married to Chlodoswintha, a daughter of King Chlothar I.[737] King Authari, before marrying Theudelinda, had tried (in vain) to be permitted to marry the sister of Childebert II of Austrasia.[738] When this proved impossible, he redirected his marital efforts towards Bavaria.[739]

Marriage alliances could also be used to appease other political factions within the Lombard kingdom itself or even incorporate some of these factions within the structure of the current régime. Thus, Paul the Deacon tells us how King Rodoald (652–53) married Gundeperga, the daughter of Agilulf and Theudelinda, and thus a member of the family that had been dethroned in 626. This particular item in the chronicle is probably a mistake on Paul's part, since Gundeperga would have been much too old for Rodoald. According to Fredegar's chronicle, Gundeperga was married to the two previous Lombard kings, Arioald and Rothari, which makes more chronological sense. Regardless of who is right, however, all of these three kings had similar reasons for wanting to assimilate the political tradition of Gundeperga's family into their own. Paul the Deacon also informs us that Gundeperga was on one occasion accused of adultery, but she was cleared of the charge by her slave Carellus, who defeated the accuser in single combat (see Fredegar's more detailed description of her troublesome history, pp. 232–34). Rodoald was eventually killed by a jealous husband, whose wife he had seduced or possibly even raped.[740] As for royal marriage alliances in the eighth century, Paul the Deacon informs us that King Liutprand (712–44) married Guntrut, a daughter of a Bavarian duke.[741]

Not only the Lombard kings, but also their subordinate dukes, were busy creating alliances through marriage. Euin, Duke of Trento at the end of the sixth century, married a daughter of Duke Garibald of the Bavarians, thus securing the northern frontier of his duchy.[742] When he wanted to gain the help of Duke Grimoald of Benevento during the civil war against his brother Perctarit, King Godepert (661–62) offered Grimoald his sister in marriage. Grimoald accepted the offer, betrayed Godepert, defeated Perctarit and took both the throne and the princess for himself in 662.[743] In order to secure his own control of Central Italy, Grimoald gave one of his daughters in marriage to Transamund I, newly appointed Duke of Spoleto, in c. 663.[744] Not content with that, Grimoald also increased his influence in the duchy of Friuli in the north-east by arranging a marriage between the daughter of the deceased Duke Lupus of Friuli, Theuderada, and his own son Romuald I, Duke of Benevento.[745] Romuald's son, Duke Grimoald II (687–c. 689), was connected to the ruling dynasty (i.e., the dynasty that had been deposed by his grandfather Grimoald and had then retaken the throne after his death) in Pavia by marriage to Wigilinda, the daughter of King Perctarit and the sister of his son King Cunincpert.[746] We are also well informed about Duke Romuald II of Benevento (c. 706–731 or 732), who first married Gumperga, the daughter of King Liutprand's sister Aurora, and later married Ranigunda, daughter of Duke Gaidoald of Brescia.[747] The son of Romuald and Gumperga, Gisulf, was brought up at the court of King Liutprand, who married him off to a woman of noble blood called Scauniperga in c. 735.[748]

Hostages and exiles: women in trouble

Paul the Deacon provides us with several examples of royal women whose power evaporated with the disappearance of their husbands through death, deposition, etc. That these women did not necessarily have to end up in precarious situations is evident from several of the stories related above: royal widows could, and often did, exert a considerable degree of influence over Lombard politics, both on the royal and on the ducal levels. The power of women is, in fact, also indicated by the mere fact that Paul the Deacon usually mentions them in their capacity as one of the items that *should* be mentioned in his accounts of their husbands. Thus, one of the few things that we do know about King Cleph (572–74) is that he was married to a woman called Masane, who is said to have ruled with him until he was murdered.[749] It would also seem that several duchesses, such as the humble Radperga, wife of Duke Pemmo of Friuli (deposed c. 738), were of great help to their husbands.[750]

Probably because everyone knew about the various possibilities that were open to widows such as Theudelinda and Romilda, usurper kings often decided to get rid of the widows and princesses by incarcerating them and/or sending them into exile. Paul the Deacon is not our only source of information on this royal habit; we are also informed about it by Fredegar (pp. 232–34). Grimoald's coup in 662 is a typical example: when King Perctarit escaped to the Avars, he left his consort Rodelinda and their son Cunincpert in Milan. Grimoald had them both exiled to Benevento, which was controlled by his own family.[751] If Rodelinda had been allowed to remain in Northern Italy, she could easily have become a focus for resistance against the new régime. In Benevento, however, she had no basis of power and could cause no harm. Perctarit immediately recalled his wife and his son to Northern Italy when he retook his throne in 672.[752]

After Aripert II had fought his way to the throne in 701, his first mission was to secure it against the threat posed by the magnate Ansprand, a leading member of the faction that had controlled the throne before the recent civil war. Ansprand himself had gone into exile in Bavaria, but his family had been captured by Aripert's troops. The king had Ansprand's oldest son Sigprand blinded, thus making him unfit for politics, but he allowed the younger son Liutprand to rejoin his father in Bavaria, since he considered this boy (who would eventually turn out to be one of the greatest kings of Lombard history) an insignificant person. However, Ansprand's wife Theuderada was another matter: she had to be unmercifully dealt with. Hearing that Theuderada had been talking about her plans to become queen some time in the future, Aripert (who knew that these plans were fully realistic) had her brutally disfigured: her nose and her ears were cut off. Ansprand's daughter Aurora was treated in a similar fashion.[753] After that, they were certainly less likely to become rallying points for rebellions. Lombard aristocrats had little love for obvious losers.

If high-ranking Lombard women ended up in the hands of the East Romans, they were clearly regarded as valuable political tools. The East Romans behaved in the same way with Frankish women, as is clear from Ingund's story (p. 151), which is retold by Paul the Deacon.[754] However, we should not forget that Byzantium was also considered the natural refuge for Western European aristocrats, men as well as women, who were in real political trouble. A Lombard example of this is Duchess Anna, who fled to Constantinople when King Liutprand conquered the duchy of Benevento and her husband Duke Godescalc was killed in 742.[755]

The first Lombard woman to fall in the hands of the imperial troops was Albsuinda, the daughter of King Alboin and Queen Chlodoswintha. She was taken to Ravenna by Rosemunda and Helmechis after her father's murder in 572. When Rosemunda and Helmechis were dead (see above), the East Roman commander Longinus sent Albsuinda all the way to Constantinople.[756] A more serious incident occurred some time around 600, when a daughter of King Agilulf was captured by the East Roman patrician Gallicinus and brought from Parma to Ravenna together with her husband Godescalc.[757] Agilulf was furious and, it would appear, continued the war with greater strength than would otherwise have been used. His ally, the leader of the Avars, sent him Slavic auxiliaries that were used in his conquest of Cremona and Mantua in 604. After yet another Lombard victory, the patrician Smaragdus released the king's daughter together with her husband and her wealth. She returned to Parma, where she died in childbirth shortly afterwards.[758] Another Lombard woman, who was regarded as an effective means of influencing political and military events, was Gisa, the daughter of King Grimoald and the sister of Duke Romuald I of Benevento. When Emperor Constans II agreed to withdraw his forces from the besieged city of Benevento in 663, he did so on condition that Romuald hand Gisa over to him as hostage. Romuald agreed, and Gisa was taken to Naples.[759] She was never able to return. The Byzantines held on to her and finally sent her to Sicily, where she died.[760]

Builders of churches

Some Lombard queens, although mentioned too briefly to give us a chance to learn what Paul the Deacon really thought about them, are nevertheless known to have excelled in piety. Thus, Gundeperga is said to have imitated the actions of her mother Theudelinda. While Theudelinda had a famous church built in Monza, Gundeperga ordered a church, likewise dedicated to Saint John the Baptist, to be built in the capital Pavia. She had it adorned with gold, silver and other precious ornaments, and she was eventually buried in it.[761] Paul the Deacon tells us a similar story of Perctarit's queen, Rodelinda, and Romuald I's duchess, Theuderada. Rodelinda was responsible for the building of a richly adorned church called Ad Perticas outside the walls of Pavia,[762] while Theuderada built a church and a nunnery outside Benevento.[763]

Not all women associated with churches acted of their own free will. King Cunincpert had his mistress Theodota sent to a nunnery in Pavia, which was later named after her. Although her position in the nunnery may have been quite elevated, Paul the Deacon makes it clear that she was sent there on the king's orders.[764]

Summary

A study of Paul the Deacon's portrayal of the only seven women in his chronicle that display a real degree of individuality and character shows that women engaging in political activities, according to the world view of *Historia Langobardorum*, were mostly to be feared and avoided. With the exception of Gambara and Frea – both of them belonging to the realm of mythology – only Theudelinda is described in a positive way. Rumetruda, Rosemunda, Sophia and Romilda are all described as villains. All of them are dangerous, never to be trusted. They often behave illogically, committing deeds that they should have realised would only bring trouble to themselves as well as to others.

Rumetruda's action leads to war, Rosemunda's result in civil war and her own exile and death. Sophia is arrogant and greedy; her attempt to rule the empire after a coup against the virtuous Tiberius II is perceived per se as an ungodly act which, of course, fails. Romilda sells her country and her people in return for sex; she is duly rewarded by being raped and impaled. Rumetruda and Rosemunda both appear in *Historia Langobardorum* as evil, seductive females equipped with poison and/or assassins.

Paul the Deacon's female characters are clearly stereotypes. The bad women are murderous, promiscuous, illogical and hungry for power. The good woman (Theudelinda) is very Christian and thus very virtuous. The old juxtaposition of Eve and Mary would seem to fit perfectly in the framework of the mind of Paul the Deacon.

However, as is clear from our overview of the other, less conspicuous, women in *Historia Langobardorum*, Paul the Deacon also provides us with a realistic background to the scenes of his stereotypical images. Most importantly, this analysis shows us the strong structural position of royal and ducal women. They were instrumental in forging alliances both with subordinate rulers and with external forces, they constituted an important political element to be reckoned with after the death of their husbands, and their very existence as, for example, hostages or prisoners could result in war. Also, they helped to construct a firm ecclesiastical power base by founding and building churches and nunneries. That their enemies sometimes dealt with them harshly was undoubtedly because they regarded them not primarily as women (i.e., as members of a weaker sex, a fact that might have induced them to behave with greater mercy) but rather as political opponents, just as dangerous as their male counterparts.

Images of female political culture from the Lives of Saints

Having looked at the major historical works from Gaul, Italy and England from the sixth century to the eighth, we will now turn to the saints' lives, the *vitae*. To the modern reader, this hagiographical material may at first sight appear tedious, boring and based on all kinds of superstitions of the pre-modern age, especially a belief in the ability to perform miracles. To read and understand the purpose of a *vita* is, for many today, very difficult. The meanings and the symbols are often hidden from our eyes; we do not possess the correct codes to unlock the texts and spot what we are supposed to read between the lines.

Perhaps the most important fact to remember when confronted by a hagiographical text, is that the chief aim of the writer was to prove beyond any reasonable doubt that the object of his (or, in Baudonivia's case, her) work is indeed a saint. This meant focusing on the virtuous *power* of the person in question. The reader had to be made fully aware of the fact that God worked through the saint, that the saint acted as a vessel for God's miraculous power. The hagiographer was also forced to make his audience understand the nature of this power: that it was clean and Christian, not founded on magical arts and paganism. A miracle was only accepted as a true miracle if it (and its hidden message) conformed to Christian teachings. Another important fact, not to be forgotten, is the actual function of the texts. The *vitae* were used to train the members of the monastic communities and give them inspiration in their own battle against whatever temptations and adversities Satan and the demons might use against them. They were intended for frequent public reading on the anniversary of the saint's death, or of the translation of the saint's relics, or of the dedication of his or her basilica, or some other important festivity. Furthermore, they had an important economic function, since they recorded land transactions and promoted cults of monastic founders (or foundresses) in order to attract new donors to the communities.

For our purpose, the biographies devoted to female saints (all of whom are connected with Gaul) that were written before the Carolingian age are of particular importance. While the actual texts are short, the biographies are still relatively numerous when seen from an early medieval perspective. Merovingian hagiography was a flourishing literary genre, and holy women were often objects of interest for clerical writers. However, I have also decided to include a couple of other texts, since the picture they provide of female political culture (such as Eddius' description of Queen Irminburga) is too important to be ignored. Most of the texts studied in the present analysis were written by contemporaries of the saints themselves, or at least by someone who lived within the same period (sometimes a couple of decades after the saint's death).[765]

Genovefa, protector of Paris

The first woman we encounter among the biographies of saints in early medieval Gaul is none other than Saint Genovefa (*Sainte Geneviève*, c. 429–502), the famous protector of Paris. Although written not long after her death (probably in the first half of the sixth century), neither the date nor the author of her biography is known.[766] Genovefa was clearly a woman of substance in fifth-century Gallo-Roman society. It appears from her *vita* that she owned fields in the vicinity of Meaux and went out to harvest them herself.[767] Since there were at the time no models of how a religious woman should live (a few monastic rules for nuns may in fact already have been written, but none of them seems to have been known in Gaul), Genovefa had to create her own models and her own way of life.[768]

She was born in Nanterre, today a suburb of the French capital, and went to live in Paris after the death of her parents.[769] By far her most famous miracle is supposed to have occurred in 451, as Attila and the Huns were approaching the city. The inhabitants were stricken by terror and sought to save their goods and money by moving them to safer cities. Genovefa, however, summoned the women of Paris and persuaded them to undertake a series of fasts, prayers, and vigils in order to ward off the danger. She also told the men to stop removing their wealth to other cities. Paris alone would be safe, she assured them, while the other cities would be devastated by the Huns. The women obeyed Genovefa's command, but the men refused to believe her. They accused her of being nothing but a false prophetess who prevented them from saving what they could from the approaching disaster. According to the *vita*, the Parisians were just about to kill her when an archdeacon from Auxerre appeared with a testimony from Saint Germanus, testifying that Genovefa was truly a servant of God. Hearing this, the men refrained from killing her. Meanwhile, the prayers of Genovefa managed to drive away the Huns and save Paris from destruction.[770]

During the remainder of her life, Genovefa lived according to her Christian principles. Among other things, she worked hard to build a church in honour of Saint Denis, she cured the sick, exorcised demons and travelled to several places in Gaul (such as Lyons and Orléans), where she was welcomed as the celebrity her biographer regarded her as being. When King Childeric I of the Franks planned to execute some captives, she persuaded him to let them live.[771] When the Franks besieged Paris, causing widespread famine, Genovefa was sent with ships on the Seine to collect the *annona* (a late Roman tax in kind, usually grain) in the town of Arcis-sur-Aube. Returning to Paris after a successful mission, her sole concern was to distribute the food to all according to their needs.[772]

Monegund, a recluse of Tours

Saint Monegund (d. c. 570) is known to us from the hagiographical work of Gregory of Tours. She appears in his *De vita patruum* ('On the Lives of the Fathers'), a collection of tales that may have been written as part of an episcopal strategy designed to subject the saints in question to ecclesiastical authority, in other words, to integrate them into the tradition of Gregory's own episcopal church.[773]

Monegund was born in Chartres. She married according to the wishes of her parents and had two daughters. Her spiritual career began as a consequence of the death of her children. After a period of mourning, she ordered a little cell to be prepared for herself, where she went to live, spurning the company of her husband. From then on, she devoted all her time to God, performing a number of good deeds such as giving food to the poor.[774] Soon, she left her household entirely and went to Saint Martin's church in Tours. She settled in a little cell and spent her time in daily prayer, fasting and vigils. However, as her fame spread, her husband became anxious to have her return home. This was apparently not to Monegund's liking, and her second attempt to settle in her cell in Tours succeeded. By now, she had acquired a following of nuns.[775] For the rest of her life, she continued to heal the sick and perform miracles.

Venantius Fortunatus and Baudonivia: the two biographers of Saint Radegund

We have already met Radegund, Queen and Saint, in the analysis of *Decem Libri Historiarum* (pp. 87–95). However, Radegund made such a great impact on contemporary society that she quickly became the object of two separate biographies, one by the great poet Venantius Fortunatus, who was her personal friend and wrote several poems about her,[776] and one by Baudonivia, a nun in the Convent of the Holy Cross.[777] The biographies are far from identical. Baudonivia knew Venantius Fortunatus' work and had no intention of copying it. On the contrary, she wanted to tell her readers about miracles that were not included in the previous biography. While Venantius Fortunatus shows Radegund as a heroic royal ascetic, Baudonivia prefers to paint a picture of her as a model nun. Aside from these two texts, we also possess a poem, probably written by Venantius Fortunatus with the help of Radegund (in fact, Radegund may have written the whole poem herself), about the Thuringian war in which most of her relatives were killed and she was taken prisoner by the Franks. The poem was directed to one of the few members of her family that was still alive, Radegund's cousin Amalafrid in Constantinople.[778]

We also have a letter written by Caesaria II (d. 559), Abbess of the convent of Saint Jean at Arles that had been founded by Saint Caesarius (whose Rule was adopted by Radegund for use in her own convent). From our point of view, one part of this letter is of special interest since its reasoning would seem to be directly related to gender attitudes and images of the day. Caesaria admonishes Radegund to avoid familiarity with men as much as possible ('the woman who does not avoid the company of men is lost one way or another', *femina, que virorum familiaritatem non vitaverit, aut se aut alium cito perdet*). Although clearly conditioned by the monastic atmosphere in which the letter was written, Caesaria's text nevertheless reveals a certain sense of agreement with those male writers who stated that women were more fragile and less morally strong than men. She appears to have taken it for granted that Radegund shared this view.[779]

Radegund was probably born in c. 525. As has already been described, she was a member of the Thuringian royal house, and she was taken to Gaul by Chlothar I after the above-mentioned war (probably in 531). Venantius Fortunatus tells us that Radegund, still a child, was brought up in the villa of Athies in Vermandois, and that her upbringing was entrusted to royal guardians. Chlothar eventually decided to marry her, a thought that was repulsive to Radegund. When he wished to bring her to Vitry, she at first managed to escape from Athies and avoid him, but the king had his will in the end. The marriage was probably consummated in c. 540, and Radegund became Queen of Soissons. As such, she is said to have piously avoided the trappings of royalty.[780] She used her position to bestow generous gifts on the poor and on various monasteries, obviously becoming well-known for her generosity. Among other things, she had a hospice for needy women built in Athies. At royal banquets, Radegund used to withdraw from the company in order to sing psalms to the Lord and provide fresh food for the paupers that had gathered at the door.[781] She did her best to intervene and save the lives of criminals that her husband had condemned to death.[782]

According to Venantius Fortunatus, the most crucial event in Radegund's life as queen was the death of her brother, another member of the Thuringian royal house who had been taken captive in c. 531. For an unknown reason, Chlothar had him killed in c. 550. Venantius Fortunatus regards the incident as instrumental in leading the queen to a life devoted to God.[783] To Radegund, the murder appears to have been a terrible blow. Her grief for the loss of her brother is one of the central issues of the poem *De excidio Thoringiae* (usually referred to in English as 'The Thuringian War'):

De nece germani cur, dolor alte, taces,
qualiter insidiis insons cecidisset iniquis
oppositaque fide raptus ab orbe fuit?
Ei mihi, quae renovo fletus referendo sepultus
atque iterum patior, dum lacrimanda loquor!
...
percutitur iuvenis, tenera lanugine barbae,
absens nec vidi funera dira soror.
...
sic miserae dulces consummavere parentes
regius ac serie sanguis origo fuit?
Quae mala pertulerim neque praesens ore referrem,
nec sic laesa tuo consulor alloquio.
Quaeso, serene parens, vel nunc tua pagina currat,
mitiget ut validam lingua benigna luem.
...
Christe, fave votis: haec pagina cernat amantes
dulcibus et redeat littera picta notis,
ut quam tarda spes cruciat per tempora longa,
hanc celeri cursu vota secuta levent.[784]

Oh deepest grief, why are you silent about my murdered brother?
How could the innocent have fallen into the wicked ambush,
Or was he ripped from the world by men of a hostile faith?
Thinking of him in the grave, all my tears well up again,
And I suffer again, and still speak tearfully.
...
The youth was struck down while in his first downy beard,
Nor did I, his absent sister, attend the dire funeral.
...
Oh, how can the sweet royal kindred end in such misery,
The whole blood line from which he sprang?
I should have endured this evil, not bring it to my lips at present
Nor be soliciting your comfort for my wounds.
Oh kindly kinsman [her cousin Amalafrid], I beseech, send me a letter now,
Sooth my raging fever with a friendly word.

...
> Christ hear my prayer: may this page find out my loved ones
> And may a letter come back with sweet painted messages.
> That my long delayed hopes after such suffering
> Will swiftly be fulfilled when your course is run.[785]

The poem clearly reflects Radegund's feelings of sorrow and loss, as well as her sense of belonging to a family (or rather what remained of it). The Radegund we hear in *De excidio Thoringiae* is certainly not an isolated individual who cares for nothing but God and her convent. Although she had been living in the convent in Poitiers for quite some time when the poem was written, she still retained a vivid interest in the world outside the convent walls, imploring her cousin to get in touch with her, at least by letter.

It would appear that Radegund left Chlothar's court at this time, possibly as a consequence of the murder. According to Venantius Fortunatus, this action should be regarded as an escape: she left the king and went straight to Bishop Médard of Noyon, begging him to consecrate her to God. Médard was thereby placed in a very difficult position. Married women were not allowed to escape from their husbands and join nunneries; it was against the law, and most husbands strongly disapproved of it. Radegund's husband, moreover, was none other than the powerful King Chlothar I, a man who was used to getting what he wanted. Frankish nobles quickly appeared on the scene, harassing Médard in order to prevent him from granting Radegund's wish. The bishop, however, managed to come up with a compromise: he did consecrate her, but not as a nun – Radegund became a deaconess.[786]

As a deaconess, Radegund continued to display her Christian generosity even more clearly than she had done as a queen.[787] She settled at a villa at Saix, not far from Tours and Poitiers, where she lived a couple of years.[788] She provided daily meals for paupers and even arranged baths.[789] For some reason, Venantius Fortunatus does not detail the end of her sojourn at Saix and her move to Poitiers. He jumps directly from her daily life at the villa to the day when she determined to seclude herself in Poitiers and begin the life of an ascetic, fasting every day and subjecting herself to what must be regarded as extreme versions of self-inflicted torture.[790] The rest of the biography is mainly devoted to the description of a number of miracles.

In the biography by Baudonivia, Radegund's early life is quickly passed over. For instance, Baudonivia does not link her move to Saix with her brother's murder. She simply says that Radegund went to Saix 'moved by divine power' (*operante divina potentia*).[791] Then, however, she describes several important episodes that are not to be found in Venantius Fortunatus' biography. According to Baudonivia, a rumour arose that Chlothar intended to take her back. On hearing this, Radegund was very afraid and began to impose even harsher torment on herself than before. Some way or another (the text is unclear) she managed to stay outside Chlothar's court. It is certain that she remained on reasonably friendly terms with her husband, since Chlothar supported her subsequent foundation of a convent in Poitiers.[792] Later, probably in 558 or 560,[793] Chlothar journeyed to Tours together with his son Sigibert, intent upon taking Radegund back once and for all. In her defence, Radegund wrote a letter to Bishop Germanus of Paris, who was accompanying Chlothar at the time. The letter was brought to Germanus by her agent Proculus, who also carried gifts to the bishop. Germanus did as he was asked: he pleaded with the king and, in the end, did manage to make him change his mind. Baudonivia describes how Chlothar prostrated himself before Saint Martin's threshold, praying Germanus to ask Radegund's forgiveness for having obeyed his evil counsellors and sinned against her. Germanus then went to Poitiers and told Radegund what had happened. She gladly forgave her husband and rejoiced that she 'had been snatched from the jaws of the temporal world' (*de saeculi faucibus ereptam*).[794]

Baudonivia has more to tell us. She maintains that Radegund, during the rest of her life as a religious in Poitiers, kept interfering in non-monastic matters, constantly striving for peace. Whenever the kings made war on one another, she prayed for the lives of all the kings and for an ending of the war. She dispatched several letters to the Merovingian rulers and made them agree to at least one temporary truce.[795] As for Radegund's activities within the convent itself, Baudonivia makes a point of stressing her ambitious attempts to collect relics, a practice that had begun already during her stay at Saix. She sent a man called Reovalis (probably the doctor mentioned by Gregory of Tours, see p. 164) all the way to the Patriarch of Jerusalem, looking for relics of saints. Imitating Saint Helena, she dreamt of securing for her nunnery a piece of the cross on which Jesus had been crucified, and in this she was assisted by King Sigibert. The king consented to her attempt to get the East Roman emperor to give up a piece of the Holy Cross, and the emperor himself readily gave Radegund what she wanted. All of these relics, especially that of the Holy Cross (which gave its name to the convent), turned Radegund's nunnery into one of the most prominent religious houses in Western Europe.[796]

However, the steadily growing importance of the Convent of the Holy Cross also created problems, both internal and external. It is clear that social equality did not exist. For instance, Baudonivia tells us a story of a housemaid called Vinoberga, who presumed to seat herself in Radegund's high seat after the queen's death. In doing so, Vinoberga crossed a social barrier that was not meant to be crossed, and she was soon punished by God. She is said to have burned for three days and nights, shouting that she had sinned against Lady Radegund and begging the saint for forgiveness.[797] We have already seen how the tensions within the walls erupted in open rebellion only a few years later (pp. 154–69).

The social and spiritual importance of Radegund and her community also resulted in a bitter cold war with the Bishop of Poitiers (Maroveus, see pp. 93, 156), who rightly regarded the convent as a forceful competitor on the ecclesiastical scene. The bishop refused to receive the relic of the Holy Cross ceremonially, and the king eventually had to ask Bishop Eufronius of Tours to do what was necessary in Maroveus's place.[798] After Radegund's death in 587, Maroveus refused to conduct her funeral; he was not even present. Again, the nuns had to turn to the neighbouring city of Tours for a bishop willing to assist them (in this case, the historian Gregory himself).[799]

As for Radegund's death, Baudonivia paints a picture of intense grief among a veritable army of assembled nuns. Apparently, the whole congregation had gathered around her bed, weeping and wailing, striking their breasts with hard fists and stones and crying to Heaven in despair. On the morning Radegund died, a great clamour is said to have penetrated the heavens. Angels were heard welcoming her, and the saint was received in Paradise.[800]

285

Eustadiola, a wealthy saint in Bourges

Eustadiola was one of apparently quite a few rich widows in sixth- and seventh-century Bourges who decided to establish themselves in a semi-retired religious life. Eustadiola's life was probably typical of the urbanised asceticism of the sixth century practised mainly by small communities without a firm institutional basis. In the end, this religious free-enterprise was doomed, since the official ecclesiastical authorities strongly disapproved of it. However, before the real spread of aristocratic monastic culture in Gaul and the spread of rules such as those of Columbanus and (especially) Benedict, women such as Eustadiola could do as they liked. After that, most of these holy people were forgotten, and it is only because her *vita* was embedded in the *vita* of her contemporary Bishop Sulpicius of Bourges (bishop from 624 to 647) that it managed to survive. The story of her life was probably written in the early eighth century.[801]

In her *vita*, Eustadiola is described as belonging to the local nobility of Bourges. Her parents owned land in several parts of Gaul, including Aquitaine. She was married off to a man of equal rank and had a son called Tetradius.[802] However, when her husband died, she decided not to remarry, but instead to devote her life to the service of God. Her anonymous biographer associates this decision with a display of pious generosity on the part of Eustadiola: she gave her goods to the poor, particularly to the poor who served God. Her houses within the city of Bourges were dedicated as basilicas in honour of the Virgin Mary and Saint Eugenia. She used her wealth to adorn the churches with gold and silver vessels, pearls and gemstones; she also had made crosses, candelabra, chalices and other vessels fitting for the sacred mysteries, as well as books and so-called turrets (reliquaries shaped like towers). In order to have a firm basis for her new life, she ordered a convent to be built, where she settled together with her maids and those women who decided to join her.[803]

During the rest of her life, Eustadiola continued to act like a generous and pious matron of her community. Her prayers, according to the *vita*, induced God to perform many cures and miracles.[804] She is said to have fed the hungry, clothed the naked and supported widows and orphans. After her death (she is supposed to have died at the age of ninety in 684), the people of Bourges mourned her greatly, and Bishop Rocco proclaimed that he had never before witnessed such enormous grief at the death of a religious. Of course, miracles soon began to occur at her tomb.[805]

Rusticula, the heiress who was kidnapped

Rusticula was abbess of the convent of Saint Jean in Arles from c. 575 to 632, a remarkably long tenure that can hardly have failed to make her something of a living institution in Provence. According to the beginning of the *vita*, her biography was written during the rule of her immediate successor Celsa.[806]

Rusticula was probably born in c. 556 to a wealthy Gallo-Roman family in the district of Hebocassiac in the territory of Vaison; her father was called Valerian and her mother Clementia. Shortly after her birth, both her father and her young brother died, leaving Rusticula alone with her mother.[807] When she was only five years old, Rusticula, because of her position as heiress to a big fortune, was kidnapped by a greedy nobleman called Ceraonius. Ceraonius entrusted the child to his mother for upbringing so that he might marry her and thus gain control of her wealth when she reached the age of consent. Ceraonius' plan would probably have succeeded if it had not been for Abbess Liliola of the convent of Saint Jean at Arles. On hearing of the incident, she persuaded King Gunthchramn to force Ceraonius into releasing the girl and sending her to Arles. Ceraonius protested and even made a formal request to the king to be allowed to marry Rusticula, but Gunthchramn supported Liliola. As a result, the young heiress was sent to the convent.[808]

When Clementia heard what had happened, she wept bitterly and tried to use what influence she had to force Liliola to give up the child and send her home. She contacted the local bishop and asked him to intervene in her favour. The bishop refused to help her and tried to make Clementia accept that her daughter was now lost to the world but not to Christ. Clementia took no consolation in this. Instead, she sent some of her relatives with various gifts to persuade Rusticula herself to abandon her life at Arles for home, where her dear mother had need of her. According to her biographer, Rusticula, 'whose faith was firmly founded on an unshakable rock' (*cuius fidei fundamenta stabilita iam erant supra petram firmissimam*), scorned the worldly presents and refused to leave the convent.[809]

When Liliola died, in about 575, Rusticula succeeded her as abbess.[810] The rest of her long life was, according to her biographer, filled with various kinds of good and pious deeds. She excelled in abstinence, vigils, fasting and praying. She also received heavenly visions and carried on a long struggle against Satan and the forces of evil. However, on one occasion (probably in 613), she got into real trouble. A bishop called Maximus and a patrician by the name of Ricomer went to King Chlothar II and accused Rusticula of secretly supporting the king's enemies. According to Jo Ann McNamara, the accusation of treason suggested a continuing loyalty, on the part of Rusticula, to Brunhild and her supporters, who had recently been defeated in the political struggles against Chlothar; in other words, Rusticula might have been guilty of the charges, a fact denied, of course, by the hagiographer.[811]

Chlothar ordered Ricomer to proceed immediately to Arles to make a thorough enquiry into the matter and summon Rusticula to trial. The way the biographer describes the nuns' reaction to this threat makes it clear that he regarded the convent as a place of real power, equal to, if not identical with, that of the temporal world. The nuns are supposed to have 'seized weapons of celestial grace' (*arma gratiae caelestis arripientes*) against the military force of Ricomer. 'Modulating their voices in psalms, they called upon the heavenly defender...' (*modulatis vocibus psallentes illum poscebant defensorem e caelis*). When a man called Audoaldus, intent upon showing his loyalty to Ricomer, sought to strike Rusticula with his sword, God caused the raised sword to fall from his hands.[812] Ricomer, however, claimed that he had found enough evidence to prove that Rusticula was indeed guilty. Hearing this, Chlothar grew furious and dispatched Duke Faraulf with orders to bring the abbess into his presence. Faraulf arrived in Arles and demanded that Rusticula be brought out from the convent. Rusticula responded that she preferred to obey the King of Heaven than the one who reigned on earth and that she would rather die than transgress the Rule of Caesarius (according to which it was clearly forbidden for a nun, even an abbess, ever to leave the convent buildings).

Faraulf understood her reasoning, but he also understood that his own life would be in jeopardy if he failed to carry out the king's orders. Therefore, he did what persons in such situations normally do: he delegated the order to someone else, in this case Nymfidius, the governor of Arles. If Nymfidius did not bring the abbess out of the nunnery, Faraulf promised to see to it that Nymfidius would be beheaded. The frightened governor begged Rusticula to come out voluntarily without violence. To prevent a tragedy, she finally agreed. There was nothing the nuns could do, except for 'ululating for their absent mother' (*pro matris absentia ululatibus*).[813]

Considered guilty without being given a chance to summon witnesses of her own, Rusticula was placed under guard in a cell of a monastery in the city. After seven days, her journey to Chlothar began. At that time, however, Bishop Domnolus of Vienne went to the king and denounced him for giving grave offense to God by condemning the abbess in an unjust judgment. Chlothar then sent two counts, both described by the biographer as God-fearing men, to lead Rusticula to him with honour and reverence. They were also to provide her with whatever she might need in every city they passed through. At last, when she had been led before the king, Rusticula's very presence testified for her, and the king and all his court began to venerate her and give her the honour that she was due. Nevertheless, Chlothar made her swear a solemn oath that the charges brought against her were untrue, and even then he still hesitated about what to do with her. The lords of the palace, however, told Chlothar that Rusticula ought to be restored to her former position, and the king finally did as he was advised. Provided with royal authorisation, Rusticula returned to her convent. When it was announced in Arles that she was near the city, a great crowd of all ages and sexes ran out, all rejoicing that she was no longer under suspicion. The nuns greeted her with chanting. Rusticula is said to have proclaimed that she owed her freedom to the prayers of the nuns, which had been instrumental in restoring her. Those who had wrongly accused her of treason turned up a few days later, confused and repentant, humbly asking her pardon. Rusticula gladly forgave her former enemies and promised to include them in her prayers.[814]

Rusticula died in c. 632 (or possibly 627). Her passing did not take place in silence. On the contrary, she was surrounded by a veritable troop of singing nuns. When on one occasion they lowered their voices, the dying abbess ordered them to sing louder. After her death, the convent is said to have exploded in groaning, weeping and wailing, as the nuns mourned the mother they had lost. When she was buried by Bishop Theodosius, even the Jews of Arles joined the throngs of people assembled to venerate her.[815]

Desiderius of Vienne, a martyr produced by Brunhild

As we have seen in the analyses of Gregory of Tours and of Fredegar's chronicle and *Liber Historiae Francorum*, there were two images of Queen Brunhild in early medieval Gaul: a positive sixth-century one and a very negative seventh-century one. The first clear evidence of the second, made possible by the victory of Chlothar II in 613, is to be found in the two *passiones* of Bishop Desiderius of Vienne, one of Brunhild's chief ecclesiastical opponents in Burgundy. One of the texts is anonymous, the other was written by King Sisebut of the Visigoths.[816]

The anonymous work known as *Passio Sancti Desiderii episcopi et martyris* was probably written shortly after 613, when such a text was needed because of the flourishing of the cult of Desiderius, and when Brunhild was safely dead and therefore could not intervene against the writer.[817] This text is the earliest evidence of the conflict between Brunhild and clergymen over a particular question: whether Theuderic's children by his mistresses were legitimate. The issue was to reappear in *Vita Columbani* by Jonas of Bobbio (see below). In the *passio*, Brunhild is introduced to the reader as a 'second Jezebel' (*tunc usurpata daemonio secunda Iezabel*),[818] a prominent political actor during the exile of the hero of the story, Bishop Desiderius, to an island.[819] Eventually, Desiderius is recalled from his exile, but the evil female persecutor is only waiting to attack him with new and deadlier weapons.[820] The conflict is brought to a climax by Desiderius' complaints to Theuderic of the latter's lack of sexual morals. When 'the above mentioned Jezebel' hears about this, she decides to kill the bishop.[821] Nothing can help Desiderius, who dies as a martyr at the hands of the queen's henchmen.[822]

King Sisebut's *Vita vel Passio Sancti Desiderii*, a text that must also have been written shortly after the events described (Sisebut died in 621), is more elaborate and differs somewhat from the anonymous *passio*; but the anti-Brunhildian tendency is similar. Sisebut begins by telling us that Desiderius was born into an old Gallo-Roman family and that he became Bishop of Vienne.[823] Theuderic and Brunhild, on the other hand, are both described as villains, Brunhild in particular as a great friend of all things evil.[824] Together, they see to it that Desiderius is sent off to an island, but he manages to get back and retake his diocese.[825] Brunhild and Theuderic respond by having him killed.[826] Not satisfied, Sisebut continues his tale by informing his readers of the divine payment due: chapter 21 is devoted the horrible, but well-deserved, death of Brunhild.[827]

These *passiones* are, of course, political texts. We must also take into account that Sisebut probably had another motive apart from wanting to denigrate Brunhild and praise Desiderius; he appears to have used his *passio* to show how a good king (such as Sisebut himself) was supposed to act by making very clear how the exact opposite of a model king was believed to live. Nevertheless, the *passiones* are a great help in understanding Brunhild as a political actor. As Ian Wood has rightly pointed out, they show Brunhild treating the Church in much the same way as she treated secular power structures. A bishop was a powerful figure, just like a duke or a count. Since a dangerous duke or count could and should be got rid of, so, she appears to have argued, could and should a bishop. Desiderius represented a threat; therefore, he was removed and finally killed.[828] Exactly why he constituted a threat is impossible to tell. I find it hard to accept that Brunhild was terrified by his complaints that Theuderic slept with mistresses instead of with his wife. Although a royal wife might weaken Brunhild's personal position at court, it did not necessarily have to be that way; she had obviously been able to co-exist with Faileuba (Childebert II's wife). It is more likely that Desiderius was dangerous because he was a leading member of the aristocratic opposition of Burgundy (for a further discussion of Brunhild's reasons for attacking clergymen, see below on Columbanus' role, pp. 294–95).

Jonas of Bobbio: the Life of Columbanus

One of the most famous of all early medieval *vitae*, the *Vita Columbani*, was written between 639 and 643 by Jonas of Bobbio.[829] It was of considerable importance to a number of other writers, such as the anonymous Burgundian chronicler referred to as 'Fredegarius' and the likewise anonymous biographers of saints such as Wandregisel and Germanus of Grandval.[830] It tells of Saint Columbanus (d. 615), a holy Irishman who made his spiritual influence felt in several parts of continental Europe, from Gaul to Italy, and of his successors Athala, Bertulf and Eustasius as abbots in the monasteries he established. Jonas himself belonged to the second generation of Columbanian monasticism, having being trained by Athala and Bertulf. He later came to be associated with secular as well as ecclesiastical leaders in Merovingian Gaul, such as Queen Balthild and Saint Amandus.[831] For our purpose, two parts of the *vita* are of particular interest: Jonas' description (in Book I) of Columbanus' quarrel with Brunhild and his tales (in Book II) of the major female saint of Columbanian monasticism, Burgundofara.

Jonas' description of Columbanus' arrival in Gaul is puzzling and probably not entirely correct. He claims that Columbanus arrived during the reign of Sigibert I[832] and that Luxeuil, where his most famous monastery was founded, was a wilderness at the time (i.e., Columbanus founded it himself without a royal benefactor).[833] None of this information would appear to be true: Columbanus probably arrived during the reign of Childebert II, and given the habit of the Merovingian kings of founding monastic houses, it is likely that Luxeuil was originally a royal foundation. The founder was probably Childebert himself or his son Theuderic, who must have actively supported Columbanus at the time.[834]

Jonas then describes how Columbanus' fame steadily increased. King Theuderic II of Burgundy often visited him at Luxeuil, and Columbanus used this opportunity to rebuke the king and tell him to get rid of his mistresses and get himself a real wife. The royal stock, Columbanus argued, should be seen to issue from an honourable queen, not from prostitutes (*ut regalis prolis ex honorabilem reginam prodiret et non potius ex lupanaribus videretur emergi*). Although Theuderic himself was soon convinced by these arguments, Columbanus had not counted on the opposition of a much more dangerous enemy than Theuderic's various mistresses: his grandmother, old Queen Brunhild. She is described as an evil old woman, a second Jezebel (*secundae ut erat Zezabelis*). Brunhild feared that the substitution of a queen for mistresses at the head of the court would deprive her of her own influence.[835] When Columbanus on one occasion visited Brunhild at the villa of Bruyères-le-Châtel, she brought the sons born to Theuderic's mistresses to the future saint and asked him to give them his blessing. Columbanus replied that these children should never hold the royal sceptre, since they were born in adultery. Brunhild became furious and immediately started planning Columbanus' downfall. She sent instructions to those living around the monastery that no monk should be allowed to leave its confines or should be allowed refuge. Afraid of what might happen, Columbanus then went to Theuderic and confronted him. According to Jonas, both the king and his grandmother begged forgiveness for what they had done. Theuderic and Brunhild promised to live better in the future, and Columbanus returned to his monastery. Very soon, however, Theuderic gave himself up to his habitual adultery. Columbanus wrote him an angry letter, threatening him with excommunication. Brunhild now launched a propaganda war against Columbanus, inflaming the king against him and beseeching all the noblemen, courtiers and magnates to influence the king against Columbanus. She also tried to get the bishops to bring him into disrepute and to examine his monastic Rule critically.[836]

In the end, an enraged Theuderic went to Luxeuil to question Columbanus on his ecclesiastical practices. Jonas gives us a lengthy description of the two men shouting at each other, both of them seething with rage. The discussion ended with Theuderic entrusting Luxeuil to a magnate called Baudulf, who was ordered to chase Columbanus into exile to Besançon. Columbanus was indeed deported, but, as it turned out, not for long.[837] When he observed that no-one actually guarded him, Columbanus returned to Luxeuil, thereby making Brunhild and Theuderic even more angry than before. A troop was sent to Luxeuil under the command of Baudulf and Count Berthar. At first, Columbanus refused to agree to their requests that he go into exile, but when the soldiers told him what might happen to them if they failed to drive him away (they risked death if they did not remove him), he agreed to go with them.[838]

This tale of royal persecution is difficult to interpret. It has usually been believed by its readers, mainly because Jonas wrote only a few decades after the events. In political history, Columbanus has therefore been perceived as a threat to the position of Brunhild in Burgundy. If he managed to get Theuderic to marry a real wife and not just sleep with his mistresses, Brunhild risked losing her influence at court. However, according to one line of interpretation, Brunhild's persecution had little to do with whatever went on in Theuderic's bedchamber. Rather, Brunhild and Theuderic are both thought to have responded to a much more serious political threat arising from Columbanus' great importance. His supporters and followers were drawn from the leading families of Austrasia and Burgundy, opponents of Brunhild and friends of the families of Pippin of Landen and Arnulf of Metz who were to come into favour following Chlothar II's victory over the old queen a few years later. As a result, Columbanus was hounded out of the country in 609 or 610.[839] This alternative interpretation is strengthened by the fact that Brunhild in all probability had very little to fear from Columbanus' refusal to bless Theuderic's children. We know that the Merovingians never cared whether their princes and princesses were born to concubines or wives. It was perfectly possible for the son of a king's mistress to become a king. The only thing that really mattered was that the father was a true Merovingian: the legal status of the mother was not an issue in determining the royal status of the child. Actually, the whole story of Brunhild's quarrel with Columbanus seems a bit suspicious, as if it was constructed by monastic scribes working decades after the events, intent upon showing how they wanted things to be, not how they actually were.

Ian Wood links Jonas of Bobbio to the régime of Chlothar II and his successors: the *Vita Columbani* thus becomes a history of the victors and a *damnatio memoriae* for the losers. We know that Luxeuil was under royal control later in the seventh century. For instance, it was used as a prison for notable political figures such as Ebroin and Leodegar of Autun. Luxeuil, in fact, appears to have functioned as a kind of propagandist centre for Brunhild's victorious enemies.[840] Not surprisingly, Jonas often flatters Chlothar II and his faction. For example, according to the *vita*, Columbanus predicted the king's ultimate success on three occasions.[841]

Looked at from these alternative perspectives, the story of the persecution of Columbanus becomes even more interesting than at first sight. While still a good source of information on how powerful women were visualised in the seventh century and how a queen such as Brunhild is supposed to have been able to act, it also tells us much about the politics of hagiography. Jonas was trying hard to make Brunhild and, to a lesser extent, Theuderic look like a villain, and he almost overdid it. From the point of view of the faction of Chlothar II, this was just as it should (and needed to) be. The hypothesis if true, as I believe it is, indirectly demonstrates how powerful, and how feared, Queen Brunhild must have been before her defeat.[842]

Reverting to Jonas' story we find that Columbanus, exiled from Burgundy, spent some time travelling in other parts of Gaul and then moved on to the Austrian Alps, where he founded a missionary centre on Lake Constance at Bregenz. His only companion in those days appears to have been Burgundofara's brother Chagnoald, who later became Bishop of Laon and was entrusted with the supervision of his sister's convent.[843] While describing these events, Jonas also makes full use of the various opportunities to make Brunhild look even worse than she already does: he tells us how she and Theuderic were responsible for the killing of Bishop Desiderius of Vienne,[844] and he delights in the tale of her gruesome death at the hands of Chlothar II's soldiers.[845] As for Columbanus, he finally ended up in Lombard Italy, where he was welcomed by King Agilulf and was allowed to establish another important monastery, Bobbio. He died at Bobbio in 615.[846]

After devoting the first book of *Vita Columbani* to the life of the saint himself, Jonas narrates the lives of Columbanus' successors at Luxeuil (which had been entrusted to Eustasius, d. 629), Bobbio and the other monasteries founded under his patronage. From our point of view, the most interesting person to appear in this context is Burgundofara (b. c. 603, d. c. 645), daughter of a wealthy magnate called Chagneric and his wife Leudegund and sister of Chagnoald.[847] Jonas tells us that Chagneric had betrothed Burgundofara and meant to give her away in marriage against her will, but that God had intervened. The young woman had been stricken with a severe affliction of the eyes and a burning fever. Eustasius, who was visiting the family at the time, then rebuked Chagneric, claiming that Burgundofara's illness was entirely his fault; the girl had previously been consecrated to the Lord by Columbanus himself and could therefore not be given away in marriage.[848] Chagneric admitted his guilt and repented. However, after Burgundofara's health had returned, her father again decided to give her away in marriage. Fearful of what might happen, Burgundofara fled from her parents' home together with a friend and sought sanctuary in a church. Chagneric was furious, sending some boys after them with orders to kill Burgundofara. Although they did not dare to violate the sanctuary, to appease her father's wrath they threatened her with death. Again, it fell to Eustasius to set things right. Reproaching Chagneric, he freed Burgundofara from custody and had the local bishop consecrate the girl and dress her in the religious habit. They then proceeded to build a convent for her on family land near Meaux, a religious house that was first called Evoriacum and was renamed Faremoutiers after her death in her honour.[849]

Burgundofara later appears in the text when Jonas relates how an opponent of Eustasius, the monk Agrestius, tried to introduce modifications to the Rule at the Columbanian monasteries. On one occasion, Agrestius made his way to Evoriacum to try to persuade Burgundofara to join his cause. Jonas says that she confounded him 'not in a feminine manner, but with a virile response' (*non femineo more, sed virili confundit responsione*), telling him to abandon his insane ways. Agrestius fled quickly to his own supporters, not troubling her further.[850]

It would appear that Jonas spent some time in the 640s collecting stories about Burgundofara and her community, since we know that he visited the neighbourhood of Meaux at this time. Since the stories are told in the first person, we may guess that they were sent to him by a nun of the community. From the eleventh chapter to the twenty-second chapter of the second book of *Vita Columbani*, the history of the nuns at Evoriacum dominates Jonas' narrative, but most of the material is of little importance to the present study. It is difficult to place Jonas' pious tales within a larger perspective. The general social and political position of the convent is seldom remarked upon, although we know from a few hints that Burgundofara's foundation must have been of great local importance. One of the leading men of

Francia, Aega, is briefly described as an enemy of the community, violating the convent boundaries and settling his own servants there. Why he did so, however, is unknown. Burgundofara and her family must have been perceived as a political threat to Aega's aristocratic faction.[851] Some instances among the stories, however, are clearly deserving of note, illustrating important aspects of the lives and mental attitudes at Evoriacum/Faremoutiers.

One such instance is Jonas' description of the nun Gibitrude's two deaths. This indicates the importance of visions and penitence, and testifies to the conceptualisation of the spiritual forces of Heaven in military terms. Gibitrude was seized with fever and died. As she described it afterwards, she saw the white-garbed troops and all the militia of heaven standing before the glory of the Eternal Judge. She then heard a voice telling her to return to her life and settle her affairs; she still nursed too many grievances for slights inflicted upon her by others. Shortly afterwards, she returned to life, confessing her guilt and living for six months before dying permanently.[852]

Death is a recurring theme of the nun stories inserted into *Vita Columbani*. Apparently, a good nun was defined as a nun deserving to depart this life accompanied by song, preferably sung by nuns and angels. This is remarked upon several times, especially with regard to the nuns Augnofledis and Landeberga.[853] On another occasion, Jonas describes a deathbed in the convent as being surrounded by 'the cohorts of the sodality' (*sodalium cohortes*), who were supposed to sing psalms as dying nuns passed from this world to the next.[854] One nun on her deathbed even maintained that an invisible group of dead nuns, who had already ascended to Heaven, came to join the chorus.[855]

Despite Jonas' wish to paint life at Evoriacum in light colours, he does not refrain from telling us that not all of the nuns were satisfied with their lot. There were those who strongly objected to Burgundofara's rule. At least once, a large group of nuns planned to flee over the convent walls with the help of a ladder. However, God stopped them and made them confess their evil intentions to Burgundofara. Two did manage to escape but were later found and forcibly returned to the community.[856] Exactly what these nuns found intolerable is impossible to tell, but Jonas does give us some hints. It would appear that Burgundofara ruled her community like a true commander, not allowing her subordinates to indulge in secular vices of any kind. For nuns of noble families, her dictatorial régime may have seemed unacceptable. Jonas specifically tells us about a girl from a wealthy family who was tempted by Satan to eat more than she was allowed: 'he goaded her with greedy gluttony until she was driven to steal food to satisfy her hunger' (*excitavit gulae aviditatem, ac esuriem furtivo cibo aggressa est satiare*). When this was discovered, she was punished with heavy penance. Another girl, who was possessed by a similar weakness for food, was punished by God by burning fever that lasted until she died.[857]

Sadalberga and Anstrude, the saints of Merovingian Laon

Sadalberga (b. c. 605, d. c. 670) belonged to a wealthy family that included many other saints (on the principle that the generosity of monastic patrons was rewarded with the subsequent establishment of cults in their names). It would appear that she founded at least two convents for nuns from her inheritance.[858]

According to her *vita*, Sadalberga was born in the suburb of Leucus outside Langres. The anonymous biographer, who instantly reveals his own dependence on the work of Jonas of Bobbio, begins by giving a short monastic background to her career by mentioning a few facts about Columbanus, Eustasius and the wickedness of Queen Brunhild.[859] He goes on to relate a few miracles that are supposed to have occurred during Sadalberga's childhood and mentions that she was, against her will, given in marriage to a man of noble birth called Richramnus. Richramnus died only two months later.[860] Sadalberga remained a widow for two years, eagerly wanting to render her life up to the Lord by becoming a nun in the convent of Remiremont.[861]

At that time, however, King Dagobert I entered the scene. We know from this as well as other sources that Dagobert had a habit of intervening in aristocratic marriages, probably to secure a balance of power among the Frankish magnates.[862] The biographer describes how an important man at Dagobert's court known as Blandinus (or Baso) was able to take Sadalberga in marriage thanks to support from the king.[863] Although both Sadalberga and the biographer regretted this, the biographer admits that Blandinus proved to be a worthy husband.

The couple had five children, among them a girl called Anstrude, to whom we will have reason to return later.[864] In the end, Sadalberga managed to convert her husband to her own way of thinking. She assumed the religious habit and, with the assistance of Blandinus, erected a convent in the suburbs of Langres on land from her paternal inheritance. She was able to recruit more than a hundred women both from the free nobility and from her own service to live in the nunnery.[865]

After a while, Sadalberga began to have second thoughts about the project. She anticipated that the region where the convent was built might suffer from civil war between the Frankish kings and the various political factions, as would indeed be the case in the 670s.[866] Therefore, she left her home and set out for Laon together with her flock. Laon, with its strong city walls and its natural defences, was deemed a far safer place than the previous location. Bishop Attila of Laon welcomed her and led the nuns into the city, 'while a chanting choir rejoiced with psalms and hymns of praise' (*cum psalmodia et hymnidicis summisque laudibus deducit in urbem*).[867] Having made a careful topographical study of Laon, Sadalberga and her company began to build their new convent. Just as before, many women from noble families gathered around the abbess.[868]

The rest of the *vita* offers little of immediate value to the present study. The nunnery appears to have flourished, and Sadalberga did her best to imitate previous holy women, especially Helena, the Emperor Constantine's mother.[869] One element in the biography, however, should definitely be remarked upon: the emphasis put on Sadalberga's material wealth. We have already seen that she used her inheritance as the basis for the foundation of her nunneries. The biographer also stresses her great generosity, the fact that she loved to give alms to the poor and that she was never backward in providing hospitality to those in need.[870] Of particular significance is a brief note at the very end of the biography, according to which her brother Bodo had usurped her right to the farms which she had bestowed on the convent through a series of charters. The text is unclear, but it appears that Bodo eventually agreed to confirm Sadalberga's charters. The biographer maintains that they remain legal 'to this day' (*hactenus rata perdurat*).[871]

Moving on to Sadalberga's daughter Anstrude, we find that she in fact inherited the office of abbess in Laon from her saintly mother. Anstrude remained head of the community until her own death at the beginning of the eighth century (d. before 709).[872] Her *vita* begins with a short tale of the marriage between her father and mother. The biographer then describes a scene that is familiar to all readers of medieval hagiographic literature on women: the struggle between the secular world, represented by a suitor, and the spiritual one, represented by divine virginity. When Anstrude was twelve years old, a young nobleman called Landramnus asked for her hand, bringing much gold, gems and clothing to her parents. Naturally, the pious Anstrude resisted this, since she had already decided to give herself to God. Instead of joining Landramnus in marriage, she followed the singing clerks to the convent in which Sadalberga 'piously commanded a troop of nuns' (*pie regendo catervam sanctimonialium*).[873] This seems to have occurred around 657. When Sadalberga passed away (c. 670), Anstrude was consecrated abbess. As such, she proved herself to be very generous ('most joyful in giving away her goods', *in distributione suarum rerum letissimam*), providing the poor with alms, and hospitable to the needy and to pilgrims. The biographer also describes her as taking an active part in the world outside the nunnery, 'visiting the sick, calming the angry, restoring disputants to peace, and finally burying the dead.'[874]

However, the world outside the walls of the convent eventually came too close for comfort. These were violent times, with one civil war and aristocratic feud following another. Since Anstrude's family was a powerful one, her relatives could not help but become entangled in the various intrigues that made life dangerous for Frankish landowners and their clients. The *vita* describes how Anstrude's brother Baldwin was called to an assembly at a villa near Laon. It turned out to be a trap laid by his enemies (at the instigation of Satan himself, according to the biographer), and Baldwin was stabbed to death.[875] The murderers are not named, and there are too many potential magnates to choose from to enable us to guess their identities. The leading protagonist on the Frankish political scene, the mayor of the palace Ebroin, may have been responsible for Baldwin's murder, but we cannot be sure. However, the *vita* makes it clear that Anstrude herself was involved in Baldwin's actions. According to the text, the abbess blamed herself for her brother's death, saying that it was she who had sent him off to the trap, foolishly acting on the advice of the evil men who planned to kill him. It would appear that she had persuaded Baldwin to attend a specific court case that proved instrumental in the arrangement of the murder. Having devoted much text to Anstrude's complaints, the biographer nevertheless maintains that the abbess managed to present 'a reasonably calm and manly face'.[876] She continued to play her role as a powerful abbess, since 'the quality of her strength was more of the masculine than the feminine kind' (*in potentia virtutis eius nec iam femineo, sed virili more consolabatur*). The biographer describes, in words echoing the impact of military life on early medieval society, how she 'armed herself with the shield of patience'.[877]

The dangers to Anstrude's family did not disappear with the murder of Baldwin. The killers are said to have accused Anstrude herself in front of Ebroin and moved him to anger. Ebroin and King Theuderic III were persuaded to deprive her of her position as abbess and drive her out of the convent.[878] The royal army entered Laon, and Ebroin ordered Anstrude to be expelled from the nunnery.[879] This would seem to have happened some time in the last years of the 670s, when Ebroin's opponents, Pippin of Herstal and his brother Martin, took refuge in Laon (Martin later went to Ebroin on a safe conduct, but he was treacherously killed).[880] The nuns, however, acting on the advice of a man called Agilbert, refused to do as the mayor of the palace had told them. The 'cohort of holy nuns' (*cohors sanctarum sanctimonialium*) launched into a loud common prayer to God and urged Him to tear Anstrude from the hands of the enemy. When Ebroin's servants and companions heard the chanting nuns, they were seized with excessive fear. As they raised their gaze to the towers of the church, they saw a globe of fire rising to the heavens. Ebroin was terrified. The biographer describes how he threw himself humbly at Anstrude's feet, devoutly begging her forgiveness.[881]

Not even Ebroin's fear of divine punishment, however, could prevent the nunnery from encountering new dangers. A couple of days later, a man called Cariveus ('instigated by the Devil', *instigante diabolo*) began to contend with the abbess. He chased her into a church and drew his sword to kill her. Relying on the forces of God, Anstrude stood valiantly against the horn of the altar, arms outstretched, and prayed. Seeing how she scorned his threats, Cariveus did not dare come near her. When he begged for her pardon, she kindly forgave him for having attacked her.[882]

Two years later, the convent was in trouble again. Under cover of darkness, a young man called Ebroard entered the fortress of Laon together with his accomplices. In his desire to kill his neighbour, Giselard, he set the greater part of the town on fire. Realising his danger, Giselard fled as fast as he could. Ebroard began a thorough search but could not find him. Guessing that he must be hiding in Anstrude's convent, he went there himself and began to revile the abbess harshly. He ordered her to bring him the keys to the house, and Anstrude did as she was asked in order to calm his madness. Shortly afterwards, at dawn, God punished Ebroard by killing him right outside the gates of the convent. Anstrude retrieved the keys and had the 'miserable little corpse' (*miserum corpusculum*) buried.[883]

As if it was not enough to have to take on powerful mayors of the palace and violent madmen such as Ebroard, Anstrude was also confronted by Bishop Madelgar of Laon, the most prominent ecclesiastical officer of the city. Madelgar intended to take possession of the convent himself, seizing it from Anstrude. The abbess did what she could to prevent this from happening: she used her network of powerful relatives to counteract Madelgar's local influence. She sent word to Pippin of Herstal, by that time (this probably occurred in the 690s) the most powerful man in Gaul, through her relative Wulfold. Pippin responded by sending his son Grimoald to Laon with instructions to see that Bishop Madelgar ceased to cause Anstrude anxiety.[884]

The final years of Anstrude's life appear to have been relatively calm. When she was about to die, she called 'her troop of sisters' (*turbam sororum*) and told them that the day of her death was swiftly approaching. In the same hour that her soul left her body, it issued from her mouth like a snow white dove and flew straight to heaven, witnessed by all the bystanders. The people at the gates wept bitterly as her body was brought for burial.[885] Needless to say, several miracles occurred at her tomb.[886]

Gertrude of Nivelles

Gertrude was the daughter of Pippin of Landen, the powerful leader of the Austrasian nobility during the reigns of Chlothar II and

Dagobert I and one of the ancestors of the Carolingian dynasty, and his wife Ida. Her *vita* was written after her sister Begga's death in 693, when Pippin of Herstal, another member of the family, was in control of the important office of mayor of the palace. Gertrude eventually became one of the most popular saints of northern Europe; indeed, her cult helped to give her dynasty the ecclesiastical legitimation it needed to stabilize the institution of medieval kingship.[887]

Gertrude was born during the 620s. Her biographer describes how her father Pippin invited King Dagobert to a noble gathering at his house. A man referred to as the son of the Duke of Austrasia then stepped forward and asked the king to grant him Gertrude's hand in marriage. Dagobert was pleased by this request, as was (according to the *vita*) Pippin himself. However, when Pippin asked his daughter whether she wanted the boy for a husband, Gertrude lost her temper and flatly rejected him with an oath, saying that she would neither have him nor any earthly spouse, but Christ. The boy left in confusion, filled with anger.[888] It is not entirely clear who this 'son of the Duke of Austrasia' (*filius ducis Austrasiorum*) really was. He might have been none other than Ansegisel, who later did become Duke of Austrasia and is believed to have married Gertrude's sister Begga. However, it is also possible that the suitor was an usurper or, which is even more likely, an aristocratic competitor for Pippin's position who wanted to strengthen his own power base by marrying into Pippin's family. In any case, Gertrude's situation is too similar to Sadalberga's to be considered an accident; both girls were targets of Dagobert I's marriage policy, undoubtedly aimed at maintaining the balance of wealth and power within the Frankish nobility. It is perfectly possible that her refusal to marry the king's candidate was dictated by her father, not only by Gertrude herself.[889]

After the death of Pippin in about 640, Gertrude and Ida became nuns and founded the monastery at Nivelles, according to the biography prompted by Bishop Amandus. In so doing, they kept their portion of the family fortune out of royal hands and made it impossible for their aristocratic competitors to acquire it through marriage. Nivelles was destined to remain a possession of the members of the family that would later be known as the Carolingians; it still belonged to them when the Carolingians replaced the Merovingians on the Frankish throne a century later. The biographer makes no secret of the fact that other members of the Frankish nobility clearly understood the implications of this monastic withdrawal. 'To prevent violent abductors from tearing her daughter away by force into the alluring charms of this world' (*ut non violatores animarum filiam suam ad inlecebras huius mundi voluptates per vim raperent*), Ida is said to have snatched up a barber's blade and quickly cut Gertrude's hair into a crown-shaped tonsure.[890]

Ida formally appointed Gertrude leader of the nuns at Nivelles. On the death of her mother (who is said to have died at the age of sixty and been buried in the convent), Gertrude commended the stewardship of external affairs to others in order to devote her own life to her constant spiritual struggle against evil through vigils, prayers, reading and fasts. She erected churches to the saints and ministered to orphans, widows, captives and pilgrims with daily sustenance.[891] Later, when she became increasingly fatigued and sick from too much abstinence and ceaseless care, she was told in a divine revelation that her end was drawing near (she is supposed to have died in 658). Gertrude then abandoned all the temporal offices that she still controlled in her capacity as abbess and appointed her niece, Wulftrude, to govern the nuns in her place.[892] According to the biographer, who maintains that he was personally summoned to view her corpse, Gertrude was thirty-three years old at the time of her passing.[893]

Saint Gertrude is claimed to have performed a number of posthumous miracles; these were recorded in a special text following immediately after her biography. From our point of view, this text offers a valuable insight into the networks of religion and family in seventh-century Austrasia. For instance, the author mentions an abbess in Trier called Modesta who was 'bound closely to holy Gertrude in divine friendship' (*sanctae Geretrude in amicitia divina familiariter constricta*; this might imply a blood relationship). The author says that they 'performed their militant service equally' (*aequalem servitutis militiam baiularunt*), in their struggle against the forces of evil.[894]

Gertrude's biographer also provides a brief outline of the years during which Wulftrude ruled the convent. Wulftrude was the daughter of Gertrude's brother Grimoald, famous for his attempt to usurp the royal throne in which he sent the young Merovingian Dagobert II into exile and appointed his own son to the throne some time during the latter half of the 650s or at the beginning of the 660s. The coup did not fail to arouse the anger of other aristocratic factions, and Grimoald eventually lost both his position and his life. According Gertrude's biographer, Grimoald's political enemies also directed their anger at Wulftrude, and thus at Nivelles. 'The queens' (*reginae*; probably Balthild, the widow of Clovis II, and Chimnechild, the widow of Sigibert III) attempted to remove Wulftrude from Nivelles and confiscate the property administered by the convent. However, Wulftrude's pious prayers to the saints protected her from her adversaries. The wicked queens, according to the biographer, were transformed into defenders and benefactors of Nivelles, giving magnificent endowments. After a tenure filled with generosity towards the needy, Wulftrude died in 669.[895]

Aldegund, a mystic of the seventh century

Aldegund was a contemporary of Sadalberga and Gertrude. Like them, she was born in the age of Chlothar II and Dagobert I, when aristocratic influence was on the rise, and the Merovingian dynasty had reached the peak of its power and was trying to defend itself from the structural threats posed by the wealthy landowners.[896] Her original *vita* appears to be a direct transcription of the notes assembled by an abbot called Subinus[897] and another anonymous brother to whom Aldegund had entrusted her own description of her visions. A later version, probably a rewrite made when her remains were transferred to Maubeuge under the direction of her niece Aldetrude, is also of interest to the present study.[898] Neither the first nor the second version is clear about where she actually lived; the tradition that makes her Abbess of Maubeuge is in all probability a much later addition to her legend. It would seem that she was consecrated soon after her first vision but that she remained at home, probably gathering some women (referred to as sisters[899]) around her and using the local church for devotions. The *vitae* do not mention her living in any monastic foundation.[900]

Her biographer, who almost immediately refers to women as being members of a fragile sex, describes Aldegund as belonging to a noble family. Her father was a man called Waldebert, and her mother's name was Bertilla.[901] The young Aldegund is depicted as a very generous woman, providing the poor with alms and doing whatever she could to spread her family's wealth to those who really needed it. Bertilla is said to have been a somewhat greedy woman with a secret hoard of coin that she often counted. As soon as her mother died, however, Aldegund dispersed Bertilla's treasure among the poor.[902] She remained a generous woman throughout her life, taking all that she had received by hereditary right – gold, silver, precious stones and valuable garments – and distributing it all to buy church ornaments and provisions for the poor, keeping only cheap clothing and enough for her own daily sustenance. In the second version of her *vita*, her generosity is specified in terms of charters and public donations.[903]

Aldegund did not want to marry but preferred to serve Christ as a virgin.[904] She began to have nocturnal visions, sent to her by God and described as gleaming miracles of signs of His majesty.[905] However, not only God but also his main adversary, Satan, decided to pay Aldegund frequent visits in her visions. Aldegund's spiritual life appears to have been a long, unceasing mystical battle between the benevolent angelic forces of heaven and the wickedness of Satan, who strove to bring her down.[906] The struggle between good and evil within the mind of Aldegund appears to the modern reader as a series of almost military events, with Satan likened to a roaring lion or portrayed as a flame-haired monster blowing his breath around her bed, and Aldegund protecting herself by singing the psalms, burning with Christ. As for the world outside her home and her contacts with other people, all that we are told is that she was a friend of Saint Amandus.[907]

After her death, Aldegund is described as having ascended straight to the celestial court, where she rejoices in a chorus of angels. Summing up her greatness, the author of the second version of her biography proclaims that it was heightened by the fact that she was a woman: 'she vanquished the Devil's power, overcame the weakness of the female sex, manfully rising above worldly delights…'.[908]

Balthild: slave, queen and saint

Balthild, Queen of Neustria, had what must be regarded as one of the most interesting lives in medieval history. To a modern reader, Balthild's story is the stuff that dreams, soap operas and tales of high adventure are made of. She was born in England, fell victim to a slave raid and was sold in Gaul. Working her way up in the household of Erchinoald, mayor of the palace of Neustria from 641 or 642, she was in some (unfortunately unknown) way spotted and picked out by King Clovis II of Neustria and Burgundy, who made her his consort. After Clovis' death in 657, she appears to have become the most powerful individual in Gaul, reigning in the name of her son Chlothar III. She continued to be on friendly terms with her former owner Erchinoald, who held the office of mayor of the palace until his death in 658. Through her alliance with Chimnechild,[909] the widow of Sigibert III of Austrasia, she also managed to extend her power into Austrasia, where her younger son Childeric II was acknowledged as king (although still a minor) in the beginning of the 660s. By appointing bishops, establishing a network of monasteries and killing those aristocrats who stood in her way, she would appear to have increased her influence even more. Her closest ally was a man called Ebroin, whom she appointed to the vacant post of mayor of the palace. Eventually, however, Balthild lost her power under mysterious circumstances that have never been satisfactorily explained. Her last known official act was a charter for the monastery of Corbie in 664. At some unknown date after this, she resigned her power and retired to the nunnery at Chelles, where she lived until her death in 680, moving on to the Kingdom of Heaven and sainthood.[910]

Balthild's colourful history is not entirely unique. Other early medieval queens began their careers as servant women, for example Queen Fredegund. Jo Ann McNamara (who also counts Theudebert II's wife Bilichild and Dagobert I's wife Nantechild among the queens who started out as slaves) goes so far as to suggest that their servile status made these women more attractive to the kings because their status ensured that they would remain dependent on the good will of their husbands. Aristocratic women, on the other hand, could be dangerous, since they had powerful friends, relatives and landed resources of their own.[911] What is especially interesting about Balthild is not so much that she went from the ship of a bunch of slavers to the bed of King Clovis, but rather the mixed reputation that she has been awarded by the writers of history. As in the case of Queen Brunhild, we are fortunate enough to have two completely different sets of opinions on Balthild's character. One appears in Balthild's own *vita*, the other in the *vita* of Bishop Wilfrid of York (which will be discussed below, see p. 318). Balthild's *vita* has traditionally been thought to have been written by a nun at Chelles shortly after Balthild's death in 680, and there is no reason to suspect that this attribution is false.[912] The biographer was clearly anxious to emphasise the saintly qualities of the dead queen, silently passing over her acts of violence as if they had never occurred. As a patron of ecclesiastical foundations, Balthild had become the favourite of a highly influential ecclesiastical faction that included Philibert, the founder of the monastery of Jumièges, and Abbot Waldebert of Luxeuil. It would appear that Balthild, Ebroin and probably Clovis II as well worked hard to balance, or even neutralise, the forces of the aristocratic opposition by using the royal treasury to found monasteries and create strong bases for royal power among the religious houses of Gaul (such as Saint-Denis, Corbie, Jouarre and Chelles). Balthild and Ebroin tried to strengthen their hold on Gaul by appointing their personal agents and allies, such as Leodegar of Autun, to bishoprics and providing their own monasteries and convents with immunity from episcopal jurisdiction. Needless to say, this aroused anger among the aristocratic factions that used monasteries and bishoprics as nuclei for local concentrations of land and power. Some bishops were undoubtedly killed on Balthild's orders, including Bishop Aunemundus of Lyons, who was replaced by Bishop Genesius.[913]

Turning to the actual text of the *vita*, the blood-stained hands of Queen Balthild immediately turn white as snow. She is introduced as 'God's most precious and lofty pearl' (*ipsa pretiosa et optima Dei margarita*) who behaved 'most honourably' (*honestissime*) while serving in Erchinoald's household. Erchinoald is said to have wanted to marry her himself, but Balthild managed to escape by hiding herself in a corner and throwing some rags over herself. Instead, she married King Clovis.[914] As queen of Neustria and Burgundy, she distributed generous alms to everyone and spent her days suggesting various pious acts to the king for the benefit of the church and the poor. She fed the needy and clothed the naked; she steadily kept on funnelling large amounts of gold and silver through her faithful friend Genesius to various monasteries and convents.[915] After the death of Clovis, Balthild's sons Chlothar III and Childeric II took over the kingdoms of the Franks under the tutelage of Balthild and her allies. According to the biographer, the three realms (Neustria, Burgundy and Austrasia) held peace and concord among themselves because of the great faith of Lady Balthild.[916]

At this point in the *vita*, the biographer begins to enumerate all the good and generous deeds that Balthild performed at the peak of her career, deeds that have been interpreted by modern scholarship as vital elements within a political strategy (see above). She gave great estates and whole forests to religious communities in order to help them construct cells and monasteries. At Chelles (near Paris), she built a great community of virgins, appointing Bertilla as abbess. At her own expense, she built the monastery of Corbie near Amiens. At Jumièges, Philibert was given a great forest and valuable pasture from the royal fisc to help him build his monastery. At Curbio (now Saint-Laumer-de-Moutier), she gave many farms and much gold and silver to Lagobert. Likewise at Fontanelle and Logium, at Luxeuil and at the other monasteries in Burgundy, at Jouarre and at Faremoutiers. She also granted great estates to the basilicas of the saints (Saint Denis, Saint Germain, etc.) and the monasteries of the city of Paris, and enriched them with many gifts. She granted immunity to a number of religious houses, freeing them from episcopal rule and making them her firm allies.[917]

According to her biographer, Balthild spent her reign redistributing the royal wealth to ecclesiastical institutions. She (if indeed the biographer is a she, as is likely) then goes on to describe how it all ended, how the queen lost her earthly power and was locked up in a nunnery. According to the *vita*, Balthild herself always wanted this to happen. She longed for a life in God's honour, far from the secular world. Then why, might we ask, did she not remove herself from the court at the time of Clovis' death? As a royal widow, she would have been free to enter any nunnery she wanted, and a number of power-hungry aristocrats would have loved to see her leave the political scene. Instead, she waited until 664 or 665. The biographer explains this in a curious way: Balthild was *forced* by the Franks to remain their leader. The Franks loved her so much that they did not want her to cease governing them. That she finally managed to escape to her beloved Chelles was wholly due to the anger aroused by the wretched and proud Bishop Sigobrand of Paris. His wickedness earned him the hatred of the Franks, and they decided to kill him. Afraid that the God-fearing Balthild would stop them from committing this sin (even if Sigobrand deserved to die, which he did, it was still a sin to murder him) or even avenge his death, the Franks suddenly relented and permitted her to enter the nunnery. Conducted by several elders, Balthild journeyed to Chelles and was received into the holy congregation. Her biographer then adds an interesting detail: the nuns did not behave as they were supposed to. Balthild had ample reason to complain against those whom she had tried so hard to help while still ruling the kingdoms of the Franks. 'For they suspected her of false motives or else simply attempted to return evil for good' (*pro qua re falso ipsi eam habuissent suspectam, vel etiam pro bonis mala ei repensarent*). Only after the intervention of various priests and a long delay was peace restored between Balthild and the congregation. In the end, of course, the nuns grew to love the future saint.[918]

Exactly why Balthild ended up in Chelles is, as stated above, unknown. Did she actually resign her power to her son of her own free will, glad to get rid of the dirty job? Or did Chlothar III have her deposed in order to reign on his own? Or did Ebroin turn on her, hungry for even more power than she had already bestowed upon him? Or was she dethroned by the ecclesiastical opposition that opposed both her and Ebroin? As far as we can guess from reading between the lines in the *vita*, it is highly unlikely that Balthild left the secular sphere voluntarily. It is clear from what the discreet biographer tells us that the nuns of Chelles were noticeably hesitant about admitting her. Something did not ring true.[919]

Balthild remained at Chelles for the rest of her life. She continued to be a pious and generous woman, caring for the poor and for the guests. When she died, her chamber glittered brightly with divine splendour as a chorus of angels came to receive her most holy soul into the Kingdom of Heaven. She was buried with great honour, and many miracles occurred at her tomb.[920] Her biographer finishes by comparing Balthild to three former Merovingian queens, likewise famous for their piety: Chlothild (Clovis I's wife), Ultrogotha (Childebert I's wife) and, of course, Radegund (Chlothar I's wife). The fact that Ultrogotha is mentioned in this saintly company is particularly interesting, since we seldom hear much about her in other sources (see p. 95). Ultrogotha is said to have been a comforter of the poor and a helper of the monks that served God. There was probably more to it than that, but whatever legends and texts once existed about Childebert I's queen have since been forgotten or destroyed.[921]

Apart from the description of Balthild in her own *vita*, she appears now and again in other biographies from the late seventh and eighth centuries. In one of these texts, the Anglo-Saxon Eddius Stephanus' *Vita Wilfridi*, she is definitely not regarded as a saint (see below). Otherwise, however, the hagiographical image of Balthild is very positive. This is especially true of the two *passiones* of Bishop Leodegar of Autun, who owed his bishopric to the queen.[922]

Bertilla, Abbess of Chelles

Bertilla was, as was mentioned above, the woman who was chosen as Abbess of Chelles by Balthild while she was still reigning as queen. Although the present manuscript of Bertilla's *vita* is clearly Carolingian, I have not hesitated to use the story, since the text was apparently derived from several earlier sources in the eighth century. The Life of Bertilla has few miracles and also suffers from a lack of descriptions of the heroic, saintly qualities of its heroine. These characteristics are undoubtedly due to the specific function the *vita* was supposed to have at Chelles. The convent rapidly developed into a training ground for missionaries of monasticism and a centre for the conversion of the countryside through the dispensation of communion and confession. The author of Bertilla's biography does not appear to have wanted (or needed) a *vita* of a miracle-working saint. What was needed was the image of an abbess functioning as a mirror of good monastic living, a good practitioner of the Rule. By hearing about the exemplary life of Bertilla, those living at Chelles would learn how to behave in their daily lives.[923]

The biographer begins by telling us that Bertilla was a native of the province of Soissons, where her parents belonged to the nobility. The bishop of Rouen once questioned her about her intentions in life, and she responded that she had been devoted to Christ from infancy. However, since she knew that her parents opposed this, she kept silent for several years. In the end, her parents gave their consent, and she was consecrated as a virgin to God, going to live at the Abbey of Jouarre (probably founded some time between 635 and 642) in Brie-sur-Marne near Faremoutiers.[924] Due to her excellent qualities as a nun, she soon achieved senior status in holy obedience, and Abbess Theudechild laid increasingly heavy duties upon her shoulders over and above those of the other nuns.[925]

Bertilla, however, was destined for more important duties than serving under Theudechild at Jouarre. Queen Balthild, whose picture is painted in light and positive colours (generous, pious, religious, etc.), built a convent at the royal villa of Chelles, where, according to the biographer, she intended to live after Chlothar III had reached his majority. The convent completed, Balthild began to look for a woman 'of worthy merits and honesty and maidenly behaviour' to whom she could safely entrust a flock of holy virgins (*quam meritis et honestate seu moribus puellarum repperiret dignam, de qua fidens, gregem sacrarum virginum ibi adunatum sub norma sanctae religionis ei committeret*). Bertilla was chosen. After due persuasion, Abbess Theudechild agreed to order Bertilla to proceed to Chelles with a cadre of nuns from Jouarre to serve in Balthild's new foundation. It would appear that Genesius, who became Bishop of Lyons at about the same time, had something to do with Bertilla's appointment; his name is mentioned in the context of the move from Jouarre to Chelles.[926]

At Chelles, Bertilla developed into a model of piety, carefully teaching religious customs to her charges both through her speech and through her own sanctity. She was also busy adorning churches and altars, and she did not hesitate to use her resources to bring comfort to paupers and pilgrims.[927] As we have already seen, Queen Balthild herself eventually abandoned her secular position and enlisted 'as a soldier of the Lord Christ' (*Christo domino militaturam in monasterio*) under Bertilla, although contrary to Balthild's biographer, Bertilla's biographer does not mention the difficulties associated with Balthild's retreat into Chelles. The former queen submitted in obedience to the abbess.[928] When Bertilla finally died (about 700), there was sorrow in the whole convent, and many mourners arrived. After her death, she performed many miracles, thus proving that she was a saint.[929]

The crisis of 675: Bilichild, Chimnechild, Claudia and her daughter

Thanks to a couple of *passiones*, or acts of martyrdom, of male saints, we are given a few glimpses of womens' roles within the political culture of the turbulent years of Childeric II's rule. Childeric is commonly regarded as one of the last great Merovingian kings who refused to obey the dictates of his mayors of the palace and who never became the willing tool of aristocratic factions. The result of his rule was a crisis in 675 that was first described in the *passio* of Praeiectus, Bishop of Clermont (martyred in 675). It was later dealt with in two *passiones* of Bishop Leodegar of Autun, who was exiled in 675, restored to his diocese in the same year but then deposed and mutilated before being martyred in 678 or 679.[930]

Childeric II became king over all the three Merovingian kingdoms in 673 (before that, he had only held Austrasia). In the beginning, everything went well, and Bishop Leodegar was one of his closest advisers. Then, tensions began to increase. Leodegar grew critical of Childeric, both for the way he ruled his kingdoms and the way he lived. Leodegar condemned him for having married his cousin Bilichild, a union that was uncanonical in the eyes of the bishop.[931] The tensions finally reached a crisis and erupted during the Easter court held at Autun in 675. According to the *passio* of Praeiectus, the crisis was provoked by a dispute involving the lands of a woman called Claudia. Claudia had piously dedicated herself to God and given her lands to Bishop Praeiectus of Clermont before her death. However, Claudia's daughter is said to have been abducted by Hector, the patrician of Marseilles. Together, Hector and Claudia's daughter accused Praeiectus of appropriating Claudia's lands. They brought the accusation to King Childeric himself, an act that turned the affair into a much larger issue than it really was.[932] Bishop Leodegar supported Hector's claims against Bishop Praeiectus, who in turn refused to plead

313

because it was the Easter vigil (according to Roman law, this was one of the holy days on which prosecution of legal actions was forbidden).[933]

Praeiectus now chose to commend his cause to the queen-mother, Chimnechild (widow of Sigibert III), a shadowy figure who appears to have been more influential than the sources allow us to see (*Cumque vir Dei se undique artatum cognovisset, necessitate conpulsus, ita respondit, se causas ecclesie Imnichilde regine commendatus fatetur*). Whether influenced by Chimnechild, the mayor of the palace Wulfoald (who was hostile to Leodegar) or someone else, Childeric and Bilichild began to lean towards Praeiectus, probably fearing that Hector and Leodegar were plotting against them. The royal couple withdrew to the monastery of Saint Symphorian, and Praeiectus was asked to say mass for the king in the cathedral.[934] Hector and Leodegar now realised that they risked losing a lot more than just Claudia's lands: they immediately fled from the court and were pursued by Childeric's men. In the end, Hector was executed, and Leodegar was imprisoned in the monastery of Luxeuil.[935] Shortly afterwards, Praeiectus was killed in the Auvergne, probably as an act of revenge for the killing of Hector.[936] As we have seen in both *Liber Historiae Francorum* and Fredegar's *Continuationes*, Childeric and Bilichild (who was pregnant at the time) were both assassinated later in the same year.[937]

Bilichild's role in the crisis of 675 is not entirely clear in the sources, but we know enough to guess that she must have meant a great deal to Childeric. He had married her despite the fact that they were closely related (thereby automatically provoking the anger of the clergy, which Childeric must have known), and she always appears to have accompanied him, even when he was travelling and she was pregnant. In certain ways, she resembles Faileuba, Childebert II's wife, who also accompanied her husband to important meetings and lived at a court that was partly dominated by a queen-mother (in Faileuba's case Brunhild, in Bilichild's case Chimnechild). The circumstances of her death should also be noted: by killing Bilichild, the child growing in her womb could not be born to constitute a threat to the factions that opposed the rule of Childeric and his allies (Chimnechild, Wulfoald, Praeiectus, etc.). Childeric's and Bilichild's deaths also destroyed the influence of Chimnechild, who otherwise might have been able to cling to her position by reigning in the name of a son of Childeric's. If Childeric's enemies wanted to get rid of the king, they were forced to get rid of his female relatives as well.

The story of Claudia and her daughter illustrates another important aspect of seventh-century society: the fact that land could be used as a power base by women as well as men. Women could inherit land, and they could often do with it as they pleased. Claudia preferred to give it to God, while Claudia's daughter and Hector wanted it for themselves. Whether the daughter was really abducted or simply chose Hector as a suitable ally (he was, after all, *patricius* of Marseilles) is impossible to determine. What is important is, rather, that Hector and Claudia's daughter both appear to have done whatever they could, even involving the king, to get their hands on Claudia's wealth. When property was involved, gender did not matter: everybody wanted to get rich.

Austreberta, Abbess of Pavilly

Austreberta, the last female saint of the Merovingian period to be discussed in this study, was born around 650 and died around 703. Her monastic career largely depended on the work of episcopal saints such as Omer and Philibert, who both helped her (or used her) in their construction of the monastic landscape of western Neustria. The man who heard her vows, Bishop Omer (d. 667), originally placed her in the convent of Port-le-Grand in Ponthieu. After a time, Philibert (d. 685) sent her on to govern the convent of Pavilly, where she ruled as abbess until her death. Philibert's action was an element of a much larger undertaking that can only sometimes be glimpsed in the sources that have been preserved. At some point after 670, Philibert was exiled to the diocese of Rouen by his political enemies. Here, he spent his time establishing the monastery of Jumièges. This was at first a double monastery, with both monks and nuns, but it eventually split into separate establishments for men and women. The former was absorbed by the community at Pavilly which came to be ruled by Austreberta. We know that this systematic spread of nunneries and monasteries in Neustria included more holy women than her, but the *vitae* of the other local saints (such as Saint Godeberta and Saint Angadrisma) have not been preserved.[938] Austreberta's biography was probably written soon after her death by a contemporary who was familiar with the internal life of the convent, either one of the nuns or monks, or a chaplain attached to their service. Although some features of the biography appear to have been added in Carolingian times, the parts that are of interest to the present study do not seem to have been greatly affected by this.[939]

Austreberta was born in Thérouanne, the daughter of a nobleman called Badefridus and his wife Framechild, whom the biographer describes as a descendant of a King of the Alamans.[940] Even as a child, Austreberta began to put the world aside; 'manfully with all her strength' she began to despise all kinds of pleasures and to desire the Kingdom of Heaven.[941] When her parents wanted her to marry, she begged the Lord incessantly to save her from this terrible danger and preserve her for a life entirely devoted to religion. Badefridus and Framechild did not favour these plans but fixed a day for her appointed marriage. In desperation, Austreberta took secretly to the road, taking her young brother with her, and ran as fast as she could to Bishop Omer. The bishop fulfilled her desire, consecrating her to Christ. He also managed to change the minds of her parents, who grew to admire their pious daughter. Although Austreberta returned to her home, she never ceased to implore her mother and brothers to help her enter a religious house. In the end, they chose a new foundation on the River Somme called Portus (Port-le-Grand), whose abbess, a woman called Burgofled, greatly rejoiced when Austreberta was brought to her.[942]

Austreberta advanced rapidly in the ranks of the nuns. She was soon promoted to prioress (according to the biographer, this happened despite her sincere unwillingness), and thus to be Burgofled's second in command.[943] Having spent fourteen years[944] at Portus, however, she was appointed as abbess to the convent of Pavilly. This house had recently been founded by a magnate called Amalbert, who had placed his own daughter Aurea among the nuns. He had committed them to Philibert's care, but the future saint would rather have Austreberta teach the women what they needed to know. Two monks were sent to Portus with instructions to bring Austreberta to Pavilly. Taking two sisters with her, she went to Philibert and was put in charge of the convent.[945]

According to the biographer, who was obviously intent upon imitating a story in the life of Saint Benedict as told by Gregory the Great, the nuns strongly disapproved of the discipline taught by their new abbess. Infected with Satan's venom, the nuns even conspired to kill Austreberta so as to be freed from her rule once and for all. After the failure of their assassination attempt, they complained to Amalbert about her, making him believe all the lies and accusations that they had fabricated against her. Amalbert sought Austreberta out and began to insult her in the harshest terms. He drew his sword and attacked her, but she was not afraid. Proving that 'the heart in her breast was in no way feminine, but virile' (*nequaquam cor faemineum, sed virile se habere ostendens in pectore*), Austreberta extended her hands and bowed her head to expose her neck to the blow that would make her a martyr. Admiring 'such fortitude in a woman as he had never seen in a man' (*admirans constantiam feminae, quam in nullo unquam viro vidisset*), Amalbert put up his sword.[946]

After this incident, Austreberta ruled the convent peacefully for many years. The nuns, in all fewer than twenty-five women, became heavily dependent on her, and she herself took an active part in the evangelisation of the countryside and the ecclesiastical building programme associated with it. She built a monastery dedicated to the Virgin Mary and constructed basilicas to Saint Peter, Saint Martin and other saints.[947] An angel revealed to her the day of her death, and a crowd of nuns, priests, abbots, monks and others, men as well as women, streamed to the nunnery to witness her passing. The biographer asserts (although it is hard to believe that this is not simply an expression of his or her poetic style), that Austreberta's own nuns, when her death drew near, broke out in a single lament, hair unbound and breasts bared. They then started singing psalms until quieted by the dying abbess herself, who wished to tell them about the multitude of saints that came to greet her.[948] After her death, Austreberta performed a number of miracles, including scaring away Satan when he once appeared 'in the guise of an Ethiopian of sootiest blackness' and tried to kidnap a child.[949]

Eddius Stephanus: the Life of Wilfrid

Eddius Stephanus' biography of Wilfrid (d. 709), the controversial Bishop of Northumbria, was written in about 720, and is regarded as the first historical biography written by an Anglo-Saxon. From our point of view, the work is of great interest, since a number of women appear at various stages of Wilfrid's stormy career. Compared to Bede, Eddius is far more informative about his feelings regarding members of the opposite sex.[950]

Many of the female characters of Wilfrid's biography are painted in dark colours: evil women intent upon doing harm to those who strive to do good. We meet one of these villains right at the beginning of the biography: Wilfrid's stepmother. According to Eddius, the reason Wilfrid left his home at the age of fourteen to seek the Kingdom of Heaven was the cruelty and harshness of his stepmother.[951] Far worse, however, was the widowed Queen Balthild, the Anglo-Saxon slave-woman who had risen to become ruler of a significant part of Merovingian Gaul. Eddius gives a colourful description of Balthild persecuting the Frankish church with the help of her subordinate dukes, acting like the wicked Queen Jezebel in the Bible. According to Eddius, Balthild had nine bishops killed, among them the Bishop of Lyons. Balthild's soldiers almost killed Wilfrid himself, but his life was spared after some consideration.[952] As was explained above, these events should undoubtedly be interpreted as elements within a Frankish power struggle between the monarchy and various aristocratic factions. Bishop Aunemundus of Lyons represented a party that opposed the rule of Balthild and the mayor of the palace Ebroin. Balthild (probably rightly) regarded him as a threat and therefore had him murdered, replacing him with her loyal agent Genesius. Since Wilfrid (and thus Eddius) was a great friend of Aunemundus and his faction, Eddius' 'Wilfridian' view of Balthild was bound to be a very negative one.

The real Jezebel of the *Life of Wilfrid*, however, is Queen Irminburga of Northumbria, Egfrith's second queen. She is introduced to the reader as nothing less than a vessel of Satan. Eddius describes how the Tempter went prowling round God's fold looking for entry. He decided to use what Eddius defines as 'his usual weapon, one by which he has often spread defilement throughout the whole world – woman' (*consueta arma arripiens, vasa fragilia muliebria quesivit, per quae totum mundum maculavit frequenter*). In this way, at Satan's prompting, Irminburga grew increasingly envious of Bishop Wilfrid. She corrupted King Egfrith's heart with poisonous tales about the bishop, 'imitating Jezebel in her onslaughts on the prophets and in her persecution of Elias' (*quasi impiissima Gezabel prophetas Dei occidens et Heliam persequens*). She kept telling Egfrith about Wilfrid's great wealth, his monasteries, his wonderful buildings and (perhaps most importantly from the point of view of the king) his countless followers, arrayed and armed like a king's retinue. Egfrith was eventually persuaded that Wilfrid represented a threat. They bribed Archbishop Theodore ('money will blind even the wisest', *cum muneribus, quae excecant etiam sapientium oculos*) into helping them, and he readily agreed to humiliate Wilfrid, whose vast diocese was given to three new bishops.[953] Two years later, in 680, Wilfrid appeared at the Northumbrian court equipped with a written judgement, handed down by the Pope in Rome, that supported his claim to the diocese. Egfrith, however, cared little about papal orders. Wilfrid was condemned to prison for nine months. Queen Irminburga took away his reliquary, which was full of relics, and wore the holy objects as a necklace both at home in her chamber and when she rode forth in public. Eddius compares this last foul deed to a famous event in the Bible, when the Philistines carried off the Ark of the Covenant and dragged it through their cities after having defeated the Israelites.[954]

Not surprisingly, in Eddius' eyes, Irminburga was punished for her wickedness. In 681, when the royal couple was visiting the nunnery of Coldingham, the queen was suddenly possessed by a devil during the night. She suffered terrible attacks, and many despaired of her life. Abbess Ebba went to Egfrith and told him the reason for Irminburga's suffering: they had behaved wrongly towards Wilfrid. If he wanted his queen to survive, Egfrith would have to release Wilfrid and restore the relics that had been taken by Irminburga. Egfrith did as he was told, and the queen recovered.[955] In the end, Eddius assures us, Irminburga turned from bad to good. After the death of Egfrith (in 685) she changed 'from a she-wolf into a lamb of God', becoming a perfect abbess.[956]

Eddius' list of bad queens also includes a queen of Mercia (Egfrith's sister) and a queen of Wessex (Irminburga's sister). When the exiled Bishop Wilfrid tried to settle in Mercia, Egfrith's sister had him driven away, and Irminburga's sister did the same when he came to the kingdom of the West Saxons. However, none of these queens receive the same negative literary treatment as Irminburga herself.[957]

Not all of the women encountered by Wilfrid are described by Eddius as being bad. However, most of them are described as *powerful*. Power appears to have come naturally to Anglo-Saxon queens and abbesses; the question was not so much whether they had power or not, but rather whether they decided to put their power to good use. In Eddius' eyes, of course, putting power to good use was equivalent to helping Wilfrid. The queens mentioned above decided not to help him; therefore they were bad. Queen Eanfled, wife of King Oswy of Northumbria, on the other hand, was always ready to offer Wilfrid her assistance. She gladly received him at her court after he had left his home as a teenager, and she granted his request that he might be allowed to give himself to the service of God under the queen's protection. Eanfled commended Wilfrid to serve a nobleman called Cudda, who had left the king's service on account of his paralysis, to live as a monk at Lindisfarne. A year or two later, on Cudda's advice, Queen Eanfled granted Wilfrid's request to be allowed to set out for Rome. She sent Wilfrid to her relative, King Earconbert of Kent, and did whatever she could to help him. She fitted him out handsomely and sent messages to convey her highest commendation of him to Earconbert. He was to stay in Kent until trustworthy companions could be found for him. As it turned out, Wilfrid had to wait a whole year in Kent, and it was not until Eanfled intervened a second time that Earconbert managed to find him a fellow-traveller.[958] Another good queen (i.e., who was friendly towards Wilfrid), was Queen Etheldreda of Northumbria, the first wife of King Egfrith, who eventually became Abbess of Ely and a famous saint (see p. 250). Eddius says that she was obedient to Wilfrid in everything and that her husband (as long as *she* was his queen) was obedient as well. Furthermore, Etheldreda provided Wilfrid with land to build a marvellous church at Hexham.[959]

Not only the queens, but also many of the abbesses that appear in the *Life of Wilfrid*, are described as influential. Hilda, of course (see p. 248), appears as one of the most prominent monastic leaders of her time, participating in the synod of Whitby and sending representatives to Rome.[960] A number of other abbesses are also mentioned in their capacity as important persons, such as Ebba (described as very holy and wise) and Aelffled.[961] Aelffled in particular is demonstrated to have been a good adviser and a constant source of strength for Northumbria. She conversed with kings and participated in important ecclesiastical meetings with bishops.[962]

Discussion and summary

The analyses of the *vitae* and *passiones* have demonstrated several aspects of great importance to the present study. These texts not only reveal the attitudes of the biographers with regard to how a saintly woman was supposed to act, they also open up windows to society in general. By reading these biographies, we are informed (sometimes implicitly, but often directly in the texts) about ecclesiastical views on gender relations as such, about the gradual development of concepts of holiness and ways of conducting holy lives, and, not to be forgotten, about the biographers' views on certain powerful people who could simply not be ignored when describing the lives of the saints.

We must accept that these texts were written within the framework of a strictly ecclesiastical culture. Their views on what is good and what is bad are derived from and strictly dependent upon the norms of Christianity. Therefore, we should not be the least bit surprised when we find that women in general are regarded as inferior beings in relation to men. Distasteful as this attitude may be to our eyes, it was perfectly natural to early medieval hagiographers; any other view would have been regarded as exotic and dangerous. Thus, Eddius clearly believes that women are weaker and easier to corrupt (i.e., from Satan's point of view) than men. Several of the *vitae* of female saints (such as Anstrude and Austreberta) use words such as 'feminine' in a negative sense and words such as 'virile' or 'masculine' in a positive sense. Burgundofara, for instance, behaves in a 'virile' fashion towards Agrestius. The fact that Aldegund belonged to the weaker sex makes her victory against Satan greater than it would have been had she been a man. This attitude was shared by the religious women themselves: Caesaria II clearly regarded women as sexually weaker than men. To remain safe from their own lusts, women had no option but to avoid the company of men altogether.[963]

Having accepted this precondition, we also understand that all the women that were granted early medieval *vitae* of their own must have been perceived as extraordinary people, individuals who struggled against impossible odds and still made it all the way to sainthood. Or rather, someone (or some political and/or religious faction) wanted them to be perceived in this way. The biographers rarely wrote their texts for the sake of personal enjoyment, and they never worked in a social vacuum: as stated above, these texts had one or many specific purposes.

Judging from the *vitae*, it would appear that the lives and the various functions of female saints changed considerably from the fifth century to the eighth. The holy women of the earliest years of the early Middle Ages (or, if you will, the last years of late antiquity) were primarily aligned with and belonged among the losers, with those who did not conquer kingdoms or found dynasties. A saint such as Genovefa might be interpreted as having acted as a mediator between the Gallo-Roman world in which she was born and the Frankish warlords that conquered it. A person in Genovefa's position had to convince both her own neighbours and the new leaders that she was an ally worth having. Her weapon, of course, was her saintly power. If she could make Gallo-Romans as well as Franks accept her power as real, they would respect her and, in a certain sense, use her. It could hardly be regarded as a sign of weakness to support and help a defenceless woman belonging to a conquered people, if this woman happened to have direct access to God.[964] Although Genovefa was clearly a person of power in Paris (indicated by, for instance, her appointment to collect the *annona*), she apparently did not always succeed. When Paris was threatened by the Huns, her charisma was sufficiently strong to dominate the women, but her biographer admits that many of the men refused to accept her authority.

In the sixth century, the concept of holy women was quickly assumed by the conquerors themselves. A number of female saints are said to have performed one miracle after another, whether as religious freelancers (eventually associated with official institutions) such as Monegund or as powerful holy queens in nunneries, such as Radegund. They are described as harbouring healing power derived directly from the supernatural sphere of God, and they often negotiated with bishops as independent actors. The power of saintly women is often described as sufficiently strong to withstand the evil plans of various secular lords, even mayors of the palace. These saints, especially Radegund, appear to have continued Genovefa's role as mediators between warlords and the people, healing the sick and begging kings to help those in need and assist them in their pious works. Thus they served to mitigate the effects of the fratricidal wars of the Merovingians and to establish rituals whereby royal women could express the merciful side of early medieval monarchy without compromising the warrior image of the king.[965]

To some extent, these functions and characteristics continued to be of importance in the seventh and eighth centuries, but some of the most important aspects of feminine sanctity underwent a profound change in the development of Frankish society and Frankish Christianity. The official representatives of the church, especially the bishops, had always been suspicious of people, men as well as women, who acted or were believed to have acted as holy individuals, preaching, performing miracles, and so on on their own. Such matters should be kept within the established ranks of the church. After the initial process of conversion and evangelisation, and partly as a result of the rapprochement between the church and the secular monarchs, the hagiographers developed a more cautious, one might say more episcopal, attitude towards their subjects.[966] The female saints no longer performed as many miracles while they lived on earth as they had done in the age of Genovefa and Radegund; their acts of power occurred mainly after they had died and been buried under the auspices of the local bishop. At the same time, the holy women themselves developed stronger ties to the episcopal hierarchy than they had previously enjoyed. True, this could sometimes result in violent conflicts (as in the case of Queen Balthild), but it usually appears to have been the other way around: women worked closely with bishops or abbots who validated their personal designs and supported them against their secular enemies (such as angry husbands and kings).[967] In the days of Genovefa, this kind of female monasticism was almost impossible to conceptualise, since its very structures (rules for nuns, establishment of convents, female monastic traditions, etc.) did not exist. In the days of Gregory of Tours, it had still been relatively easy for women such as Monegund to experiment on their own. Gregory did not like it, but he was powerless to prevent it; the best he could do was to try to assimilate these women into his own episcopal traditions (especially the cult of Saint Martin).[968] In the seventh century, some women still got away into living like nuns in their own homes, as, for example, Aldegund, but they were quickly associated with proper monastic traditions (unless they were forgotten).

Trying to sum up the evidence from the study of holy women, it would seem that they followed a path that could, if they were successful (as were all those we know of; no *vitae* were written about the losers), lead to considerable social influence, at least locally, and sometimes, as in the case of royal widows such as Radegund, at a high political level. Life as a holy person was an alternative way to attain a position of power. For many women, it must have been a far easier path to walk than the one we normally think of when we attempt to construct models of social influence (i.e., the path associated with marriages, land-holding, queenship, control of minors, etc.). Of course, the ecclesiastical path was also open to men – all priests were male after all – but the female spiritual strategies are in several ways more conspicuous. Women did not have as many strategic opportunities as the men; they had to make the most of the opportunities that did exist.

This alternative way to gain influence over other people – a strategy that could, of course, be combined with more secular tactics – might also be tentatively understood as forming a part of a complex, perhaps not entirely conscious, attempt on the part of the new rulers in Western Europe to recover a charisma that had been nullified by the conversion to Christianity. After all, many of the new saints, male as well as women, belonged to the secular nobility.[969] By taking control of ideological assets, the magnates added spiritual power to their unquestioned secular power. If a dead relative could be regarded as a saint, the tomb of this man or woman could easily be transformed into a focal point for family prestige. According to one of the leading scholars in the field, Jo Ann McNamara, women were particularly well suited to this role because they shared the noble blood of their families but could not actively enter into the violent competition of the secular world. In other words, they were prevented from going to war or gaining lands by becoming the clients of kings, but they were *not* (at least not always) prevented from securing their own lands by transferring them to God through the founding of convents. Since they still controlled the convents, whether as abbesses or as the ones who appointed the abbesses, they were just as rich as before, but their lands could no longer be confiscated by greedy kings and dukes without a long struggle with the Church. They could also use their convents as ideological power bases by creating prestige on earth and favour in heaven.[970]

In order to walk the saintly path towards power and holiness successfully, you had to be wealthy, and it helped if you belonged to the nobility. Poor women had little or no hope of becoming saints in the early Middle Ages. As is easy to observe in most of the *vitae*, the outstanding virtue associated with saintly women during the centuries covered by this study was one that made wealth a necessity: charity. Several rich women chose to bring their inheritance to the Church in one form or another. Just as the kings and the warlords continually redistributed their wealth, their holy female relatives had to display their might and prestige by giving gifts to the poor. For instance, Monegund and Eustadiola often handed out part of their husbands' wealth both to the poor and to the Church. Rusticula was a wealthy heiress who became the target of the plans of both a greedy nobleman and a greedy religious house (later, her position within the convent was undoubtedly related to the fact that her wealth made her important: in the early Middle Ages as today, money talks). Both Sadalberga and her daughter Anstrude are explicitly described as very generous, as are Gertrude and Wulftrude of Nivelles, the mystic Aldegund, Queen Balthild, Bertilla of Chelles and Austreberta of Pavilly. Radegund, while queen, spent her days making donations to churches and monasteries, building a hospice and feeding the poor. We also learn that Ultrogotha, an otherwise fairly invisible queen, was famous for being a comforter of the poor.[971]

As far as belonging to the nobility is concerned, their family ties to local magnates, bishops and secular officials assured the holy women of strong support in their hour of need. These ties made it easier for them to administer estates and publicise their relics, miracles and convents; it also gave them a social platform from which they were able to recruit new members to their communities. The apparent ease with which Sadalberga's convent managed to attract women from the nobility was probably due to the fact that Sadalberga herself came from a noble family. Some abbesses were handpicked from suitable aristocratic houses, such as Bertilla, Wulftrude and Anstrude (who inherited her position as abbess from her mother Sadalberga). Austreberta came from a wealthy family, as did Gertrude and Burgundofara. One female saint, Rusticula, was even kidnapped into becoming a future abbess.

In this way, the religious houses developed into convenient pools for landed resources. Through the family monasteries, the aristocrats could store their wealth beyond the reach of kings, suitors and other ecclesiastical institutions. Gertrude and Burgundofara became the leaders of big aristocratic convents instead of getting married, possibly as a means of securing property within their families. We know that Burgundofara's convent was of great political and economic value: on at least one occasion, the powerful mayor of the palace Aega saw fit to attack its property. The strategy is even more evident in the stories of Sadalberga and (especially) Anstrude. The latter was wooed by a greedy suitor but managed to preserve her wealth by joining a nunnery where she was eventually to rule as abbess, with far more social and economic influence than if she had been the wife of a magnate. The kings, queens and the Frankish mayors of the palace behaved in a similar manner, but, at least in the seventh century, they grew to resent the fact that so much aristocratic land was beyond their influence; sometimes, like Aega, they even attacked the convents. Kings such as Dagobert I tried to plan ahead by arranging suitable marriages that would prevent certain families from becoming or remaining too wealthy: this is evident from the stories of Sadalberga and Gertrude. Ecclesiastical leaders who were regarded as too powerful, such as Bishop Wilfrid of Northumbria and Bishop Leodegar of Autun, were imprisoned or forced into exile.

Looking more closely at the female saints, we observe that they were not only rich, they also possessed an entirely different sexual status than that of the typical high medieval nun. Most of them spent a considerable part of their lives *not* living in chastity. Several of them were married, and most of those had children. It would seem that sexual status had little or nothing to do with the concept of holiness and of sainthood. Whether virgin, widow or separated wife, the woman in question could never succeed as a holy woman unless she was rich. Wealth and noble status were far more important than virginity. Even if they escaped from the world and isolated themselves in a cell in a convent, they refrained from alienating themselves so completely from their husbands or fathers that they risked losing them as allies. The abbesses and the holy nuns, no matter how ascetic, remained family members who grieved for all the tragic events that occurred outside the walls of the convent, such as the murder of their brothers. Radegund is the most famous example, but she was hardly the only one to react the way she did, as is made clear by the story of Anstrude's reaction to the death of Baldwin.[972]

The typical holy woman of the early medieval *vitae* might be characterised as 'the great monastic lady, withdrawn from worldly power and worldly comfort but not from the world's misery and strife'. She was generous towards the needy, she cared for the sick, she intervened in politics as peacemaker, protector of fugitives and prisoners, and participant at conferences, and she became, at least on some occasions, so deeply entangled in secular rivalries that the convent walls could not prevent violence from entering her life.[973] Many of the abbesses knew each other personally and may have corresponded (a letter from Caesaria to Radegund has, as we have seen, been preserved). Several of them, such as Gertrude and Austreberta, were part of a network of family and religion with close connections to other abbesses, bishops and religious houses. Furthermore, the position of abbess or holy woman in monastic retirement was perceived as an alternative route to power and influence for queens who, for some reason, could or would no longer pursue their secular careers. Radegund may have entered the monastic world of her own free will, but Balthild probably did not. The same was true of queens and princesses in England – Hilda went gladly, but Irminburga would hardly have joined a convent unless her husband had been killed. Needless to say, former queens, accustomed to giving orders, would in any case have made bad subordinates.

The fact that nunneries evolved into focal points within seventh-century political culture is proved by several episodes in the *vitae*. For instance:

(1) Radegund had male agents, such as Proculus, who did what she asked of them outside the walls of the convent. She intervened in politics and tried to make peace; she used her contacts with King Sigibert in her search for relics. Her power made her a dangerous enemy in the eyes of Bishop Maroveus, whose influence in Poitiers must have been drastically diminished through Radegund's activity.

(2) Rusticula was accused of treason and may in fact have been guilty. She had to travel to the king and was forced to swear an oath that the charges were untrue. Her position in the convent, and in the whole city of Arles, was very strong, whether based solely on religious charisma or in combination with the socio-economic influence of the convent. This is revealed in the passages of the text that describe the attempt of the royal officers to arrest her, her return in triumph and her burial.

(3) Anstrude took an active part in life outside the convent walls. She tried to make peace and considered herself partly responsible for her brother's death. Through a network of relatives and allies, she was connected to the faction of Pippin of Herstal. In her position as local leader, she often confronted enemies, such as Ebroin and the local bishop.

(4) Wulftrude of Nivelles appears to have been threatened by Queen Balthild and Queen Chimnechild. This would have made no sense unless Wulftrude had played an important role in secular society and was probably connected to her father Grimoald and his political gambles.

As leader of her convent, the early medieval abbess not only acted on a political stage together with kings and bishops, she was also the ruler of a specific kind of community that is difficult to conceptualise today. Perhaps the best way to describe it is to reason in terms of (1) the creation of an artificial family and (2) the process of social militarisation.

Beginning with the family, it is clear that monastic life as such was regarded as family life – a better and closer family life than the secular world could provide. The members of a typical aristocratic Frankish convent became the adopted children of the founding family. In Latin terminology, the usual word for an early medieval abbess was *mater* ('mother'); the word for a nun was *soror* ('sister'). The sisters came from every rung of the social ladder, from the poor and the helpless to the daughters of kings. Some had entered the nunnery of their own free will, earnestly desiring to live a pious life, while others (such as Chrodechild and Basina) had been placed there by their relatives and strongly disliked their situation. Despite rules to the contrary, various references in the *vitae* make it clear that the convents were not characterised by social equality, especially not if we consider that servants and servant-girls were employed in the houses. Consequently, the 'families' of the abbesses were bound to experience problems, sometimes even resulting in rebellion.[974] The best example, of course, is the chain of events in Poitiers in 589–90. Another example is Baudonivia's story of the Vinoberga incident in the same convent.

Turning to what I term social militarisation, it becomes necessary to view the convents as elements within a fundamental process of societal transformation. As antiquity developed into the Middle Ages, several aspects of European society underwent profound changes. To make this easier to understand, historians have decided to put various labels on them, like 'christianisation', 'territorialisation' and 'feudalisation'. One aspect that is often forgotten, mainly because it is too obvious to be noticed, is the fact that life in general, as well as patterns of thought and culture, was heavily influenced by the military sphere. This development as such is too complex and far-reaching to be dealt with here,[975] but its consequences for female monastic life should be noted. Society was more violent during the early Middle Ages than it had been during antiquity, and the constant need for defence made military responsibilities more common among ordinary males than had ever been the case in the years of Pax Romana. A judge was also a military leader (count, duke, gastald, etc.); the inhabitants of a walled town formed a military unit that could be deployed by their leaders in times of need. Within the monastic 'family' of a convent, nuns bonded in a fashion that was otherwise reserved for men, and, as a result, the sisters acquired a set of early medieval male (i.e., militarily influenced) values. In the *vitae* of the female saints, there is an undercurrent of virility, athletic competition and military service. In Bertilla's *vita*, Balthild is explicitly referred to as a soldier of Christ. The need for discipline amongst the nuns made these values more than welcome to the abbesses. Not surprisingly, life in the convents developed along lines that strongly resemble those of military units. The life of the sisterhoods became dominated by regular rounds of collective prayer and psalm singing. The enemy was Satan and the forces of evil: they were to be defeated with help of strict discipline and solidarity. Some holy women, especially the mystic Aldegund, appear to have confronted the Devil himself on several occasions. The hagiographic texts served as training manuals, and there were several famous holy women from the past to look up to as models (such as Helena). The daily exercises were supposed to result in an almost miraculous strength and self-control in the face of the enemy, much in the same way as the subjects of the *vitae* proved themselves superior to both their secular and their spiritual opponents.[976] Consequently, some of the *vitae* display a great interest in discipline and ascetic behaviour. This is especially true of Jonas' account of life at the convent of Burgundofara, where the abbess ruled like a monastic dictator, a theocratic master whose lordship led to several attempts at escape. Even sins that from our point of view seem relatively harmless (such as a fondness for eating, in those days interpreted as gluttony) were harshly condemned.

The military atmosphere was especially obvious in times of death. When a religious woman lay dying, a united sisterhood would gather like a military cohort next to her bed to sing her into heaven. The groups of nuns we meet are 'troops', not just ordinary gatherings of individuals. In the material studied above, we have seen these cases several times: in the descriptions of the deaths of Radegund, Rusticula and Austreberta, in Jonas' tale of Gibitrude's vision of the armed forces of Heaven (not to mention the many singing nuns who appear when someone at Burgundofara's convent is about to die), in the *vitae* of Anstrude and Gertrude (with their troops of nuns serving in the war against Evil), and so on. The death of an important nun, and especially an abbess, was apparently a great event for the entire city or district, at least if we are to believe the authors of *vitae* such as those of Eustadiola and Rusticula. In the same way, saintly relics came to be regarded as weapons in the battle against Satan. Radegund used all her resources and even contacted the East Roman emperor in order to get her hands on valuable relics. As we have seen in Gregory's description of the civil war in Poitiers, both Leubovera and Chrodechild tried to use the relic of the Holy Cross to further their own causes even in the middle of a raging battle. Although seventh-century saints such as Gertrude of Nivelles and Aldegund performed fewer miracles than their holy predecessors are said to have done, they were instead often credited with extraordinary powers of prophecy and vision.[977]

Thus, to understand the position of an early medieval abbess, we must realise that her situation was made up of several elements that we today consider to be unrelated. In the minds of early medieval men and women, however, these elements were readily thought of as interconnected. In fact, the very analytical separation undertaken below would probably have seemed ridiculous, if not unfathomable, to the abbesses themselves:

- Wealth and nobility
- Spiritual charisma
- Social and political influence outside the convent
- 'Motherly' leadership of the nuns
- Ability to enforce strict discipline

Turning from the holy women themselves, what do the *vitae* and the *passiones* tell us about wealthy and high-ranking women in general?

The first, and by far the most significant, impression we get of these people is that they were powerful: they had a clear potential for doing good as well as for doing bad. In any case, their help was gratefully appreciated, and their patronage was considered of immense value. Wilfrid's career was launched with the help of Queen Eanfled, and it was almost terminated by Queen Balthild, if we are to believe Eddius. Having returned to England from the continent, Wilfrid had to spend the rest of his life fighting a network of powerful female opponents from Northumbria in the north to Wessex in the south. Another impression, closely linked to the first, is that female actors on the political scene, both in Gaul and in England, were wealthy. They usually had a lot of land: resources that could be donated to the saint in question (such as Wilfrid or Praeiectus), or be used as a basis for recruitment of henchmen and soldiers, or act as financial backing for monastic foundations. Competition for women's land could result in severe political crises, as in the case of Claudia's inheritance, executions and even martyrdom. The use of wealth in attempts to strengthen the positions of a queen and thus the central authority of the kingdom is most clearly demonstrated by Balthild's career: she used her and her late husband's property to recruit allies among bishops, magnates, abbots and abbesses. In doing so, she and her allies (especially Ebroin) became feared. They began to threaten aristocratic factions that felt a need to fight back. The balance in society was broken, and feuds erupted. One result of this is that we have two completely different versions of Queen Balthild at our disposal: the one provided by her enemies (Wilfrid, Aunemundus and others, preserved by Eddius) and the one provided by those who venerated her as a saint.

The early medieval queens could use their position to influence their men, both their husbands and their sons (or, in Brunhild's case, grandsons). When influencing their husbands, they used the same weapons as they did in the work of Gregory of Tours: charisma, sexual charm and various tactics of persuasion. Balthild must have been exceptionally good at this, going from slave to queen and ending up as saint. Other wives also managed to create strong emotional ties to their husbands. From what we can read in the *passiones*, Bilichild would appear to have accompanied (and thus influenced) Childeric II at all times. Eddius clearly regarded Irminburga, not her husband, as the key to understanding Wilfrid's fall from grace. As for influencing their children and grandchildren, this would have been facilitated by several factors. The queens and their young relatives often had common enemies within the aristocracy; the queens had not only accumulated riches but also valuable knowledge; the queens had had ample time to recruit allies and to work out strategies that they were happy to share with close relatives who shared their political point of view. Mother/grandmother and son/grandson depended on each other. Brunhild's power was, at least to a certain extent, tied to her position as Theuderic's grandmother. She could influence Theuderic; she could use him and tell him what to do. If (as Brunhild's ecclesiastical opponents and victims wanted) Theuderic got married, her position might, in theory, be jeopardised. As stated above, however, we must be careful not to accept the tale of Brunhild's fear of competition as a genuine historical fact. This alleged fear could be used by writers searching for a reason that might explain why Brunhild behaved the way she did. Brunhild herself may not have regarded the prospect of a royal wife as a threat to herself. She was probably more interested in weakening the internal opposition of Burgundy by crushing men such as Desiderius of Vienne, and in securing the royal succession. She had been able to co-operate with her son's wife Faileuba, and she would probably have been able to co-operate with Theuderic's wife as well if he had ever acquired one. Likewise, Chimnechild appears to have coexisted with Bilichild without any problems, at least none that are revealed in the sources.

The really bad women of the *vitae*, the Jezebels, are those who, for whatever reason, become the enemies of the saint who acted as hero in the text. The fact that they thus have a distinct literary function serves to make them far worse than they must have been in real life. For Jonas, the Jezebel is Brunhild: her name must be as blackened as possible. For Eddius, the chief Jezebels are Balthild and Irminburga: female monsters of Biblical proportions. If we are to learn anything from these studies in black, aside from the obvious fact that the writer belonged to, or worked for, a faction that was hostile towards the so-called Jezebels, it is that these women must have been worth hating. A powerless Brunhild would not have aroused anybody's anger. That she was described the way she was is a clear indication of the fear she inspired. Regardless of whether she was guilty or not, it was assumed by everybody that Brunhild was fully capable of efficiently persecuting a powerful abbot such as Columbanus and killing a bishop such as Desiderius.

Part 3

Conclusion

Women in the four major chronicles

A comparison between Jordanes, Gregory of Tours, Bede and Paul the Deacon reveals a remarkable similarity in the relative number of women that appear in the texts. As is obvious from the table, all of these writers preferred chronicling the deeds of male protagonists.

Author	Percentage of women among all individuals mentioned
Jordanes	11
Gregory of Tours	15
Bede	12.5
Paul the Deacon	13

Only between 11 and 15 percent of all the people mentioned in the early medieval chronicles were women. Jordanes, in fact, makes his intention to paint his world in male colours explicit, even going so far as to apologise for writing too much about the Amazons. He (and the other writers, although they are less explicit) clearly regarded women's history as less important than the history of men. Gender was far from irrelevant to them; on the contrary, it was apparently crucial in defining who was to be included in their histories and who was not.

However, if we turn to the descriptions of those women who are endowed with characters of their own, the differences between the authors are considerable. In Gregory's *Decem Libri Historiarum*, 27 people are depicted as bad women and 24 as good women, while 8 women are difficult to place in either category. Princess Rigunth, for instance, is sometimes shown as a good woman and sometimes as a bad one. In Paul the Deacon's *Historia Langobardorum*, most women engaged in any kind of political activity are described as bad (with a few extraordinary exceptions, such as Gambara and Theudelinda).

Jordanes gives us a similar picture: on those rare occasions that we actually do encounter female individuals in *De origine actibusque Getarum*, they are either morally inferior, sex-hungry beings whose actions are dangerous to their own country (such as Honoria), or they are mythical Amazons or witches from the past. On the other hand, in Bede's *Historia ecclesiastica gentis Anglorum*, hardly any politically active woman is described as really bad. For example, Bede refrains from providing us with a real characterisation of a murderous queen.

These differences should be taken as evidence of the fact that early medieval gender attitudes were not as rigidly constructed as has often been argued in the past. The attitudes that are supposedly referred to in one of the introductory chapters of this book ('In the shadow of Dark Age misogyny...') were hardly shared by everybody. This would be instantly apparent if we were to compare, say, the images of women in *Decem Libri Historiarum* with the images of women in a seventh-century *vita*. However, and this is an important point, it is also apparent in a comparison of the various chroniclers themselves. Jordanes, Gregory, Bede and Paul the Deacon were all individuals with a capacity for making up their own minds and having their own opinions on men, women, politics and history. If early medieval mentality had contained a structural feature of misogyny, this feature would have had to have been sufficiently strong to make its presence felt in the texts of these writers despite their individual differences. It does not. While gender-specific stereotypes definitely did exist (see below), there was no general acceptance of the idea that all women were supposed to be bad and sinful. Their activities in the political and social arenas were remarked upon to a much lesser extent than the activities of their husbands, fathers and sons, but that does not mean that a writer such as Gregory of Tours regarded women in general as being worse than men. He simply thought of them as less important and, consciously or unconsciously, neglected their political culture.

Summing up the results, we may conclude that all the four major chroniclers of the period studied in this book had a tendency to avoid mentioning women in politics. That it not to say that women lacked political influence. What it means is that the writers of history forgot about them or neglected them, probably since women were less conspicuous in the specific political arenas that were of interest to the authors themselves. While power can be visualised and felt in a number of different ways depending on the prevailing political culture, not all of these ways need be apparent to the contemporary writer of history. The male ways of exerting power were far more apparent to Jordanes, Gregory of Tours, Bede and Paul the Deacon than the female ways. They appear to have automatically looked for kings, sieges and battles, and they found what they were looking for. As for their personal views on what powerful women were like, their ideas differed just as much as those of the historians of today.

Stereotypical images of powerful early medieval women

During the course of this study, we have encountered a number of stereotypical ideas of what women were like (or rather: what women could be like if they were perceived as typically extreme examples of their sex). The subject has been approached before, but rarely in detail, a fact that makes the present analysis all the more interesting. For instance, a collection of essays edited by Barbara Garlick, Suzanne Dixon and Pauline Allen appeared in 1992, aimed at interpreting stereotypes of women in power according to the paradigm of private versus public – a bipolarity that I saw fit to criticise in one of the introductory chapters of this book (see above, pp. 45–51). The collection contains brief analyses of male images of prominent women in a number of different societies such as ancient Egypt, ancient Rome, early Byzantium and Ming China. If we are to believe the authors, women who crossed over into the public realm were always portrayed as perversions of good women, either in the shape of domineering dowagers or as conniving concubines. Freedom of movement from one sphere to the other was the male's prerogative. The only public women that were accepted (and still are, for the study reaches into our own age) were those that fell (or fall) into the category of the so-called first-lady icon – the loyal wife of the great man. Other than that, few societies have had legitimate public roles for women, hence the stereotypes.[978]

As is evident from the present study, interpretations such as those presented by Garlick, Dixon and Allen should be read with great caution. Reality, even stereotypical reality, was far more complex than they are willing to admit. For instance, not all images of powerful women need have been negative. There were good girls as well as bad girls. If we are to understand stereotypes, we must begin by realising that these images should be tentatively interpreted as the outcome of historical discrepancies arising from specific cultural traumas. Thereby, the process of stereotyping may turn into a useful key in our attempts to make sense of early medieval mentality.

It is clear that the negative stereotypes could be, and often were, used as weapons directed against the historical memory of the woman in question. Brunhild's fate in seventh-century literature (the *Vita Columbani*, Fredegar's chronicle, etc.) is a perfect example of this kind of *damnatio memoriae*. Gregory of Tours' descriptions of foreign queens (Amalaberg, Goiswinth, Amalasuntha, etc.), all of them unknown to him personally and all either dead or living at a safe distance, serve as ideal examples of bad queens *in extremis*. In a similar fashion, the positive stereotypes were employed to enhance the memory of saints and political allies. Thus, even to the writers themselves, the stereotypes had little to do with reality in our sense of the word. The stereotypical images existed in early medieval culture; they were part of the mental arsenal of biographers, historical writers, priests, and, we may suspect, ordinary village slanderers. However, this cultural omnipresence of ideas concerning gender-specific extremes is of great significance. It turns the stereotypical picture of someone like Balthild (portrayed both as a saint and as a Jezebel) into an informative *manifestation* of the gender structure of the early Middle Ages. Balthild, Brunhild, Theudelinda and all the others were not described in their respective bright or dark colours by chance. The particular stereotypes used to paint their pictures contain important messages about the gendering of early medieval politics.

Since this is a study of gender and political culture, I have concentrated on those stereotypes that are informative from this particular perspective. It should be remembered, however, that gender was not always of prime concern to an early medieval writer intent upon describing an event or a person. Sometimes, categories and aspects that transcended gender-specific roles and traditional ways of describing men and women proved to be far more influential. In those cases, the gendering of the historians' descriptions of the individuals in question was drowned out in favour of other stereotypes and other patterns of description. For instance, Gambara and Frea are not described in the same way as later (and more historical) women in *Historia Langobardorum*. In the eyes of Paul the Deacon, these two mythical female beings were women of a quite different sort than queens such as Theudelinda and duchesses such as

Romilda. In the world that Paul the Deacon knew from his own experience, legendary creatures such as Gambara and Frea did not exist. If we are to understand their purpose in his chronicle, it is far more important to observe and analyse other elements, such as their functions within the cosmological explanations of the very existence of the *gens Langobardorum*, than the element of gender.

Stereotypes 1: the bad girls

Sexuality. Judging from what we know of prejudice within the learned world of early medieval Europe, we would expect our writers to associate their female villains with sexuality (compare with pp. 40–41 above). In this, we are not mistaken. Even the most pious and venerable woman in early medieval Europe, such as the wife of Bishop Urbicus of Clermont, could turn into a sex-hungry animal, forcing her unholy lusts upon her male victims. The male writers of history all associated sexuality in general and sexual immorality in particular with women. All of the major chronicles included in this study provide us with an abundance of evidence as to the existence of the idea of woman as a being potentially obsessed with sinful, dirty thoughts about sex. This is true even of Jordanes' short work, in the description of Honoria. In Paul the Deacon's *Historia Langobardorum*, we stumble across the hideous examples of Romilda and Rosemunda, both of whom paid with their lives for their almost unnatural longing for carnal pleasure. Bede, who otherwise rarely mentions bad women, accuses the nuns of Coldingham of being guilty of enjoying fine clothes and wanting to attract strange men. Gregory of Tours often accuses the women he does not like, including a couple of queens (such as Deuteria, who killed her daughter out of fear that her husband would soon find her more sexually interesting than he found Deuteria herself), of being prone to various kinds of crime and excess ultimately linked to sexuality. The worst of the lot would appear to be Magnatrude, the wicked, sadistic wife of Bishop Badegisil of Le Mans, who is reported to have delighted in cutting off or burning the sexual organs of men and women alike.

Murder (through male agents). Most of the bad women who appear in narrative texts from the early Middle Ages were intimately associated with the concept of assassination. That is, they did not actually stab people in the back with their own daggers, but they found male allies, agents or subordinates who were willing to commit the crimes on their behalf. Bede, who is usually silent about female murderers, nevertheless feels that he must report a rumour that Peada, King of the South Mercians, was assassinated through the treachery of his wife. Paul the Deacon is far more specific in his detailed relation of the abhorrent activities of *femmes fatales* such as Rumetruda and Rosemunda. In *Decem Libri Historiarum*, one evil female plot after another darkens the lives of many of the individuals mentioned by Gregory. The methods employed by the women differed: sometimes they used poison, sometimes the more direct approach of dispatching assassins armed with daggers. Marcatrude, for instance, was believed to have poisoned her stepson Gundobad. Fredegund, by far the most evil woman in Gregory's chronicle, is accused of having dispatched an entire troop of hired assassins to kill Childebert II. Even in death, a Merovingian queen was capable of reaching out to kill through agents: the dying Queen Austrechild made her husband Gunthchramn promise to kill the doctors who had failed to save her life. The king did as he had promised – hardly an action suitable for a future saint such as Gunthchramn. In Fredegar's chronicle, the same kind of evil behaviour that Gregory associates with Fredegund is linked to Brunhild, whose constant attempts to kill everyone of importance in the end prove to be her own undoing. The list of evil women continues in Fredegar's *Continuationes*, where Anseflid is accused of being responsible for the murder of Berchar after the battle of Tertry.

Stupidity: lack of intelligence and common sense. Not only are the bad girls of the early Middle Ages described as cruel individuals obsessed with thoughts of murder and sex, they are also shown to have been stupid. The stereotypical image of a stupid woman could take several different forms, some of which are just as alive today as in the days of Bede and Paul the Deacon. For instance, men of all times appear to have regarded women as fickle beings who are to be expected to change their minds over and over again. Today, we find this stereotype in comic books and television series including scenes of husbands waiting for their wives trying to decide which clothes to buy. Variants of this stereotype appear in early medieval literature, for instance in Paul the Deacon's description of the dangerously fickle Rumetruda.

Rumetruda is demonstrated to have been a vain girl whose brain was ruled by illogical emotions. One minute, she invites an innocent young man to share a cup of wine with her. The next minute, taking offence, she has him killed. As a result of her fickleness, war erupts between two kingdoms. There are similar examples in *Decem Libri Historiarum*, such as Berthegund's sudden change of mind after her brother Bertram's death. Gregory also uses this incident to denounce Berthegund's mother Ingitrude as stupid ('what a fool I have been to listen to the advice of my stupid mother'). The stereotypical message of examples like these is clear: you cannot trust a woman to stick to her original purpose.

The essence of this female stupidity would appear to be an inability to control the emotions. The women in question are described as people incapable of using reason and logic. Rather, their actions are governed by feelings and impulses. In *Historia Langobardorum*, Romilda fails to understand the dangers, both to herself and to her people, that would follow her submission to the Avars. In the biography of Saint Cuthbert, Aelffled, otherwise described as a rather good woman, displays a sense of curiosity and bewilderment of which Bede definitely seems to have disapproved. In Gregory's detailed description of the trial in Poitiers in 590, Chrodechild's wild verbal eruptions and accusations, aimed at discrediting Leubovera, are clear indications that Gregory wanted to give his readers a picture of Chrodechild as an illogical woman who made up her mind quickly, without planning ahead. Remember that we only have Gregory's words for the inherent weakness of Chrodechild's accusations. For all we know, they may have been perfectly valid; Leubovera may have been guilty. From Gregory's point of view, however, the entire incident served as an example of Chrodechild's dangerous, feminine way of reasoning.

Ambition: the will to rule. Many of the bad women who turn up in early medieval chronicles are governed by their longing for power. Not content with whatever powers they already possess, they always want more. Gregory of Tours provides us with a typical example in his description of Queen Amalaberg of Thuringia, who prompts her husband Hermanfrid to commit evil deeds by telling him that 'a king who is deprived of half his kingdom deserves to find half his table bare.' Paul the Deacon does not fail to point out that Rosemunda wanted to control Ravenna (*dum optat Ravennatium domina fieri*), and Sophia's arrogance, haughtiness and greed is evident both in Gregory's text and in Paul the Deacon's work.

Bad advisers. When it comes to male relatives, especially their husbands, the bad women of early medieval chronicles delight in providing them with ideas spawned in Hell rather than in Heaven. Amalaberg wants Hermanfrid to go to war and cause destruction. Magnatrude persuades Bishop Badegisil to follow in her evil footsteps. Irminburga, inspired by Satan himself, corrupts Egfrith's heart with poisonous tales about Bishop Wilfrid. In this way, the wicked actions of several male sinners are blamed on their women.

Stereotypes 2: the good girls

Beauty. Many of the positively described female protagonists of early medieval chronicles are said to have been good-looking. In reality, many of the 'bad' women must have been beautiful as well (otherwise, Fredegund would hardly have been able to work her way up through the king's bedchamber), but the writers preferred not to say so in their texts. In the Middle Ages, beauty was not believed to be merely skin deep: a beautiful body denoted a beautiful soul. This is very evident in Gregory's introduction of Brunhild ('elegant in all that she did, lovely to look at, chaste and decorous in her behaviour, wise in her generation and of good address'). A century later, Balthild is described by her hagiographer as *ipsa pretiosa et optima Dei margarita*, a precious pearl of a woman who, despite her being a foreigner and a slave, became the object of both Erchinoald's and Clovis' marital plans. It should be noted that both Brunhild and Balthild are described, in other texts, as female villains. However, no mention of their beauty is made in connection with these alternative versions of their characters.

Piety. All 'good' women are described as pious. They were all, in one way or another, associated with the ecclesiastical sphere of society. A prominent example is Paul the Deacon's description of Theudelinda: a genuinely pious queen, who restores the Church to its former glory, establishes good relations with the Pope and works to secure the peace. While it is easy for us (and, it would seem, for Fredegar) to argue that Theudelinda must have had quite a few dirty tricks up her sleeve to have survived in politics for as long as she did, this is never mentioned by Paul the Deacon. In *Historia Langobardorum*, Theudelinda is portrayed as a model of a good, Christian queen. She has several parallels in *Decem Libri Historiarum* – noblewomen who promoted Catholicism, founded convents and were held in high esteem by the clerical writers themselves, examples being Chlothild, Radegund and Brunhild.

Not surprisingly, the association of good women with piety is especially strong in works that were written with a specific purpose within the ecclesiastical sphere itself. In Bede's *Historia ecclesiastica gentis Anglorum*, a history of the English church and not the English kingdoms, the good woman is always a nun, living in a religious house and abstaining from all worldly concerns. In the saints' lives, all the female heroines are a priori defined as pious.

Peace-weaving. While often appearing as diplomats and peacemaking brides, the image of the peace-weaving woman can hardly be said to constitute a stereotype in the early medieval chronicles. The closest we get to a stereotypical image of a queen making peace is Paul the Deacon's picture of Theudelinda. However, it is definitely a recurring image in the saints' lives. Genovefa struggled to bring peace and security to her war-torn land, and subsequent female saints are demonstrated to have carried on the tradition. As Pauline Stafford has rightly pointed out, the idea of the queen as a peacemaker developed into a prominent hagiographical motif.[979] Michael Enright, in his article on the motif of the 'Lady with a Mead-Cup' (1988), likewise assigns the role of *mediatrix* between the king and his followers to the queen.[980]

Resources, tactics and strategies

Fathers and other biological relatives

The first asset of an early medieval girl, and often the most important of all, was her biological network of relatives: her father, mother, brothers and sisters. Of course, this family network could just as easily have been perceived as a dangerous liability. The members of the older generation, in most cases the fathers, used their daughters (for example, by marrying them off to suitable allies) in ways that often determined the remainder of the girls' lives. However, as far as the women studied in this book are concerned, the majority of them had everything to gain and little to lose by maintaining as close links as possible with their relatives. To Visigothic outsiders such as Galswinth and Brunhild, links with relatives south of the Pyrenees were essential. Even Radegund, whose Thuringian family had almost been wiped out, did whatever she could to stay in touch with her only living relative, even though he lived in Constantinople and she was confined to her convent in Poitiers.

The fact that the marriages that brought women such as Wisigarda and Brunhild to Gaul were usually elements within political alliances made the links between fathers/relatives and daughters problematic. Alliances could be broken while marriages remained intact, and vice versa. To a Frankish queen of foreign extraction, her biological ties to the leaders of other kingdoms could in theory be used against her by her enemies. To this political game should be added the natural feelings parents and children had for their own family. Fathers and mothers cared, then as well as now, about the well-being of their children. In an age characterised by the political importance of individual actors, the sorry fate of a daughter far from home could easily dominate the political agenda of kings and queens. The best example in the present study is that of Ingund and her son. In the end, Brunhild was unable to intervene on Ingund's behalf, but she devoted a considerable amount of time and energy to helping her. Gunthchramn used the incident as a perfectly logical *casus belli*, a reasoning that resulted in large-scale destruction in Septimania.

Many of the problems experienced by the Merovingian daughters mentioned in *Decem Libri Historiarum* were, one way or another, linked to a family crisis. A lack of paternal allies, the death of a father or a brother, usually resulted in a loss of power. Generally speaking, most of these Merovingian women were, despite the deaths of their fathers, rather better off than most of their female contemporaries. From a personal point of view, however, the sudden loss of influence was undoubtedly a terrible blow of psychologically dramatic proportions. To women grown used to wielding power, this change of fortune could prove disastrous. Many of them displayed considerable difficulties in adapting to the new situation and accepting their new roles. Some women entirely refused to accept their subordinate roles, in a few cases (Chrodechild and Basina) even going so far as to launch an armed rebellion. Others responded to their bad luck by over-compensating through other pleasant activities, such as gluttony (Gregory describes Berthefled as 'a woman who ate and slept a lot') and promiscuity (Fredegund was furious with Rigunth for her habit of sleeping with every man she could talk into bed).

Husbands

The second asset of an early medieval woman was her husband. Normally, she had little or no choice in the matter, at least not with regard to her first marriage. She was married off to a suitable candidate from another good family. If, however, the woman was a widow with a potential for political action of her own, she could often exert considerable influence, as did Theudelinda and Brunhild. The longer a woman remained on the political scene, the more chances she had of influencing politics through her own marriage.

While some early medieval kings, especially the Merovingians, chose their consorts from among the women they fell in love with or found sexually appealing, a number of the more important marriages of the era were pre-arranged alliances between royal houses. Bede and Paul the Deacon supply us with much information on Anglo-Saxon and

Lombard kings establishing alliances by recruiting sons-in-law among the members of neighbouring dynasties. Paul the Deacon is especially interesting from this point of view, since he makes it abundantly clear that the Lombards used marriage, in the sense of a political tool, both as an external and as an internal way of forming alliances and keeping the peace. For instance, Lombard kings gave away their daughters to the leaders of strategically important duchies. Duke Euin of Trento married a daughter of his northern neighbour, Duke Garibald of the Bavarians. We might at least suspect that the liaison between Duchess Romilda of Friuli and the Avar khakhan was an attempt to secure peaceful relations in the frontier zone between Friuli and present-day Slovenia.

For a woman married to a king, the chief asset inherent in a good marriage was her *access to power*. That this was extremely important is reflected in one of the stereotypes analysed above: the fact that bad women were often thought to be giving their husbands bad advice. Queens and royal concubines lived next door to the king. They slept in his bed, whispered in his ear and could twist his mind in the particular direction *they* wanted. For example, Fredegar indicates that Berthetrude and Sichild were particularly good at exerting influence at court, since Chlothar II is reported to have paid too much attention to the advice of his women. Thus, royal women could influence politics; they could decide on crucial matters that the king had been persuaded to delegate to them; they could talk the king into accepting the queen's favourite as mayor of the palace, as Master of the Stables or as army commander, and so on. It is not hard to see how the above-mentioned stereotype developed and became popular: anyone who felt slighted by the king could blame the queen for blocking his path. In many cases, the accuser would probably be right. If a dissatisfied faction of magnates planned to strengthen their own position at court, the queen was often perceived as an obstacle that had to be dealt with as a preliminary, but necessary, move to gain influence over the king. The dissatisfied magnates in Austrasia spent several decades trying to get rid of Brunhild – sometimes with success, sometimes with disastrous consequences for themselves.

Enjoying the king's favour meant that a woman could do things that would otherwise have been impossible. Even in the case of Radegund, who appears to have voluntarily ceded her position at court for a life dedicated to the glory of God, her influence over her husband (Chlothar I) enabled her to establish one of the most important monastic foundations of seventh-century Western Europe.

However, the queen's or concubine's position was structurally insecure, as is repeatedly demonstrated in Gregory's chronicle of the Franks and in the brief glimpses Fredegar allows us of seventh-century Lombard Italy. The king's women were only the king's women as long as this arrangement pleased the king. When he got tired of them or when another woman, such as Fredegund in the case of Chilperic, made him turn against them, they were literally finished – forgotten, banished or murdered. The various tactics employed by a royal woman in order to remain a powerful partner of her husband's (and thereby secure a good position, hopefully the entire kingdom, for her children) had no parallel in the political culture of early medieval men. Kings did not have to please their queens the way the queens always had to manipulate the kings into remaining sexually interested in them and into transferring power and material resources into their greedy hands.

At a lower level, this picture is valid for magnate women as well as for royal women. The material rewards of a magnate wife were usually not as impressive as those awarded a successful queen, although some magnate wives (such as Rauching's) were richer than most. The dangers were not quite as alarming as the risks of being at a royal court frequented by murderous queens such as Fredegund and uxorious kings such as Dagobert I and Charibert I. Nevertheless, they were sufficient to make several magnate women seek sanctuary when news reached them of their husbands' death. Although quite powerful on a local scale, those female aristocrats, such as Tetradia, who lacked male allies usually appear to have lost their struggles against male enemies. Not surprisingly, widowed female aristocrats often remarried wealthy magnates soon after the deaths of their husbands. Everybody benefited from this: both parties grew richer, and the woman's legal position was strengthened.

Children

As far as assets in human form were concerned, children constituted the third and final step. For most of the really powerful women, queens such as Theudelinda and Brunhild, neither fathers nor husbands could compete with children in their capacity as keys to power and influence. As has been demonstrated many times in this study, royal motherhood was far more important than royal marriage. A king's wife could be discarded and locked up in a convent. The king's mother, on the other hand, was destined to remain a powerful individual for as long as she or her royal sons were alive, either at the royal court or (as in the case of Clovis I's widow, Chlothild) at a residence of her own.

The acquisition of children changed the queen's status *immediately*. She did not have to wait for the king to die in order to improve her position by controlling the upbringing of the next generation of rulers. Faileuba's position at the Austrasian court clearly indicates that the aristocratic opposition in the kingdom feared the queen's position as a mother just as much as they feared her position as a wife. Faileuba's enemies wanted to remove her from Austrasia entirely, not only from her immediate access to Childebert II. As long as Faileuba was allowed the possibility of staying in touch with her son, she would remain dangerous. Some magnates would always gamble on her chances of a comeback. Her very existence in the kingdom would destabilise the political situation her enemies wanted to construct.

However, a position of royal motherhood appears to have been difficult to acquire. Even if the woman in question had managed to produce a couple of male heirs by the king, she was far from secure. The king could grow tired of the woman, making her children a potential source of future power rather than a key to present influence. Moreover, other women could also produce royal heirs, and these competitors were bound to do everything in their power to further the interests of their own sons and daughters to the detriment of other children (and their mothers). Audovera, whose prospects might have appeared quite promising in the beginning, ended up having lost everything: her children, the king's favour, and, eventually, her own life. Female rivalry at a royal court was an inherent part of early medieval political culture; people took it for granted. If a prince died from unclear causes, his stepmother (if he had one) was automatically presumed guilty of murder. Thus, we do not know if Marcatrude actually did poison her stepson Gundobad, but Gregory of Tours (and, we might suspect, everybody else) regarded such an action as typical of a woman in her position. While actions such as murder were not, are not and should not be approved of in any epoch, we must be careful not to think of these stepmothers, with all their poison and daggers, as more evil than the other political actors of the early Middle Ages. A stepmother such as Fredegund primarily did what she had to do in order to create the best possible chances of survival for herself and her children. If she did not take her chances, she risked ending up like Audovera, Ultrogotha and Theudechild.

While of great importance during the royal husband's lifetime, motherhood became crucial to the fortunes of a royal widow. Without a son to inherit the kingdom and thus preserve the position of the mother/widow, the political career of the woman in question was usually terminated. She would be deprived of her position and sent off to some estate or convent, where she would spend the rest of her life outside the secular political sphere. Gregory of Tours supplies us with several examples of these sudden changes of fortune. For instance, Ultrogotha was quickly removed from her position by Chlothar I in 558; it would seem from other sources that she devoted the rest of her life to committing pious deeds instead of trying to manipulate politics. Theudechild, Charibert's widow, fared worse. King Gunthchramn confiscated her treasure and had her locked up in a nunnery in Arles. After her failed attempt at escape, Theudechild was mercilessly beaten and confined to a cell.

Theudechild could have been spared all her anguish if only her son by Charibert had survived infancy. The existence of a son, not the son's age, was what mattered. Thus, Fredegund was able to make a highly successful political comeback after Chilperic's murder despite the fact that her son Chlothar II was only an infant. As long as she had influence over Chlothar's upbringing, she was powerful. Even if that influence was withheld from the mother/widow (as was the case for Brunhild's relation to Childebert II in the first years after Sigibert's murder), her very potential for reacquiring access to her son was enough to ensure her a certain amount of political influence. Merovech definitely regarded the recently widowed Brunhild as a useful ally – he even went so far as to marry her.

Brunhild's success as a royal widow is a clear indication of the overwhelming importance of children. Childebert II remained an asset, someone she could return to from her exile and use as a firm point of reference in her subsequent attempts to construct a network of allies. Without Childebert, it is hard to imagine Brunhild being able to retain her position in Austrasia after 575. Many Austrasian magnates made no secret of their intention of getting rid of her. Still, Brunhild was able to influence Frankish politics for forty-six years (567–613), almost half a century! I find it impossible to agree with Ian Wood in his evaluation of Brunhild as an unremarkable woman.[981] Brunhild's fame should, however, not make us forget that several other royal widows were equally successful in holding on to the reins of power after the death of their husbands. In Lombard Italy, Theudelinda outlived two kings and continued to exert considerable influence during the reign of her son Adaloald. In seventh-century Francia, Nantechild (together with Aega) assumed the regency of Neustria after Dagobert I's death in 637. Balthild's influence was crucial in the years following the death of Clovis II. We know less about Chimnechild, but everything seems to hint at her being just as influential as the other royal widows of her time.

Aggressiveness and sexual charisma

Biological relatives, husbands and children: these were the three major external human assets that were available within female political culture in the early Middle Ages. These assets formed the backbone of most successful careers. They do, however, only give us a very incomplete picture. Not all queens had strong biological allies. For instance, Fredegund's parents were poor; she began her career as a servant. Balthild's position was even worse: she started out as a foreign slave in the household of a magnate. More than that, these human assets are, at least to a certain extent, to be regarded as structural features of life, over which the woman herself had little influence. None of us has the power to choose our own parents. Early medieval girls lacked the power to choose their husbands. Nobody could tell if an infant was to survive or to die.

To achieve a better understanding of early medieval political culture, we ought to keep in mind the important point made in the theoretical chapter at the beginning of this book: that political culture should be understood as political practice. Political culture consists of the actions, whether innovative or based on routine, that are carried out by the political actors themselves. By analysing textual manifestations, for example in the form of stereotypical images, we may catch a few glimpses of the various patterns of behaviour resulting from these actions and tactics. In doing so, it also becomes possible in theory to differentiate between gender-specific patterns of political culture.

The logical place to begin to look for these patterns would be in the chambers and in the minds of the women themselves: in their personalities and their ways of life. It comes as no surprise to find that many of the successful royal women that appear in the chronicles are described as ambitious and aggressive. They are always ready to grasp an opportunity, to dispose of their enemies and to create ties of dependence and alliance with whoever happens to be available. There is nothing gender-specific about this. What we see is early medieval politics in action: everyone, man or woman, who wanted to emerge victorious in the dangerous political game *had* to behave aggressively. If that kind of behaviour did not suit you, you could always join the clergy and hopefully become a saint (such as Chlodovald/Saint Cloud, Chlodomer's only surviving son). Being aggressive and charismatic was part of the job description for an early medieval politician regardless of age or gender.

However, writers such as Gregory of Tours and Paul the Deacon did associate some aspects of aggressiveness with women in particular. Looking at the analysis of stereotypical images above, we find that 'bad' women were constantly portrayed as sexually depraved individuals. When acting in their own personal arena (which, by the very personal nature of early medieval politics was also a public, political scene), they used their sexuality to a degree that their male contemporaries did not. Men were not associated with sexuality in its capacity as a weapon. Rather, their sexual interests are described as incidental, apolitical features of their lives, directed towards rape victims and good-looking girls in general. Sexuality formed a part neither of their negative identity nor of their positive identity to the same extent as it did for a stereotypically described woman (whether a promiscuous princess or an explicitly asexual virgin).

There is, I believe, an important reason for this association of politically active women with sexuality. While the general association of sexuality with women went far beyond the boundaries of the political sphere discussed in this book, the particular cases of female sexuality linked to political activity cannot simply be explained by referring to a set of misogynist mental preconceptions. For instance, Paul the Deacon (and the source that he used) could easily have supplied another reason than sexual desire for Romilda's agreement with the Avars. For some reason, the particular idea of women as potential sex-hungry monsters appears to have agreed with the political circumstances to a degree that made this particular stereotype appealing to the writers.

This correspondence of ideas and circumstances is, in fact, quite obvious if we look at the first phases of the career patterns of several of the Frankish queens. Some, such as Brunhild and Wisigarda, arrived on the political scene because of marriage alliances, but a significant number of the future queens worked their way up by way of the king's bedchamber. If Fredegund had failed to get Chilperic sexually interested in her, she would never have become Queen of Soissons. Deuteria might – Gregory's relation of the events is unclear – have actively seduced the future Theudebert I; she is reported to have worked very hard (even killing her own daughter) to keep his favour. Bilichild, the wife of Theudebert II, was originally a slave girl who was bought by Brunhild and placed at the Austrasian court. She eventually managed to get into her owner's grandson's bed and openly compete with Brunhild. Balthild, an Anglo-Saxon slave girl, first made herself popular at Erchinoald's household and was later able to impress the king into marrying her.

Viewed from the men's point of view, this list of beautiful young Cinderellas ending up as queens can be read as evidence of male domination in a society characterised by patriarchal ideas. Chlothar I, Charibert I, Chilperic I and Dagobert I can be seen as immoral and powerful males grabbing hold of any girl they want. From the point of view of female political culture, however, it soon becomes clear that this interpretation misses the point completely. True, a king such as Chilperic probably did grab hold of any girl he fancied, but *he did not confer power* on all of them. To perceive Fredegund, Balthild, Bilichild and all the others as passive victims of a patriarchal system would be to neglect completely both the actual influence wielded by these women as queens and their personal capacity for thought and action.

I find it impossible to believe that Clovis II married Balthild simply because she was as pious and pleasant as her *vita* would have us believe. There were several girls, far more easily accessible, who could have acted sufficiently pious and submissive for the king to marry them, if that had been his only motivation. After all, Balthild did not even live at the royal court. It is more likely that Clovis married her simply because he found her sexually appealing or because he fell in love with her. The subsequent history of Balthild (her personal reign after Clovis' death, her persecution of bishops, her monastic policy, etc.) shows her to have been exactly the kind of aggressive politician that the early medieval political scene demanded. It is hard to think of the young Balthild as a passive creature in Erchinoald's household. On the contrary, I think we may safely assume that she did whatever was in her power to influence both Erchinoald and Clovis. Any other conclusion would be an insult to early medieval women and to their ability to think and act. In fact, on those rare occasions when the early medieval writers allow us to see women manipulating the people in their environment, the queens exhibit a considerable amount of persuasive charm. God only knows what Fredegund did to get Gunthchramn on her side in the autumn of 584, but it was certainly enough to save her political life. Gunthchramn had ample reasons to regret his actions a few years later, when he referred to Fredegund as *inimica Dei atque hominum.*

Likewise, while the horrible story of Romilda surely contains elements of pure fiction and misogyny, the idea of a female ruler of a frontier duchy trying to secure her position by a sexual liaison and/or marriage alliance to a foreign ruler is far from improbable per se. For all we know, Lombard tradition, as it appears in the text of Paul the Deacon, may be false; Romilda's strategy might have worked. After all, her family remained dominant in the duchy of Friuli for several decades.

What is hinted at in the stereotypical image and what is revealed by a study of female career patterns can be interpreted as a gender-specific aspect of early medieval political culture. Women (not men) used the various aspects of their sexual charm (persuasion, seduction, intercourse, etc.) to attain power. The men did not, mainly because they did not have to. If you were already king, you did not have to work your way upward by way of someone else's bed. Sometimes, however, when the queen in question was so powerful that her position was equivalent to that of a king, the gender roles would have been reversed. There are very few examples of this, but it can easily be argued that Protadius attained his position in Burgundy because of his ability to make himself appealing in the eyes of Brunhild.

Wealth and generosity

Let us assume that an early medieval woman has managed to climb the first important ladders towards political power. She is married to a king or a duke, either because her father arranged it or because the king thought she looked pretty. She has a few children, preferably male ones. That would still hardly be enough to make her feel secure. No matter how elevated the position of a medieval king or queen, medieval power was manifested through (and limited by) his or her ability to get others to obey orders. For instance, if the Austrasian magnates wanted to go to war with their Thuringian or Slavic neighbours to the east, regardless of his personal inclination, eastwards the king would probably have to lead them. If he failed to make them happy, he would lose their support in future crises. In order to counterbalance this structural weakness in early medieval positions of power, the holders of offices such as king, duke and count worked hard to recruit allies in the form of institutions (churches, monasteries, etc.) and people (bishops, warriors, allied kings, etc.). The more such allies you had, the more secure your position would be. There was nothing gender-specific about this; as in the case of aggressiveness, this rule affected everybody. However, the constant need for institutional and personal support also meant that there was a constant need for material funds (land, treasure, money, etc.). Warriors demanded payment; churches and monasteries needed lands and revenues; foreign rulers had to be bribed into action. Is it, we might ask, possible to discern gender-specific attitudes towards the acquisition and treatment of wealth?

In most cases, the answer would have to be no. Everybody wanted to get rich; greed was not, and is not, a gendered phenomenon. All of the men and women appearing on the political scene in the early medieval chronicles belonged to the landed class, whether by birth or as a consequence of their careers. They owned land, sometimes even entire cities, and they had servants. When an opportunity appeared that promised to make them even richer, both men and women hastened to use it. A few examples will suffice to demonstrate that early medieval women fully understood the value of material wealth. Chrodechild confiscated the lands of the nunnery of the Holy Cross during the revolt of 589. Berthegund's confiscations were worthy of a Barbarian warlord. Brunhild killed Aegyla and transformed his property into a part of the fisc. Nantechild held on to a third of Dagobert's treasure during the conference at Compiègne. Theudechild, Charibert's widow, tried to use her wealth to continue her life as a queen (or at least as a free woman), but she failed because of the fact that Gunthchramn was even greedier than she was. Many of the wives of magnates that appear in *Decem Libri Historiarum* were only too aware of the dangers awaiting their personal funds if and when their husbands died. If that happened, they did what they could to save what could be saved.

Furthermore, all our sources clearly indicate that men as well as women understood what to do with material funds once they got hold of them. Land and money could be used to buy warriors, assassins and other useful agents (see below). Above all, everybody understood the importance of *generosity*. In an economic and political system partly based on the logic of gift-exchange, the one who gave away property was automatically regarded as somebody important, someone to whom you owed thanks and service. Not only was this self-evident to men as well as women, it was also an inherent feature of both the secular and the ecclesiastical spheres. Kings and queens had to be generous; so did abbots and abbesses. We meet this attitude over and over again in the saints' lives: one biographer after another praises his or her respective saint as a generous giver of alms to the needy. Thus, the convent – and its leader – grew in social importance. The more grateful clients and supporters the convent (and the abbot/abbess) had, the more influential it would be.

However, the fact that generosity as well as greed was universal, and the fact that everybody understood this, does not mean that the *consequences* of possessing wealth were always the same. Sometimes, possession of too much land might prove fatal. Kings, queens and magnates of both sexes could easily decide to kill a wealthy landowner-cum-victim whose defences were perceived as sufficiently weak. As far as female political culture was concerned, this became crucial when it coincided with other crises. For instance, wealthy wives of Frankish magnates who suddenly became powerless (such as Duke Ragnovald's wife) appear to have been free targets for those with swords in their hands. The same rule applied to royal women without additional assets such as children. If Theudechild had been left destitute after Charibert's death, nobody would have paid attention to her. She might have married an ordinary farmer and disappeared from history, probably a lot happier than in her cell in Arles. As it turned out, Theudechild was a rich but defenceless woman, an easy victim for King Gunthchramn. Still, it might have been a lot worse. The richest of all the women mentioned in the early medieval sources, Galswinth, was so rich that Chilperic or Fredegund simply had to kill her once it was clear that the marriage between her and Chilperic was a failure. With all those resources at her disposal, Galswinth could easily have bought an army and set up a court of her own. Chilperic could not afford to let her live.

Thus, we must conclude that wealth had much the same function within female political culture as within male political culture. Everybody wanted it, and nobody ever seemed to have enough of it. When the women were faced with a personal crisis, however, the possession of wealth could turn against them in a way that seldom happened to the men.

Networks of clients and allies

Having established that a normal early medieval queen had a lot of land and a store of treasure that could be used to buy support, we must also ask our sources what this support looked like and whether we are dealing with gender-specific aspects of political culture or not.

We must always remember that queens, especially those who worked their way up through the bedchamber, came *into* a situation of power. While the kings might have inherited a system (or at least a tradition of having a system) of clients and allies, the queens had to construct their own systems from scratch. This provided them both with fresh opportunities and with structural opposition from all those magnates who risked losing influence through the creation of new social networks in local society.

Despite the scantiness of the material at our disposal, we can discern two basic levels of client relationships centred on the queens. Both levels demanded an active, personal approach to the issue, from the point of view of the women as well as from the point of view of the potential clients themselves. There is no reason to suppose that there was a lack of the latter: a wealthy queen with access to the king was powerful, and her friendship was worth having per se. However, there was a big difference between constructing a primary network of household agents and a secondary network of politically powerful clients. The primary network might be constructed in a few weeks, once the ambitious candidates had made themselves known to the queen. In this way, most queens would have constructed a primary network of clients at their own court, as in the case of Marcovefa (client: Leudast) and possibly Wisigarda (client: Asteriolus). In all probability, the differences between the various kingdoms in Western Europe were marginal from this point of view. Judging from *Historia ecclesiastica gentis Anglorum*, Anglo-Saxon queens such as Etheldreda and Eanfled had courts and thegns of their own.

The secondary level of client relationships was more important and demanded that the queen invested much wealth, time and energy in the project – especially if her husband was dead (in which case the network would be of far greater value to her than if he were alive). Thanks to Gregory of Tours and Fredegar, we are able to glimpse both Fredegund and Brunhild constructing, working with and protecting their secondary networks. Powerful individuals all over the kingdom were drawn into their webs of influence: bishops, dukes, counts, even popes (Gregory the Great maintained very good relations with Brunhild). If they suffered political setbacks, they had to start all over again, using the various resources that were still at their disposal. Thus, the events of 602–04 show us Brunhild, deposed from her position in Austrasia, creating a new network in Burgundy. Just as she had been doing for decades in Austrasia, she promoted her friends and attacked those factions that opposed her activity. Another good example is Nantechild: as a widow, she continued to rule the country together with her mayors of the palace (Aega, Erchinoald and Flaochad). The appointment of Flaochad as mayor of the palace in Burgundy in 641 or 642 clearly shows how Nantechild was able to intervene in a kingdom where she had previously wielded little power, extending her influence by way of a client.

A queen with a secondary network was always a very powerful queen, whether married or widowed. If she got that far, her court was automatically one of the major centres of power in the kingdom. Other assets (such as fathers) could, in that case, be dispensed with. However, that kind of power also demanded that the queen be prepared to fight. Her political system depended on reciprocity. Local landowners, counts and bishops had agreed to be her clients so that they would be handsomely rewarded, so that their enemies might be her enemies, so that they would be feared. Just as she could count on them to perform certain political services for her, she had to help them whenever necessary. Brunhild, the best known 'Godmother' of this early medieval political Mafia, appears to have had her client Innocentius (Count of Javols) kill Abbot Lupentius in 584, later rewarding the murderer with a bishopric. However, three years previously, she had been forced to intervene in person on the battlefield to help another of her allies, Duke Lupus of Champagne.

As is evident from these examples, the political system of a powerful early medieval queen included an element of violence. It also included many other aspects, such as ecclesiastical patronage, but we are comparatively well informed about the particular incidents that either resulted in or were expected to result in bloodshed. This is not surprising: medieval chroniclers enjoyed writing about warfare and destruction. However, there is something peculiar about the way these 'Godmothers' are described, if we compare them with descriptions of their equally bloodthirsty male contemporaries. This brings us back to the stereotypical images. As already stated, writers such as Gregory of Tours and Paul the Deacon regularly associated politically active 'bad' women with *murder through agents*.

As in the case of the stereotype concerning sexuality, I believe that there is a reason grounded in political culture for this textual manifestation. Why should a woman such as Rosemunda be associated with one attempted murder after another, first in Verona and then in Ravenna? Why is Fredegund repeatedly accused of trying to assassinate most of her royal colleagues in Gaul? Why is murder mentioned over and over again in association with powerful women? True, kings had murders committed as well, but they also acted in a number of other ways when in the process of causing destruction or taking revenge. For instance, Gunthchramn is not reported having dispatched assassins to kill his Visigothic enemies – instead, he sent armies with orders to devastate and, if possible, occupy Septimania.

The stereotype could hardly have been used to the degree that it actually was if early medieval writers and readers had not been able to recognise it, understand it and, at least on a subconscious level, agree with it. In some way, the stereotype told them something about society, about the kind of political culture that they instinctively associated with women. The fact that queens such as Rosemunda were associated with assassination is, I believe, to be explained as an element in their political culture that was linked to the fact that the early medieval gender structure prohibited them from leading armies and starting rebellions in the same way as kings did. The structural dilemma provoked a change in cultural attitudes. Despite the hypothesis of Megan McLaughlin (see above, pp. 46–48), there is very little in the sources to indicate that women usually went to war. Brunhild's interference on behalf of Duke Lupus of Champagne is an exception to the rule; it is not the way Brunhild and Fredegund normally behave in *Decem Libri Historiarum*. They had to work behind the scenes, using agents, dispatching murderers and manipulating courtiers. While Paul the Deacon's story of the murder of Alboin in 572 may to a large extent be fictitious, his description of the secret machinations of Rosemunda must nevertheless have been based upon his implicit knowledge of how female political culture worked. If Rosemunda wanted to get rid of Alboin, she would have had to behave in a way very similar to that described in *Historia Langobardorum*.

The ecclesiastical sphere

Apart from creating networks of allies such as bishops, abbots, dukes and counts, many rich women of the early Middle Ages sought to establish permanent institutional power bases (and bases of wealth) in the form of monasteries and convents. So did a number of rich men; indeed, the foundation of monastic institutions developed into one of the main political and economic strategies of the magnate class in seventh-century Merovingian Gaul, and the Anglo-Saxons were soon to follow the Frankish example. While these foundations undoubtedly corresponded to an urgent spiritual need of a number of truly pious individuals, it is our chief purpose in this book to analyse them as exponents of political culture.

It is easy to find supposedly pious women in the early medieval sources. As was explained above, piety as such developed into a stereotypical element in the picture of 'good' women. Many politically important women are primarily known to us in their capacity as generous benefactors of the church. In *Historia Langobardorum*, we meet Theudelinda, Gundeperga, Rodelinda and Theuderada. In Bede's works, pious queens, abbesses and nuns dominate the female scene entirely. The abundance of references enables us to establish that the relationship of powerful women to monastic institutions and churches could develop into networks and even myths, such as Chlothild's legendary persuasion of Clovis to accept Christianity. We know that Chlothild, who appears to have been a fairly normal powerful royal widow – bloodthirsty, vengeful and careful of her own favourite grandsons – worked hard to create a network of episcopal allies. She apparently did not become a nun, but she did gain a certain reputation for piety. Regardless of whether she actually did convert Clovis or not, the story fitted perfectly in the picture of Chlothild as it was known in the days of Gregory of Tours.

Chlothild eventually became Saint Chlothild, just as Radegund and Balthild were eventually venerated as holy women of God. It is not up to us to decide whether they deserved this honour; the Burgundian victims of Chlothild's revenge and the bishops killed at Balthild's command would undoubtedly have found their sainthood hard to countenance. From our point of view, the very existence of the saint-making process (which, of course, began once the women in question were already dead and unable to influence it personally) deserves attention. The myths of Saint Chlothild, Saint Radegund and Saint Balthild were constructed within their own spiritual circles. The *vitae* of Radegund and Balthild were written by their own friends in their own convents. The queens had been so deeply associated with their active interference in the religious sphere of society that myths of sainthood developed quickly. During the period studied in this book (especially during the seventh century), this development of saintly fame affected comparatively more women than in most other periods of history (see p. 54).

This is hardly a coincidence. Early medieval women used the various ecclesiastical resources to a very high degree, not only because they were pious (which many of them probably were). Association with the church strengthened the general position of a woman within the early medieval political structure. If she combined it with other resources, such as personal links to members of the royal house, a resourceful and charismatic woman such as Radegund could use her spiritual status and her convent in order to gain power. Backed by the Convent of the Holy Cross, Radegund was safe from the dangers that put an end to the political careers of women such as Theudechild. Not only was she safe, she was also capable of reaching out from her cell to intervene in politics, even to the point of establishing good relations with Constantinople. A Western European king in the early Middle Ages could seldom, if ever, afford to make enemies of rich abbesses armed with powerful relics, mighty episcopal and royal friends, and lots of land protected by the fact that it was theoretically owned by the church. The power of the abbesses is further illuminated by Bede's stories of the holy women of seventh-century England, many of them members of royal houses. Hilda was a prominent adviser of kings and a spiritual mother to several bishops. She participated in, and in fact hosted, the important synod of Whitby in 664. When they were about to die, these abbesses, such as Heriburg, arranged the succession just as if they had been petty kings trying to preserve the power of their own family into the next generation.

In many cases, the women themselves would have been actively responsible for the creation of their ecclesiastical assets. Radegund, of whom we know more than of most other individuals in the sixth century, definitely worked according to *her* agenda, not Chlothar I's. Others were not so fortunate but made the best of their situation. While Balthild, as a royal widow, was very active in creating a vast network of ecclesiastical allies comprising monastic institutions as well as bishops, her withdrawal to Chelles appears to have been forced upon her by her enemies. Most likely, she was the victim of a coup d'état, the swiftness of which prevented her from activating her own network of allies. The nuns at Chelles were initially reluctant to accept her as a member of their community, and it is not hard to guess why. Before her fall, Balthild (together with Ebroin) had laboured to balance, or even neutralise, the forces of the aristocratic opposition by creating strong bases for royal power among the religious houses of Gaul. She had not hesitated to kill those who disapproved of her policy, including several bishops with family connections to wealthy (and possibly vengeful) magnates. In 665, Balthild, having lost her power, could easily have been seen as a dangerous liability to any community bold enough to accept her presence. It is also possible that her previous activities had caused ill feeling within nunneries that she had dominated. Nevertheless, Balthild, being the resourceful woman that she was, appears to have survived and spiritually prospered at Chelles. After her death, sainthood was quick to follow.

However, the analysis of the saints' *vitae* indicates that several women had little choice in their association with the church. Monasteries and nunneries, especially in seventh-century Gaul, were used by aristocratic families to balance the powers of the crown. When Balthild and her allies at the Merovingian court tried to use this strategy to their own advantage, they were only doing what many other families were doing as well. The ecclesiastical sphere appealed to seventh-century aristocrats: it served a spiritual need at the same time as it helped them in their attempts to consolidate their power in local society. As has been pointed out by Jo Ann McNamara, the tendency of many Frankish crown officers to end their careers as bishops may reflect this use of the church as an alternative to the dangers of secular office or as a strategic repository of wealth. In the same way, the fact that many noble women entered convents with all their wealth suggests a family strategy that sought to oppose the king's desire to dispose of these rich heiresses among his own followers. Columbanus' rule and its adaptations were ideally suited to large monastic foundations in rural areas. This new pattern of monastic culture reflected the dynastic system of moving property and power through women to enable them to share in the responsibilities of the great families without risking a loss of patrimony to their husbands. Therefore, the pattern proved particularly effective for the establishment of female foundations.[982] Harshly speaking, fathers and mothers founded convents for their daughters to preserve their accumulated family lands through the church. They knew that kings could confiscate private property. They knew that kings could arrange marriages that destroyed vast collections of family lands. However, they also knew that kings found it considerably more difficult to abolish religious institutions out of pure greed. Sometimes, of course, secular leaders such as Aega and Charles Martel would attack the lands of ecclesiastical institutions anyway, but that kind of behaviour had still not become a permanent feature of Frankish political culture.

Jonas of Bobbio provides us with a detailed description of how Chagneric tried to force his daughter Burgundofara into marriage (pp. 295–96). He failed, and Burgundofara became a powerful abbess instead of the wife of a magnate. Following McNamara's hypothesis, the various difficulties of a religious nature with which Columbanus and Eustasius strewed Chagneric's path may in fact have been Chagneric's own way of creating a good excuse for sending Burgundofara to her nunnery. If the king tried to press a marriage candidate upon Chagneric (thereby destroying whatever plans he might have had of maintaining his family wealth), the clever father could use this religious excuse to explain why Burgundofara simply had to become a nun.

This chain of events is hypothetical. Jonas may very well be telling the truth. However, the hypothetical tactic employed by men such as Chagneric would in any case have had to be disguised in the *vita* in question. Chagneric's family would not have been shouting to the world that they had been planning to fool the king and that Burgundofara's saintly fame was the consequence of economic planning. Furthermore, we know that planning like this was essential for the preservation of family lands, since kings' intentions were far from hypothetical. What we know of King Dagobert's history proves without a shadow of a doubt that he fully understood the importance of well-chosen marriages. His attempts to force

Sadalberga and other future female saints into marriage can only be interpreted as part of a strategy to gain some control over the Frankish aristocracy and to prevent family alliances that might be harmful to Merovingian power.[983] Dagobert was not stupid: he wanted his own faithful clients to have sufficient landed assets. Why else should he have bothered to interfere in the marriage plans of members of the aristocracy?

It would be wrong to say that ecclesiastical assets constituted a particularly feminine resource in the early Middle Ages. There were, after all, far more male saints than female saints, and the nunneries were few compared with the monasteries. Nevertheless, ecclesiastical assets appear to have been more significant for women than for men. A politically active woman had more to gain from association with the church than a politically active man. The reason is, we might suspect, that women had fewer alternative assets. Male politicians did not need monasteries to the same degree that female politicians needed convents. How often do we read of kings exerting influence from behind the walls of institutions such as the Convent of the Holy Cross in Poitiers? The answer is never. When men such as Ebroin and Leodegar of Autun joined the monastery of Luxeuil, they did so because they were forced to. The monasteries served as prisons. Other men joined monasteries because they were genuinely pious. This pattern was not confined to the sixth and seventh centuries – eighth-century monastic kings such as Ratchis (in Lombard Italy 744–49, 756–57) and Carloman (in Austrasia, Alamannia and Thuringia 741–47) had little, if any, influence while they remained behind the walls of their Italian and Frankish monasteries. To many women, however, the church offered ideological assets that could help them assert their social position in the absence of male resources such as links of military dependence, patronage and fosterage. As an abbess, women like Anstrude and Rusticula could influence society to the same degree as an abbot. As a powerful religious armed with other resources as well as the purely ecclesiastical ones (wealth, ties to the royal house, etc.), the woman could do even more. She could develop into a local and regional nuisance, as in the case of Ingitrude of Tours, or even into an actor on the international scene, as in the case of Radegund.

Dangers

Summarising the various analyses of the resources and tactics of individual women in the present study, it is also important not to forget the dangers that lurked around every corner of their lives. All the politically active people in the early Middle Ages acted within a common framework of insecurity. While political assassinations do not form a part of contemporary Western European political culture, they were quite normal in the sixth and seventh centuries. That is not to say that the practice was approved of. On the contrary: King Gunthchramn openly declared that it was his firm intention to 'put an end to the abominable habit of murdering kings' (*consuetudo auferretur iniqua, ne reges amplius interficerentur*, p. 115).

To many of the royal women, especially the wives of kings, the chief danger was constituted by competition within the court itself. If they were unable to keep the king emotionally interested in them, they could easily get in trouble. The king might decide to promote a seductive young servant-woman who, if she were anything like Fredegund, might eventually attain so much power that the very lives of her competitors were in jeopardy. We even hear of kings murdering their own wives, for instance in the case of Theudebert II and his consort Bilichild in 610 (Theudebert preferred the company of an otherwise unknown girl called Theudechild). Some courts would appear to have been entirely characterised by the competition between wives and concubines (for example the courts of Charibert I, Theudebert I, Chilperic I, Theuderic II and Dagobert I). The core of this competition was the struggle for access to the king. Since individual actors, especially kings, mattered so much in medieval society, anyone interested in improving his or her lot through politics had to do so by way of the king himself, not by way of an institution. As a consequence, not only wives but also royal mothers, grandmothers and sisters were involved in the constant struggle for access. Theuderic II's Burgundian court in 606–07 is a good example. Brunhild, whose position was for the moment relatively secure, and Theudila (the king's sister), managed to oust their rival Ermenberga, the king's consort, from her position of access.

Furthermore, apart from being subjected to fierce competition from other women, the queens and princesses also had to deal with the prospect of being killed or imprisoned while performing their official duties. Just as the kings could be killed by their enemies, so could their female relatives. Their social influence (whether through access to the king or through their own networks) made them logical targets. For instance, King Agilulf's daughter was captured by the East Romans some time around 600 and brought to Ravenna together with her husband Godescalc. She was eventually released as part of a peace agreement. Others were not so lucky: Ingund died in Carthage, Gisa in Sicily. Bilichild, Childeric II's consort, was killed together with her husband in 675, apparently by members of an aristocratic faction hostile to the royal couple. Early medieval warlords were no gentlemen. They respected and feared those with power, and they behaved towards powerful women in a similar fashion as they behaved towards powerful men, all according to principle of do to others before they do to you. The brutal, almost paranoid behaviour of some royal women, exemplified by Brunhild's actions towards Columbanus, becomes understandable if viewed from this perspective. Brunhild, if indeed she was guilty of the persecution of which Jonas accuses her, undoubtedly had good political reasons for her action. She was afraid of becoming the victim of her aristocratic enemies; she wanted to decrease their influence by turning on their chief ecclesiastical ally. Furthermore, we *know* that her fears were justified. A few years after the incident, Brunhild lost the political game she had been playing for almost half a century, and she was, despite her old age, subjected to one of the most horrible executions known in early medieval history.

Death was, of course, the worst fate imaginable for all political actors. There were, however, a number of other consequences to be feared if and when a woman ended up at the mercy of her enemies. Being killed, like the two sisters Brunhild and Galswinth, was in a certain sense a mark of respect: their enemies were so afraid of them that they did not dare let them escape. Less dangerous female captives could get away with maltreatment and exile. Ansprand's wife Theuderada and his daughter Aurora were both brutally disfigured on the orders of Aripert II. Rodelinda and Ultrogotha were exiled. Albsuinda, Ingund, Gisa and Agilulf's daughter became hostages (or some kind of official guest) of the East Roman Empire. Above all, many undesirable young women of noble blood were incarcerated in nunneries. Under the rule of an abbess and surrounded by a multitude of nuns, they were thought to be safely out of the way. We know that this tactic, while far more lenient than death, led to personal tragedy for many women. While some, such as Balthild, appear to have managed rather well even as nuns, others loathed their new lives. Theudechild paid for her failed attempt to escape from the convent in Arles with subjection to even harsher treatment than before. Berthefled escaped from Tours to Le Mans when the leader of her convent (Ingitrude) was temporarily out of the way in 589. Chrodechild and Basina, in the same year, grew so desperate that they felt that they had to start a rebellion. Open warfare was, they argued, the only way to improve their lot. As Merovingians, they were supposed to rule, not take orders from abbesses.

The best thing that could possibly happen to woman who had lost her position of power was to retain, or regain, a freedom of choice (i.e., whether to be a secular female landowner or join a nunnery). As widows without male heirs, their positions were delicate. Although some extraordinary individuals, undoubtedly with powerful social networks of their own, nevertheless continued to fight for a while (as Plectrude did in 714–17), most such widows would, unless they quickly found a new royal husband, be faced with a life of political obscurity and danger. Their riches, if they had any left, could easily be stolen. Their lands could be confiscated. In fact, most of these women disappear entirely from history the moment their husbands die or lose interest in them. Those that do resurface are difficult to evaluate. Take, for example Queen Ingoberg, one of Charibert I's wives. What happened to her after her loss of the king's affection? We do not know. However, she reappears in 589, a few months before her death, summoning Gregory of Tours to carry out a few pious commands. Gregory describes Ingoberg as a wise woman, devoted to the religious life. We can only guess that Ingoberg would have been fairly well off, living off her lands and seeking solace in her religion. Her material situation might have been similar to that of Chrodechild, the rebel nun, after her rehabilitation at the court in Metz in 590 – with one crucial exception: Ingoberg was probably able to arrange her situation peacefully, while Chrodechild had to fight for her estate.

Social militarisation

With the ominous *revertar*, 'I will be back', Chrodechild finishes her opening sally in her verbal battle with Gregory of Tours. Chrodechild, daughter of Charibert of Paris, the princess of bandits and the scourge of Poitiers, is one of the most fascinating individuals of early medieval literature. We literally hear her voice shouting at us down the centuries, as she haughtily orders Bishop Gregory to do his duty by the poor defenceless rebel nuns while she heads off to meet her royal relatives. She stands there, in the cold early spring of 589, wet and chilly from the pouring rain, in front of the bishop's desk, informing Gregory of his duties as if he were a servant in the nunnery. Gregory was old when this happened; he was to die only a few years later. His relation of the conversation must be fairly contemporary with the events themselves, and his report on what Chrodechild had to say does not contain any suspicious-looking pieces of rhetoric. For all we know, he may have preserved her exact words. Though a barbarous villain in the eyes of Gregory, Chrodechild emerges as a heroine of almost mythical proportions to the modern reader: a woman fighting to regain her right of freedom of choice; an Emmeline Pankhurst of the sixth century.

Yet Chrodechild was no feminist. She was an ordinary Merovingian woman – as far as Merovingians can ever be regarded as ordinary – who, due to the current crisis in the ecclesiastical affairs of Poitiers (the strained relations between the convent and the local bishop, the weakness of the recently elected abbess, and so on) was able to respond with violence to her lack of power. Nobody appears to have been surprised by her tactics. The kings and the bishops surely did not approve of her rebellion (above all since it caused problems for themselves), but there is no hint in *Decem Libri Historiarum* that they found her general pattern of behaviour unnatural. Her one and only action in the entire rebellion that Gregory finds worthy of specific mention, undoubtedly since he found it peculiar, is her sudden appearance on the battlefield outside the walls of the nunnery. As we see the scene in Gregory's chronicle, Chrodechild walks out amidst the bodies of her slain thugs, brandishing the relic of the Holy Cross and speaking words of future revenge. This – the appearance of a woman on a battlefield – was obviously something out of the ordinary. The same is true of Gregory's stories of Brunhild's dealings with her Austrasian enemies: her appearance at the side of Duke Lupus in 581 was obviously not expected by Ursio; Gregory does not appear to have expected it either.

In other words, women who actually fought were sufficiently rare to merit attention, but women who were capable of taking command, assemble warbands and order others to fight were not. The first part of this paradox is not hard to explain. Women have always been physically weaker than men. In ancient and medieval combat, they would have been comparatively easy to kill if confronted by strong men wielding big swords. This must have been obvious to everybody even at the dawn of history. Thus, Jordanes finds it necessary to provide us with a myth to explain why there was once a tribe of Gothic Amazons. However, to explain the second part of the paradox, we must venture deeper into the early medieval mentality in search of a transformation of cultural attitudes.

The basic reason for Bishop Gregory's lack of surprise in finding a Merovingian nun becoming a female warlord should, I believe, be sought in the changing patterns of political structure in the *Völkerwanderungszeit* and in the way this affected the cultural attitudes of both men and women. I define this new element in early medieval society as *social militarisation*. The military sphere of life – with all its symbols, values and needs – mentally as well as physically invaded the lives of the people. A man who acted as judge in times of peace automatically became a commander in times of war. New settlements were not only surrounded by walls but also often located on well-defended hills. The civic élite of the Roman Empire was gradually being replaced by a medieval élite that favoured martial values. The age of the warriors, the knights and the kings with swords and armour (whether real or symbolic) had begun, an age that would last throughout the medieval and early modern periods until crushed by the combined forces of capitalism, industrialism and liberalism.

Perhaps the easiest way to spot the change in the material surveyed in the present study is by way of an analysis of language. In the *vitae* of the seventh century, even nuns begin to appear in 'cohorts' and 'troops'. Furthermore, their activities take on a distinctly military form: they congregate to sing their dying sisters into heaven, to defeat the forces of Evil as if Satan had actually brought forth a real army of demons in order to besiege the convent and steal the souls of the nuns. In the nunneries as well as in the royal courts and aristocratic manors, this wave of social militarisation made its influence felt each time a project was to be launched or a conflict arose. An abbot and an abbess fought Satan with spiritual tools, just as a king or a queen would oppose their evil enemies with whatever means were at their disposal. Since the power of saints and relics was thought of as being as concrete as the power of swords and spears, the actual difference between the military aspects of the secular sphere and of the ecclesiastical sphere was blurred.

From the point of view of female political culture, early medieval social militarisation meant that politically active women began to respond to demands and threats in ways that in many anachronistic studies of history have been relegated to the 'public' or male-dominated sphere of society. This cultural transformation affected patterns of organisation as well as the actual means employed by the people in question. A 'cohort of holy nuns' (*cohors sanctarum sanctimonialium*) such as that in Anstrude's convent in Laon was essentially a new kind of organisation that had not existed in the political or the spiritual culture of late antiquity. The political activity of abbesses such as Rusticula and Anstrude corresponded to the actions of queens such as Fredegund and Brunhild: neither the abbesses nor the queens were prepared to surrender to their enemies, be they Satan or Ebroin, without a fight. They used their respective resources in a way that to our eyes appears violent and forbidding, but which was quite natural to everybody in the early Middle Ages. Powerful women were *supposed* to defend themselves with the weapons that were theirs to command, whether secular or ecclesiastical. They intervened in feuds to help their friends and/or to secure the peace; they ritually assembled to help the souls of dying nuns reach across the dangerous gap of death and arrive in the bosoms of the angels. Thus, when Fredegund violently solved the feud in Tournai in 591, she was simply doing her duty. As *de facto* reigning queen, she was responsible for keeping the peace. Having failed to talk some sense into the antagonists, she had them killed, thereby making the streets of Tournai safer than before.

Summary

Judging by the results of the various analyses from in this study, a brief summary of the major elements of early medieval female political culture might look something like this:

- Fathers and other biological relatives. These assets were of great initial importance, especially with regard to marriage alliances. Powerful relatives could also be counted upon to intervene in case of later troubles, even if the woman in question ended up on another continent (such as Ingund in Africa). However, the existence of powerful relatives also served to limit drastically the social horizons of the daughters. Freedom of choice (in marriage and career) did not exist.
- Husbands. Even more important than fathers, a woman's ability to influence her environment depended to a large extent on her husband's power and status. A queen with direct access to a king was a woman to be feared and envied.
- Children. To an early medieval queen, children acted as a kind of career insurance. With the birth of a male heir, the queen's future prospects brightened considerably. After the king's death, the very existence of children could keep the queen in politics. As mother of the next king, she was automatically important.
- Aggressiveness and sexual charisma. All medieval politicians had to be aggressive and ruthless. If they were not, their enemies would soon see to it that they did not remain politicians. As far as the early medieval women were concerned, many queens actually managed to use their personal talents to advance from complete obscurity by way of the royal bedchamber.
- Wealth and generosity. All medieval politicians had to be rich. They also had to spread their wealth around abbots, abbesses, dukes, counts, foreign monarchs and everybody else that counted. In order to do this, they were forced to behave very aggressively against enemies or potential enemies who were sufficiently weak to be safely used as victims of confiscations.
- Networks of clients and allies. With the help of their gifts of land, their promises of support in various local conflicts and their patron-

age in general, the queens could construct powerful networks of episcopal and magnate allies.
- The ecclesiastical sphere. Many queens, princesses and magnate women developed strong ties to the church. They founded convents, retired to religious institutions, appointed bishops and were sometimes even awarded a posthumous career as saints.
- Dangers. The life of a powerful early medieval woman was structurally insecure, even if we leave out a number of typically feminine dangers (such as the ever-present danger of dying in childbirth). They faced many of the same dangers as their husbands faced, such as the risk of being killed by political opponents. However, they were also forced to contend with their personal rivals (other queens, concubines, stepsons, etc.).
- Social militarisation. Although rarely appearing in person on the battlefield, early medieval abbesses and queens shared a mentality that was far more imbued with military values and models than the one we are accustomed to today. Nuns fought spiritual battles against the Devil. Secular women did not hesitate to gather warbands and, on occasion, take command.

Ultimately, the cultural differences between early medieval male and female political culture were rooted in the fact that the structural patterns of male careers and female careers were entirely different. The men usually inherited a considerable potential for power – that is, the potential would turn into real power if they managed to stay alive until adulthood. Most of the women within the political circles of early medieval Europe either had to start from scratch (if they had no powerful relatives) or were placed on the political scene according the wishes of their parents. This could cause a number of difficulties, all of them emanating from the structural insecurity inherent in the women's situation. As a result, even at the beginning of their political lives, women were driven to act according to other strategies than their male contemporaries. They had to be prepared for sudden losses of strength due to the death of key male relatives; they had to create alternative bases for their power, whether in the form of loyal husbands, male heirs or social networks. As far as husbands were concerned, this human asset was not to be trusted as a permanent source of support.

Firstly, husbands often died while the wives were still fairly young. Secondly, competition for the king's or the magnate's favour was often very tough. A queen who had managed to attain access to the king's bed and the king's ear could never take it for granted that she had exclusive access. As long as she did, she wielded a lot of power, and she could easily construct a primary client network of her own. However, the king could cast her off in favour of another woman, in which case she might lose everything she had tried hard to achieve. This problem was both structural and gender-specific: the structure could not be changed, and it only affected women. As a result, the political culture arising out of the need to respond to the structural dilemma appears to have chiefly affected the female protagonists of the political drama.

Children were far better assets than husbands and fathers. The very existence of a male royal heir was enough to make the mother's position immensely stronger than would otherwise have been the case. A royal heir could save the political career of a royal widow. While an ambitious son could prove extremely dangerous to a king, few queens had cause to be wary of their offspring. In most cases, the enemies of the son were also the enemies of the mother, as in the case of Childebert II and Brunhild. There were a few exceptions, such as when Brunhild lost her ability to influence her grandson Theudebert II. We can only guess the reason – perhaps the combined persuasive abilities of concubines such as Bilichild and a number of Austrasian aristocrats at a time when Brunhild was away from court.

Despite the importance of children, some widows were nevertheless sufficiently strong to hold on to their position without immediate heirs. Pippin's widow, Plectrude, was a powerful actor in the Frankish civil war that followed her husband's death in 714. She made peace with her stepson Charles and disappeared from the political scene in 717, but three years of power is still, by early medieval standards, quite an achievement. Plectrude would hardly have been able to remain in command for so long without additional assets, such as personal charm and material wealth.

As far as charm is concerned, this asset could, quite literally, turn a poor slave-girl into a wealthy queen. While the early medieval male political career was barred to most non-nobles, the female one was characterised by an impressive degree of social mobility. It is easy to see why various chroniclers found it natural to associate powerful women with an unnatural degree of sexuality. In many other historical periods, pretty girls at the king's court might, at best, end up as royal mistresses, but at the Merovingian royal court, they could become the legal wives of the kings and assume command of the *regnum* when their husbands died. Within the female political culture of the time, sex was a tactical weapon to be used to attain power and keep it.

Just as important as the ability to persuade people and lure them into friendship was the possession of material wealth. When the husband was dead and the children were too young to fight, money, land and precious stones were an early medieval girl's best friends. When news reached her that Chilperic had been murdered, his sensible wife Fredegund grabbed as much of her treasure as possible (she had wisely hidden a sizeable amount in a safe place, just in case) and fled to a church, where it would appear that she began to milk her assets to the very best of her ability. Women in particular had to be careful to plan ahead, as Fredegund had wisely done. Their wealth could, it would appear, be stolen rapidly once their male protectors were removed from the scene. Rigunth's immense treasure dwindled away on her journey from northern Francia towards the kingdom of the Visigoths.

Material assets could be used to buy allies and clients. They could be employed as persuasive tools when dealing with would-be murderers such as Claudius, the 'empty-headed and greedy fellow' who committed sacrilege in Tours in order to be handsomely rewarded by Fredegund. Powerful women, as well as powerful men, understood the importance of being both rich and above all generous. In order to serve its purpose, money and land should be constantly redistributed to well-chosen aristocrats, monasteries, nunneries and foreign allies. Carl Barks' Scrooge McDuck, hoarding his coins in a huge money bin, would not have lasted many weeks in the political game of the early Middle Ages.

If a rich early medieval queen used her wealth to create a network of allies, her power would increase considerably. Bishops, dukes and counts would come to her and ask for protection and patronage. Reciprocal bonds would be created, and the queen would be feared. The same general rule applied to male leaders, but there is an important difference. While the prime form of male political culture was conceptualised as one of warfare, not even the most powerful early medieval queens were thought of as warriors. Rather, they used intermediaries. Men as well as women employed assassins, but women had to rely on them to a much greater extent than men had to do. Men had far more options. However, we must not make the mistake of thinking of all early medieval female politicians as hardened criminals who routinely ordered murders. They only did so when they thought that they had to. When acting within the more peaceful sphere of ordinary politics, they had no need for male intermediaries. Several women personally acted as peacemakers, diplomats trying to bridge the gaps between dynasties and kingdoms. For instance, Fredegar found it remarkable that Bilichild on one occasion failed to attend a peace conference. As a woman of power, she was supposed to have been at the meeting. Likewise, Fredegund intervened to stop a feud in Tournai but, being the particular kind of practical person that she was, she had her own bloody way of solving the issue.

Finally, there was the Church. While a prison to some, it was an asset for others. The career of an abbess (or a powerful religious ruling behind a puppet, as in the case of Radegund) was a worthy alternative to the career of a queen or that of a wife of a landowner. By founding convents, a queen could gather institutional support for her position, and a magnate (whether male or female) could preserve landed wealth from the greedy hands of his or her enemies. Abbots and abbesses were perceived as just as materially powerful as secular landowners, but their spiritual power – their access to God and His saints – made them even stronger. Radegund, Sadalberga, Anstrude, Burgundofara, Rusticula, Hilda and all the other influential women of religion that we have met in the course of this study clearly belonged to the leading political stratum of their time. As in the case of client relationships, this feature of early medieval political mentality was, in itself, not gender-specific. However, it turned out to be of greater significance for women than for men, since women lacked several of the alternative options that were readily available to men. Thus, political practice contributed to making the ecclesiastical career a prominent one in the history of early medieval women.

Evaluating the results of our investigation, we must conclude that the differences between male and female political culture in the early

Middle Ages were considerable. The very goals and career patterns were entirely different. While men, even at an early age, would begin to fight for even more power and influence than they had been given by their fathers, women had to spend a long time (sometimes their entire lives) fighting for the *survival* of themselves and of their children. Secondly, when survival appeared to be temporarily assured, they had to lay the foundations for continued presence on the political scene, a presence that most kings and magnates took for granted. Only thirdly (and for many women, this third step was never reached) could they begin to wield power equal to that of kings and mayors of the palace. Even the most powerful women in the early Middle Ages were politically weaker than their male counterparts. They had to be more careful than the men; they had to plan ahead in a strategic fashion that was not necessary for most kings and male landowners; they had to use consistently whatever resources were at their disposal (and they had fewer resources than the men) in their unceasing battle for survival, presence and power.

Still, women were not perceived as aliens as far as politics was concerned. The chroniclers and the biographers of saints' lives, all the way from Northumbria to Monte Cassino, took for granted that women exerted influence over secular as well as ecclesiastical matters. The reason why we meet so few of them (women only amount to between 11 and 15 percent of the individuals mentioned in the major texts from period) is because their political culture was different from that of the men. Political chroniclers such as Paul the Deacon and Gregory of Tours were men, and they had been brought up to think in terms of male political culture. They seldom bothered to think about the Other Half of politics. They undoubtedly knew about it, but they instinctively refrained from making it manifest in their texts, thereby perpetuating the near-invisibility of female political culture into the future. We only encounter early medieval women in politics on those rather rare occasions when female strategies and tactics were so conspicuous in the political arena that they simply had to be mentioned. All the other actions and projects of early medieval queens, abbesses and magnate women are doomed to remain hidden from our view, although we may glimpse them through studies such as this. The channels through which these women acted were different, and they belonged to a political culture that was different, from the cultural patterns that the chroniclers a priori associated with political action. In their attempts to explain the discrepancies between the two cultures, the chroniclers employed stereotypical images focusing on aspects that they, consciously or unconsciously, found suitable for the characterisation of women associated with power. Thus, we find evil queens who live for the joy of sex and murder, and we meet beautiful ladies who piously and generously devote their lives in the convent or at court to weaving peace on earth and bringing glory to God. Slowly, through a process of political and scholarly routine, early medieval gender roles are constructed and made manifest.

Epilogue

At a certain point in the course of the work resulting in this book, I came up with the bright idea of calling the finished product *Cinderellas and Godmothers*. 'Cinderellas' because many powerful women in the early Middle Ages started out as poor servant-women in the households of kings or mayors of the palace. Eventually, a young prince or a king caught sight of them, fell in love and raised them to queenhood. True, the heroes in question were hardly the dashing Prince Charmings of the fairy-tales; rather, they were dirty, lusty young Barbarians reeking of ale. Nevertheless, they were members of the royal house and the servant-women did become queens. 'Godmothers' because the Cinderellas had a tendency to evolve into early medieval female versions of Don Corleone. Those ex-Cinderellas who were in a position to do so recruited clients/torpedoes, who were always ready to kill, and some of them (at least Fredegund) even employed whole gangs of professional assassins. At the same time, they were in the habit of benevolently exerting their patronage in a fashion similar to that of Cinderella's Fairy Godmother. They could raise their own favourites to positions of honour, transform a poor adventurer with a price on his head into an honoured master of stables, appoint bishops and found convents. One day, they made offers to aristocrats that the aristocrats could not refuse; the next day, they used their magic wands to transfer riches and happiness to their friends. Furthermore, a few of them even performed some of the very religious acts that have been associated with the word 'Godmother' – Brunhild, one of the most powerful of all medieval women, actually stood sponsor to the magnate Berthefried's daughter at her baptism. Berthefried then betrayed her good faith and turned into an enemy. As in all good gangster plots, he eventually paid for his betrayal with his life. His blood was shed in the church of Verdun, despite strong episcopal disapproval, in the year of Our Lord 587. Ergo, 'Godmothers'.

Then it dawned upon me that I was being grossly unfair to another literary tradition. Rereading what I had been writing, I found that the character known as the Wicked Stepmother was far more prominent than Cinderella and the Godmother. You have all met her: the very evil, very beautiful queen who keeps asking her magic mirror if any woman in the entire kingdom is prettier than she is. When the mirror replies that Snow White is prettier, the evil queen (turning into a Godmother) orders one of her male torpedoes to take her for a last ride. Just like the queens in this book, she does not perform the dirty work herself; she orders her men to do it for her. When forced to sully her dainty hands, she uses poison (just like many of 'my' queens) and she wears a disguise. Queen Deuteria is even reported to have killed her own daughter because of her fears that the daughter's beauty might put ideas into the king's head...

Raised from poverty and obscurity, sometimes even from slavery, into becoming powerful queens, then turning evil, persecuting their stepsons and their daughters with gangs of hired assassins – these were the women of Gregory of Tours, Fredegar and Paul the Deacon. Perhaps there actually is a link with the stories of Snow White and Cinderella as we know them today. However, I know too little about the evolution of fairy tales and legendary themes to pursue this idea, and it would in any case be beside the point. What I have been trying to argue is, rather, that these stereotypical images of early medieval powerful women served an urgent need for the early medieval writers of history. The stereotypes made sense to them; they helped them understand and conceptualise society. Behind the stereotypes were real women of flesh and blood, women who were probably neither inherently good nor inherently evil but rather female individuals following the unwritten rules of their own political culture, and in doing so also transforming it and forcing the other actors to respond. Since the majority of these women were either abbesses or queens, I decided to at least honour their, admittedly not always bright, memory by naming the book after these professions.

The sixth, seventh and eighth centuries were indeed an age of abbesses and queens. During the first decades of the seventh century, two of the most powerful political entities of Western Europe, Merovingian Gaul and Lombard Italy, were dominated by two queens, Brunhild and Theudelinda. Both began their political careers as foreign outsiders; both survived two husbands; both ruled as royal widows; both have left colourful traces in the history books. Brunhild was unfortunate: her enemies dominated the historiographical scene and decided to portray her as a Jezebel. Theudelinda was fortunate: her supporters made her look a paragon of virtue. It is only because of a rumour reported in an anonymous Burgundian chronicle that we begin to suspect that there was more to her character. Only a madman would have argued that these two women were weak and inferior compared with their male contemporaries. However, it would nevertheless appear that most people in the early Middle Ages, men as well as women, believed that women were by nature weaker than men. This attitude did not include a moral judgement: there was no generally accepted doctrine that proclaimed that women as such were bad and evil, like Brunhild (or, for that matter, that they were particularly good and saintly, like Theudelinda). It was not a given fact that early medieval queens were to be portrayed with the help of the particular stereotypes that have been elucidated in the present study. Some stereotypes did exist (and still do), but the actual manifestations of stereotypical images of women in politics were by no means predictable. I am not saying that I have explained the early medieval pattern of gender-specific stereotypical manifestations in this book, but I would definitely argue that the present study serves to illuminate a number of crucial aspects associated with the parts played by women through their participation in political culture.

Like everybody else, the writers of the early Middle Ages believed that women were inferior beings. At least, that is the message inherent in their choice of words, for instance by describing the actions of a good woman as 'virile'. The word 'feminine' was used in a pejorative sense. It implied weakness and a certain kind of stupidity. Just like numerous other men in many other societies and periods, Western European men in the early Middle Ages regarded women as strange creatures ruled by their emotions to an extent that they found both puzzling and dangerous. The stereotype of the Stupid and Emotional Woman – hysterical, impulsive and illogical – is therefore present in many of the works analysed in the course of this study.

Add to this the Bad Adviser: the woman who transmits ideas of murder and betrayal through the whispers in her husband's ear in the darkest hours of the night; the woman who is not content with her position, who always wants more power and more riches; the woman who leaves a trail of corpses wherever she walks, whose wickedness drives innocent stepsons and stepdaughters into monasteries or exile. The sexual demon and the pious saint. Step by step, we see a kaleidoscope of stereotypes forming before our eyes, a kaleidoscope in which one and the same woman, be she Brunhild or Theudelinda, is quickly transformed from one extreme to another depending on which artist is responsible for the particular image in question.

What we see is gender in the process of being constructed, at least the particular aspect of gender that is associated with political culture. The ideas that are manifested in the form of stereotypes grew stronger with each reading of a *vita*, each reading of a chronicle and each brief reflection along the same lines of thought that prompted Gregory of Tours and Paul the Deacon to write the way they did. As an evil man once said: if a lie is repeated often enough, you begin to believe in it. Stereotypical images become a part of the very culture from which they emanate.

Bibliography

Sources

Abbreviations:

AS	*Acta Sanctorum*
Bede	Beda Venerabilis, *Historia ecclesiastica gentis Anglorum*, in *Bedae opera historica*, ed. C. Plummer, Oxford 1896.
Fredegar	Fredegarius, *Chronicae*, in *MGH SRM* 2, Hannover 1888.
Gregory of Tours	Gregorius Turonensis, *Historia Francorum* (more correctly *Decem libri historiarum*), ed. W. Arndt, in *MGH SRM* 1:1, Hannover 1884–85.
Jordanes	Jordanes, *De origine actibusque Getarum*, in *MGH Auctores antiquissimi 5*, Berlin 1882–83.
PD	Paulus Diaconus, *Historia Langobardorum*, in *MGH Scriptores rerum langobardicarum et italicarum, saec. VI–IX*, Hannover 1878.
MGH	*Monumenta Germaniae historica*
SRM	*MGH Scriptores rerum merovingicarum*

Other sources:

Vita Aldegundis (2nd version), in *AS*, January 30, Venice 1734.

Vita Amandi episcopi I, in *MGH SRM* 5, Hannover and Leipzig 1910.

Vita Anstrudis abbatissae Laudunensis, in *MGH SRM* 6, Hannover and Leipzig 1913.

Vita Audoini episcopi Rotomagensis, in *MGH SRM* 5, Hannover and Leipzig 1910.

Vita Austrebertae, in *AS*, February 10, Venice 1735.

Vita Balthildis, in *MGH SRM* 2, Hannover 1888.

Vita Bertilae abbatissae Calensis, in *MGH SRM* 6, Hannover and Leipzig 1913.
Bieler, Ludwig (ed. and transl.), *The Irish Penitentials*, Dublin 1963.
Caesaria's letter to Radegund: *MGH Epistolae* 3, pp. 450–53.
Vitae Columbani abbatis discipulorumque eius libri duo auctore Iona, *MGH SRM* 4, Hannover and Leipzig 1902.
Vita sancti Cuthberti auctore Beda, in *Two Lives of Saint Cuthbert*, ed. Bertram Colgrave, Cambridge 1940.
Passio sancti Desiderii episcopi et martyris, in *MGH SRM* 3, Hannover 1896.
Sisebut, Vita vel Passio Sancti Desiderii a Sisebuto rege composita, *MGH SRM* 3, Hannover 1896.
Epistolae Austrasiacae, in *MGH Epistolae* 3, Berlin 1891–92.
Vita Eustadiolae, in *AS*, June 8 (embedded in a *vita* of Saint Sulpicius of Bourges), Venice 1742.
Fredegarii Continuationes, in *MGH SRM* 2, Hannover 1888.
Vita Genovefae, in *AS*, January 3, Venice 1734.
Vita Geretrudis, in *MGH SRM* 2, Hannover 1888.
Gregory of Tours (Gregorius Turonensis): Liber I de virtutibus beati Martini episcopi, in *MGH SRM* 1:2, Hannover 1885.
Passio Leudegarii episcopi Augustodunensis I, in *MGH SRM* 5, Hannover and Leipzig 1910.
Passio Leudegarii episcopi Augustodunensis II, auctore Ursino, in *MGH SRM* 5, Hannover and Leipzig 1910.
Liber Historiae Francorum, in *MGH SRM* 2, ed. B. Krusch, Hannover 1888.
De beata Monegunde (by Gregory of Tours), in *Liber vitae patrum*, *MGH SRM* 1:2, Hannover 1885.
Panazza, G., 'Catalogo delle iscrizioni e sculture paleocristiane e pre–romaniche di Pavia', *Arte del primo millennio*. Atti del II° convegno per lo studio dell'arte dell'alto medio evo, tenuto presso l'Università di Pavia nel settembre 1950, Turin 1953.
Passio Praeiecti episcopi et martyris Arverni, in *MGH SRM* 5, Hannover and Leipzig 1910.
Vita Radegundis (by Baudonivia), in *MGH SRM* 2, Hannover 1888.
Vita Radegundis (by Venantius Fortunatus), in *MGH SRM* 2, Hannover 1888.

De excidio Thoringiae, in *MGH Auctores antiquissimi* 4:1, Berlin 1881.
Vita Rusticulae sive Marciae abbatissae Arelatensis, *MGH SRM* 4, Hannover and Leipzig 1902.
Vita Sadalbergae abbatissae Laudunensis, in *MGH SRM* 5, Hannover and Leipzig 1910.
Venantius Fortunatus, Carmina, in *MGH Auctores antiquissimi* 4:1, Berlin 1881.
Vita Wilfridi I. episcopi Eboracensis auctore Stephano, in *MGH SRM* 6, Hannover and Leipzig 1913.

Translations mentioned in the book:
Gregorius av Tours, *Frankernas historia*, övers. i urval av Alvar Eriksson, Stockholm 1963.
McCarthy, Mary Caritas (trans.), *The Rule for Nuns of Saint Caesarius of Arles*, Washington, D.C. 1960.
McNamara, Jo Ann et al. (eds.), *Sainted Women of the Dark Ages*, Durham and London 1992.
Wallace–Hadrill, J.M., *The Fourth Book of the Chronicle of Fredegar with its Continuations*, London 1960.

Secondary works

Affeldt, Werner, 'Frühmittelalter und historische Frauenforschung', in *Frauen in der Geschichte VII: Interdisziplinäre Studien zur Geschichte der Frauen im Frühmittelalter. Methoden – Probleme – Ergebnisse*, eds. Werner Affeldt and Annette Kuhn, Düsseldorf 1986.
Affeldt, Werner, and Reiter, Sabine, 'Die Historiae Gregors von Tours als Quelle für die Lebenssituation von Frauen im Frankenreich des sechsten Jahrhunderts', in *Frauen in der Geschichte VII: Interdisziplinäre Studien zur Geschichte der Frauen im Frühmittelalter. Methoden – Probleme – Ergebnisse*, eds. Werner Affeldt and Annette Kuhn, Düsseldorf 1986.
Affeldt, W.; Nolte, C.; Reiter, S.; Vorwerk, U. (eds.), *Frauen im Frühmittelalter: Eine ausgewählte, kommentierte Bibliographie*, Frankfurt 1990.
Aigrain, René, *Sainte Radegonde*, Parthenay 1987 (reprint).

Almond, Gabriel A. and Verba, Sidney (eds.), *The Civic Culture Revisited*, Boston and Toronto 1980.
Andersson, Gudrun, *Tingets män och kvinnor. Genus som norm och strategi under 1600– och 1700-tal*, Uppsala 1998.
Aronsson, Peter, *Bönder gör politik*, Lund 1992.
Artaeus, Irene, *Kvinnorna som blev över. Ensamstående stadskvinnor under 1800-talets första hälft – fallet Västerås*, Uppsala 1992.
Arvizu, Fernando de, 'La femme dans le Code d'Euric', *Revue historique de droit français et étranger* 4, 62, 1984.
Atkinson, Clarissa W., *The Oldest Vocation. Christian Motherhood in the Middle Ages*, Ithaca and London 1991.
Aubrun, Jean, *Radegonde: reine, moniale et sainte*, Poitiers 1986.
Badinter, Elisabeth, *Om Mannens identitet*, Juva 1994.
Baltrusch–Schneider, Dagmar Beate, 'Klosterleben als alternative Lebensform zur Ehe?', in *Weibliche Lebensgestaltung im frühen Mittelalter*, ed. Hans–Werner Goetz, Cologne, Weimar and Vienna 1991.
Bandel, Betty, 'The English Chroniclers' Attitude toward Women', *Journal of the History of Ideas*, vol. 16, I, Lancaster, New York 1955.
Bitel, Lisa, 'Sex, Sin and Celibacy in Early Christian Ireland', *Proceedings of the Harvard Celtic Colloquium* 7, 1987.
Bitel, Lisa, *Land of Women. Tales of Sex and Gender from Early Ireland*, Ithaca and London 1996.
Bloch, R. Howard, *Medieval Misogyny and the Invention of Western Romantic Love*, Chicago and London 1991.
Blomqvist, Karin, *Myth and Moral Message in Dio Chrysostom. A Study in Dio's Moral Thought, with a Particular Focus on his Attitudes towards Women*, Lund 1989.
Breisch (now Ney), Agneta, 'Hervor – en kvinna på svärdssidan. Om genusidentitet och gränsöverskridande i äldre nordisk historia', in *Historiska etyder. En vänbok till Stellan Dahlgren*, eds. Janne Backlund, Anders Florén, Åsa Karlsson, Hans Norman and Maria Ågren, Uppsala 1997.
Brown, Peter, 'The Rise and Function of the Holy Man in Late Antiquity', *Journal of Roman Studies* LXI, 1971, also in *Society and the Holy in Late Antiquity*, London 1982.
Brown, Peter, 'Eastern and Western Christendom in Late Antiquity: A Parting of the Ways', in *The Orthodox Churches and the West, Studies*

in Church History XIII, Oxford 1976, also in *Society and the Holy in Late Antiquity*, London 1982.

Brown, Peter, *The Cult of the Saints. Its Rise and Function in Latin Christianity*, London 1981.

Brown, Peter, 'Relics and Social Status in the Age of Gregory of Tours', in *Society and the Holy in Late Antiquity*, London 1982.

Brown, Peter, *The Body and Society. Men, Women and Sexual Renunciation in Early Christianity*, New York 1988.

Brundage, James, *Law, Sex, and Christian Society in Medieval Europe*, Chicago 1987.

Buc, P., 'Italian Hussies and German Matrons: Liutprand of Cremona on Dynastic Legitimacy', *Frühmittelalterliche Studien* 29, 1995.

Cadden, Joan, *Meanings of Sex Difference in the Middle Ages. Medicine, Science, and Culture*, Cambridge 1993.

Carlsson Wetterberg, Christina, 'Från patriarkat till genussystem – och vad kommer sedan?', *Kvinnovetenskaplig tidskrift* 3, 1992.

Clover, Carol, 'Maiden Warriors and Other Sons', in *Matrons and Marginal Women in Medieval Society*, eds. Robert R. Edwards and Vickie Ziegler, Woodbridge 1995.

Collins, Roger, *Early Medieval Spain. Unity in Diversity, 400–1000*, London 1983.

Condren, Mary, *The Serpent and the Goddess. Woman, Religion, and Power in Celtic Ireland*, San Francisco 1989.

Consolino, Ela, 'Due agiografi per una regina: Radegonda di Turingia fra Fortunato e Baudonivia', *Studi storici, Rivista trimestrale dell'Istituto Gramsci* 29, 1988.

Cristiani, Marta, 'La sainteté féminine du haut moyen âge. Biographie et valeurs', in *Les fonctions des saints dans le monde occidentale (IIIe–XIIIe siècle)*, Colloque de l'école française de Rome 14, Rome 1991.

Dalarun, Jacques, 'Eve, Marie ou Madelaine? La dignité du corps féminin dans l'hagiographie médiévale (VIe–XIIe siècles)', *Médiévales* 8, 1985.

Damsholt, Nanna, *Kvindebilledet i dansk højmiddelalder*, Copenhagen 1985.

Davidoff, Leonore, 'Class and Gender in Victorian England', in *Sex and Class in Women's History*, ed. Newton, Ryan and Walkowitz, London, Boston, Melbourne and Henley 1983.

Davidoff, Leonore and Hall, Catherine, *Family Fortunes. Men and Women of the English Middle Class 1780–1850*, London 1987.
Davids, A. (ed.), *The Empress Theophano*, Cambridge 1995.
Davis, Natalie Zemon, *Women on the Margins. Three Seventeenth–Century Lives*, Cambridge, Mass., 1995.
Demertzis, Nicolas, *Cultural Theory and Political Culture. New Directions and Proposals*, Lund 1985.
Demyttenaere, Albert, 'The Cleric, Women and the Stain. Some Beliefs and Ritual Practices Concerning Women in the Early Middle Ages', in *Frauen in Spätantike und Frühmittelalter. Lebensbedingungen – Lebensnormen – Lebensformen*, ed. Werner Affeldt, Sigmaringen 1990.
Dienst, Heide, 'Zur Rolle von Frauen in magischen Vorstellungen und Praktiken – nach ausgewählten mittelalterlichen Quellen', in *Frauen in Spätantike und Frühmittelalter. Lebensbedingungen – Lebensnormen – Lebensformen*, ed. Werner Affeldt, Sigmaringen 1990.
Dubois, Jacques and Beaumont–Maillet, Laure, *Sainte Geneviève de Paris*, Paris 1982.
Duggan, A., *Queens and Queenship in Early Medieval Europe*, ed. A. Duggan, Woodbridge 1997.
Effros, Bonnie, 'Images of Sanctity: Contrasting Descriptions of Radegund by Venantius Fortunatus and Gregory of Tours', *UCLA Historical Journal* 10, 1990.
Effros, Bonnie, 'Symbolic Expressions of Sanctity: Gertrude of Nivelles in the Context of Merovingian Mortuary Custom', *Viator* 27, Berkeley, Los Angeles and London 1996.
Enright, Michael J., 'Lady with a Mead–Cup. Ritual, Group Cohesion and Hierarchy in the Germanic Warband', *Frühmittelalterliche Studien* 22, Berlin and New York 1988.
Erkens, Franz–Reiner, 'Die Frau als Herrscherin in ottonisch–frühsalischer Zeit', in *Kaiserin Theophanu. Begegnung des Ostens und Westens um die Wende des ersten Jahrtausends*, eds. Anton von Euw and Peter Schreiner, Cologne 1991.
Erler, Mary and Kowaleski, Maryanne, 'Introduction', in Erler, M. and Kowaleski, M. (eds.), *Women and Power in the Middle Ages*, Athens (Georgia) 1988.

von Euw, A. and Schreiner, P. (eds.), *Kaiserin Theophanu: Begegnung des Ostens und Westens um die Wende der ersten Jahrtausends*, Cologne 1991.

Fell, Christine (together with Cecily Clark and Elizabeth Williams), *Women in Anglo–Saxon England and the Impact of 1066*, Bloomington 1984.

Ferrante, Joan, *Woman as Image in Medieval Literature from the Twelfth Century to Dante*, New York 1975.

Florin, Christina and Johansson, Ulla, *'Där de härliga lagrarna gro...' Kultur, klass och kön i det svenska läroverket 1850–1914*, Kristianstad 1993.

Folz, Robert, *Les saintes reines du moyen âge en Occident (VIe–XIIIe siècles)*, Subsidia Hagiographica 76, Brussels 1992.

Fouracre, Paul, 'Merovingian History and Merovingian Hagiography', *Past and Present* 127, 1990.

Frantzen, Allen J., 'When Women aren't Enough', *Speculum* 68:2, 1993.

Gäbe, Sabine, 'Radegundis: Sancta, Regina, Ancilla. Zum Heiligkeitsideal der Radegundisviten von Fortunat und Baudonivia', *Francia* 16/1, Sigmaringen 1989.

Garlick, Barbara; Dixon, Suzanne; Allen, Pauline (eds.), *Stereotypes of Women in Power. Historical Perspectives and Revisionist Views*, New York 1992.

Gillis, John R., 'Alltid lika problematiskt att göra fäder av män', *Kvinnovetenskaplig tidskrift* 1, 1993.

Given, J.B., *Society and Homicide in Thirteenth–Century England*, Stanford (California) 1977.

Goetz, Hans–Werner, *Frauen im frühen Mittelalter. Frauenbild und Frauenleben im Frankenreich*, Weimar, Cologne and Vienna 1995.

Goffart, Walter, *The Narrators of Barbarian History (A.D. 550–800). Jordanes, Gregory of Tours, Bede and Paul the Deacon*, Princeton 1988.

Goffart, Walter, 'The Fredegar Problem Reconsidered', *Rome's Fall and After*, London 1989.

Graus, František, *Volk, Herrscher und Heiliger im Reich der Merowinger. Studien zur Hagiographie der Merowingerzeit*, Prague 1965.

Grimshaw, Jean, *Feminist Philosophers. Women's Perspectives on Philosophical Traditions*, Brighton 1986.

Hagemann, Gro, 'Postmodernismen en användbar men opålitlig bundsförvant', *Kvinnovetenskaplig tidskrift* 3, 1994.
Halsall, Guy, 'Female Status and Power in Early Merovingian Central Austrasia: The Burial Evidence', *Early Medieval Europe* 1996:1.
Hanawalt, Barbara, *Crime and Conflict in English Communities, 1300–1348*, 1979.
Harrison, Dick, *Krigarnas och helgonens tid. Västeuropas historia 400–800 e.Kr.*, Stockholm 1999 (forthcoming).
Heidrich, Ingrid, 'Von Plectrud zu Hildegard. Beobachtungen zum Besitzrecht adliger Frauen im Frankenreich des 7. und 8. Jh. und zur politischen Rolle der Frauen der frühen Karolinger', *Rheinische Vierteljahresblätter* 52, 1988.
Heidrich, Ingrid, 'Besitz und Besitzverfügung verheirateter und verwitweter freier Frauen im merowingischen Frankenreich', in *Weibliche Lebensgestaltung im frühen Mittelalter*, ed. Hans–Werner Goetz, Cologne, Weimar and Vienna 1991.
Heinzelmann, Martin and Poulin, Jean–Claude, *Les vies anciennes de Sainte Geneviève de Paris*. Bibliothèque de l'école des hautes études, scientifiques, historiques, et philologiques 329, Paris 1986.
Herlihy, David, 'Land, Family, and Women in Continental Europe, 701–1200', *Traditio* 18, 1962.
Hillmann, Michael, ''Geschlecht' als Maßstab der Rechtsordnung. Überlegungen zur Geschlechterpolarität in den altenglischen Gesetzen', in *Frauen in der Geschichte VII: Interdisziplinäre Studien zur Geschichte der Frauen im Frühmittelalter. Methoden – Probleme – Ergebnisse*, eds. Werner Affeldt and Annette Kuhn, Düsseldorf 1986.
Hirdman, Yvonne, 'Genussystemet – reflexioner kring kvinnors sociala underordning', *Kvinnovetenskaplig tidskrift* 3, 1988.
Hochstetler, Donald, 'The Meaning of Monastic Cloister for Women According to Caesarius of Arles', in *Religion, Culture and Society in the Early Middle Ages. Studies in Honor of Richard E. Sullivan*, eds. Thomas F. X. Noble and John J. Contreni, Kalamazoo 1987.
Hoebanx, Jean Jacques, *L'abbaye de Nivelles des origines au XIVe siècle*. Mémoires de l'académie royale de Belgique 46, Brussels 1952.
Hollis, Stephanie, *Anglo–Saxon Women and the Church. Sharing a Common Fate*, Woodbridge 1992.

Howell, Martha C., 'Citizenship and Gender: Women's Political Status in Northern Medieval Cities', in Erler, M. and Kowaleski, M. (eds.), *Women and Power in the Middle Ages*, Athens (Georgia) 1988.

Hunt, Lynn, *The Family Romance of the French Revolution*, London 1992.

Hyam, Jane, 'Ermentrude and Richildis', in *Charles the Bald: Court and Kingdom*, eds. Margaret Gibson, Janet Nelson and David Ganz, BAR International Series 101, Aldershot 1990.

Jarrick, Arne, *Kärlekens makt och tårar. En evig historia*, Stockholm 1997.

Jäschke, Kurt–Ulrich, *Notwendige Gefährtinnen. Königinnen der Salierzeit als Herrscherinnen und Ehefrauen im römisch–deutschen Reich des 11. und beginnenden 12. Jahrhunderts*, Saarbrücken 1991.

Johnson, Penelope D., *Equal in Monastic Profession. Religious Women in Medieval France*, Chicago and London 1991.

Keller, H., 'Widukind's Bericht über die Aachener Wahl und Krönung Ottos I', *Frühmittelalterliche Studien* 29, 1995.

Kroeschell, Karl, 'Söhne und Töchter im germanischen Erbrecht', in *Studien zu den germanischen Volksrechten. Gedächtnisschrift für Wilhelm Ebel*, Frankfurt and Bern 1982.

Laiou, Angeliki E., 'The Role of Women in Byzantine Society', in XVI. Internationaler Byzantinistenkongress (Wien 1981), Akten I/1, *Jahrbuch der Österreichischen Byzantinistik* 31/1, 1981.

Laiou, Angeliki E., *Gender, Society and Economic Life in Byzantium*, Variorum Reprints, Brookfield 1992.

Landes, Joan, *Women and the Public Sphere in the Age of the French Revolution*, New York 1988.

Laporte, Jean–Pierre, 'La reine Balthilde ou l'ascension sociale d'une esclave', in *La femme au moyen âge*, eds. Michel Rouche and Jean Heuclin, Paris 1990.

Lennartsson, Malin, 'De som älskar varandra måtte få komma tillsammans', in *Jämmerdal och fröjdesal. Kvinnor i stormaktstidens Sverige*, ed. Eva Österberg, Stockholm 1997.

Lennartsson, Malin, review of Jarrick, Arne ('Kärlekens makt...') in *Historisk tidskrift* 1998, Stockholm 1998.

Leonardi, Claudio, 'Fortunato e Baudonivia', in *Aus Kirche und Reich.*

Studien zu Theologie, Politik und Recht im Mittelalter. Festschrift Friedrich Kempf, Sigmaringen 1983.
Leyser, Karl J., *Herrschaft und Konflikt. König und Adel im ottonischen Sachsen,* Göttingen 1984.
Luecke, Janemarie, 'The Unique Experience of Anglo–Saxon Nuns', in *Medieval Religious Women 2: Peaceweavers,* eds. John A. Nichols and Lillian Thomas Shank (Cistercian Studies Series 72), Kalamazoo 1987.
McKitterick, Rosamond, *The Carolingians and the Written Word,* Cambridge 1989.
McKitterick, Rosamond, 'Frauen und Schriftlichkeit im Frühmittelalter', in *Weibliche Lebensgestaltung im frühen Mittelalter,* ed. Hans–Werner Goetz, Cologne, Weimar and Vienna 1991.
McLaughlin, Megan, 'The Woman Warrior: Gender, Warfare and Society in Medieval Europe', *Women's Studies* 17, 1989.
McNamara, Jo Ann, 'Muffled Voices: The Lives of Consecrated Women in the Fourth Century', in *Medieval Religious Women 1: Distant Echoes,* eds. John A. Nichols and Lillian Thomas Shank (Cistercian Studies Series 71), Kalamazoo 1984.
McNamara, Jo Ann, 'A Legacy of Miracles: Hagiography and Nunneries in Merovingian Gaul', in *Women of the Medieval World. Essays in Honour of John H. Mundy,* eds. Julius Kirschner and Suzanne F. Wemple, Oxford 1985.
McNamara, Jo Ann, 'The Ordeal of Community: Hagiography and Discipline in Merovingian Convents', *Vox Benedictina* 3, 1986.
McNamara, Jo Ann, 'Living Sermons: Consecrated Women and the Conversion of Gaul', in *Medieval Religious Women 2: Peaceweavers,* eds. John A. Nichols and Lillian Thomas Shank (Cistercian Studies Series 72), Kalamazoo 1987.
McNamara, Jo Ann, 'The Need to Give. Economic Restriction and Penitential Piety among Late Medieval Nuns', in *Images of Sainthood in Medieval and Renaissance Europe,* eds. Renate Blumenfeld–Kozinski and Timea Szell, Ithaca 1991.
McNamara, Jo Ann et al. (eds.), *Sainted Women of the Dark Ages,* Durham and London 1992.
McNamara, Jo Ann and Wemple, Suzanne F., 'Marriage and Divorce

in the Frankish Kingdom', in Stuard, Susan Mosher (ed.), *Women in Medieval Society*, Philadelphia 1976.

McNamara, Jo Ann and Wemple, Suzanne F., 'The Power of Women through the Family in Medieval Europe, 500–1100', in Erler, M. and Kowaleski, M. (eds.), *Women and Power in the Middle Ages*, Athens (Georgia) 1988.

Merta, Brigitte, 'Helenae conparanda regina – secunda Isebel. Darstellung von Frauen des merowingischen Hauses in frühmittelalterlichen Quellen', *Mitteilungen des Instituts für Österreichische Geschichtsforschung* 96, Vienna, Cologne and Graz 1988.

Meyer, Marc A., 'Land Charters and the Legal Position of Anglo–Saxon Women', *The Women of England. From Anglo–Saxon Times to the Present. Interpretative Bibliographical Essays*, ed. Barbara Kanner, London 1980.

Moreira, Isabel, 'Provisatrix Optima: St. Radegund of Poitiers' Relic Petitions to the East', *Journal of Medieval History* 19, 1993.

Nelson, Janet, 'Queens as Jezebels: the Careers of Brunhild and Balthild in Merovingian History', in Derek Baker (ed.), *Medieval Women*, Oxford 1978.

Nelson, Janet, 'Perceptions du pouvoir chez les historiennes du haut moyen âge', in *La femme au moyen âge*, eds. Michel Rouche and Jean Heuclin, Paris 1990.

Nelson, Janet, 'Commentary on the Papers of J. Verdon, S.F. Wemple and M. Parisse', in *Frauen in Spätantike und Frühmittelalter. Lebensbedingungen – Lebensnormen – Lebensformen*, ed. Werner Affeldt, Sigmaringen 1990.

Nelson, Janet, 'Women and the Word in the Earlier Middle Ages', in *Women in the Church*, eds. W.J. Sheils and Diana Wood, Studies in Church History 27, Oxford 1990.

Nelson, Janet, 'Gender and Genre in Women Historians of the Early Middle Ages', in *L'historiographie médiévale en Europe*, ed. Jean–Philippe Genet, Paris 1991.

Nelson, Janet, 'Early Medieval Rites of Queen–Making and the Shaping of Medieval Queenship', *Queens and Queenship in Early Medieval Europe*, ed. A. Duggan, Woodbridge 1997.

Nicholson, Joan, '*Feminae Gloriosae*: Women in the Age of Bede', in Derek Baker (ed.), *Medieval Women*, Oxford 1978.

de Nie, Giselle, *Views from a Many–Windowed Tower: Studies of Imagination in the Works of Gregory of Tours*, Amsterdam 1987.
Niederhellmann, Annette, *Arzt und Heilkunde in den frühmittelalterlichen Leges. Eine wort– und sachkundliche Untersuchung*, Arbeiten zur Frühmittelalterforschung 12, Berlin and New York 1983.
Nolte, Cordula, 'Klosterleben von Frauen in der frühen Merowingerzeit. Überlegungen zur Regula ad virgines des Caesarius von Arles', in *Frauen in der Geschichte VII: Interdisziplinäre Studien zur Geschichte der Frauen im Frühmittelalter. Methoden – Probleme – Ergebnisse*, eds. Werner Affeldt and Annette Kuhn, Düsseldorf 1986.
Noonan, John T., *Contraception. A History of Its Treatment by the Catholic Theologians and Canonists*, Cambridge, Mass. 1965.
Ó Cróinín, Dáibhí, *Early Medieval Ireland 400–1200*, London and New York 1995.
von Olberg, Gabriele, 'Aspekte der rechtlich–sozialen Stellung der Frauen in den frühmittelalterlichen Leges', in *Frauen in Spätantike und Frühmittelalter. Lebensbedingungen – Lebensnormen – Lebensformen*, ed. Werner Affeldt, Sigmaringen 1990.
Ortner, Sherry B. and Whitehead, Harriet (eds.), *Sexual Meanings: The Cultural Construction of Gender and Sexuality*, Cambridge 1981.
Österberg, Eva, 'Bönder och centralmakt i det tidigmoderna Sverige. Konflikt – kompromiss – politisk kultur', *Scandia* 1989:1, Lund 1989.
Österberg, Eva, 'Vardagens strävja samförstånd', in *Tänka, tycka, tro. Svensk historia underifrån*, eds. Gunnar Broberg, Ulla Wikander and Klas Åmark, Stockholm 1993.
Österberg, Eva, 'Stark stat och starkt folk. En svensk modell med långa rötter', in *Innsikt og utsyn. Festskrift til Jørn Sandnes*, eds. Kjell Haarstad, Anders Kirkhusmo, Dagfinn Slettan and Steinar Supphellen, Trondheim 1996.
Österberg, Eva, 'Den förmoderna kvinnan – variationer och tvetydigheter', in *Jämmerdal och fröjdesal. Kvinnor i stormaktstidens Sverige*, ed. Eva Österberg, Stockholm 1997.
Österberg, Eva, 'Makt, stat och kön – begreppens tyranni, ambivalenta tolkningar och kvinnorna på 1600–talet', in *Kjønn, makt, samfunn i Norden i et historisk perspektiv*, vol. 1, Konferansrapport fra

det 5. Nordiske kvinnehistorikermøte, Klækken 08.–11.08.96, eds. B. Gullikstad and K. Heitmann, Dragvoll 1997.

Österberg, Eva and Lindström, Dag, *Crime and Social Control in Medieval and Early Modern Swedish Towns*, Uppsala 1988.

Papa, Cristina, 'Radegunda e Baltilde: Modelli di santità regia femminile nel regno Merovingio', *Benedictina* 36, 1989.

Parisse, Michel, *Les nonnes au moyen âge*, Le Puy 1983.

Payer, Pierre J., *Sex and the Penitentials. The Development of a Sexual Code 550–1150*, Toronto, Buffalo and London 1984.

Pernoud, Régine, *La femme au temps des Cathédrales*, Paris 1984.

Pohl–Resl, Brigitte, "Quod me legibus contanget auere'. Rechtsfähigkeit und Landbesitz langobardischer Frauen', *Mitteilungen des Instituts für österreichische Geschichtsforschung* 101, 1993.

Portmann, Marie–Luise, *Die Darstellung der Frau in der Geschichtsschreibung des früheren Mittelalters*, Basler Beiträge zur Geschichtswissenschaft 69, Basel and Stuttgart 1958.

Prinz, Friedrich, *Frühes Mönchtum im Frankenreich. Kultur und Gesellschaft in Gallien, den Rheinlanden und Bayern am Beispiel der monastischen Entwicklung (4.–8. Jh.)*, Munich and Vienna 1965.

Prinz, Friedrich, 'Heiligenkult und Adelsherrschaft im Spiegel merowingischer Hagiographie', *Historische Zeitschrift* 204, 1967.

Pye, Lucian W. and Verba, Sidney (eds.), *Political Culture and Political Development*, Princeton 1965.

Roper, Michael and Tosh, John, 'Introduction. Historians and the Politics of Masculinity', in *Manful Assertions. Masculinities in Britain since 1800*, London 1991.

Rosaldo, Michelle Zimbalist, 'A Theoretical Overview', in Rosaldo, M. Z. and Lamphere, L., *Woman, Culture, and Society*, Stanford 1974.

Rosaldo, Michelle Zimbalist, 'The Use and Abuse of Anthropology: Reflections on Feminism and Cross–Cultural Understanding', *Signs* 5, 1980.

Ruether Radford, Rosemary, 'Virginal Feminism in the Fathers of the Church', *Religion and Sexism*, New York 1974.

Ryan, Mary P., *Cradle of the Middle Class. The Family in Oneida County, New York, 1790–1865*, Cambridge 1981.

Sasse, Barbara, 'Frauengräber im frühmittelalterlichen Alamannien', in *Frauen in Spätantike und Frühmittelalter. Lebensbedingungen – Lebensnormen – Lebensformen*, ed. Werner Affeldt, Sigmaringen 1990.

Sasse, Barbara, and Dübner–Manthey, Birgit, 'Frühmittelalterliche Frauengräber – Archäologische Untersuchungen zu Frauen im westlichen und südlichen Mitteleuropa', in *Frauen in der Geschichte VII: Interdisziplinäre Studien zur Geschichte der Frauen im Frühmittelalter. Methoden – Probleme – Ergebnisse*, eds. Werner Affeldt and Annette Kuhn, Düsseldorf 1986.

Sawyer (formerly Strand), Birgit, 'Sköldmön och madonnan – kyskhet som ett hot mot samhällsordningen', *Kvinnovetenskaplig tidskrift* 1986:2, 1986.

Scheibelreiter, Georg, 'Königstöchter im Kloster. Radegund (d. 587) und der Nonnenaufstand von Poitiers (589)', *Mitteilungen des Instituts für Österreichische Geschichtsforschung* 87, Vienna, Cologne and Graz 1979.

Schmidt–Wiegand, Ruth, 'Der Lebenskreis der Frau im Spiegel der volkssprachigen Bezeichnungen der Leges barbarorum', in *Frauen in Spätantike und Frühmittelalter. Lebensbedingungen – Lebensnormen – Lebensformen*, ed. Werner Affeldt, Sigmaringen 1990.

Schreiner, Klaus, "Hildegardis regina'. Wirklichkeit und Legende einer karolingischen Herrscherin', *Archiv für Kulturgeschichte* 57, 1975.

Schulenburg, Jane Tibbetts, 'Strict Active Enclosure and its Effects on the Female Monastic Experience (500–1100)', in *Medieval Religious Women 1: Distant Echoes*, eds. John A. Nichols and Lillian Thomas Shank (Cistercian Studies Series 71), Kalamazoo 1984.

Schulenburg, Jane Tibbetts, 'Female Sanctity: Public and Private Roles, c. 500–1100', in Erler, M. and Kowaleski, M. (eds.), *Women and Power in the Middle Ages*, Athens (Georgia) 1988.

Scott, Joan Wallach, 'Gender: A Useful Category in Historical Analysis', *Gender and the Politics of History*, New York 1988.

Skinner, Mary, 'Benedictine Life for Women in Central France, 850–1100: a Feminist Revival', in *Medieval Religious Women 1: Distant Echoes*, eds. John A. Nichols and Lillian Thomas Shank (Cistercian Studies Series 71), Kalamazoo 1984.

Skinner, Patricia, 'Women, Wills and Wealth in Medieval Southern Italy', *Early Medieval Europe* 2, 1993.

Sommestad, Lena, 'Mejerskor, industrialisering och välfärdspolitik – argument för en komparativ genusforskning', in *Fra kvinnehistorie til kjönnshistorie?*, From the 22nd Nordiske Historikermöte, Oslo 1994.
Stafford, Pauline, 'Sons and Mothers: Family Politics in the Early Middle Ages', in *Medieval Women*, ed. Derek Baker, Oxford 1978.
Stafford, Pauline, *Queens, Concubines and Dowagers. The King's Wife in the Early Middle Ages*, London 1983.
Stenton, Doris, *The English Woman in History*, London 1957.
Strand (now Sawyer), Birgit, *Kvinnor och män i Gesta Danorum*, Gothenburg 1980.
Taylor, Charles, 'Interpretation and the Science of Man', *Review of Metaphysics*, vol. 25, 1971.
Thompson, Sally, *Women Religious. The Founding of English Nunneries after the Norman Conquest*, Oxford 1991.
Thraede, Klaus, 'Zwischen Eva und Maria: das Bild der Frau bei Ambrosius und Augustin auf dem Hintergrund der Zeit', in *Frauen in Spätantike und Frühmittelalter. Lebensbedingungen – Lebensnormen – Lebensformen*, ed. Werner Affeldt, Sigmaringen 1990.
Ulvros, Eva Helen, *Fruar och mamseller. Kvinnor inom sydsvensk borgerlighet 1790–1870*, Lund 1996.
Van Dam, Raymond, *Leadership and Community in Late Antique Gaul*, Berkeley 1985.
Verdon, J., 'Les femmes et la politique en France au Xe siècle', *Économies et sociétés au moyen âge: Mélanges offerts à E. Perroy*, Paris 1973.
Verdon, J., *Grégoire de Tours*, Le Coteau 1989.
Verdon, Jean, 'Les femmes laïques en Gaule au temps des Mérovingiens: les réalités de la vie quotidienne', in *Frauen in Spätantike und Frühmittelalter. Lebensbedingungen – Lebensnormen – Lebensformen*, ed. Werner Affeldt, Sigmaringen 1990.
Vogelsang, T., *Die Frau als Herrscherin im hohen Mittelalter*, Frankfurt 1954.
Wallace–Hadrill, J.M., *The Fourth Book of the Chronicle of Fredegar with its Continuations*, London 1960.
Ward, Elizabeth, 'Caesar's Wife. The Career of the Empress Judith, 819–29', in *Charlemagne's Heir. New Perspectives on the Reign of*

Louis the Pious (814–40), eds. Peter Godman and Roger Collins, Oxford 1990.

Ward–Perkins, Bryan, *From Classical Antiquity to the Middle Ages. Urban Public Building in Northern and Central Italy AD 300–850*, Oxford 1984.

Wemple, Suzanne Fonay, *Women in Frankish Society. Marriage and the Cloister, 500 to 900*, Philadelphia 1981.

Wemple, Suzanne Fonay, 'Female Spirituality and Mysticism in Frankish Monasteries: Radegund, Balthild and Aldegund', in *Medieval Religious Women 2: Peaceweavers*, eds. John A. Nichols and Lillian Thomas Shank (Cistercian Studies Series 72), Kalamazoo 1987.

Wemple, Suzanne, 'Sanctity and Power: The Dual Pursuit of Medieval Women', in Bridenthal, R. and Koonz, C., *Becoming Visible: Women in European History*, Boston 1987.

Wemple, Suzanne Fonay, 'Female Monasticism in Italy and its Comparison with France and Germany from the Ninth through the Eleventh Century', in *Frauen in Spätantike und Frühmittelalter. Lebensbedingungen – Lebensnormen – Lebensformen*, ed. Werner Affeldt, Sigmaringen 1990.

Wittern, Susanne, 'Frauen zwischen asketischem Ideal und weltlichem Leben. Zur Darstellung des christlichen Handelns der merowingischen Königinnen Radegunde und Balthilde in hagiographischen Lebensbeschreibungen des 6. und 7. Jahrhunderts', in *Frauen in der Geschichte VII: Interdisziplinäre Studien zur Geschichte der Frauen im Frühmittelalter. Methoden – Probleme – Ergebnisse*, eds. Werner Affeldt and Annette Kuhn, Düsseldorf 1986.

Wittern, Susanne, *Frauen, Heiligkeit und Macht. Lateinische Frauenviten aus dem 4. bis 7. Jahrhundert*, Stuttgart and Weimar 1994.

Wood, Ian, 'The *Vita Columbani* and Merovingian Hagiography', *Peritia* 1, 1982.

Wood, Ian, 'Forgery in Merovingian Hagiography', *MGH Schriften* 33, *Fälschungen im Mittelalter* V, Hannover 1988.

Wood, Ian, *The Merovingian Kingdoms 450–751*, London and New York 1994.

Notes

Introduction

[1] Vita Audoini 15: regnante Theuderico et Chrodochilde regina, administrante Warattone subregulo.
[2] Liber Historiae Francorum 49.
[3] This is the term used in this book for the Latin *maior domus*.
[4] Gregorius av Tours, *Frankernas historia*, övers. i urval av Alvar Eriksson, Stockholm 1963.

Theoretical and historiographical background

[5] The literature on this subject is considerable. For an introduction, see for instance Badinter 1994; Davidoff 1983; Davidoff and Hall 1987; Frantzen 1993; Hunt 1992; Landes 1988; Ortner and Whitehead 1981; Roper and Tosh 1991; Ryan 1981.
[6] Scott 1988, pp. 42–50.
[7] In the Swedish academic milieu, the one I know best, Andersson 1998; Artaeus 1992; Florin and Johansson 1993 and Ulvros 1996, among others, are clearly inspired by Scott.
[8] Carlsson Wetterberg 1992, p. 37.
[9] Hirdman 1988.
[10] See Carlsson Wetterberg 1992; Hagemann 1994; Ulvros 1996, pp. 16–17.
[11] Davis 1995; Österberg 1997 ('Den förmoderna kvinnan…'); Österberg 1997 ('Makt, stat och kön…').
[12] Andersson 1998, especially p. 30; Sommestad 1994.
[13] Goetz 1995, pp. 402–03.
[14] Goetz 1995, p. 407.
[15] Grimshaw 1986.
[16] Jarrick 1997, esp. pp. 251, 269, 272–73
[17] Jarrick 1997, p. 247.
[18] Jarrick 1997, p. 251.
[19] Jarrick 1997, pp. 257–62.
[20] In this respect, Jarrick has been justly criticised by Malin Lennartsson. See Lennartsson 1998 and (for a specific case study) Lennartsson 1997.
[21] Blomqvist 1989, p. 266.
[22] Strand 1980, pp. 199, 224, 230. See also Sawyer 1986. Generally for views on women in high medieval Denmark, see Damsholt 1985 (stressing the great impact of the church).
[23] For a brief overview of previous research on theological views on women in the early

Middle Ages, see Goetz 1995, pp. 58–60. More specifically, see Damsholt 1985, pp. 63–73; Demyttenaere 1990; Portmann 1958 and (although not on the early part of the Middle Ages) Bloch 1991.
24 Ruether Radford 1974; Strand 1980, pp. 30–32.
25 Dalarun 1985; Thraede 1990 (on late antiquity).
26 Strand 1980, p. 59.
27 Thraede 1990, p. 137.
28 Hollis 1992.
29 Stenton 1957, arguing that Anglo–Norman military society relegated women to an honourable but essentially unimportant position; Fell (with Clark and Williams) 1984, especially pp. 13–14. Post–1066 development is described on pp. 148–93. See also Bandel 1955.
30 Hollis 1992, pp. 5–7.
31 Hollis 1992, pp. 12–13. A significant part of Hollis' work is devoted to revealing the misogynist tendencies of Bede's texts. See pp. 179–207 (on the *Life of Cuthbert*) and 208–70 (on the *Historia ecclesiastica gentis Anglorum*), especially pp. 250–52.
32 Bitel 1996, pp. 14–16.
33 Bitel 1996, pp. 19–27.
34 Bitel 1996, p. 33.
35 Bitel 1996, pp. 34–36.
36 Bitel 1996, pp. 206–16.
37 Clover 1995. See also Breisch 1997.
38 Bitel 1996, pp. 216–22.
39 Goetz 1995, pp. 62–63. See also Dienst 1990; Niederhellmann 1983; Stafford 1983, pp. 29–30.
40 Bitel 1996, p. 158.
41 Bitel 1996, pp. 161–66.
42 Condren 1989, p. 48.
43 Condren 1989, especially pp. 50, 79–80.
44 Condren 1989, pp. 112–13, 143–210.
45 Bitel 1996, pp. 167–203.
46 Atkinson 1991, pp. 79–81; Bieler 1963, pp. 90–93, 116–17, 222–23, 264; Bitel 1987, p. 80; Bitel 1996, pp. 66–83; Brown 1988, pp. 361–64, 401–08; Brundage 1987, pp. 160–63; Noonan 1965; Payer 1984.
47 Bitel 1996, pp. 53, 62.
48 Bitel 1996, p. 69.
49 Bitel 1996, p. 71.
50 Cadden 1993, pp. 48–53.
51 Goetz 1995, especially pp. 58–60, 71–103 (on Eve), 161–62 (on saints' lives), 399, 404–07, 414–15.
52 Goetz 1995, especially pp. 359, 390–91: 'Die Anschauungen aber, die uns heute als von männlichen Normen bestimmt oder gar als frauenfeindlich erscheinen mögen, wurden von den Frauen selbst mitgetragen, im frühen Mittelalter also offensichtlich nicht in dieser Weise empfunden. Das weibliche Selbstverständnis orientierte sich an dem zeitgenössischen Frauenbild, den Vorstellungen von einem schwachen

Geschlecht und von vermeintlich weiblichen Handlungsweisen sowie an dem Vorbild männlichen Verhaltens. Feminines Selbstverständnis schien weit stärker integrativ als abgrenzend. Das Klischee weiblicher Schwäche verband sich sicherlich mit einer sozialen Underordnung, es führte jedoch weder zur Handlungsunfähigkeit noch zur funktionellen Abwertung.' (quotation from p. 359).

53 Goetz 1995, p. 402: 'Aus solchen Anschauungen erwuchsen jedoch keine getrennten Lebensbereiche oder gar Lebensformen, und selbst die Suche nach spezifisch weiblichen Verhaltensweisen stößt auf beträchtliche Schwierigkeiten...'.

54 Erler and Kowaleski 1988, pp. 3–5. The early medieval situation, according to this theory, is most clearly stated in Schulenburg 1988, p. 114: 'During this early period, the intersection of public and private spheres favored the acquisition of wealth and the exercise of power by women.' See also, for more information on the general theory, Rosaldo 1974.

55 McNamara and Wemple 1988.

56 McLaughlin 1989. For examples of medieval female warlords, see also Fell (with Clark and Williams) 1984, pp. 91–92, 170; Stafford 1983, pp. 117–20.

57 See, for instance, Howell 1988; McNamara and Wemple 1988; Wemple 1987 ('Sanctity and Power...').

58 Rosaldo 1980.

59 Nelson 1978, p. 75.

60 See, for instance, Given 1977; Hanawalt 1979; Österberg and Lindström 1988.

61 Bitel 1996, especially chapter VII ('The Land of Women'), pp. 138–66.

62 Bitel 1996, pp. 93–103.

63 Halsall 1996, especially p. 21. See also Sasse 1990; Sasse and Dübner–Manthey 1986.

64 Effros 1996, p. 2.

65 Effros 1990; Effros 1996, p. 3.

66 Effros 1996, p. 8 (with references).

67 General historiographical overviews are available in Affeldt 1986; Goetz 1995, pp. 13–68.

68 Arvizu 1984, Kroeschell 1982; von Olberg 1990; Schmidt–Wiegand 1990. The general situation is outlined in Wemple 1981.

69 On Frankish women, see Heidrich 1988; Heidrich 1991; Herlihy 1962; McNamara and Wemple 1988, pp. 87–90. On Lombard women, see Pohl–Resl 1993; Skinner 1993. See also the general discussion in Goetz 1995, pp. 38–40, 199–242.

70 Fell (with Clark and Williams) 1984, pp. 56–57, 75–78; Hillmann 1986; Meyer 1980.

71 Bitel 1996, p. 115.

72 Ó Cróinín 1995, p. 127. See also Bitel 1996, pp. 39–44, 151–52.

73 Nelson 1990 ('Commentary...'), p. 326. See also Stafford 1983, pp. 73–75.

74 See, for instance, Affeldt and Reiter 1986, p. 200; McNamara and Wemple 1976, p. 99; Wemple 1981, pp. 38–40; Stafford 1983, pp. 71–79.

75 Verdon 1990, pp. 246–47. See also (generally on marriage and the position of the wife) Goetz 1995, pp. 41–43, 165–242; McNamara and Wemple 1976.

76 Goetz 1995, pp. 270–78. See also Bitel 1996, pp. 123–37.

77 See, for instance, Bitel 1996, pp. 120–21; Goetz 1995, pp. 226–31. On the varying

importance of male participation in rituals and phases concerning reproduction, see the provocative works of John R. Gillis, e.g. Gillis 1993.
78 See the bibliography in Goetz 1995, pp. 45–50. For good examples, see Johnson 1991; Luecke 1987; McNamara 1987; Parisse 1983; Skinner 1984; Thompson 1991; Wemple 1990. On the development of early medieval monasticism in general, see Prinz 1965.
79 McNamara 1985; Wemple 1981, pp. 190–91.
80 Goetz 1995, pp. 48, 105–62, 400.
81 Baltrusch–Schneider 1991.
82 Nicholson 1978; Schulenburg 1988; Wemple 1981, pp. 181–87. See also the overview by Goetz 1995, pp. 61–62.
83 Nelson 1990 ('Perceptions du pouvoir...'); Nelson 1990 ('Women and the Word...'); Nelson 1991. See also the works by Rosamond McKitterick: McKitterick 1989; McKitterick 1991.
84 Consolino 1988; Gäbe 1989; Leonardi 1983; Wemple 1981, pp. 181–85.
85 Wittern 1986; Wittern 1994. See also Cristiani 1991.
86 Wemple 1987 ('Female Spirituality...').
87 Schulenburg 1988. For a critical evaluation and a much more comprehensive study of the Frankish *vitae*, see Goetz 1995, pp. 105–62, especially pp. 112–13.
88 Folz 1992.
89 The terms 'politics' and 'political' used in this book are, of necessity, very vague; they are of less theoretical importance than the concepts of gender and (political) culture. By politics, I refer to what can briefly be characterised as relations of social power, whether economic, military or legal.
90 Merta 1988.
91 Stafford 1983, p. 174.
92 Stafford 1983, pp. 99–114.
93 Stafford 1983, pp. 113, 146–48.
94 Wemple 1981, especially pp. 54–56, 59, stressing the importance of marriage alliances and children.
95 Nelson 1978, p. 37.
96 Nelson 1978, pp. 53–56, 67–72.
97 Enright 1988, p. 201.
98 Enright 1988, p. 200.
99 Affeldt et al 1990, Section 9, pp. 225–66; Buc 1995; Duggan 1997; Keller 1995; Stafford 1983 (although the book covers the period 500–1050, most examples belong to the tenth century); Verdon 1973; Vogelsang 1954.
100 Fell (with Clark and Williams) 1984, pp. 89–107.
101 Erkens 1991; Jäschke 1991; see also some parts of Leyser 1984.
102 Hyam 1990; Schreiner 1975; Ward 1990.
103 Wemple 1981, especially the concluding discussion on pp. 189–97.
104 See the collection of articles in Laiou 1992.
105 Laiou 1981, pp. 250–52.
106 Nelson 1978; Stafford 1983, pp. 13–15.
107 Wood 1994, especially pp. 120–39.

[108] Nelson 1997.
[109] On Theophanu, see von Euw and Schreiner 1991; Davids 1995.
[110] Atkinson 1991, p. 82: 'The important relationships were those of the heroes who fought side by side in battle and slept side by side in the lord's hall. Women, even the queen, were peripheral, and women of the lower classes had no existence, at least in the literary remains of the culture.'
[111] Goetz 1995, pp. 52–53, 408–14.
[112] Goetz 1995, especially p. 231; Stafford 1978; Stafford 1983, pp. 104–06; Nelson 1978; Wood 1994, especially pp. 124–25.
[113] Atkinson 1991, pp. 90–91.
[114] Merta 1988. See also Atkinson 1991, p. 82; Goetz 1995, p. 52.
[115] Pye and Verba 1965.
[116] See the historiographical description in Aronsson 1992. See also Almond and Verba 1980; Taylor 1971.
[117] Demertzis 1985, chapter 5, especially p. 160. Demertzis, inspired by Gramsci and Williams, further develops this line of reasoning into a two–part typification of political cultures, hegemonic and counter–hegemonic (pp. 166–72).
[118] Demertzis 1985, p. 160.
[119] Aronsson 1992, pp. 337–44; Österberg 1989; Österberg 1993; Österberg 1996.

The women of Jordanes

[120] See the chapter on Jordanes in Goffart 1988.
[121] Jordanes 49–57.
[122] Jordanes 121–122.
[123] Jordanes 58: (immediately after a description of the deeds of the Amazons) Sed ne dicas: de viris Gothorum sermo adsumptus cur in feminas tamdiu perseverat? Audi et virorum insignem et laudabilem fortitudinem. 'So that you should not say: why does he, after having begun to tell us about the Gothic men, devote so much time to speaking about women? Listen now to tales of the famous and praiseworthy fortitude of the men.'
[124] Jordanes 49–50.
[125] Jordanes 49–50.
[126] Jordanes 57.
[127] Jordanes 223–224.
[128] Jordanes 306.
[129] Jordanes 184, referring to the evil behaviour of King Huneric of the Vandals.
[130] Jordanes 49–50.
[131] Jordanes 56–57.
[132] Jordanes 57.
[133] Jordanes 223.
[134] Jordanes 224: prorsus indignum facinus, ut licentiam libidinis malo publico conpararet.

The women of Gregory of Tours

135 Gregory of Tours V:32.
136 Gregory of Tours VI:13.
137 On Gregory, see the chapter in Goffart 1988 (with references). See also de Nie 1987, Van Dam 1985, pp. 179–276, and Verdon 1989. A specific study of Gregory's general description of women is available in Affeldt and Reiter 1986.
138 Gregory of Tours II:12: 'Novi', inquid, 'utilitatem tuam, quod sis valde strinuus, ideoque veni, ut habitem tecum. Nam noveris, si in transmarinis partibus aliquem cognovissem utiliorem tibi, expetissem utique cohabitationem eius.'
139 Gregory of Tours II:12.
140 Briefly on Chlothild, see Merta 1988, pp. 5–6, 24–25; Pernoud 1984, pp. 13–17.
141 Gregory of Tours II:28.
142 Gregory of Tours II:28: Qui cum ea vidissent elegantem atque sapientem et cognovissent, quod de regio esset genere...
143 Gregory of Tours II:28.
144 Gregory of Tours II:29: ut Saturnus, qui filio, ne a regno depelleretur, per fugam elapsus adseritur, ut ipse Iovis omnium stuprorum spurcissimus perpetratur, incestatur virorum, propinquarum derisor, qui nec ab ipsius sororis propriae potuit abstenere concubitu...
145 Gregory of Tours II:29: Deus vero vester nihil posse manefestatur, et quod magis est, nec de deorum genere esse probatur.
146 Gregory of Tours II:29.
147 Gregory of Tours II:29: Sed orante matre, Domino iubente convaluit.
148 Gregory of Tours II:30.
149 Gregory of Tours II:31: Mitis depone colla, Sigamber; adora quod incendisti, incende quod adorasti.
150 Gregory of Tours II:43.
151 Gregory of Tours II:43.
152 Gregory of Tours III:6: Non me paeneteat, carissimi, vos dulciter enutrisse; indignate, quaeso, iniuriam meam et patris matrisque meae mortem sagaci studio vindecate.
153 Gregory of Tours III:6.
154 Gregory of Tours III:6.
155 Gregory of Tours III:18: utrum incisa caesariae ut reliqua plebs habeantur, an certe his interfectis regnum germani nostri inter nosmet ipsius aequalitate habita dividatur.
156 Gregory of Tours III:18: Dirige parvolus ad nos, ut sublimentur in regno.
157 Gregory of Tours III:18: utrum incisis crinibus eos vivere iubeas, an utrumque iugulare.
158 Gregory of Tours III:18: Satius mihi enim est, si ad regnum non ereguntur, mortuos eos videre quam tonsus.
159 Gregory of Tours III:18.
160 Gregory of Tours III:18.
161 Gregory of Tours III:28: Quod nullus ambigat, hanc per obtentum reginae beati Martini fuisse virtutem.
162 Gregory of Tours IV:12.
163 Gregory of Tours X:31.

NOTES

[164] Gregory of Tours III:18: Chlodigildis vero regina talem seque exhibuit, ut ab omnibus honoraretur; assiduae in elymosinis, pernocte in vigiliis, in castitate atque omni honestate puram se semper exhibuit; praedia eclesiis, monastyriis vel quibuscumque locis sanctis necessaria praevidit, larga ac prona voluntate distribuit, ut putaretur eo tempore non regina, sed propria Dei ancilla ipsi sedolo deservire, quam non regnum filiorum, non ambitio saeculi nec facultas extulit ad ruinam, sed humilitas evexit ad gratiam.

[165] Gregory of Tours IV:1.

[166] Gregory of Tours III:1. On his marriages, see Stafford 1983, pp. 51–52.

[167] Gregory of Tours III:6.

[168] Gregory of Tours IV:3.

[169] Gregory of Tours VI:24.

[170] Gregory of Tours IV:3.

[171] Gregory of Tours IV:9.

[172] See also the section on Radegund on pp. 280–85 (with bibliographical references).

[173] Gregory of Tours III:4.

[174] Gregory of Tours III:7.

[175] Gregory of Tours III:7.

[176] Gregory of Tours III:7: Quae orationibus, ieiuniis atque elymosinis praedita, in tantum emicuit, ut magna in populis haberetur.

[177] Gregory of Tours IX:39. The Rule is available in translation: McCarthy 1960. See also Hochstetler 1987; Nolte 1986.

[178] Gregory of Tours IX:42: Et quoniam olim vinclis laicalibus absoluta, divina providente et inspirante clementia, ad religionis normam visa sum voluntariae duce Christo translata, ac pronae mentis studio cogitans etiam de aliarum profectibus, ut, annuente Domino, mea desideria efficerentur reliquis profutura, instituente atque remunerante praecellentissimo domno rege Chlothario, monastirium puellarum Pectava urbe constitui, conditumque, quantum mihi munificentia regalis est largita, facta donatione, dotavi…

[179] Gregory of Tours IX:42.

[180] Gregory of Tours IX:42.

[181] Gregory of Tours V:39

[182] Gregory of Tours IX:40, 42, X:16.

[183] Gregory of Tours VI:29: Vel licuisset prius causas inquirere, et sic de potestate nostra fuisset ablata haec anima.

[184] Gregory of Tours VI:29: Princeps vero noster, quem vos diabolum nominatis…

[185] Gregory of Tours VI:29.

[186] Gregory of Tours IX:40.

[187] Gregory of Tours IX:40. See also Brown 1982, p. 239; Scheibelreiter 1979.

[188] Gregory of Tours IX:40.

[189] Gregory of Tours IX:2.

[190] Gregory of Tours VI:34: Non est enim dignum, ut puella Christo dedicata iterum in saeculi voluptatibus revertatur.

[191] Gregory of Tours VII:36.

[192] Gregory of Tours V:42.

193 Gregory of Tours IV:20.
194 Gregory of Tours: Liber I de virtutibus beati Martini episcopi 12.
195 Venantius Fortunatus, carm. VI:6. See also Stafford 1983, p. 175.
196 Vita Balthildis 18.
197 Gregory of Tours III:1.
198 Gregory of Tours III:5.
199 Gregory of Tours III:20. On this marriage as an example of a political alliance, see Stafford 1983, p. 51.
200 Gregory of Tours III:21.
201 Gregory of Tours III:22: Nullus tibi, domine piissime, resistere potest. Cognuscemus dominum nostrum; veni et quod bene placitum fuerit in oculis tuis facito.
202 Gregory of Tours III:22–23.
203 Gregory of Tours III:23.
204 Gregory of Tours III:25.
205 Gregory of Tours III:27.
206 Gregory of Tours III:26.
207 Gregory of Tours III:27. On Deuteria, see Merta 1988, pp. 6–7, 25.
208 Gregory of Tours III:33.
209 Gregory of Tours IV:3.
210 Gregory of Tours IV:22.
211 Gregory of Tours IX:26.
212 Gregory of Tours IV:25.
213 Gregory of Tours IV:25.
214 Gregory of Tours IV:26: percussa iuditio Dei obiit.
215 Gregory of Tours IV:26.
216 Gregory of Tours V:48. See also Stafford 1983, p. 98.
217 Gregory of Tours IV:26: Accedere ad me ei non pigeat cum thesauris suis. Ego enim accipiam eam faciamque magnam in populis, ut scilicet maiorem mecum honorem quam cum germano meo, qui nuper defunctus est, potiatur.
218 Gregory of Tours IV:26: Rectius est enim, ut hi thesauri penes me habeantur, quam post hanc, quae indigne germani mei torum adivit.
219 Gregory of Tours IV:26.
220 Gregory of Tours IV:26: non mediocribus adtrita passionibus. McNamara 1992, p. 119, suggests that Liliola might have co-operated with Gunthchramn in robbing and imprisoning Theudechild in order to secure a much-needed addition to the endowment of the convent. On the Theudechild incident, see also Enright 1988, p. 195; Merta 1988, pp. 9–10.
221 Gregory of Tours IX:26.
222 Gregory of Tours IV:3. On his women, see Merta 1988, p. 10.
223 Gregory of Tours IV:22.
224 Gregory of Tours IV:25.
225 Gregory of Tours IV:25.
226 Gregory of Tours IV:25, V:20.
227 Gregory of Tours V:17.
228 Gregory of Tours V:35: Quaeso, et cum sacramenti interpositione coniuro, ut, cum

ab hac luce discessero, statim ipse gladio trucidentur; ut, sicut ego amplius vivere non queo, ita nec ille post meum obitum glorientur, sed sit unus dolus nostris pariter ac eorum amicis.

[229] Gregory of Tours V:35. See the discussion in Stafford 1983, pp. 186–87.
[230] Gregory of Tours IV:3.
[231] Gregory of Tours IV:22.
[232] Gregory of Tours IV:28.
[233] Gregory of Tours VI:34.
[234] Gregory of Tours V:2.
[235] Gregory of Tours V:39.
[236] She became the object of a long poem by Venantius Fortunatus ('de Gelesuintha', carm. VI:5).
[237] Gregory of Tours IV:28: a quo etiam magno amore diligebatur. Detulerat enim secum magnos thesauros.
[238] Gregory of Tours IV:28.
[239] Gregory of Tours IX:20.
[240] There are alternative explanations as to why Galswinth was murdered. Pauline Stafford (Stafford 1983, p. 187) says that 'Chilperic wanted to marry Fredegund and the crime may have been one of passion, though he could have taken Fredegund to his bed without murdering Galswinth. The gratuitous act seems another testimony to the violence of the man.'
[241] She also appears, together with Chilperic, in Venantius Fortunatus, carm. IX:2–3. Generally on Fredegund, see Merta 1988, pp. 10–12, 26–27.
[242] Gregory of Tours IV:28.
[243] Gregory of Tours IV:51.
[244] Gregory of Tours V:3.
[245] Gregory of Tours V:2, 18.
[246] Gregory of Tours V:14.
[247] Gregory of Tours V:14.
[248] Gregory of Tours V:18.
[249] Gregory of Tours V:18.
[250] Gregory of Tours VII:16.
[251] Gregory of Tours VIII:31.
[252] Gregory of Tours V:22.
[253] Gregory of Tours V:34.
[254] Gregory of Tours V:39: ideoque moneo, ne speres de te melius, cum tibi spes per quam regnare debueras sit ablata.
[255] Gregory of Tours V:39. According to a story related by Gregory (VIII:10), Fredegund was afraid that Clovis' body would one day be discovered and receive honourable burial. She therefore ordered it to be thrown into the River Marne. However, a local fisherman accidentaly caught the royal corpse in a fish trap. The fisherman recognised Clovis, buried him under a heap of turves and eventually, in 585, told King Gunthchramn where to find the corpse. Gunthchramn had it uncovered and buried at Saint Vincent's church (later Saint–Germain–des–Près).
[256] Gregory of Tours VI:35.

[257] Gregory of Tours VI:34.
[258] Gregory of Tours VI:45. See also Stafford 1983, p. 58.
[259] Gregory of Tours VI:46.
[260] Gregory of Tours VII:9.
[261] Gregory of Tours VII:10.
[262] Gregory of Tours VII:15.
[263] Gregory of Tours VII:39.
[264] Gregory of Tours IX:34: Post ista vero inter easdem inimiciae vehementius pullulantes…
[265] Gregory of Tours VI:41.
[266] Gregory of Tours VIII:9.
[267] Gregory of Tours VII:7. Childebert II first accused her of the murder during his negotiations with King Gunthchramn shortly after the event.
[268] Liber Historiae Francorum 35.
[269] Stafford 1983, pp. 14–15.
[270] Gregory of Tours VI:46, VII:4.
[271] Gregory of Tours VII:5.
[272] Gregory of Tours VII:7: Redde homicidam, quae amitam meam suggillavit, quae patrem interfecit et patruum, quae ipsius quoque consobrinus meus gladio interemit.
[273] Gregory of Tours VII:7.
[274] Gregory of Tours VII:14.
[275] Gregory of Tours VII:7–8, 18.
[276] Gregory of Tours VII:19.
[277] Gregory of Tours VII:19–20: cum esset valde maesta, quod ei potestas ex parte fuisset ablata.
[278] She was certainly there in 586 when she had Bishop Praetextatus killed, according to Gregory of Tours VIII:31.
[279] Gregory of Tours VII:20.
[280] Gregory of Tours VII:21–22.
[281] Gregory of Tours VII:29: Si eam videro, elicere ab ea aliquid muneris possum. Scio enim, eam esse homini ad quem directus sum inimicam.
[282] Gregory of Tours VII:29. See also Brown 1982, pp. 231–32.
[283] Gregory of Tours VII:39.
[284] Gregory of Tours VIII:28: Inimicos nostros, id est Childebertum et matrem eius, velociter interemite et cum rege Gunthchramno pacem inite, quod praemiis multis coemite. Et si vobis minus est fortassis paecunia, nos clam mittemus, tantum ut quae petimus impleatis. Cum autem de inimicis nostris ulti fuerimus, tunc Amelio episcopo ac Leubae matronae bona tribuite, per quos missis nostris ad vos accedendi aditus reseratur.
[285] Gregory of Tours VIII:29.
[286] Gregory of Tours VIII:31.
[287] Gregory of Tours VIII:31: Nam et omnes nos erimus inquisitores mali huius, ut tibi diucius non liceat tam crudelia exercere.
[288] Gregory of Tours VIII:31.
[289] Gregory of Tours VIII:31.

NOTES

[290] Gregory of Tours VIII:41.
[291] Gregory of Tours VIII:42.
[292] Gregory of Tours VIII:43.
[293] Gregory of Tours VIII:44.
[294] Gregory of Tours IX:13.
[295] Gregory of Tours IX:20: Dic, o Felix, iam enim plenissime conexuistis amicicias inter sororem meam Brunichildem et inimicam Dei atque hominum Fredegundem?
[296] Gregory of Tours IX:20: Non dubitet, rex, quia illae amiciciae inter easdem custodiuntur, quae antea hos annus plurimus sunt legati. Nam certe scias, quia odium, quod inter illas olim statutum est, adhuc pullulat, non arescit. Utinam tu, o rex gloriosissime, minus cum eam caritatem haberes! Nam, ut saepe cognovimus, dignius eius legationem quam nostram excepis.
[297] Gregory of Tours IX:20: Nam ibi amicicias legare non possum, de qua saepius processerunt, qui mihi vitam praesentem auferrent.
[298] Gregory of Tours X:9.
[299] Gregory of Tours X:18.
[300] Gregory of Tours X:17.
[301] The immediate cause of this conflict was that two young men began arguing about a woman, the sister of one and the wife of the other. The brother accused the husband of neglecting his wife and chasing after loose women. When the husband continued to behave in this way, the girl's brother finally killed him.
[302] Gregory of Tours X:27.
[303] Gregory of Tours X:11.
[304] Gregory of Tours X:28: Proficiscatur dominus meus rex usque Parisius, et arcessitu filio meo, nepote suo, iubeat eum baptismatis gratia consecrare; ipsumque de sancto lavacro exceptum, tamquam alumnum proprium habere dignetur.
[305] Gregory of Tours X:28. The baptism of Chlothar could have happened a lot sooner, and Gunthchramn had obviously been prepared for it ever since Chilperic's death. According to Suzanne Fonay Wemple, Fredegund deliberately postponed the baptism, since this act would serve to formalise the guardianship of Gunthchramn as Chlothar's godfather (Wemple 1981, pp. 64–65).
[306] Fredegar IV:17; Liber Historiae Francorum 37.
[307] Gregory of Tours VII:15: non metuebat Deum.
[308] Gregory of Tours V:47, 49.
[309] Gregory of Tours V:49.
[310] Gregory of Tours V:49.
[311] Gregory of Tours VI:32: Conpraessa a multis aliud facere non potui, nisi ut eum abire permitterem. Nunc autem rogo, ut pacem tuam non mereatur neque eologias de manu tua suscipiat, donec a nobis quid agi debeat plenius pertractatur.
[312] Gregory of Tours VI:32: Vae mihi, quae video inimicum meum, et nihil ei praevaleo.
[313] Gregory of Tours VI:32.
[314] Gregory of Tours V:49: Commota autem regina, quod scilicet locus Deo sacratus taliter pollueretur, iussit eum a basilica sancta eici.
[315] Wood 1994, pp. 123–24.
[316] Wood 1994, pp. 125–26.

317 See also the section on Brunhild on pp. 222–27. Generally on Brunhild: Merta 1988, pp. 12–15, 27–29; Wemple 1981, pp. 65–67, 69–70.
318 She also features prominently in Venantius Fortunatus, carm. VI:1, X:7–8.
319 Gregory of Tours IV:27: Erat enim puella elegans corpore, venusta aspectu, honesta moribus atque decora, prudens consilio et blanda colloquio.
320 Gregory of Tours IV:27, 38.
321 Gregory of Tours IV:51.
322 Gregory of Tours V:1: conturbata dolore ac lucto, quid ageret ignoraret.
323 Gregory of Tours V:1.
324 Gregory of Tours V:1.
325 Gregory of Tours V:2. Merovech probably married Brunhild to be able to lay claim to the kingdom of Sigibert (Stafford 1983, p. 49).
326 Gregory of Tours V:3, 14.
327 Gregory of Tours V:18.
328 Gregory of Tours V:18.
329 Gregory of Tours V:40.
330 Gregory of Tours VI:4: Nolite, o viri, nolite hoc malum facere; nolite persequi innocentem; nolite pro uno hominem committere proelium, quo solatium regionis intereat.
331 Gregory of Tours VI:4: Recede a nobis, o mulier. Sufficiat tibi sub viro tenuisse regnum; nunc autem filius tuus regnat, regnumque eius non tua, sed nostra tuitione salvatur. Tu vero recede a nobis, ne te ungulae equorum nostrorum cum terra confodiant.
332 Gregory of Tours VI:4.
333 Gregory of Tours VI:37.
334 Gregory of Tours VI:38.
335 Gregory of Tours VII:20, VIII:28. See also the remarks by Gunthchramn and Gregory in IX:20.
336 Gregory of Tours VII:33.
337 Gregory of Tours IX:28.
338 Gregory of Tours VII:34.
339 Gregory of Tours VII:43: et ab ea susceptus, cum muneribus et gratia est demissus.
340 Gregory of Tours VIII:4: Verum, quia mater eius Brunechildis me minatur interemere, sed nihil mihi ex hoc formidinis est. Dominus enim, qui me eripuit de manibus inimicorum meorum, et de huius insidiis liberavit me.
341 Gregory of Tours VIII:22.
342 Gregory of Tours VI:371, VIII:28.
343 Gregory of Tours VIII:21: sed parum consolacionis emeruit.
344 Epistolae Austrasiacae 27–28, 43–45.
345 Gregory of Tours VIII:28.
346 Gregory of Tours VIII:29.
347 Gregory of Tours V:14.
348 Gregory of Tours IX:8.
349 Gregory of Tours IX:10.
350 Gregory of Tours IX:11

[351] Gregory of Tours IX:11, 20.
[352] Gregory of Tours IX:9.
[353] Gregory of Tours IX:12.
[354] For instance, she is mentioned in the famous text of the treaty of Andelot (in 587) between Childebert and Gunthchramn as having been present at the conference resulting in the treaty. According to the text, Gunthchramn promised to help ensure that she could hold on to her property in the future (Gregory of Tours IX:20). She is also reported to have accompanied Childebert and his wife to the neighbourhood of Strasbourg in 589 (Gregory of Tours IX:36).
[355] Gregory of Tours IX:16.
[356] Gregory of Tours IX:20.
[357] Gregory of Tours IX:28.
[358] Gregory of Tours IX:19.
[359] Gregory of Tours IX:32.
[360] Gregory of Tours IX:38.
[361] Gregory of Tours IX:38.
[362] Gregory of Tours X:19.
[363] Gregory of Tours X:19: Si radix cuiuslibet rei incisa non fuerit, culmis, qui terris est editus, non ariscit.
[364] Gregory of Tours X:19: nam ego novi, me ob crimen maiestatis reum esse mortis, qui semper contra utilitatem huius regis matrisque eius abii.
[365] Gregory of Tours X:19.
[366] Venantius Fortunatus, carm. V:3 (see also 8–17); Wood 1994, p. 126.
[367] Wood 1994, p. 127.
[368] Wood 1994, pp. 129–30.
[369] Gregory of Tours IX:10. She is also mentioned, together with her daughters, in the text of the treaty of Andelot, IX:20. According to Merta (Merta 1988, p. 4), Faileuba was unimportant, a weak girl standing in the shadow of Brunhild.
[370] Gregory of Tours IX:38.
[371] Gregory of Tours II:31.
[372] Gregory of Tours III:31.
[373] Gregory of Tours III:1.
[374] Gregory of Tours III:10.
[375] Gregory of Tours IV:3.
[376] Gregory of Tours IV:41.
[377] Gregory of Tours IV:26, IX:26.
[378] Gregory of Tours IX:33: Erat enim gulae et somno dedita et nullam de officio Dei curam habens.
[379] Gregory of Tours IX:20.
[380] Gregory of Tours V:1.
[381] Gregory of Tours V:38. See also IX:24.
[382] Collins 1983, pp. 45–49.
[383] Gregory of Tours V:38.
[384] Gregory of Tours VI:40.
[385] Gregory of Tours VIII:18.

[386] Gregory of Tours VIII:21, 28.
[387] Gregory of Tours IX:10. She is also mentioned in the text of the treaty of Andelot, IX:20.
[388] Gregory of Tours IX:16.
[389] Gregory of Tours IX:20.
[390] Gregory of Tours IX:25.
[391] Gregory of Tours IX:25, 28.
[392] Gregory of Tours V:49.
[393] Gregory of Tours VI:18, 34, 45.
[394] Gregory of Tours VI:45.
[395] Gregory of Tours VII:27–28.
[396] Gregory of Tours VII:9–10, 15.
[397] Gregory of Tours VII:27.
[398] Gregory of Tours VII:32, 35.
[399] Gregory of Tours VII:39.
[400] Gregory of Tours IX:34.
[401] The incident has been analysed by Scheibelreiter 1979 and (briefly) by McNamara 1986, pp. 311–12; Wittern 1986, p. 283.
[402] Gregory of Tours V:39, VI:34, IX:39.
[403] Gregory of Tours IX:39: Depraecor, sanctae sacerdos, ut has puellas, quae in magna humilitate ab abbatissa Pectavinse redactae sunt, custodire digneris ac cibum praebere, donec ego eam ad reges parentes nostros exponamque eis quae patimur et revertar.
[404] Gregory of Tours IX:39–40.
[405] Gregory of Tours IX:2, 40.
[406] Gregory of Tours IX:40.
[407] Gregory of Tours IX:40: Reginae sumus, nec prius in monastyrio nostro ingrediemur, nisi abbatissa eiciatur foris.
[408] Gregory of Tours IX:41.
[409] Gregory of Tours IX:41.
[410] Gregory of Tours IX:43.
[411] Gregory of Tours IX:43.
[412] Gregory of Tours X:15–16.
[413] Gregory of Tours X:15: Relinque abbatissam, ut in his diebus in hoc carcere non reteneatur; alioquin non celebrabo pascha Domini, neque baptismum in hac urbe ullus catecuminus obtinebit, nisi abbatissa a vinculo quo tenetur iubeatur absolvi. Quod si nec sic volueritis, collectis civibus, auferam eam.
[414] Gregory of Tours X:15.
[415] Gregory of Tours X:16.
[416] Gregory of Tours X:15: vix praeteriit dies sine homicidio, hora sine iurgio vel momentum aliquod sine fletu.
[417] Gregory of Tours X:15: Nolite super me, quaeso, vim inferre, quae sum regina, filia regis regisquae alterius consubrina; nolite facere, ne quando veniat tempus, ut ulciscar ex vobis.
[418] Gregory of Tours X:15.

419 Gregory of Tours X:16.
420 Gregory of Tours X:16.
421 Gregory of Tours X:16.
422 Gregory of Tours X:16.
423 Gregory of Tours X:16.
424 Gregory of Tours X:16.
425 Gregory of Tours X:15.
426 Gregory of Tours X:15: Quae enim sanctitas in hac abbatissa versatur, quae viros eunuchus facit et secum habitare imperiali ordine praecipit?
427 Gregory of Tours X:15.
428 Gregory of Tours X:16: de levioribus causis paterna communitione contestati sumus, ut haec nullatinus deinceps pro reprehensione repeteret.
429 Gregory of Tours X:16.
430 Gregory of Tours X:16.
431 Gregory of Tours X:17.
432 Gregory of Tours X:18.
433 Gregory of Tours X:17.
434 Gregory of Tours X:20.
435 In his evaluation of the rebellion, Scheibelreiter (1979) argues that Chrodechild and Basina were unable to bridge the gap between the values of the Germanic warrior nobility and the values of Christianity. Radegund was able to combine asceticism with the life of a member of the nobility, but the two princesses failed: 'Chrodhild dagegen versuchte, die christlichen Institutionen unreflektiert ihrem starren Selbstverständnis zu unterwerfen' (Scheibelreiter 1979, p. 37). However, as Wittern correctly remarks, Chrodechild did not object to Christian values (like piety) as such. She objected to her lack of career prospects. (Wittern 1986, p. 283). To early medieval aristocrats, there was no contradiction between being of noble rank and being a humble Christian. Most of the prominent Christians (such as the new saints) were themselves members of the nobility. – Another explanation of the rebellion has been put forward by Jane Schulenburg, who argues that the revolt might have been spurred on by the very real material poverty that the nuns were forced to endure (as is evidenced by Chrodechild's complaints about the food). See Schulenburg 1984, p. 72.
436 Gregory of Tours VI:43.
437 Gregory of Tours X:9.
438 Gregory of Tours IV:4.
439 Gregory of Tours III:4: 'Qui', inquid, 'a medio regno spoliatur, decet eum mensae medium habere nudatum.'
440 Gregory of Tours III:4.
441 Gregory of Tours III:5–6.
442 Gregory of Tours III:31.
443 Gregory of Tours IV:41.
444 Gregory of Tours IV:38.
445 Gregory of Tours V:38: lumen, quod mens non habebat, pepulit a palpebris.
446 Gregory of Tours V:38. See also IX:24.
447 This is true of the treacherous Fausta and the pious Helena, in Gregory of Tours I:36.

[448] Gregory of Tours V:19: Quod ego multis annis congregavi, tu infra pauco tempus prodegi dispergis.
[449] Gregory of Tours V:19.
[450] Gregory of Tours V:30.
[451] Gregory of Tours VI:30: Valde strinuus et sacax vir isti. Nam et sepius contra inimicos rei publicae demicans, victurias obtenuit.
[452] Gregory of Tours VI:30.
[453] Gregory of Tours VII:17.
[454] Gregory of Tours VII:29.
[455] Gregory of Tours VIII:18, X:22.
[456] Gregory of Tours V:49, VI:32.
[457] Gregory of Tours IV:46.
[458] Gregory of Tours IV:17, 20.
[459] Gregory of Tours IV:20.
[460] Gregory of Tours IX:12.
[461] Gregory of Tours VIII:19.
[462] Gregory of Tours VIII:36.
[463] Gregory of Tours IX:13.
[464] Gregory of Tours IX:27.
[465] Gregory of Tours V:3, IX:9.
[466] Gregory of Tours VII:29.
[467] Gregory of Tours IX:10.
[468] Gregory of Tours VI:12.
[469] Gregory of Tours VII:10.
[470] Gregory of Tours VII:38.
[471] Gregory of Tours VII:40.
[472] Gregory of Tours VIII:21.
[473] Gregory of Tours IX:38.
[474] Gregory of Tours VIII:28.
[475] Gregory of Tours II:37.
[476] Gregory of Tours III:2: 'Sufficiat, domne sancte, senectute tuae, quod es episcopus ordenatus. Permittat', inquiunt, 'pietas tua servo tuo Apollonari locem huius honoris adipisci. Ille vero cum ad hunc apicem ascenderet, sicut tibi placitum fuerit obsequitur; tu quoque imperabis, et ille tuae parabit in omnibus iussioni; tantum ut humili suggestioni nostrae aurem benignitatis acommodis.'
[477] Gregory of Tours III:2.
[478] Gregory of Tours III:9.
[479] Gregory of Tours III:11.
[480] Gregory of Tours III:12.
[481] Gregory of Tours III:36.
[482] Gregory of Tours IV:13.
[483] Gregory of Tours IV:39.
[484] Gregory of Tours IV:36.
[485] Gregory of Tours IX:19.
[486] Gregory of Tours V:25.

487 Gregory of Tours VIII:32.
488 Gregory of Tours VIII:32.
489 Gregory of Tours VIII:43.
490 Gregory of Tours IX:40.
491 Gregory of Tours IX:35.
492 Gregory of Tours VIII:39.
493 Gregory of Tours VIII:39.
494 Gregory of Tours X:5.
495 She is said to have been about eighty years old at the time of her death in 590 (Gregory of Tours X:12). Generally on Ingitrude and Berthegund, see McNamara 1986, pp. 303–04, 310–11; Wemple 1981, pp. 62–63.
496 Gregory of Tours V:21.
497 Gregory of Tours VII:36.
498 Gregory of Tours VIII:2: Scire enim te oportuerat, dilectissime pater, quod parens eras nobis ex matre nostra, et super gentem tuam non debueras inducere pestem extraneam.
499 Gregory of Tours IX:33: Relinque virum tuum et veni, ut faciam te abbatissam gregi huic, quem congregavi.
500 Gregory of Tours IX:33.
501 Gregory of Tours IX:33.
502 Gregory of Tours IX:33: Quia sine consilio parentum eam coniugio copulasti, non erit uxor tua.
503 Gregory of Tours IX:33.
504 Gregory of Tours IX:33: Abstulisti uxorem meam cum famulis eius. Et ecce, quod sacerdotem non decit, tu cum ancillis meis, et illa cum famulis tuis, dedecus adulterii perpetrasti.
505 Gregory of Tours IX:33.
506 Gregory of Tours IX:33.
507 Gregory of Tours VIII:22.
508 Gregory of Tours IX:33: Vae mihi, quae audivi consilio matris iniquae. Ecce frater meus obiit; ecce a viro derelicta sum, a filiis separata; et quo ibo inflex, vel quid faciam?
509 Gregory of Tours IX:33.
510 Gregory of Tours IX:33.
511 Gregory of Tours X:12.
512 Gregory of Tours X:12: Tantaque ibi mala gessit, quae vix ex ordine potuerunt enarrari.
513 Gregory of Tours X:12.
514 Gregory of Tours X:8. See also Wemple 1981, p. 43.
515 Gregory of Tours X:8.
516 Gregory of Tours X:8.
517 Gregory of Tours X:8.
518 Gregory of Tours X:8.
519 Gregory of Tours VIII:27.
520 Gregory of Tours X:8.

[521] Gregory of Tours VIII:45.
[522] Gregory of Tours X:8.
[523] Eve appears in Gregory of Tours I:1; Noah's wife and his three daughters-in-law in I:4; Rebecca in I:8; Rachel in I:9; Bathsheba in I:12; the two wives who quarrelled in front of Solomon in I:13; Judith in IX:27; Martha in X:13. And, of course, the Virgin Mary is mentioned often, most conspicuously in I:16 and I:19.
[524] Gregory of Tours VI:36.
[525] Gregory of Tours IX:21.
[526] Gregory of Tours VI:36.
[527] Gregory of Tours II:7.
[528] Gregory of Tours II:13.
[529] Gregory of Tours II:17.
[530] Gregory of Tours III:13: Si ita est hodie pessumdatus, numquam eregeris.
[531] Gregory of Tours III:13.
[532] Gregory of Tours VIII:33.
[533] Gregory of Tours X:29: semper orationem Domino, tanquam odorem incensi acceptabilis offerebat.
[534] Gregory of Tours IX:40, 42. She is also mentioned (as abbess) in VI:29.
[535] Gregory of Tours IV:26.
[536] Gregory of Tours VI:16.
[537] Gregory of Tours I:44.
[538] Gregory of Tours II:22.
[539] Gregory of Tours I:40.
[540] Gregory of Tours IV:1.
[541] Gregory of Tours IX:40, 42.
[542] Gregory of Tours I:47.
[543] Gregory of Tours II:2.
[544] Gregory of Tours VIII:12: O sceleste et inveterate dierum, qui pro inimico nostro Theodoro oracionem fundis ad Dominum. Ecce nos cotidie querimus, qualiter ab his Galliis extrudatur, qui nos cotidianis incendiis conflat; et tu pro eo rogare non desinis!
[545] Gregory of Tours VI:6.
[546] Gregory of Tours X:29.
[547] Gregory of Tours I:45.
[548] Gregory of Tours V:39.
[549] Gregory of Tours VII:44.
[550] Gregory of Tours V:14.
[551] Gregory of Tours X:25.
[552] Gregory of Tours VIII:33: vidi per somnium a basilica sancti Vincenti venientem virum inluminatum, tenentem manu caereum et domus neguciantum ex ordine succendentem.
[553] Gregory of Tours VIII:33.
[554] Gregory of Tours IX:42.
[555] Gregory of Tours IX:40.
[556] The need for a widow to remarry has also been remarked upon by Affeldt and Reiter 1986, p. 203.

The women of Fredegar

557 Wallace-Hadrill 1960, the introduction. On Fredegar, see also Goffart 1989; Wood 1994, p. 248.
558 Fredegar IV:4.
559 Fredegar IV:9 and PD IV:50.
560 Fredegar IV:48.
561 Fredegar IV:54.
562 Fredegar IV:3, 17.
563 Fredegar III:35. Here it is said that King Chilperic I was killed by an assassin called Falco, sent by Brunhild.
564 Fredegar IV:7.
565 Fredegar IV:18.
566 Fredegar IV:16. See also Paul the Deacon IV:11.
567 The year 599 might be an error on Fredegar's part. Other evidence (from Gregory the Great) points to 602. See Wood 1994, p. 131.
568 Fredegar IV:19. The bishop in question is probably Bishop Desiderius of Auxerre. It is highly unlikely that Fredegar is telling us what actually happened: local Auxerre tradition holds Desiderius to have been of royal blood.
569 Fredegar IV:21.
570 Fredegar IV:24.
571 Fredegar IV:24.
572 Fredegar IV:27: Cum esset nimium argutissimus et strenuus in cunctis sed saeua illi fuit contra personas iniquitas, fiscum nimium stringens, de rebus personarum ingeniose fisco uellens implere et se ipsum ditare; quoscumque de gentem nobilem repperiret, totusque humiliare conabat, ut nullus repperiretur qui gratum quem adriperat potuisset adsumere.
573 Fredegar IV:27.
574 Fredegar IV:28.
575 Fredegar IV:29.
576 Fredegar IV:30.
577 Fredegar IV:34.
578 Fredegar IV:35.
579 Fredegar IV:32.
580 Fredegar IV:36.
581 Fredegar IV:38–39.
582 Fredegar IV:40.
583 Fredegar IV:41.
584 Fredegar IV:42.
585 The situation at the court of Theuderic II has been discussed by Stafford 1983, pp. 67–69, 101.
586 Fredegar IV:30–31.
587 Fredegar IV:36.
588 Fredegar IV:21.
589 Fredegar IV:24.

[590] Fredegar IV:29.
[591] Fredegar IV:30.
[592] Fredegar IV:42.
[593] Fredegar IV:35.
[594] Fredegar IV:37. Why was Bilichild murdered? Fredegar gives us no hints. Pauline Stafford (Stafford 1983, p. 87) guesses that she was killed because she was sterile. Later in her book, Stafford merely states that 'the full circumstances are unclear' (p. 187). See also the speculations of Nelson 1978, p. 44. Generally on Bilichild: Merta 1988, pp. 15, 21, 29.
[595] Fredegar IV:42.
[596] Fredegar IV:46.
[597] Fredegar IV:43.
[598] Fredegar IV:44. See also Stafford 1983, pp. 49, 104.
[599] Fredegar IV:46.
[600] Fredegar IV:53–54.
[601] Vita Amandi 17: *Dagobertus rex, amore mulierum plus quam oportebat deditus omnique spurcitia libidinis inflammatus...*
[602] Fredegar IV:53.
[603] Fredegar IV:58.
[604] Fredegar IV:76. Clovis appears to have been born in or around 633.
[605] Fredegar IV:59.
[606] Fredegar IV:60.
[607] Fredegar IV:79.
[608] Fredegar IV:80.
[609] See Wemple 1981, p. 67; Wood 1994, p. 156.
[610] Fredegar IV:85.
[611] Fredegar IV:83.
[612] Fredegar IV:84.
[613] Fredegar IV:89.
[614] Fredegar IV:90. Generally on Nantechild: Merta 1988, pp. 15–16, 29.
[615] Fredegar IV:34.
[616] Fredegar IV:49.
[617] Fredegar IV:51. See also Enright 1988, p. 193; Stafford 1983, pp. 96–97.
[618] Fredegar IV:70.
[619] Fredegar IV:71.

The women in the Continuations of Fredegar

[620] Wallace-Hadrill 1960, pp. xxv–xxviii.
[621] This is the case for Remistanius' wife: *Fredegarii Continuationes* 51.
[622] *Fredegarii Continuationes* 12.
[623] *Fredegarii Continuationes* 25.
[624] *Fredegarii Continuationes* 1.
[625] *Fredegarii Continuationes* 2.
[626] *Fredegarii Continuationes* 5.

[627] Fredegarii Continuationes 5.
[628] Fredegarii Continuationes 6.
[629] Fredegarii Continuationes 8–10.
[630] Fredegarii Continuationes 6.
[631] Fredegarii Continuationes 7.
[632] Fredegarii Continuationes 33.
[633] Fredegarii Continuationes 49.
[634] Fredegarii Continuationes 50.
[635] Fredegarii Continuationes 51.
[636] Fredegarii Continuationes 52.
[637] Fredegarii Continuationes 53.

The women in *Liber Historiae Francorum*

[638] Wood 1994, pp. 257–58. The focus on the Carolingians is even clearer in Annales Mettenses Priores, written in c. 806, a work that is not included in the present study.
[639] Liber Historiae Francorum 37–38. She keeps feeding her grandson bad advice: Brunchildis enim cotidie peiora consilia ipsius Theuderico ministrabat… See also Stafford 1983, p. 14: 'Brunhild had become fixed as the utterly evil genius of Merovingian politics'.
[640] Liber Historiae Francorum 39: In odium nimium habita, pocionem venenatam, per manus ministrorum maleficium ei porrigens. Theudericus rex haec ignorans, bibit, elanguensque, inicum spiritum in peccatis deficiens, mortuus est. Filios eius parvulos ipsa Brunchildis occidit.
[641] Liber Historiae Francorum 40.
[642] Liber Historiae Francorum 35.
[643] Liber Historiae Francorum 43.
[644] Liber Historiae Francorum 44: omne spurcicia deditus, fornicarius et inlusor feminarum, gulae et ebrietate contentus.
[645] Liber Historiae Francorum 45: una cum regina eius pregnante.
[646] Liber Historiae Francorum 48: instigante Anseflide, post haec Pippinus Theuderico rege coepit esse principale regimen maiorum domus.
[647] Liber Historiae Francorum 49.
[648] Liber Historiae Francorum 50.
[649] Liber Historiae Francorum 48, 51–53.

The women of Bede

[650] See the chapter on Bede in Goffart 1988.
[651] Bede II:9, V:24.
[652] Bede II:20.
[653] Bede III:15.
[654] Bede III:14, 24.
[655] Bede III:25.
[656] Bede V:19.

[657] Bede IV:26.
[658] Bede III:24.
[659] Bede III:8.
[660] Bede III:8.
[661] Bede IV:21.
[662] Bede III:11.
[663] Bede V:24.
[664] Bede III:11.
[665] Bede III:24.
[666] Bede IV:26.
[667] Bede III:24.
[668] Bede's description of Hilda has been critically analysed by Hollis 1992, pp. 253–70.
[669] Bede III:24, IV:23.
[670] Bede III:25.
[671] Bede IV:23, V:24.
[672] On Bede's treatment of her, see Hollis 1992, pp. 67–74.
[673] Bede IV:19.
[674] Bede IV:3.
[675] Bede IV:22.
[676] Bede IV:19.
[677] Bede IV:6.
[678] Bede IV:7–10.
[679] Bede IV:9.
[680] Bede IV:10.
[681] Bede IV:23.
[682] Bede IV:19.
[683] Bede IV:25. See also Fell (with Clark and Williams) 1984, pp. 124–25; Hollis 1992, p. 245, on Bede's negative attitude towards Coldingham; Nicholson 1978, pp. 15–16.
[684] Bede V:3.
[685] An interesting study of this *vita* from a gender perspective is to be found in Hollis 1992, pp. 179–207.
[686] Bede: Vita Cuthberti 10.
[687] Bede: Vita Cuthberti 35, 37.
[688] Bede: Vita Cuthberti 23.
[689] Bede: Vita Cuthberti 24.
[690] Bede: Vita Cuthberti 34.
[691] According to Stephanie Hollis, Bede's under–representation of women's social participation 'reflects an aspiration towards their actual marginalization' (Hollis 1992, pp. 12–13). She also suggests that the absence of reigning queens in *Historia ecclesiastica gentis Anglorum* is because 'the attention of the church in the early 8th century was still focused on the conversion of the king and that it had, as yet, no blue–print for the role of the queen as the king's partner in his protection and patronage of the church' (Hollis 1992, p. 220). Compare Hollis' evaluation of Bede with the one made by Luecke 1987, pp. 59–61. Luecke regards Bede as considerably less hostile to women than does Hollis.

[692] Bede II:11.
[693] Bede: Vita Cuthberti 27–28.
[694] Hollis 1992, pp. 219, 234–42, also emphasises the importance of royal marriages and the actual power wielded by queens in their husbands' countries. According to Luecke 1987, pp. 57–59, the typical Anglo–Saxon queen, acting as 'wife–ambassador', brought peace and Christianity to the English political scene.
[695] Bede III:24.
[696] Bede III:24.
[697] Bede V:19.

The women of Paul the Deacon

[698] PD II:28.
[699] On Paul the Deacon, see the chapter in Goffart 1988 (with references).
[700] PD I:3, 7–8.
[701] PD I:8.
[702] PD I:20.
[703] PD I:27, II:28–30.
[704] PD II:5, III:11–12, 15.
[705] PD III:30, 35, IV:5–6, 8–9, 21–22, 25, 40–41.
[706] PD IV:37.
[707] PD I:3.
[708] PD I:7.
[709] PD I:8, 10.
[710] PD I:20.
[711] PD I:27.
[712] PD II:28.
[713] PD II:28.
[714] PD II:29.
[715] See for instance PD I:17.
[716] PD II:5.
[717] PD III:11.
[718] PD III:12.
[719] PD III:15.
[720] PD III:30. On this and on Theudelinda in general, see Enright 1988, pp. 192–93, 199–200.
[721] PD III:30: Cum ille: 'Ego quidem', inquid, 'occidi possum; nam certe ad hoc ista in hanc patriam femina venit, ut tuis debeat nuptiis copulari.'
[722] PD III:35.
[723] PD IV:5.
[724] PD IV:6.
[725] PD IV:8.
[726] PD IV:9.
[727] PD IV:21.
[728] PD IV:22.

[729] PD IV:25.
[730] PD IV:41.
[731] PD IV:37: Cum eum cerneret iuvenili aetate florentem, meretrix nefaria concupivit, eique mox per nuntium mandavit, ut, si eam in matrimonium sumeret, ipsa eidem civitatem cum omnibus qui aderant traderet.
[732] PD IV:37: Talem te dignum est maritum habere!
[733] PD IV:37: Igitur dira proditrix patriae tali exitio periit, quae amplius suae libidini quam civium et consanguineorum saluti prospexit.
[734] PD IV:37.
[735] PD VI:51.
[736] PD I:21.
[737] PD I:27.
[738] PD III:28.
[739] PD III:30.
[740] PD IV:47–48.
[741] PD VI:43.
[742] PD III:10.
[743] PD IV:51, V:1, 33.
[744] PD V:16.
[745] PD V:25.
[746] PD VI:2.
[747] PD VI:50.
[748] PD VI:55.
[749] PD II:31. Paul's description of the empress Martina's situation in Constantinople is similar, although Martina is mentioned primarily in her capacity as royal mother (PD IV:49).
[750] PD VI:26.
[751] PD IV:51.
[752] PD V:33.
[753] PD VI:22.
[754] PD III:21.
[755] PD VI:57.
[756] PD II:29–30.
[757] PD IV:20.
[758] PD IV:28.
[759] PD V:8–9.
[760] PD V:14.
[761] PD IV:47.
[762] PD V:34.
[763] PD VI:1.
[764] PD V:37. As for her position in the nunnery, it would appear that she became abbess. On her sarcophagus, her convent is declared to be more beautiful than any other building except for the palaces of kings. See Panazza 1953: 66 and Ward–Perkins 1984, p. 168.

NOTES

Images of female political culture from the Lives of Saints

[765] On Merovingian hagiography in general, see Graus 1965, pp. 60–139, 438–50. See also McNamara 1985 and the introductory pages in McNamara 1992.

[766] The best edition is the one in *AS*, January 3. For more detailed discussions of Saint Genovefa, see Dubois and Beaumont–Maillet 1982; Heinzelmann and Poulin 1986; McNamara 1992, pp. 17–37.

[767] Vita Genovefae 49.

[768] On religious women in late antique society, see McNamara 1984; McNamara 1986. Generally on the situation for religious women in late antique Gaul, see Van Dam 1985, pp. 74–77.

[769] Vita Genovefae 1, 7.

[770] Vita Genovefae 10–12.

[771] Vita Genovefae 25.

[772] Vita Genovefae 34–40.

[773] McNamara 1992, p. 51. The text is to be found in *MGH SRM* 1:2, pp. 736–41.

[774] De beata Monegunde 2.

[775] De beata Monegunde 5.

[776] These were published in *MGH AA* 4:1, Berlin 1881. See especially carm. VIII:5 and the various poems in XI.

[777] Both biographies are to be found in *MGH SRM* 2.

[778] For more information on Radegund, see Aigrain 1987 (reprint); Aubrun 1986; Folz 1992; McNamara 1992, pp. 60–105; Merta 1988, pp. 7–9, 25–26; Stafford 1983, pp. 9–11. On the various descriptions of her in the *vitae*, see Consolino 1988; Effros 1990; Gäbe 1989; Leonardi 1983; Papa 1989; Wemple 1981, pp. 181–85; Wittern 1986.

[779] The letter is published in *MGH, Epistolae* 3, pp. 450–53. See also the translation and discussion in McNamara 1992, pp. 112–18, and the comments by Goetz 1995, pp. 368–71.

[780] Venantius Fortunatus: Vita Radegundis 2.

[781] Venantius Fortunatus: Vita Radegundis 3–4.

[782] Venantius Fortunatus: Vita Radegundis 10. According to Jo Ann McNamara, this kind of intervention by women on behalf of prisoners may indicate an aspect of the division of labour whereby the harsh military face of kingship could be softened through the merciful quality of queenship without making the king appear weak or indecisive. See McNamara 1992, p. 74, note 47.

[783] Venantius Fortunatus: Vita Radegundis 12.

[784] De excidio Thoringiae, verses 124–28, 133–34, 153–58 and 169–72. The poem is printed in *MGH AA* 4:1.

[785] I have used the translation of verses 124–28, 133–34, 153–58 and 169–72 in McNamara 1992, pp. 65–70.

[786] Venantius Fortunatus: Vita Radegundis 12. There is no reason to suppose that a deaconess was bound to celibacy. See McNamara 1992, p. 75, note 53.

[787] Venantius Fortunatus: Vita Radegundis 13–14.

[788] Venantius Fortunatus: Vita Radegundis 15–20.

[789] Venantius Fortunatus: Vita Radegundis 17.

[790] Venantius Fortunatus: Vita Radegundis 21–26.

791 Baudonivia: Vita Radegundis 3.
792 Baudonivia: Vita Radegundis 4–5.
793 McNamara 1992, p. 62 and p. 89 (note 90).
794 Baudonivia: Vita Radegundis 6–7.
795 Baudonivia: Vita Radegundis 10.
796 Baudonivia: Vita Radegundis 13–16. According to Isabel Moreira, Baudonivia's attention to Radegund's search for relics indicates that Baudonivia tried to raise Radegund's saintly status to a more ambitious level (Moreira 1993).
797 Baudonivia: Vita Radegundis 12. See also Wemple 1981, p. 165.
798 Baudonivia: Vita Radegundis 16.
799 Baudonivia: Vita Radegundis 23, 25.
800 Baudonivia: Vita Radegundis 21–22.
801 The Vita Eustadiolae is now to be found in *AS*, June 8 (embedded in a *vita* of Saint Sulpicius of Bourges). For a brief discussion, see McNamara 1992, pp. 106–111.
802 Vita Eustadiolae 1–2.
803 Vita Eustadiolae 3.
804 Vita Eustadiolae 4–5.
805 Vita Eustadiolae 7–11.
806 Her *vita* is to be found in *MGH SRM* 4: 337–51. See also the discussion and translation in McNamara 1992, pp. 119–36; McNamara 1985, p. 44.
807 Vita Rusticulae 1.
808 Vita Rusticulae 3. According to McNamara 1992, p. 120, Gunthchramn's refusal to help Rusticula's mother was because he owed Liliola a favour for imprisoning Theudechild, King Charibert's widow.
809 Vita Rusticulae 5. Needless to say, little Rusticula can hardly have had much choice in the matter. Abbess Liliola must have been entirely responsible.
810 Vita Rusticulae 7.
811 McNamara 1992, p. 121.
812 Vita Rusticulae 9.
813 Vita Rusticulae 10–11.
814 Vita Rusticulae 11–18.
815 Vita Rusticulae 22–25.
816 Generally on Desiderius, see Graus 1965, pp. 375–76; Nelson 1978, pp. 56–57.
817 Wood 1988, pp. 373–74.
818 Passio sancti Desiderii 2.
819 Passio sancti Desiderii 2–3.
820 Passio sancti Desiderii 7: ...tunc persecutrix...temptat dolo occidere, quem antea ex falsitate nulla ratione potuit immolare.
821 Passio sancti Desiderii 8: Sed ut haec suasio iam dictae Iezabel est fama currente perlata, tunc de repente ardenti consilio vernaculum Christi conatur occidere.
822 Passio sancti Desiderii 9. At this point, the author stops referring to the villain with words such as 'Iezabel' and 'persecutrix', instead calling her by her real name: Heu virum sanctum a Brunichilde regina nequiter fuisse dampnatum!
823 Sisebut, Vita vel Passio 2–3.
824 Sisebut, Vita vel Passio 4: regnante simul scilicet Theodorico, totius hominem

NOTES

stultitiae dignum, et fautricem pessimarum artium, malis amicissimam Brunigildem...etc.

[825] Sisebut, Vita vel Passio 4, 10–11.
[826] Sisebut, Vita vel Passio 15–18.
[827] Sisebut, Vita vel Passio 21.
[828] Wood 1994, p. 133.
[829] It is to be found in *MGH SRM* 4.
[830] Wood 1982; Wood 1994, pp. 247–48.
[831] Wood 1994, p. 197.
[832] Vita Columbani I:6.
[833] Vita Columbani I:10.
[834] Wood 1994, p. 195.
[835] Vita Columbani I:18.
[836] Vita Columbani I:19.
[837] Vita Columbani I:19.
[838] Vita Columbani I:20.
[839] McNamara 1992, pp. 155–56.
[840] Wood 1994, pp. 195–96; see also Passio Leudegarii I:6, 12–14, 16 and Passio Leudegarii II:4,7.
[841] Vita Columbani I:20, 24, 29.
[842] See Nelson 1978, especially pp. 57–59.
[843] Vita Columbani I:27.
[844] Vita Columbani I:27: Theudericus atque Brunichildis non solum adversum Columbanum insaniebant, verum etiam et contra sanctissimum Desiderium Viennensis urbis episcopum adversabantur.
[845] Vita Columbani I:29.
[846] Vita Columbani I:30.
[847] On Burgundofara and her role in Vita Columbani, see McNamara 1992, pp. 155–75.
[848] Vita Columbani I:26, II:7.
[849] Vita Columbani II:7.
[850] Vita Columbani II:10.
[851] Vita Columbani II:17.
[852] Vita Columbani II:12.
[853] Vita Columbani II:14, 20.
[854] Vita Columbani II:16.
[855] Vita Columbani II:17.
[856] Vita Columbani II:19.
[857] Vita Columbani II:22.
[858] The biography of Saint Sadalberga (*MGH SRM* 5) has sometimes been regarded as a ninth-century forgery, but the latest study accepts it as a genuine seventh-century creation. See McNamara 1992, pp. 176–94 (especially the note on p. 176).
[859] Vita Sadalbergae 1–2.
[860] Vita Sadalbergae 4–6.
[861] Vita Sadalbergae 9.
[862] McNamara 1992, p. 183, note 23 (with references).

[863] Vita Sadalbergae 10.
[864] Vita Sadalbergae 11.
[865] Vita Sadalbergae 12.
[866] Vita Sadalbergae 13.
[867] Vita Sadalbergae 14.
[868] Vita Sadalbergae 17.
[869] Vita Sadalbergae 25.
[870] Vita Sadalbergae 17, 25.
[871] Vita Sadalbergae 29.
[872] The *vita* is to be found in *MGH SRM* 6. See also the translation and discussion in McNamara 1992, pp. 289–303.
[873] Vita Anstrudis 1–3.
[874] Vita Anstrudis 4: egrotos visitando, irascentes mitigando, discordes in pacem revocando, ad ultimum mortuos sepeliendo.
[875] Vita Anstrudis 5.
[876] Vita Anstrudis 6–7: rationabiliter tamen virilis apparebat eius vultus et mitis.
[877] Vita Anstrudis 9: patientiae se clipeo armabat.
[878] Vita Anstrudis 11.
[879] Vita Anstrudis 12.
[880] McNamara 1992, pp. 291, 297. See Fredegarii Continuationes 3.
[881] Vita Anstrudis 13.
[882] Vita Anstrudis 14.
[883] Vita Anstrudis 15.
[884] Vita Anstrudis 16. See also Schulenburg 1984, p. 74. Schulenburg, however, chooses to regard the incident as an example of the *vulnerability* of early medieval nunneries!
[885] Vita Anstrudis 21–22.
[886] Vita Anstrudis 23–38.
[887] Her *vita* is to be found in *MGH SRM* 2. See also McNamara 1992, pp. 220–34. For the early years of the monastery at Nivelles, see Hoebanx 1952.
[888] Vita Geretrudis 1.
[889] McNamara 1992, pp. 220–23.
[890] Vita Geretrudis 2. See also McNamara 1992, pp. 221 and 224.
[891] Vita Geretrudis 3.
[892] Vita Geretrudis 6.
[893] Vita Geretrudis 7. On her burial, see Effros 1996.
[894] Of Miracles Performed after the Death of the Holy Abbess Gertrude (appendix to Vita Geretrudis) 2.
[895] Vita Geretrudis 6.
[896] On Aldegund, especially in her capacity as a mystic, see Wemple 1981, p. 185; Wemple 1987 ('Female Spirituality'), pp. 45–48.
[897] Vita Aldegundis (1st version) 18.
[898] The oldest version is to be found in *Acta Sanctorum Belgae* 4. Unfortunately, I have not been able to get hold of this collection (instead, I used the translation in McNamara 1992). The second version is printed in *AS*, January 30. See also the translation and the discussion in McNamara 1992, pp. 235–54. The transfer to Maubeuge

is mentioned in Vita Aldegundis (2nd version) 27.
899 Vita Aldegundis (1st version) 12.
900 McNamara 1992, p. 236.
901 Vita Aldegundis (1st version) 2.
902 Vita Aldegundis (1st version) 3, 19. See also the more explicit reference to her mother's death in Vita Aldegundis (2nd version) 15.
903 Vita Aldegundis (1st version) 23. See also McNamara 1992, p. 251, note 57.
904 Vita Aldegundis (1st version) 3.
905 Vita Aldegundis (1st version) 6.
906 Vita Aldegundis (1st version) especially the chapters 8, 15 and 17.
907 Vita Aldegundis (1st version) 14.
908 Vita Aldegundis (2nd version) 26: diabolica devicit tentamenta, sexus feminei domuit blandimenta, saecularia viriliter superavit oblectamenta.
909 Chimnechild probably enjoyed a position similar to that of many other powerful royal widows, but we have too little information about her to be sure (see Merta 1988, pp. 17–18; Wood 1994, pp. 223–24). That she did have the resources and the allies necessary to influence society is indicated in Passio Praeiecti 24: Cumque vir Dei se undique artatum cognovisset, necessitate conpulsus, ita respondit, se causas ecclesie Imnichilde regine commendatus fatetur.
910 McNamara 1992, pp. 264–66. See also Folz 1992; Graus 1965, pp. 411–14; Laporte 1990; Merta 1988, pp. 16–17, 22, 29–30; Nelson 1978, pp. 46–52, 60–72; Papa 1989; Wemple 1981, pp. 67–69; Wittern 1986; Wood 1994, pp. 197–201.
911 McNamara 1992, p. 264.
912 The *vita* is to be found in *MGH SRM* 2. See also McNamara 1992, pp. 264–78.
913 McNamara 1992, pp. 265–66.
914 Vita Balthildis 2–3.
915 Vita Balthildis 4.
916 Vita Balthildis 5.
917 Vita Balthildis 7–9.
918 Vita Balthildis 10–11.
919 Compare with Wittern 1986, p. 279, who despairs of finding an answer to the question of why she withdrew to Chelles.
920 Vita Balthildis 12–16.
921 Vita Balthildis 18.
922 Passio Leudegarii I: 2, 4. Passio Leudegarii II: 3.
923 The *vita* is to be found in *MGH SRM* 6. See also the translation and the discussion in McNamara 1992, pp. 279–88.
924 Vita Bertilae 1.
925 Vita Bertilae 2.
926 Vita Bertilae 4.
927 Vita Bertilae 5–6.
928 Vita Bertilae 7.
929 Vita Bertilae 8.
930 On these saints and their sources, see Graus 1965, pp. 376–79; Wood 1994, pp. 225–27.

[931] Passio Leudegarii I:8.
[932] Passio Praeiecti 23. On Hector's action: Qui filiam suprascripte Claudiae raptam ex scelere sibi sociaverat, et deinceps concubinarum miseria adorsus, ad Hildericum principem...'
[933] Passio Praeiecti 24.
[934] Passio Praeiecti 24–25.
[935] Passio Praeiecti 25–26; Passio Leudegarii I:9–12.
[936] Passio Praeiecti 30. See also Fouracre 1990, p. 22.
[937] Liber Historiae Francorum 45; Fredegarii Continuationes 2.
[938] McNamara 1992, pp. 304–05.
[939] The Vita Austrebertae is to be found in *AS*, February 10. See also the translation and the discussion in McNamara 1992, pp. 304–25.
[940] Vita Austrebertae 4: accepit uxorem Alemannorum regis ex prosapia, nomine Framechildem.
[941] Vita Austrebertae 5: Coepit nempe toto nisu mundum postponere, voluptatum oblectamenta viriliter calcare, et caelestia totius cordis medullis desiderare.
[942] Vita Austrebertae 5–9.
[943] Vita Austrebertae 9.
[944] Vita Austrebertae 10.
[945] Vita Austrebertae 11.
[946] Vita Austrebertae 12.
[947] Vita Austrebertae 13.
[948] Vita Austrebertae 17–18.
[949] These miracles are collected in an appendix of their own (twenty–five chapters) called *Miracula S. Austrebertae*. The story of Satan appearing as a black African (*in similitudine Aethiopis fuligine nigrioris*) is to be found in chapter 20.
[950] See the analysis in Hollis 1992, pp. 165–78. See also Nicholson 1978, pp. 25–26, 28; Stafford 1983, p. 15.
[951] Vita Wilfridi 2.
[952] Vita Wilfridi 6.
[953] Vita Wilfridi 24.
[954] Vita Wilfridi 34.
[955] Vita Wilfridi 39.
[956] Vita Wilfridi 24: Nam de lupa post occisionem regis agna Dei et perfecta abbatissa materque familias obtima commutata est.
[957] Vita Wilfridi 40.
[958] Vita Wilfridi 2–3. See also Hollis 1992, pp. 175–76.
[959] Vita Wilfridi 19, 22.
[960] Vita Wilfridi 10, 54.
[961] Vita Wilfridi 39, 43, 59, 60, 66.
[962] Vita Wilfridi 60.
[963] On this attitude in the chronicles, see Merta 1988, p. 23.
[964] McNamara 1992, p. 4. See also Brown 1981, p. 47, on women's roles within the cult of saints in late antiquity.
[965] McNamara 1992, pp. 5–6.

NOTES

[966] The late antique–early medieval development of holiness and holy persons has been investigated in several important works by Peter Brown. See especially Brown 1981, pp. 23–42 and 86–105 (on saints and relics and the increasing importance of bishops); Brown 1971 (arguing that the 'rise' of the living holy person coincided with the erosion of classical institutions, while the decline of the holy person coincided with the re-assertion of a new sense of the importance of the community); Brown 1976; Brown 1982.
[967] McNamara 1992, pp. 6, 9. On Balthild, see Wood 1994, pp. 197–201.
[968] See, for instance, Van Dam 1985, pp. 230–76 (particularly on the role of the cult of Saint Martin).
[969] Prinz 1967. Compare this with the general picture of aristocratic episcopal careers in Van Dam 1985, pp. 205–11.
[970] McNamara 1992, p. 7.
[971] Compare this attitude with the later practice discussed in McNamara 1991. On the general situation (the importance of wealth and noble heritage), see Goetz 1995, pp. 138–39. The most important study of the relationship between holiness and wealth/secular power in early medieval Gaul is Graus 1965.
[972] McNamara 1992, p. 10.
[973] McNamara 1992, pp. 8–9.
[974] McNamara 1992, p. 10–11.
[975] Discussed in Harrison 1999.
[976] McNamara 1992, pp. 12–15.
[977] McNamara 1992, pp. 12–15.

Stereotypical images of powerful early medieval women

[978] Garlick 1992. The study of female stereotypes in later periods than are dealt with in this book is wide-ranging, and this is not the right place to delve into the subject. For an introduction to the high medieval literary image of women, see Ferrante 1975. Ferrante's main argument is that the history of female stereotypes should be regarded as a reflection of the general development of society.
[979] Stafford 1983, p. 45.
[980] Enright 1988, p. 202.

Resources, tactics and strategies

[981] Wood 1994, p. 136.
[982] McNamara 1992, p. 159.
[983] McNamara 1992, p. 177

Index

Ababa 69
Adaloald 232, 267, 353
Adalperga 259
Adalulf 232, 233
Adam 36
Adamnan 251, 252
Aega 231, 234, 297, 326, 353, 361, 366
Aegyla 223, 358
Aelffled 247, 248, 253, 254, 256, 321, 344
Aetherius of Lisieux 198
Aetius 198
Ageric of Verdun 138, 203
Agilbert 301
Agilulf 232, 235, 265–267, 270, 271, 274, 295, 369
Agin 196
Aginus 140
Agnes 89, 90, 92, 200, 205
Agrestius 296, 321
Ahab 57
Aidan of Lindisfarne 248, 249
Aio 260
Albinus 200
Albofled 149
Alboin 149, 172, 226, 259, 262–264, 271, 274, 362
Albsuinda 263, 274, 369
Alchima 180, 181
Alcuin of York 259
Aldegund 305, 306, 321, 324, 325, 330, 331
Aldetrude 305
Aldfrith 253
Aldwin of Partney 247
Aldwulf of East Anglia 248
Alethius 229, 230, 235
Allen, Pauline 340
Almond, Gabriel 60
Alpaida 239
Amalaberg 18, 169, 170, 172, 174, 213, 341, 344, 345
Amalafrid 280, 282
Amalaric 149
Amalasuntha, *Amalasuintha, Amalasuentha* 69–71, 149, 169, 171, 172, 174, 213, 341
Amalbert 316, 317

Amalo 177, 178
Amandus 230, 292, 303, 306
Ambrose, Saint 40
Ambrosius 74
Amelius [of Bigorra] 117
Anastasius 83
Andarchius 176
Andica 169
Angadrisma 315
Anna 260, 274
Anna, King of East Anglia 247, 249
Anseflid 238, 239, 240, 242, 243, 343
Ansegisel 303
Ansovald 108, 118, 128
Ansprand 273, 274, 369
Anstrude 298–302, 321, 325–328, 330, 367, 373, 378
Apollinaris 180, 181, 186
Arcadius (messenger) 82, 83
Arcadius (aristocrat) 181, 186
Aredius 199, 202
Aregund 86, 87, 103
Arichis 259
Aridius of Lyons 223, 225
Arioald 232, 233, 236, 271
Aripert II 273, 274, 369
Arnebert 221, 222, 230
Arnulf of Metz 226, 294
Aronsson, Peter 61
Asteriolus 97, 98, 210, 360
Athala 292
Athanagild, King of the Visigoths 104, 130, 131, 143, 148, 151, 172
Athanagild (Ingund's son) 136, 151
Atkinson, Clarissa 59, 60
Attila 71, 278
Attila of Laon 299
Aubedo 233, 234
Audoaldus 288
Audofleda 149, 170, 171
Audoin of Rouen 17
Audolenus 230
Audovera 91, 103–106, 109, 132, 152, 155, 209, 211, 351, 352
Augnofledis 297
Augustine, Saint 40

433

Aunemundus of Lyons 308, 318, 332
Aurea 316
Aurora 272, 274, 369
Ausanius 181
Austreberta 315–317, 321, 325, 326, 327, 330
Austrechild 102, 214, 343
Austrigusa 271
Authari 152, 265, 266, 267, 271

Baddo 120
Badefridus 316
Badegisil of Le Mans 112, 184, 186, 213, 342, 345
Baderic 170
Baldwin 300, 301, 327
Balthild 33, 50, 55–57, 95, 167, 238, 242, 243, 256, 292, 305, 307–312, 318, 323, 325, 327–329, 331–333, 341, 345, 353, 355, 356, 363–365, 370, 431
Baltrusch-Schneider, Dagmar 53
Barks, Carl 377
Basina (wife of Childeric I) 76, 77
Basina (daughter of Chiperic I) 18, 91, 93, 103, 109, 122, 152, 154, 155, 157–170, 197, 204–206, 329, 348, 370, 415
Bathsheba 418
Baudonivia 53, 277, 280, 284, 285, 329, 426
Baudulf 293
Bede 36, 37, 58, 65, 245–257, 318, 337, 338, 339, 342–344, 346, 348, 363, 364, 402, 421, 422
Begga 303
Begu 249
Beletrude 238
Benedict, Saint 286, 317
Benedict Biscop 245
Beppolen 108, 118–122, 129, 130, 177
Berchar 239, 240, 242, 343
Berchild 230
Beretrude 180, 183, 185
Bertha (daughter of Charibert I) 150
Bertha (magnate woman) 221, 222
Berthar, Thuringian king 87, 170
Berthar (count) 293
Berthefled 150, 154, 187, 348, 370
Berthefried 133, 134, 137, 138, 141, 145, 147, 176, 217, 381
Berthegund 150, 186–194, 212, 344, 358, 417
Berthetrude 229, 230, 234, 349
Bertilla (Aldegund's mother) 306
Bertilla of Chelles 309, 311–313, 325, 326, 329
Bertoald 223
Bertrada 58, 238, 239, 240
Bertram of Bordeaux 124,187–189, 192–194, 344
Bertram of Le Mans 184
Bertulf 292

Bilichild (d. 610) 225, 227–229, 234, 235, 307, 355, 356, 368, 376, 378, 420
Bilichild (d. 675) 238, 313, 314, 332, 333, 369
Bisinus 76, 77
Bitel, Lisa 37, 41, 44, 48, 63
Bladast 117, 180
Blandinus 298, 299
Blomqvist, Karin 34
Bobilla 102
Bobolen 183, 186
Bodo 299
Boniface V 254
Borgia, Lucrezia 264
Boso of Étampes 230
Breguswith 245, 248
Brigit 38
Britanus 182, 185
Brunhild 19, 47, 56, 57, 61, 65, 77, 83, 93, 101, 103–107, 115, 117, 121, 128–151, 167, 172, 175, 179, 182, 186, 205, 207, 208, 210, 213, 215–218, 222–229, 232, 234–236, 241–243, 288, 290–295, 298, 308, 314, 332, 333, 341, 343, 345–349, 351–353, 355, 357, 358, 360–362, 368, 369, 372, 373, 376, 381–384, 412, 413, 419
Burgofled 316
Burgolen 182, 185
Burgundofara 292, 295, 296, 297, 321, 326, 330, 366, 378

Cadden, Joan 42
Caesara 220
Caesaria 180–182, 185, 186
Caesaria, Saint 201
Caesaria II 100, 280, 281, 321, 327
Caesarius 88, 93, 280, 288
Carellus 271
Cariveus 301
Carloman 367
Cassiodorus 69
Cautinus of Clermont 83, 194
Celsa 287
Ceraonius 287
Chagneric 295, 296, 366
Chagnoald 295
Chainulf 231
Chalda 176
Charibert I 86, 90, 98–101, 150, 154, 155, 187, 200, 203, 207, 210, 350, 352, 355, 358, 359, 368, 370, 371, 426
Charivald 122
Charlemagne 59, 219, 237, 259
Charles Martel 237–239, 242, 366, 376
Charles the Bald 59
Charoald 232
Childebert I 81–84, 95, 98, 149, 172, 181, 208, 311
Childebert II 106, 107, 111, 113–118, 120–123, 127–129, 131–142, 144, 145,

INDEX

147, 148, 150–152, 158, 160, 166, 167, 169, 177–179, 190, 193, 206, 207, 217, 218, 222–225, 232, 271, 291, 292, 314, 343, 351–353, 376, 410, 413
Childebert III 18
Childebert (son of Theuderic II) 228
Childebrand 237
Childeric I 76, 77, 149, 279
Childeric II 18, 238, 242, 307, 309, 313–315, 332, 369
Childeric the Saxon 157, 175
Childeric (son of Chlothar I) 86
Chilperic I 61, 73, 86, 90, 91, 93, 94, 103–116, 118, 123–129, 131–134, 137, 142, 152, 153, 155, 178, 208, 209, 215, 216, 222, 227, 236, 242, 350, 352, 355, 356, 359, 368, 377, 409, 411, 419
Chilperic, Burgundian king 77
Chilperic II 18, 239, 242
Chiltrude 238, 240
Chimnechild 305, 307, 313, 314, 328, 333, 353, 429
Chlodomer (King of Orléans) 79–82, 84, 85, 101, 171, 210, 354
Chlodomer (son of Gunthchramn) 102
Chlodosinda (daughter of Sigibert I) 132, 138, 148, 150–152
Chlodoswintha 18, 86, 149, 271, 274
Chlodovald (Saint Cloud) 81, 82, 354
Chlothar I 81–89, 94, 95, 98, 101, 103, 149, 172, 176, 181, 187, 207, 208, 218, 271, 281, 283, 284, 311, 350, 352. 355, 365
Chlothar II 112–115, 117–119, 121–123, 126–130, 208, 218, 221, 222, 226–230, 233, 234, 241, 288–290, 294, 295, 302, 305, 349, 352, 411
Chlothar III 238, 307, 309, 310, 312
Chlothar (son of Gunthchramn) 102
Chlothar (son of Theudeberth II) 227
Chlothild, Saint 55, 77–85, 149, 210, 211, 311, 346, 351, 363, 364
Chlothild (daughter of Clovis I) 149, 154
Chlothild (daughter of Gunthchramn) 150, 154
Chramn 168, 176, 181, 182, 185, 186, 218
Chramnesind 139, 140
Chramnulf 221
Chrodechild 18, 91, 109, 122, 150, 154, 155, 156, 157, 158, 159, 160, 161, 162, 163, 164, 165, 166, 167, 168, 169, 183, 191, 197, 198, 204, 205, 206, 210, 329, 330, 344, 348, 358, 370, 371, 415
Chrodoberga 95
Chrodochild 17, 18, 242
Chrodoswintha 95
Chroma 78
Chunsina 86, 87
Chuppa (Master of the Stables) 116
Chuppa (magnate) 184–186
Ciarán, Saint 41
Claudia 313, 314, 315, 331

Claudius 116, 129, 175, 377
Clementia 287
Cleph 273
Clover, Carol 38
Clovis I 77–80, 82, 84, 85, 95, 149, 154, 180, 210, 211, 311, 351, 363
Clovis II 230, 231, 233, 238, 242, 243, 305, 307–309, 345, 353, 356, 420
Clovis (son of Chilperic I) 91, 103, 109, 110, 114, 126, 202, 203, 409
Coenburg 252
Columbanus 225, 228, 286, 291, 292, 293, 294, 295, 296, 298, 333, 366, 369
Condren, Mary 39, 40, 42
Constans II 274
Constantina 180, 183, 185
Constantine 80, 299
Corbus 227
Cudda 320
Cunimund 262, 263
Cunincpert 272, 273, 275
Cuthbert 245, 252, 253, 254, 344, 402
Cyniburg 245
Cynwise 255

Dagobert I 221, 230, 231, 234, 236, 298, 303, 305, 307, 326, 350, 353, 355, 358, 366–368
Dagobert II 18, 304
Dagulf 176
Demertzis, Nicolas 61, 62, 64
Desiderius (deacon) 157
Desiderius (duke) 111, 153, 157, 178, 195–197
Desiderius of Auxerre 419
Desiderius of Vienne 223, 225, 290, 291, 295, 333
Deuteria 96–98, 207, 208, 214, 342, 355, 382, 408
Didimia 162, 163
Dinifius 83
Dio Chrysostom 35
Disciola 92
Dixon, Suzanne 340
Domnola 180, 183, 185, 186
Domnolus of Vienne 289
Don Corleone 381
Droctulf 141, 148, 179
Drogo 239

Eanfled 246, 248, 255, 320, 331, 360
Earconbert, King of Kent 246, 247, 250, 320,
Earcongota 247
Earconwald 250
Ebba 250, 251, 252, 319, 321
Eberulf 115, 116, 126, 128, 129, 178, 185
Ebrachar 139
Ebregisel (retainer) 139, 144
Ebregisel of Cologne 160

435

Ebroard 302
Ebroin 294, 300, 301, 307, 308, 310, 318, 328, 332, 365, 367
Eddius Stephanus 36, 278, 311, 318,–321, 331–333
Edwin of Northumbria 246, 248, 254
Effros, Bonnie 50
Egfrith, King of Northumbria 249–251, 253, 318–320, 345
Egidius of Rheims 141, 142, 145, 166
Elafius of Châlons-sur-Marne 133, 144
Elias 319
Emerius 195
Ennodius 142
Enright, Michael 56, 57, 60, 346
Erchinoald 231, 234, 307, 308, 345, 355, 356, 361
Erkens, Franz-Reiner 57
Ermenberga 225, 228, 235, 368
Ermenfred 231
Ethelberga 246, 247, 254
Ethelbert, King of Kent 98, 150, 254
Ethelburga 250, 251
Etheldreda 248, 249, 250, 255, 320, 360
Ethelhild 247, 248
Ethelred of Mercia 247
Ethelwin of Lindsey 247
Eufronius of Tours 93, 156, 285
Eugenia 286
Euin, Duke of Trento 272, 349
Eulalius 194–197, 212
Eustadiola 286, 325, 330
Eustasius 292, 295, 296, 298, 366
Eustenia 106
Eve 35, 36, 43, 201, 276, 418

Faileuba 18, 137, 140, 148, 179, 186, 207, 218, 223, 291, 314, 333, 351, 413
Falco 419
Faraulf 288, 289
Fausta 415
Felix of Châlons-sur-Marne 120, 121
Felix of Nantes 200, 201
Fell, Christine 36, 37, 56
Firminus 181, 182, 185, 186
Flaochad 231, 234, 361
Flavianus 160
Flavinius 140
Framechild 316
Frea 260, 261, 275, 341, 342
Freddy Krueger 269
Fredegar 58, 142, 219, 220, 221, 222, 223, 224, 225, 226, 227, 228, 229, 230, 231, 232, 233, 234, 235, 236, 237, 238, 239, 240, 241, 242, 267, 271, 272, 273, 290, 314, 341, 343, 345, 349, 350, 360, 378, 382, 419, 420
Fredegund 33, 58, 59, 61, 77, 83, 91, 93, 94, 101, 103, 104, 105, 106, 107, 108, 109, 110, 111, 112, 113, 114, 115, 116, 117, 118, 119, 120, 121, 122, 123, 124, 125, 126, 127, 128, 129, 130, 131, 132, 134, 135, 136, 143, 146, 147, 148, 152, 153, 166, 167, 172, 180, 183, 202, 203, 204, 206, 208, 209, 210, 213, 214, 215, 216, 217, 222, 223, 225, 234, 242, 307, 343, 345, 348, 350, 352, 353, 355, 356, 359, 360, 362, 368, 373, 377, 378, 381, 409, 411

Gaidoald, Duke of Brescia 272
Galienus 124
Gallicinus 274
Gallomagnus 141
Galswinth 103, 104, 105, 106, 114, 137, 205, 207, 209, 347, 359, 369, 409
Gambara 260, 261, 275, 337, 341, 342
Garibald, Duke of Bavaria 87, 265, 271, 272, 349
Garlick, Barbara 340
Genesius 308, 309, 312, 318
Genovefa, Saint 201, 278, 279, 322, 323, 346, 425
Germanus, Saint 279
Germanus of Grandval 292
Germanus of Paris 98, 284
Gertrude of Nivelles 50, 53, 302–305, 325–327, 330, 331
Gibitrude 297, 330
Gisa 274, 275, 369
Giselard 302
Gisulf II, Duke of Friuli 267, 268
Gisulf (son of Romuald II) 272
Godan 260, 261
Godeberta 315
Godepert 272
Godescalc, Duke of Benevento 274
Godescalc (Agilulf's son-in-law) 274, 369
Godin 178, 185
Godinus 221, 222
Godomar 80, 81
Goetz, Hans-Werner 28, 43, 44, 53, 54, 59, 63
Goiswinth 18, 130, 150, 169, 172–175, 204, 213, 341
Gomatrude 230
Gregory I the Great 266, 267, 317, 360, 419
Gregory of Tours 18, 58, 65, 73–88, 91–93, 95–100, 102–131, 133–139, 141–145, 147–157, 159–161, 163, 167, 169–182, 184, 186–192, 195, 197–207, 210–215, 219, 220, 222, 227, 234, 243, 245, 279, 284, 285, 290, 324, 330, 332, 337–339, 341–345, 348, 350, 352, 354, 355, 360, 361, 363, 370–372, 379, 382, 384
Grimoald, King of the Lombards 272–274
Grimoald (son of Pippin of Herstal) 239, 242, 302
Grimoald (son of Pippin of Landen) 304, 305, 328
Grimoald II, Duke of Benevento 272

436

INDEX

Grimshaw, Jean 29
Gumperga 272
Gundegisel of Bordeaux 157, 165
Gundeperga 232, 233, 235, 236, 271, 275, 363
Gundoald 232, 265, 267
Gundobad, Burgundian king 77, 78, 80,
Gundobad (Gunthchramn's son) 101–103, 209, 214, 343, 352
Gundovald (duke) 132
Gundovald (pretender) 86, 93, 116, 128, 135, 139, 140, 144, 147, 153, 179, 187, 188, 196
Gunthar (son of Chlodomer) 81, 82
Gunthar (son of Chlothar I) 86
Gunthchramn 86, 90, 99, 101–103, 107, 113–123, 127–129, 134–141, 145, 147, 148, 150–152, 154, 157, 160, 169, 178, 179, 183, 187, 188, 191, 196, 198, 200, 206, 209, 211, 214, 216, 220, 222, 223, 287, 343, 348, 352, 356, 358, 359, 362, 368, 408–413, 426
Gunthchramn Boso 107, 136, 137, 178, 179, 203
Guntheuc 85–87
Guntrut 260, 272

Hadwald 254
Halsall, Guy 49
Hector 313, 314, 315, 430
Heiu 251
Helena 285, 330, 415
Helmechis 263, 264, 274
Hereric 248
Hereswith 248
Heriburg 252, 364
Herlihy, David 51
Hermanfrid 87, 94, 170, 344, 345
Hermelinda 260
Hermenigild 136, 143, 150, 151
Hilary, Saint 90, 125, 157, 159, 165, 205
Hilda of Whitby 19, 53, 248, 249, 320, 327, 364, 378, 422
Hildilid 251
Hirdman, Yvonne 27
Hollis, Stephanie 36, 37, 402, 422
Honoria 69, 71, 72, 338, 342
Hospicius 202
Huneric 405

Ibor 260
Ida 303, 304
Imma 250, 255
Ingitrude 94, 150, 186, 187, 188, 189, 190, 191, 192, 193, 194, 212, 344, 367, 370, 417
Ingoberg 98, 100, 370
Ingomer 79
Ingund (wife of Chlothar I) 86, 87, 98, 101, 149, 187

Ingund (daughter of Sigibert I) 132, 136, 143, 144, 150–152, 154, 172, 173, 206, 235, 274, 347, 369, 374
Injuriosus 201
Innocentius 134, 146, 196, 361
Irminburga 278, 318, 319, 320, 327, 332, 333
Isidore of Seville 42

Jarrick, Arne 30, 31, 33, 401
Jason 269
Jesus 285
Jezebel 57, 226, 290, 293, 318, 319, 333, 341, 383
John 195, 196
John of York 252
Jonas of Bobbio 222, 226, 236, 290, 292–298, 330, 333, 366, 369
Jordanes 21, 58, 65, 77, 80, 81, 82, 337, 338, 339, 342, 372
Judith (Biblical) 418
Judith (empress) 57
Jupiter 78
Justin II 92, 173, 264, 265
Justina 159, 167
Justinian I 97
Justinian (nephew of Justin II) 265
Jäschke, Kurt-Ulrich 57

Lagobert 309
Laiou, Angeliki 57
Lampeto 69, 70
Landeberga 297
Landramnus 300
Lanthechild 149
Leodegar of Autun 294, 308, 311, 313, 314, 326, 367
Leuba 117, 180
Leubovera 76, 122, 154, 155, 157, 159, 160, 162–169, 198, 200, 206, 330, 344
Leudast 99, 100, 124–126, 175, 207, 210, 360
Leudegund 295
Leudemund of Sion 229, 230
Leudovald of Bayeux 118, 120, 122
Leunard 112, 153
Leuvigild 110, 116, 117, 136, 138, 150, 151, 172, 173, 180
Liliola 100, 287, 288, 408, 426
Liutprand 259, 270, 272–274
Longinus 263, 264, 274
Louis the Pious 57
Lupentius 134, 146, 361
Lupus, Duke of Champagne 133, 134, 147, 217, 361, 372
Lupus, Duke of Friuli 272
Lupus (citizen of Tours) 74
Lytigius 199

Macco 158, 160, 161, 166

437

Macha 39
Macliaw 170
Madelgar of Laon 302
Magnachar 101, 102
Magnatrude 180, 184, 185, 186, 213, 214, 342, 345
Magnovald 177
Magnulf of Toulouse 153
Marcatrude 101, 102, 103, 209, 214, 343, 352
Marcovefa 98, 99, 100, 207, 210, 360
Maroveus of Poitiers 93, 95, 156–160, 162, 190, 285, 328
Marpesia 69, 70
Martha 418
Martin, Saint 80, 82–84, 88, 90, 100, 107, 116, 122, 123, 132, 136, 176, 178, 186, 187, 189, 199, 280, 284, 317, 324, 431
Martin (brother of Pippin of Herstal) 301
Martina 424
Mary (Virgin Mary) 36, 90, 112, 153, 276, 286, 317, 418
'Mary' (follower of a bogus Christ) 204
Masane 273
Matesuentha 69
Maurice 174, 265
Maximus 288
McLaughlin, Megan 46–48, 51, 362
McNamara, Jo Ann 45, 46, 53, 288, 307, 324, 365, 366, 425
Médard of Noyon 283
Medopa 69
Melania the Younger, Saint 50
Melanius of Rouen 115, 119, 128, 129
Merofled 98, 100
Merovech (son of Chilperic I) 103, 106, 107, 114, 126, 132, 133, 136, 144, 145, 203, 227, 353, 412
Merovech (son of Chlothar) 227
Merovech (son of Theuderic II) 228
Merta, Brigitte 55, 60
Michael, archangel 92
Modesta 304
Modestus 124
Monegund 75, 279, 280, 322, 324, 325
Mummolus (victim of Fredegund) 110
Mummolus (warlord) 179, 220

Namatius of Clermont 198
Nantechild 230, 231, 232, 234, 307, 353, 358, 361, 420
Narses 264
Nectarius (brother of Badegisil) 112
Nectarius (husband of Domnola) 183
Nelson, Janet 47, 52, 53, 56–58
Nibelung 237, 239
Nicetius 182
Noah 418
Nymfidius 289

Odilo, Duke of Bavaria 238
Omer 315, 316

Österberg, Eva 61
Osthryd 247, 248
Oswald, King of Northumbria 247, 248
Oswin, King of Deira 246
Oswy, King of Northumbria 246–248, 251, 253, 320
Otto II 57
Owini 250, 255

Palladius (count) 182
Palladius of Saintes 120
Pankhurst, Emmeline 371
Papianilla 180, 181, 185
Pappolen 200, 201
Parthenius 181
Paul the Deacon 19, 21, 58, 65, 66, 172, 173, 220, 223, 232, 235, 236, 243, 245, 259, 260–276, 337–339, 341–346, 348, 349, 354–356, 361, 362, 379, 382, 384, 423, 424
Paulinus 246, 248
Peada, King of the South Mercians 256, 343
Pelagia 199
Pemmo, Duke of Friuli 273
Penda, King of Mercia 248, 255
Penthesilea 69, 70
Perctarit 272, 273
Peredeo 263
Peter (physician) 224
Philibert 308, 309, 315, 316
Pippin of Herstal 238, 239, 242, 301–303, 328, 376
Pippin of Landen 226, 294, 302, 303
Pippin the Short 58, 237–240
Pitto 233
Placidana 180, 181
Plato 124
Plectrude 238, 239, 240, 242, 243, 370, 376
Praeiectus of Clermont 313, 314, 331
Praetextatus of Rouen 106, 107, 108, 115, 118, 119, 126, 128, 129, 133, 147, 410
Priscus of Lyons 182, 186
Proculus of Tours 83
Proculus (Radegund's agent) 284, 328
Promotus of Châteaudun 175
Protadius 223, 224, 227, 357
Pye, Lucian 60

Quintianus, Saint 180, 181, 199

Rachel 418
Radbod, Duke of the Frisians, 239, 242
Radegund 19, 49, 50, 53, 86–89, 91–95, 155, 156, 162, 164, 165, 168–170, 187, 194, 197, 200, 202, 205–207, 211, 212, 217, 280, 281, 283–285, 322–325, 327, 328, 330, 346, 347, 349, 363, 364, 367, 378, 415, 425, 426
Radperga 273

Ragamfred 239, 242
Ragnemod of Paris 73, 107, 113
Ragnetrude 230
Ragnobertha 231
Ragnovald 178, 179, 359
Ranicunda 271
Ranigunda 260, 272
Ratchis 259, 367
Rauching 137, 141, 178, 185, 350
Rebecca 418
Recared 110, 138, 139, 151, 152, 173
Remigius 79, 80
Remistanius 420
Reovalis 164, 284
Richramnus 298
Ricomer 288
Ricula 245
Riculf 124
Rigunth 18, 76, 110–112, 116, 126, 152–154, 206, 337, 348, 377
Rocco 287
Rodelinda 273, 275, 363, 369
Rodoald 271, 272
Rodulf 261, 262
Romanus 246
Romilda 19, 49, 167, 168, 243 260, 267–269, 270, 273, 275, 276, 342, 344, 349, 355, 356
Romuald I 272, 274, 275
Romuald II 272
Rosario, Michelle Zimbalist 46
Rosemunda 172, 260, 262, 263, 264, 271, 274–276, 342–344, 362
Rothari 233, 236, 271
Rumetruda 260–262, 275, 276, 343, 344
Rusticula 287–289, 325, 326, 328, 330, 367, 373, 378, 426
Rusticus 198

Sadalberga 298–300, 303, 305, 325, 326, 367, 378
Saethryd 247
Salinga 271
Salvius of Albi 92
Samo 220
Samson 108
Sapphira 204
Saturn 78
Saxo Grammaticus 35
Scauniperga 272
Schulenburg, Jane 54, 415
Scott, Joan 26
Scrooge McDuck 377
Secundinus 97
Septimima 140, 141, 148, 179, 180, 186
Severus 182
Sexburg 247, 250
Sichar 139, 140, 147, 182, 185
Sichild 230, 234, 349
Sidonia 220
Sidonius Apollinaris 180, 201

Sigeric 170, 171
Sigibert I 61, 86, 90, 92–94, 103, 105–107, 111, 114, 115, 130–133, 136, 138, 142–148, 150, 151, 154, 156, 172, 175, 208, 215, 216, 227, 236, 284, 285, 292, 328, 352, 412
Sigibert II 226, 228
Sigibert III 230, 231, 305, 307, 314
Sigismund 80, 81, 85, 95, 170, 171
Sigobrand of Paris 310
Sigprand 273
Sisebut 290, 291
Smaragdus 274
Socratius 195
Solomon 418
Sophia 92, 173, 174, 260, 264, 265, 275, 276, 345
Stafford, Pauline 55, 56, 60, 346
Stenton, Doris 36
Strand (now Sawyer), Birgit 35
Subinus 305
Sulpicius of Bourges 286, 426
Sunilda 69
Sunnegisil 141
Sunnichild 238, 240
Susanna 180, 182, 186

Taso 233
Tato 261
Tetradia 194, 195, 196, 197, 212, 350
Tetradius 286
Thatcher, Margaret 62
Thecla, Saint (originally Melania) 201
Theodora 264
Theodore of Marseilles 202
Theodore of Canterbury 319
Theodorus of Tours 83
Theodosius 290
Theodota 275
Theophanu 57, 58, 59, 405
Theudat 171, 172
Theudebald 87, 96, 97, 209, 271
Theudebert I 82, 83, 95–97, 172, 181, 205, 208, 271, 355, 368
Theudebert II 121, 140, 223–229, 241, 307, 355, 368
Theudebert (son of Chilperic) 103
Theudechild (wife of Gunthchramn) 98–101, 200, 211, 352, 358, 359, 364, 370, 408, 426
Theudechild (wife of Theudebert II) 229–368
Theudechild (abbess) 312
Theudelinda 19, 47, 49, 58, 59, 225, 232, 236, 260, 265, 266, 267, 270, 271, 273, 275, 276, 337, 341, 345, 346, 348, 351, 353, 363, 383, 384, 423
Theuderada (wife of Romuald I) 272, 275, 363
Theuderada (wife of Ansprand) 273, 274, 369

Theuderic I the Great 149, 170, 171
Theuderic (son of Clovis I) 78, 82, 87, 95, 96, 170, 180, 181, 186
Theuderic II 223–229, 241, 290–295, 332, 333, 368, 419
Theuderic III 17, 242, 301
Theuderic (son of Chilperic I) 110, 111
Theudesinda 242
Theudila 225, 226, 228, 235, 368
Theudoald 239
Theudovald 81, 82
Theuthar 158, 190
Thraede, Klaus 36
Tiberius II 173, 174, 265, 276
Tondbert 249
Tortgyth 251
Traguilla 171
Tranquilla 180, 182, 185
Transamund I 272
Trumhere 246

Ultrogotha 95, 208, 311, 325, 352, 369
Uncelen 224
Urbicus of Clermont 201, 214, 342
Ursicinus 95
Ursio 133, 134, 137, 138, 141, 145, 176, 217, 372
Ursus 175, 176

Valerian 287
Venantius Fortunatus 50, 95, 143, 280, 281, 283, 284, 409
Veneranda 101
Verba, Sidney 60
Verca 253
Victorius 183, 185

Vinoberga 285, 329
Virus 195
Vuldetrada 18, 86, 87, 271
Waccho 87, 95, 271
Waddo 135, 152, 167, 180, 183, 184, 185
Waiofar, Duke of Aquitaine 239, 240
Waldebert (assassin) 221
Waldebert (Aldegund's father) 306
Waldebert of Luxeuil 308
Waldin 122
Wallace-Hadrill, J.M. 219
Wandalmar 223
Wandelenus 135, 145
Wandregisel 292
Waratto 238
Warnachar 221, 222, 226, 227
Waroch 121–123, 128, 170
Warrato 242
Wemple, Suzanne 45, 46, 53, 54, 56, 57, 60, 411
Wigilinda 272
Wilfrid of York 246, 250, 308, 318–320, 326, 331, 332, 345
Wiliulf 177
Willichar 176
Winiperga 260
Wintrio 223
Wisigarda 18, 95–98, 205, 210, 271, 347, 355, 360
Witteric 225
Wittern, Susanne 54
Wood, Ian 57, 126, 145, 291, 294, 353
Wulf 224
Wulfegund 230
Wulfoald 314
Wulfold 302
Wulftrude 304, 305, 325, 326, 328

ALSO AVAILABLE
FROM NORDIC ACADEMIC PRESS

Susanne Lundin and Malin Ideland (eds). *Gene Technology and the Public: An Interdisciplinary Perspective.*

Tom O'Dell. *Culture Unbound: Americanization and Everyday Life in Sweden.*

Martin Åberg and Martin Peterson (eds). *Baltic Cities: Perspectives on Urban and Regional Change in the Baltic Sea Area.*

Jonas Frykman, Nadia Seremetakis and Susanne Ewert (eds). *Identities in Pain.*

Gunnar Dahl. *Trade, Trust, and Networks. Commercial Culture in Late Medieval Italy.*